Film Review

2012-2013

Film
Review
2012-2013

Michael Darvell and Mansel Stimpson

EXECUTIVE EDITOR:
JAMES CAMERON-WILSON

SIGNUM BOOKS

*In memory of composer, jazz pianist and singer Sir Richard Rodney Bennett who, apart from his concert and choral works, operas and songs, wrote many fine film scores; and Graham Dalling, fellow former librarian.
Both died on Christmas Eve 2012 – MD*

To Neil Brand whose brilliant piano accompaniments have helped to sustain interest in silent cinema worldwide and whose orchestral score for the 2013 reissue of Anthony Asquith's Underground *(1929), an absolute model of its kind, revealed depths in that film that had previously eluded me – MS*

Acknowledgements

The editors of *Film Review 2012-2013* would like to thank the following, without whose invaluable help this book might not have appeared:

Charles Bacon, Alex Buchan, Jeremy Clarke, Peri Godbold, Marcus Hearn, Marshall Julius, Penny Lucas, Jonathan Rigby, George Savvides, Paul Taylor and Derek Winnert.

Frontispiece: Suraj Sharma in *Life of Pi*.

First published in Great Britain in 2013 by Signum Books, an imprint of Flashpoint Media Ltd
173 Mill Road
Cambridge
CB1 3AN

© Michael Darvell and Mansel Stimpson 2013

A CIP catalogue record for this book is available from the British Library.

ISBN 978 0 956653 49 9

Designer: Peri Godbold
Managing editor: Marcus Hearn

Printed and bound in China by 1010 Printing International Ltd.

Contents

FILM REVIEW
A SURVEY OF THE WORLD CINEMA

F. MAURICE SPEED

Introduction

by **Michael Darvell**

There appears to be no let-up in UK film releases, but does more mean less in terms of quality?

In 2011 around 500 films were released to British cinemas and for 2012 the figure was slightly up, with 525 titles. Not all of them received a wide showing, as some films tend to sink without trace almost as soon as they're released. For this volume (the 68th since *Film Review* was first published in 1944) we have managed to cover 488 out of the 525 releases; the missing titles are mostly Bollywood films that still get short shrift in previews and are increasingly screened only at UK Asian specialist cinemas.

Of course, with so many titles to cover, we cannot guarantee that the general standard of films reviewed will be high. Quality seems to be in short supply if you check out *Film Review*'s star-rating system.

Three stars mean it's a good film, four is very good and five is excellent. At the lower end of the scale one star means poor and two stars mean mediocre. There isn't a 'no star' rating, much as we would sometimes love to award a negative mark, in the way that *Sight & Sound* magazine used to give 'a blob for antipathy' for those films thought to be critically beyond the pale. (Incidentally, I've always thought that 'A Blob for Antipathy' would make the ideal title for a jobbing film reviewer's autobiography. If I ever get around to writing mine, that's what I shall call it.) The panel of critics on *Film Review* are a fairly amenable bunch and will always give credit where it's due. The films of 2012 turned up some memorable titles to which we have awarded the appropriate three, four or five stars. However, nearly a third of the films released in the UK have, in our review section, fallen into the categories of poor or mediocre.

Now, we are not *Sight & Sound*, so we aren't necessarily looking for high cinematic art, cult movies or films with a message. What we are looking for, generally speaking, is good entertainment, with a credible screenplay, something that is filmically worth viewing and that adds to the art of the film without going overboard in the direction of pretension.

With one third of the year's output lacking any sort of appeal to the wide range of opinion of our ten reviewers, it seems that 2012 was not a vintage year in the cinema. (Is it ever, I hear you murmur.) Admittedly, if you survey the films of any one year you will always find plenty of dross stashed away among the gold. Can we then assume that the gold standard for 2012 was quite low and that filmmakers were making an awful number of mistakes and losing a lot of money on duff movies? I think it safe to say that most of the poor to mediocre films will be those that failed at the box-office anyway. With the cost of making films spiralling all the time, a line should be drawn under certain projects that were obviously doomed to failure before they even started shooting. No names, no pack drill, but the evidence is right there in our reviews of the Releases of the Year. The end-of-year report for 2012 should probably read: 'Not bad but could certainly do better.'

Let's hope that the British Film Institute, which has now taken over the work of the UK Film Council (deceased), will heed the trend and act accordingly by supporting only projects that are worthwhile.

How do you view your films? Most people in the UK don't go to the cinema nowadays, but watch on television via a loan scheme such as Love Film or Netflix, or view on Sky or the increasing number of film channels like Virgin or Now TV. New films are released to satellite stations very promptly, so you needn't wait too long to catch up with the latest blockbusters. However, film rental stores are closing at a rate of knots, with companies like Blockbuster going bust in the UK.

Similarly, if you want to buy DVDs you'll find many stores, such as HMV, have also closed. The press have blamed online suppliers such as Amazon and Play.com, as well as supermarkets and other stores, for stocking discounted DVDs at prices lower than HMV could offer. However, most national newspapers have their own online shops selling books, CDs and DVDs amongst other items, so they are also partially to blame. With the advent of online shopping the same thing happened to independent booksellers. Once upon a time we had specialist shops, but now the big stores have to sell absolutely everything for that one-stop marketing experience. The good news is that HMV has been bought out, so some of their outlets will now survive.

Living in Hertfordshire I am reasonably near the Rex, the single-screen cinema at Berkhamsted, now lovingly restored to its original 1930s Art Deco style. There I can watch

Opposite:
The more things change... In 1964, Audrey Hepburn in *My Fair Lady* graced the cover of the 21st *Film Review* annual. Five decades on, this year's cover is strikingly similar.

films in luxurious comfort with no adverts, no trailers and no hot dogs or popcorn – that is when and if I can get in, for the Rex is a victim of its own success, with most performances sold out in advance. Sometimes, therefore, I am forced to see films at a multiplex and it is always a chastening experience.

During 2012 I needed to catch up with *Skyfall* and *Argo*, as I had missed them at the Rex. I saw *Skyfall* at the Vue in Harrow, a typical multi-screen venue with very little atmosphere. For *Argo* I hit the West End at what used to be called 'The Showplace of the Nation'. The famous Empire in Leicester Square, once a huge single-auditorium cinema, now comprises nine screens on the old Empire and Ritz sites.

I think *Argo* must have been screened in the Empire's attic, as I counted some 50 stairs in order to reach it. On arrival I found it had about six rows of some 40 seats. Mind you, they were comfortable, but Screen 9 was so small it didn't seem to be much bigger than the average sitting room. Admittedly the screen was huge, but it still felt like being at home watching the film on a massive TV screen. What it cost me to see the film would have easily bought the DVD of *Argo* to view at home, but would I have enjoyed the same collective experience I had at the Empire, however small the audience may have been? I left Leicester Square musing on how much better any film is when shown on the truly big screen at my 'local', the Rex.

Below: Some of Britain's oldest cinemas were the subject of Thomas Lawes' engaging documentary *The Last Projectionist*.

Another single-screen cinema for enjoying movies in luxurious surroundings is the Electric Cinema Club on Portobello Road in London's Notting Hill area. It now seats only around 100 patrons, as every other row of seats was removed in its renovation some ten years ago. Dating from 1910, it's one of the earliest purpose-built cinemas still operating today; it's a mere two months younger than its namesake, the Electric Cinema in Birmingham. In the 1930s it became the Imperial Playhouse, showing mainly re-runs in an area that was beginning to decline. I remember it as a useful source for double-bills of old movies during the mid-1960s, when many seats were broken or non-existent and rats could be seen running about.

It was then revamped and run by Mainline Pictures, showing mostly independent and art-house films. Further redevelopment occurred in 2001 when the wide leather seats were installed, along with 'double-beds' in the back row where couples could lie down while enjoying the film or each other. Following a fire in 2012 the Electric re-opened with the double-beds moved to the front of the auditorium, immediately below the screen, which could prove to be a distraction for the rest of the audience. Still, it's something else to watch if the film gets boring… The Electric Cinemas in London and Birmingham are featured in one of the best documentaries of 2012, *The Last Projectionist*, which is reviewed in our Releases of the Year section.

Every ten years *Sight & Sound* publishes a list of the 'Greatest Films of All Time'. Starting in 1952, this has hitherto been a worldwide poll of film critics but, because of the changing nature of publishing and the current domination of electronic media, the magazine decided to broaden its scope in 2012 to include a much wider range of commentators. These now include many critics who have made their names online rather than in print. The magazine took on board over a thousand critics, programmers, directors, academics, distributors, writers and other cinephiles, and the ensuing results drew 846 Top Ten lists covering 2,045 different film titles.

The brief was left open to interpretation, so the choices could be made from films that have been most important to film history, or those that have achieved the pinnacle of artistic achievement, or simply those that the contributors have most enjoyed in the course of their cinema-going lives. In 1952 the film in the Number 1 position was Vittorio De Sica's *Bicycle Thieves* – by common consent, both then and now, one of the all-time great films of that or any other decade. By 1962, however, it had been replaced by Orson Welles' *Citizen Kane*, which was to remain in the Number 1 spot for decades. *Citizen Kane* is still up there but is now at Number 2 in the list, while *Bicycle Thieves* has slipped to 33.

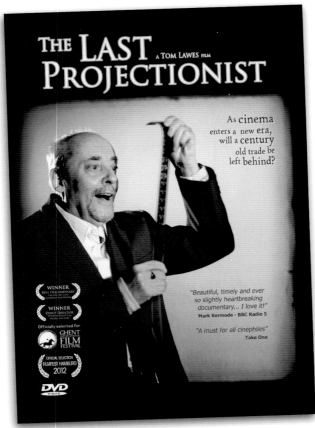

THE LAST PROJECTIONIST

A TOM LAWES FILM

As cinema enters a new era, will a century old trade be left behind?

"Beautiful, timely and ever so slightly heartbreaking documentary... I love it!"
Mark Kermode - BBC Radio 5

"A must for all cinephiles"
Take One

WINNER
BEST DOCUMENTARY

WINNER
DEBUT DIRECTOR

Officially selected for
GHENT FILM FESTIVAL

OFFICIAL SELECTION
FILMFEST HAMBURG
2012

DVD
VIDEO

In the 2012 list *Citizen Kane* was ousted by Alfred Hitchcock's *Vertigo*. Not a great critical or commercial success when it first appeared in 1958, over the years it has developed a reputation it possibly doesn't deserve. Robert Burks' beautiful cinematography is the essence of clarity and, as a piece of sheer Grand Guignol, the film works superbly well, especially with Bernard Herrmann's Gothic score heightening the action to fever pitch. But *Vertigo* is problematic in that its plot is unsatisfactorily convoluted and at times not always credible. An odd choice then, but one that reflects not only current attitudes to popular cinema but also the diversity of personnel involved in the latest *Sight & Sound* poll.

It's a shift reflected in the editorial policy of the magazine's current editor, Nick James. Since 1991 and the demise of the British Film Institute's *Monthly Film Bulletin*, *Sight & Sound* (also published by the BFI) has reviewed all the UK releases, making the magazine more democratic and less elitist than it was under previous editors such as Gavin Lambert and Penelope Houston. BFI Southbank (formerly the National Film Theatre) has also widened its brief in recent years by showing a greater range of popular films alongside the regular art-house choices.

In the Top 20 of the *Sight & Sound* poll is a typical selection of classic films that will end up on any list of the Greatest Films of All Time, including one, Jean Renoir's *La Règle du jeu*, which has appeared on the *S&S* list in every decade since the poll began. Other French films that still make the Top 50 include Dreyer's *La Passion de Jeanne d'Arc* (made by the Danish director in France), as well as his *Ordet* and *Gertrud*, Vigo's *L'Atalante*, Godard's *À Bout de souffle*, *Le Mépris*, *Pierrot le fou* and *Histoire(s) du cinéma*, Bresson's *Au Hasard Balthazar*, Chantal Akerman's *Jeanne Dielman 23 Quai du Commerce 1080 Bruxelles*, Truffaut's *Les quatre cents coups*, Tati's *Playtime* and Chris Marker's *La Jetée*.

Look through the Top 50 films and you will find many other familiar titles, such as Fellini's *8½* and *La Dolce Vita*, Ozu's *Tokyo Story* and *Late Spring*, Eisenstein's *Battleship Potemkin*, Kurosawa's *Seven Samurai* and *Rashomon*, Bergman's *Persona*, Antonioni's *L'avventura*, Fritz Lang's *Metropolis*, Tarkovsky's *Andrei Rublev* and *Stalker*, Rossellini's *Journey to Italy*, Ray's *Pather Panchali*, Pontecorvo's *The Battle of Algiers* and Mizoguchi's *Ugetsu Monogatari*.

However, it's not all 'foreign' films that become classics, for American cinema is still well represented in the Top 50, not just by *Vertigo* and *Citizen Kane* but also by *Sunrise: A Song of Two Humans* (FW Murnau's silent film made in the US in 1927), John Ford's *The Searchers*,

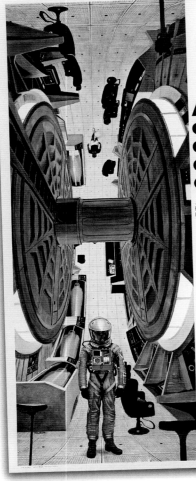

Above: Kubrick's psychedelic masterpiece *2001*... British? Or not?

Right: Number One no longer. Orson Welles in *Citizen Kane*.

Coppola's *Apocalypse Now*, *The Godfather* and *The Godfather Part II*, Gene Kelly and Stanley Donen's *Singin' in the Rain* (at Number 20), David Lynch's *Mulholland Drive*, Scorsese's *Taxi Driver*, Buster Keaton's *The General*, Hitchcock's *Psycho*, Billy Wilder's *Some Like It Hot* and Chaplin's *City Lights* (the last at Number 50).

On the other hand, if you check the list for the UK contingent there isn't a single British film until you reach Number 73, *The Third Man*. After that the only other British films to make the Top 100 are *Lawrence of Arabia* (at 82 – but is it really British?), *A Matter of Life and Death* (at 92) and *The Life and Death of Colonel Blimp* (at 97). There is, however, one film in the Top 10 of the *S&S* list that could be termed British. Coming in at Number 6, it was filmed in Britain by a director who was American but a long-time UK resident, was financed and distributed by an American company, and had two American stars in the lead roles but British actors as supporting players. The film is MGM's *2001: A Space Odyssey*, directed by Stanley Kubrick. For the sake of argument, and to save face for the UK film industry, we will call it British.

Personally I'm glad *2001* is near the top of the list as it is my favourite science fiction film,

although I know I'm in a minority. Moreover, I can never see *Citizen Kane* too often, or John Ford's *The Searchers* come to that. And if I would have placed *Singin' in the Rain* much nearer the top of my list, I am nevertheless glad that it is at least in the Top 20. After all, it's the finest original film musical ever made and one of the best movies about Hollywood too. As much as I admire *Vertigo*, given a choice I would prefer to see Hitchcock's *Psycho* again and would have put it very near the top of the *S&S* list.

Another Top 100 list of films came out during 2012, the personal choice of former television movie pundit and *Radio Times* columnist Barry Norman. As you can imagine, his choice comprised an even wider mix of general and art-house releases. His list is in alphabetical order, so that any one entry is as good as the next, from *The Adventures of Robin Hood* with Errol Flynn to *The Wizard of Oz* with Judy Garland. Whereas *Sight & Sound*'s latest list has no films made after 2002 in its first 100 titles, Norman comes right up to date by including *Chicago* (2002), *Master and Commander* (2003), *No Country for Old Men* (2007), *The Hurt Locker* (2008) and the *Harry Potter* series (2001-11). Even in the *S&S* list's second 100 titles there are only four post-2002 films. Obviously recent cinema lacks the pulling power of old movies; either that or they're just not making memorable films in the 21st century.

Norman also has a good sprinkling of classic British films: *Brief Encounter*, *The Cruel Sea*, David Lean's *Great Expectations*, *Gregory's Girl*, *I Know Where I'm Going*, *Kind Hearts and Coronets*, *Lawrence of Arabia*, *A Matter of Life and Death*, *Monty Python and the Holy Grail*, *The Railway Children* and *The Third Man*; oh, and *2001* and *Dr Strangelove*, another film Kubrick made in Britain. Norman's list also overlaps with *Sight & Sound* on 20 titles, including *Apocalypse Now*, *Blade Runner*, *Casablanca*, *Chinatown*, *Citizen Kane*, *The Godfather*, *North by Northwest*, *Psycho*, *Raging Bull*, *The Searchers*, *Seven Samurai*, *Shoah*, *Singin' in the Rain*, *Some Like It Hot*, *Sunset Blvd* and *The Wild*

Bunch. Is this a question of great minds thinking alike or are certain films, defying criticism, universally loved?

Would you believe there's yet another list of favourite films, this time from the Critics' Circle? As part of the celebrations for its centenary year in 2013, the Circle asked some of its distinguished members to curate a season, at the Barbican Cinema in London, of 'Films That Changed My Life'. It's an odd assortment, but some of them match those on the *Sight & Sound* and Barry Norman lists: David Gritten chose *The Battle of Algiers*, Sukhdev Sandhu *Les quatre cents coups*, Peter Bradshaw *Raging Bull*, Kate Muir *I Know Where I'm Going* and Jason Solomons *Annie Hall*. Other life-changing titles were Grigori Kosintsev's *Hamlet*, Derek Jarman's *The Garden*, Jacques Rivette's *Celine and Julie Go Boating*, Preston Sturges' *The Lady Eve*, Lindsay Anderson's *If....*, Anand Gandhi's *Ship of Theseus*, John Sturges' *Bad Day at Black Rock* and Nathan Juran's *East of Sudan* and *First Men in the Moon*. (The last two are both from 1964 and presumably were a double life-changing whammy for critic Kim Newman at that time.) It all goes to show the breadth of the cinematic experience.

So, what do these lists tell us, if anything? That the more cinema changes, the more it stays the same? Or are we just indulging in nostalgia?

Future nostalgics may well remember the year 2012 for the London Olympics and Paralympics, particularly for the contribution that film, theatre and television writer-director Danny Boyle made to the opening ceremony, when HM The Queen finally became a Bond girl. Who would or could possibly top that now?

Also in 2012, a real blast of nostalgia was provided by the Victoria & Albert Museum's highly successful exhibition devoted to Hollywood Costume. Here were the original outfits from the heyday of movie glamour that marked out the cinema as something special. Spread over three galleries were items from the days of silent films through the Golden Age of Hollywood, including costumes worn by Vivien Leigh in *Gone With the Wind* and Bette Davis in *The Virgin Queen*, and on to more recent designs for *Taxi Driver*, *Fight Club*, *Shakespeare in Love*, *Pirates of the Caribbean*, *Avatar* and *Black Swan*.

The first two sections demonstrated how designers research their subjects, whether real or imaginary, in order to come up with an authentic mode of dress for each character in a film. The final section was the most interesting, as it comprised a gallery of models of famous actors dressed in their original costumes. They included Travis Banton's designs for Marlene Dietrich in *Morocco*, Orry-Kelly's black chiffon dress for Marilyn Monroe in *Some Like It Hot*, Givenchy's little black number for Audrey Hepburn in *Breakfast at Tiffany's*, Irene Sharaff's outfits for Barbra Streisand in *Funny Girl*, Deborah

Nadoolman's costumes for Harrison Ford in *Raiders of the Lost Ark*, Colleen Atwood's couture for Renée Zellweger in *Chicago*, and Judianna Makovsky's costume designs for *Harry Potter*, among many, many others.

Judy Garland's ruby slippers from *The Wizard of Oz* were there, along with her little blue-gingham pinafore dress that MGM designer Adrian ran up for her on an old sewing machine, using cheap material for a truly authentic look. There were several dresses made but the one on show at the V&A was the very last surviving original; after more than 70 years, it's now fairly faded. During the run of the V&A's Hollywood Costume exhibition there was a sale at Julien's Auctions in Hollywood at which Judy's little blue dress fetched all of $480,000. At the same auction Marilyn Monroe's skirt from *River of No Return* fetched $50,000 and Julie Andrews' dress from *The Sound of Music* went for $38,400.

But enough of all this nostalgia… For something more up to date, turn to Mansel Stimpson's Afterword at the end of this volume. There he picks out some of the more striking titles of 2013, films that are merely touched on for now but will be reviewed more fully in the next edition of *Film Review*.

Below: Judy Garland and Jack Haley in *The Wizard of Oz*. Garland's dress recently fetched close to $500,000.

Top 20 UK *Box-Office Hits*

1 January – 31 December 2012

1. Skyfall
2. The Dark Knight Rises
3. Avengers Assemble
4. The Hobbit: An Unexpected Journey
5. The Twilight Saga: Breaking Dawn Part 2
6. Ted
7. Ice Age: Continental Drift
8. Life of Pi
9. The Amazing Spiderman
10. Prometheus

11. Taken 2
12. The Hunger Games
13. Brave
14. The Woman in Black
15. Madagascar 3: Europe's Most Wanted
16. Men in Black III
17. The Best Exotic Marigold Hotel
18. War Horse
19. The Muppets
20. The Pirates! In an Adventure with Scientists!

Top 10 *Box-Office Stars*

Star of the Year: *Liam Neeson*

2. **Daniel Radcliffe**
3. **Judi Dench**
4. **Kristen Stewart**
5. **Christian Bale**
6. **Sacha Baron Cohen**
7. **Channing Tatum**
8. **Meryl Streep**
9. **Tom Cruise**
10. **George Clooney**

What were the names that audiences clamoured for in 2012? Easy: James Bond, Batman, Iron Man, Bilbo Baggins, Bella Cullen (née Swan) and a foul-mouthed teddy bear. There was also a woolly mammoth, a Bengal tiger called Richard Parker and Spider-Man. The cold fact is that whoever was playing these characters, it would have made little difference to the commercial outcome. So we need to dig a bit deeper to work out which stars actually attracted audiences on the basis of their names alone.

Taken 2 is unlikely to have been anywhere near as successful without Liam Neeson. He was also in *Wrath of the Titans* and *Battleship*, both of which charted in the Top 40, and reprised his role of Ra's al Ghul in the second highest-grossing film of the year, *The Dark Knight Rises* (albeit in a cameo). Neeson seemed to be everywhere, which was not bad for an actor in his 60th year.

Daniel Radcliffe – 36 years Neeson's junior – was also the predominant reason people queued up to be scared witless by *The Woman in Black*, proving that the 23-year-old (12 inches shorter than Neeson) had plenty of drawing power even without a wand and spectacles. But perhaps the most surprising entrant is Judi Dench, whose prominent appearance in *Skyfall* and starring role in the unexpected hit *The Best Exotic Marigold Hotel* proved once and for all that audiences can't get enough of this actress.

The rest of the names in the chart are based on both the box-office performance of their films and their previous track record.

James Cameron-Wilson

Faces of the Year

by **James Cameron-Wilson**

Samantha Barks in *Les Misérables*.

SAMANTHA BARKS
Born: 2 October 1990, Laxey, Isle of Man.

It helped that *Les Misérables* was as successful as it was. But casting agents would still have beaten a path to Samantha Barks' door.

A genuine head-turner, she first caught the attention of the public on the BBC talent show *I'd Do Anything*, in which viewers were asked to vote for who they thought would make the ideal Nancy in a new West End production of *Oliver!* While Barks failed to win the part (she was placed third), she won a good many hearts and minds. She certainly earned the support of her fellow Manx: her homeland, the Isle of Man, was renamed the Isle of Sam in her honour (it was a tourist gimmick, but signs at the airport and Douglas Sea Terminal were changed). Barks' new-found fame led to good parts: Sally Bowles in a UK tour of *Cabaret*, the title role of *Aladdin* at the Theatre Royal Windsor and Éponine in the West End production of *Les Misérables*.

From Éponine, Barks went on to play Nancy in a UK tour of *Oliver!* and, while appearing in the latter, embarked on a gruelling round of auditions to play Éponine in the film version of *Les Misérables*. It was after an *Oliver!* curtain call that the producer Cameron Mackintosh walked on stage and announced to the audience that Barks had won the role. It was a sage choice. Barks can belt out a tune like the best of them and her screen rendition of 'On My Own' will put any doubters in their place. It's a song, she says, she used to sing into her hairbrush when she was just eight years old.

Les Misérables went on to snare eight Oscar nominations, a Golden Globe for best film and $433 million at the worldwide box-office. Next, Barks landed the female lead in the family fantasy *The Christmas Candle*, alongside Hans Matheson, Lesley Manville, John Hannah and Susan Boyle, another talent show contestant. It's a strange old world.

HENRY CAVILL
Born: 5 May 1983, Jersey, Channel Islands.

Henry Cavill is in the business of playing iconic figures. In his very first film he was Albert Mondego, son of Fernand Mondego (Guy Pearce), in Kevin Reynolds' *The Count of Monte Cristo*. Four years later he was back in period dress for the role of Melot in Kevin Reynolds' *Tristan & Isolde*. He was the Duke of Suffolk in TV's *The Tudors* (for four years) and when that ended he signed on to play Theseus in Zack Snyder's rollicking *Immortals*. More significantly, he is playing Superman in this year's *Man of Steel*.

Like Samantha Barks [qv], Cavill was born off the coast of Britain, on Jersey in the Channel Islands. He was a fan of acting at school and was already a professional actor at 19. He hasn't looked back since. If Cavill hadn't been so instantly successful he'd like to have gone to university to study Egyptology – but will no doubt play some heroic Pharaoh instead.

Henry Cavill in *Man of Steel*.

At 6' 1", the actor follows in the vapour trail of George Reeves, Christopher Reeve and (cough) Brandon Routh, playing the kid from Krypton in red trunks. Zack Snyder's *Man of Steel*, with an estimated budget of $225 million, is primed for big things and comes with an estimable pedigree. Scripted by David S Goyer (*Batman Begins*) and produced by Christopher Nolan, it co-stars Amy Adams as Lois Lane, Kevin Costner as Clark Kent's dad and Russell Crowe as Jor-El. And that's an impressive support act. Cavill was actually in the running to play the lead in *Superman Returns* seven years ago, but was pipped to the post by Routh. However, as that film flopped so dramatically, Cavill was spared the fatal ignominy. And by the time you read this, *Man of Steel* will have already dominated the multiplexes. And whether it turns into *Man Stillborn* or another *Dark Knight*, Cavill will probably be a rather famous chap.

On a personal note, he's romantically linked to Gina Carano, the mixed martial artist who starred in Steven Soderbergh's *Haywire*.

SAM CLAFLIN
Born: 27 June 1986, Ipswich, England.

It helps that Sam Claflin has the looks of a male model, but his upward trajectory is impressive nonetheless. The son of an accountant (his father) and a classroom assistant (his mother), Sam was hardly born with a silver thespian spoon. But, after getting into the London Academy of Music and Dramatic Art, he has been pretty damned busy.

There were the inevitable TV parts – but no ordinary TV parts. His first notable credit was a good role in Tony and Ridley Scott's adaptation of Ken Follett's *The Pillars of the Earth*, which secured a Golden Globe nomination for best mini-series. Then there was the

Sam Claflin in *The Hunger Games: Catching Fire*.

role of Logan Mountstuart in the Channel 4 adaptation of William Boyd's *Any Human Heart*, which marched off with the Bafta for best drama serial. Indeed, Claflin counts the Baftas as a highlight of his career so far: standing on stage at the Royal Opera House, no less, presenting an award for best production design with Minnie Driver.

On film, he played Philip Swift in *Pirates of the Caribbean: On Stranger Tides* (worldwide gross: $1,044 million) and was then Prince Charming in *Snow White & The Huntsman* (worldwide gross: $241 million). Perhaps even more meteoric is the casting of Claflin opposite Jennifer Lawrence in the follow-up to *The Hunger Games*. In the sequel (*The Hunger Games: Catching Fire*), Claflin plays Finnick Odair, the champion of the 65th Hunger Games tournament, a role originally rumoured to be going to Armie Hammer or Taylor Kitsch. In all the excitement, *Entertainment Weekly* featured Claflin and Lawrence on the cover of their 2013 Preview Special, an endorsement of imminent glory if ever there was one.

Meanwhile, Claflin is rumoured to be playing the poet Robert Graves – opposite Imogen Poots – in *The Laureate* and is to pair up with Lily Collins (*Mirror Mirror*) in the Anglo-American romcom *Love, Rosie*. After that, anything could happen.

Idris Elba in *Prometheus*.

IDRIS ELBA

Born: 6 September 1972, Hackney, East London, England.

Idris Elba has been around so long he hardly qualifies as a Face of the Year. He's paid his dues in episodes of *The Bill*, *2point4 Children*, *Silent Witness* and even *Absolutely Fabulous*. But this year he gets to play Nelson Mandela.

Adapted from Mandela's own memoir, Justin Chadwick's *Mandela: Long Walk to Freedom* is scripted by William Nicholson (*Shadowlands*, *Gladiator*, *Les Misérables*) and was already generating Oscar buzz in early 2013. Add this to Guillermo del Toro's SF behemoth *Pacific Rim* and you can bet that this is the year that will move Idris Elba from an inside secret to a global movie star. And the fact that he's playing Heimdall the Asgardian in *Thor: The Dark World* can hardly dampen his chances of world domination.

Like his fellow Englishmen David Harewood and David Oyelowo, Elba has become accepted in the US as a native African-American. Notably, it was his role as the charismatic drugs baron Stringer Bell in the absurdly popular *The Wire* that established this fallacy. Like the two Davids, Elba has an uncanny understanding of the American twang. However, he scuppered this with his portrayal of Lenny, an English handyman and painter who beds Laura Linney in Showtime's award-winning *The Big C*. And a year later he landed his own TV series in the UK, playing the title role of Chief Inspector John *Luther* for the BBC.

On film, Elba's most prominent roles have been in the US, in *The Gospel*, *Daddy's Little Girls*, *This Christmas* and *Obsessed* (in which he top-billed Beyoncé Knowles), but none of them really made a mark at the box-office. It was as a supporting actor in *American Gangster*, *Thor* and *Prometheus* that Elba was noted at the multiplexes, roles far from the precincts of Hackney and East London. For now, he's making his name playing Yanks, extra-terrestrial (and mythical) beings – and a South African visionary.

Soon, maybe, he might star in a major film as a Brit.

TOM HIDDLESTON

Born: 9 February 1981, Westminster, London, England.

If Tom Hiddleston betrayed a certain 'stiff upper lip' demeanour in films like *The Gathering Storm*, *War Horse* and *The Deep Blue Sea*, it's hardly surprising. The man went to Eton, then Cambridge (Pembroke College), then RADA. That's a pretty impressive (and uncommon) track record.

Hiddleston not only cuts his vowels precisely but looks the very part of a patrician Englishman, although his father is Scottish. While still at Cambridge he was cast in a TV production of *Nicholas Nickleby* and as Randolph Churchill in *The Gathering Storm* – and was then accepted by RADA. Fresh out of drama school, he won a leading role in Joanna Hogg's *Unrelated*, a low-budget film that received ecstatic reviews. He then had the lead in Hogg's *Archipelago* which, if anything, attracted even more glowing notices, and soon he was hobnobbing with the likes of Steven Spielberg and Kenneth Branagh. And the future looks good.

Following the title role in the BBC's *Henry V* (produced by Sam Mendes), Hiddleston was cast in the lead (as a vampire) in Jim Jarmusch's *Only Lovers Left*

Tom Hiddleston in *Avengers Assemble*.

Oscar Isaac in *W.E.*

Elizabeth Olsen in *Martha Marcy May Marlene.*

Alive, with Tilda Swinton, Mia Wasikowska and John Hurt in support. Being British, he was also cast as the villain in the $150-million *Thor*, and then played him, Loki, again in *Avengers Assemble*, the highest grossing film of 2012. He will repeat his duty as the Norse god of mischief (and what mischief) in *Thor: The Dark World*, released this year (2013). He is now reunited with Hogg for *London Project* and has been signed up to star as an escaped convict in the crime thriller *Black Wings Has My Angel*, co-starring Anna Paquin and Elijah Wood.

Bearing a passing resemblance to Michael Fassbender (they could play brothers), Hiddleston has not been entirely constrained by his English accent. After all, he played F Scott Fitzgerald in Woody Allen's *Midnight in Paris*.

OSCAR ISAAC
Born: 5 January 1980, Guatemala.

Oscar Isaac has been slowly creeping up on the outside. If you're a film buff, the likelihood is you've seen him – but not necessarily clocked him. That's because he's so damned chameleonic.

Yet get this: he's played Joseph in *The Nativity Story*, Orestes in *Agora* (opposite Rachel Weisz), Prince John in Ridley Scott's *Robin Hood* and the romantic rival of Ryan Gosling – for the attentions of Carey Mulligan – in *Drive*. And in the Coen brothers' *Inside Llewyn Davis* he's Llewyn Davis and back with Carey Mulligan – and is already being tipped for an Oscar nomination. In the latter he plays the eponymous singer-songwriter in a film based on Dave Van Ronk's posthumously published memoir *The Mayor of MacDougal Street*.

While Isaac has portrayed a wide variety of nationalities (Israeli, Iraqi, Roman, English, Russian), this is the first time he's got to sing. But that's not a problem: he started out as a singer (also playing lead guitar) with his own band, The Blinking Underdogs, in Miami. And drawing on his innate musical skills, Isaac even got to play piano in Madonna's *W.E.* (wooing Abbie Cornish).

The question we have to ask ourselves is: why isn't Oscar Isaac already a household name? Well, this time next year…

ELIZABETH OLSEN
Born: 16 February 1989, Sherman Oaks, California, USA.

Nobody saw Elizabeth Olsen coming. The younger sister of media darlings Mary-Kate and Ashley Olsen (who, on a creative level, nobody took seriously), she emerged from the shadow of her more celebrated family and proved that she had the acting chops to make her own name.

That Olsen came out of nowhere so fast is a testament to her seriousness as a performer: after years of acting (and ballet) classes she further honed her craft in Moscow. When she landed the title role (several, actually) in *Martha Marcy May Marlene*, she was ready to show us what she was made of. A dark and complex tale, *Martha Marcy…* explored the alternating mind states of a young woman recovering from the traumas of an upstate New York cult. Olsen was totally convincing in the role, even consented to a nude scene, and earned herself a fistful of awards.

It was one of those debuts that caught the imagination of the press and Olsen was prime material for media coverage: the famous twins' little sister who made good. In fact, she had already tucked one film under her belt – playing Jane Fonda's granddaughter in Bruce Beresford's *Peace, Love & Misunderstanding* – but nobody seemed to have seen (or even heard of) it. The starring role in the horror opus *Silent House* was hardly more successful – it grossed just $346,889 outside America – but the future looks good.

She starred opposite Josh Radnor in *Liberal Arts*, Daniel Radcliffe in *Kill Your Darlings* (in which he plays the Beat poet Allen Ginsberg and she the wife of Jack Kerouac) and then paired up with Dakota Fanning in *Very Good Girls*, with Demi Moore and Richard Dreyfuss in support. She then landed the title role in *Thérèse Raquin*, with Oscar Isaac and Jessica Lange co-starring, and has the female lead in Spike Lee's *Oldboy*, a remake of the cult South Korean thriller. And while the upcoming *Godzilla* is unlikely to stretch her thespian potential, it's a tent-pole production that will give her her greatest exposure yet.

Either way, at the moment Elizabeth Olsen seems pretty unstoppable.

IMOGEN POOTS
Born: 5 June 1989, London, England.

Imogen Poots had been brightening up films for several years but kept on disappearing. Until she popped up again. But now she's here.

She was a scene-stealer in the Danny Boyle-produced *28 Weeks Later*, had a blink-and-you'll-miss-it in *Me and Orson Welles*, was one of the schoolgirls (alongside Juno Temple) in Jordan Scott's rather too pretty *Cracks*, and then went to America to bed Michael Douglas in the little-seen *Solitary Man*. Small parts ensued in *Waking Madison* and *Centurion* and then a lead in the British, low-budget and critically reviled *Chatroom*. She was Blanche Ingram in Cary Fukunaga's *Jane Eyre* and reminded us how good she can be (complete with convincing American accent) in the entertaining *Fright Night* remake. She had the female lead in the little-seen British romantic thriller *Comes a Bright Day* and was in the American *Greetings from Tim Buckley*, which was well received but virtually ignored.

At this point, most British actresses would slither into TV. But Poots' prospects suddenly changed. She played a violinist in the small scale *A Late Quartet*

Imogen Poots in *Comes a Bright Day*.

and more than held her own against Philip Seymour Hoffman and Catherine Keener. She then got to work with director Michael Winterbottom, playing Paul Raymond's daughter Debbie in *The Look of Love*. She was the best thing in it. She then starred opposite James McAvoy in the big-screen adaptation of Irvine Welsh's controversial novel *Filth*, paid lip service (literally) to Zac Efron in the romantic comedy *Are We Officially Dating?* and was cast opposite Christian Bale ("one of my favourite actors in the world") in the romantic drama *Knight of Cups*. Directed by Terrence Malick ("a hero of mine"), the last named is likely to put her on the map.

There's also a Jimi Hendrix biopic, *All Is By My Side*, a starry British comedy-drama with Aaron Paul and Pierce Brosnan called *A Long Way Down*, and another Aaron Paul vehicle, the all-action *Need For Speed*. After that, she's pencilled in for *The Laureate*, a British drama in which she plays the American poet and novelist Laura Riding.

JUNO TEMPLE
Born: 21 July 1989, London, England.

For one so young, Juno Temple has a formidable list of credits, with 29 films under her belt and – at the time of writing – another two in pre-production.

She was 11 when her father, the English filmmaker Julien Temple, cast her as Emma, the daughter of Robert Southey, in *Pandaemonium* (2000), a lush, soap operatic and occasionally rather fun look at the lives of the Lake Poets. However, it wasn't until 2007 that the actress made a true impression in two very different, high-profile productions, *Atonement* and *St Trinian's*. In the former she was the prissy, curly-haired Lola Quincey and in the latter she was the precious, eco-friendly Celia. These were meaty character parts and Juno was still only 18.

She trotted out more snotty, rebellious schoolgirl roles until revealing a new side to her talent in Noah Baumbach's *Greenberg*, an American comedy-drama starring Ben Stiller, playing a fun-loving Australian. This led to a slew of American indies, including Gregg Araki's SF comedy *Kaboom* (in which she played a promiscuous British student), the title role in *Dirty Girl* (as a high school slut), another lead – as a rebellious, suicidal runaway – in *Little Birds*, and the lead in *Jack & Diane*, as a werewolf.

But it was another American film, *Killer Joe*, in which the actress parlayed her Lolita image to striking effect – and it was a movie that got a wide release and a whole lot of attention. Directed by William Friedkin, it featured Temple as a piece of young trailer-trash who ends up becoming the sexual bait of contract killer Matthew McConaughey. Looking at *Killer Joe*, it's hard to believe that this is the same actress who played Anne Boleyn's sister-in-law in *The Other Boleyn Girl*. No wonder, then, that she won the Rising Star award at the 2013 Baftas.

Future film parts include the starring role in the comic fantasy *The Brass Teapot*, Linda Lovelace's best

Juno Temple in *Killer Joe*.

friend Patsy in *Lovelace*, the female lead in Alexandre Aja's fantasy thriller *Horns* – opposite Daniel Radcliffe – and Sally in Frank Miller and Robert Rodriguez' *Sin City: A Dame to Kill For*.

MARY ELIZABETH WINSTEAD

Born: 28 November 1984, Rocky Mount, North Carolina, USA.

To horror lovers, Mary Elizabeth Winstead was a rather magnificent scream queen. To action fans, she was Bruce Willis' daughter Lucy in the *Die Hard* franchise. But then Mary Elizabeth starred in a little film called *Smashed* (2012) and jolted critics to attention. Deservedly nominated for an Independent Spirit Award as best female lead, the actress showed that she was just that: an actress.

As Kate Hannah, an elementary school teacher and alcoholic, she went through the usual melodramatic motions of what heavy drinkers are prone to: wetting the bed, throwing up in front of her students, urinating on the floor of the local corner shop, waking up on the street and, worst of all, singing Nick Lowe's 'Cruel To Be Kind' at a karaoke bar. But Mary Elizabeth also gave us a little more. Her irrational outbursts and scenes of denial rang scarily true. This was a performance to rank with the great celluloid drunks: Lee Remick in *Days of Wine and Roses*, Elizabeth Taylor in *Who's Afraid of Virginia Woolf*, Meg Ryan in *When a Man Loves a Woman*. Maybe better.

For the record, this Southern Belle studied ballet then switched careers to concentrate on acting: Broadway (*Joseph and the Amazing Technicolor Dreamcoat*), TV soaps (*Passions*, *Wolf Lake*) and then a

spot of Disney (*Sky High*, in which she played a school senior who could control machines with her mind). Then there were all the horrors: *Final Destination 3* (in which she had the lead), *Black Christmas*, Quentin Tarantino's grisly *Death Proof*, *The Thing* and *Abraham Lincoln: Vampire Hunter* (as Mary Todd Lincoln). In between she managed to land the lead role of Ramona Flowers (great name) in Edgar Wright's *Scott Pilgrim vs. the World*. And then there was *Smashed*.

Reflecting her new maturity, she took character parts in *A Glimpse Inside the Mind of Charles Swan III* (with Charlie Sheen), *The Spectacular Now* and *A.C.O.D.* (standing for 'Adult Children of Divorce'). Interestingly, all three films are comedies, indicating a new career path for Winstead. It will be fascinating to see where she goes next.

Mary Elizabeth Winstead in *Smashed*.

Releases *of the* Year

This section contains details of all the films released in the UK between 1 January and 31 December 2012.

Each film review is followed by the main credits for the film, beginning with names of the leading actors, then the Director, Producer(s), Screenplay Writer, Cinematographer, Production Designer or Art Director, Editor, Soundtrack Composer and Costume Designer.

For technical credits the normal abbreviations operate and are as follows:

Dir – for Director; Pro – for Producer; Ph – for Cinematographer; Pro Des – for Production Designer; Art Dir – for Art Director; M – for Composer; and Cos – for Costume Designer.

The production companies involved are listed, with the final name in the list being the distributor. The credits end with the film's running time, the country or countries of origin, the year of production, the UK release date and the British Board of Film Classification certificate.

Reviewers: Charles Bacon (CB), James Cameron-Wilson (JC-W), Jeremy Clarke (JC), Michael Darvell (MHD), Marshall Julius (MJ), Penny Lucas (PL), Jonathan Rigby (JR), George Savvides (GS), Mansel Stimpson (MS) and Derek Winnert (DW).

Star ratings

★★★★★ **Exceptional**
★★★★ **Very Good**
★★★ **Good**
★★ **Mediocre**
★ **Poor**

2 Days in New York ★

The talented Julie Delpy sadly takes a mis-step here. Although imperfect, her directorial debut *2 Days in Paris* was genuinely engaging, but this sequel taking some of the characters to America is ill-judged. Delpy's previously sympathetic heroine becomes tiresomely kooky and other characters are equally unappealing and larger than life. By the time Vincent Gallo rolls up to buy the heroine's soul and keep it in his underpants the extent of the disaster is clear. MS

❯ Julie Delpy, Chris Rock, Albert Delpy, Alexia Landeau, Alex Nahon, Dylan Baker, Kate Burton, Daniel Brühl, Vincent Gallo.
❯ *Dir* and *M* Julie Delpy, *Pro* Christophe Mazodier, Delpy and others, *Screenplay* Delpy and Alexia Landeau, *Ph* Lubomir Bakchev, *Pro Des* Judy Rhee, *Ed* Isabelle Devinck, *Cos* Rebecca Hofherr.

A Polaris production/Tempête sous un Crane/Protozoa Pictures etc-Network Releasing.
96 mins. France/Germany/Belgium. 2012.
Rel: 18 May 2012. Cert. 15.

21 Jump Street ★★½

Co-written and executive produced by Jonah Hill, this update of the cult 1987-91 TV series certainly knows itself. Police boss Ice Cube sets the record straight from the word go, deploring the lack of imagination in recycling old ideas before promptly dispatching a pair of under-achieving cops – dumb jock Jenko (Tatum) and timorous nerd Schmidt (Hill) – to pose as schoolboys at a drug-infiltrated high school. The idea certainly has comic potential, but the film quickly resorts to the crass, crude formula of most teen comedies, albeit with a very violent streak. Some of it is quite amusing, although it fails to work up any real comic momentum. JC-W

❯ Jonah Hill, Channing Tatum, Ice Cube, Brie Larson, Dave Franco, Rob Riggle, Johnny Depp.
❯ *Dir* Phil Lord and Christopher Miller, *Pro*

Opposite:
The unstoppable Jennifer Lawrence (Oscar winner, box-office champ) as Katniss Everdeen in Gary Ross' *The Hunger Games.*

Stephen J Cannell and Neal H Moritz, *Screenplay* Michael Bacall and Jonah Hill, *Ph* Barry Peterson, *Pro Des* Peter Wenham, *Ed* Joel Negrone, *M* Mark Mothersbaugh, *Cos* Leah Katznelson.

Columbia Pictures/MGM/Relativity Media/Original Film/SJC Studios-Sony.
109 mins. USA. 1012. Rel: 16 Mar 2012. Cert. 15.

360 ★★★½

A range of interconnected stories feature here even if, contrary to publicity, the emphasis on sexual relationships does not echo the structure of *La Ronde*. Making it the opening night film of the 2011 London Film Festival put too great a weight on a relatively slight and uneven movie, but it's entertaining enough. It's very well acted too, not least by Anthony Hopkins, who gives a powerful, committed performance. MS

▸ Anthony Hopkins, Ben Foster, Jude Law, Rachel Weisz, Jamel Debbouze, Dinara Drukarova.
▸ *Dir* Fernando Meirelles, *Pro* Andrew Eaton, David Linde, Olivier Delbosc etc, *Screenplay* Peter Morgan, *Ph* Adriano Goldman, *Pro Des* John Paul Kelly, *Ed* Daniel Razende, *Cos* Monika Buttinger.

BBC Films/UK Film Council/Unison Films etc-Artificial Eye.
110 mins. UK/Austria/France/Brazil. 2011. Rel: 10 Aug 2012. Cert. 15.

388 Arletta Avenue ★★★★

James Deakins (Nick Stahl) and his wife Amy (Mia Kirschner) live a comfortable life in a fashionable area of Toronto, completely unaware that they're being watched 24 hours a day. But when Amy mysteriously disappears, James is accused of foul play... This is a taut and gripping thriller despite the done-to-death filming style (the action is seen from the point of view of surveillance with handheld cameras). Stahl is excellent as the caring husband who gradually descends into a world of paranoia and despair. GS

No redress: Nick Stahl at *388 Arletta Avenue*.

▸ Nick Stahl, Mia Kirschner, Devon Sawa, Aaron Abrams, Charlotte Sullivan, Krista Bridges.
▸ *Dir* and *Screenplay* Randall Cole, *Pro* Steven Hoban and Mark Smith, *Ph* Gavin Smith, *Pro Des* Peter Cosco, *Ed* Kathy Weinkauf, *Cos* Patrick Antosh.

Copperheart Entertainment-Optimum Releasing.
87 mins. Canada. 2011. Rel: 27 Apr 2012. Cert. 15.

5 Broken Cameras ★★★★

This fine documentary puts one in mind of *Wall* (2004) as it shows from the Palestinian side the tragic consequences of the wall on the West Bank erected by the Israelis. It's a family tale captured as it happened between 2005 and 2010 on video cameras (five in all as replacements became necessary). Sparked by the birth of a son, this is a vivid portrait of growing up in a virtual war zone and it concludes with unforced poignancy. Recommended. MS

▸ With Emad Burnat.
▸ *Dir* Emad Burnat and Guy Davidi, *Pro* Davidi, Burnat, Serge Gordey and Christine Camdessus, *Ph* Burnat, *Ed* Véronique Lagoarde-Ségot and Davidi, *M* Le Trio Joubran.

Alegria Productions/Burnat Films Palestine/Guy DVD Films etc-New Wave Films.
94 mins. France/Israel/The Netherlands/UK/USA/ Canada/Republic of Korea/Finland/Switzerland. 2011. Rel: 19 Oct 2012. Cert. 15.

666: The Prophecy ★★

Tormented by the deaths of his beloved wife and child, American atheist writer Joe Crone meets Sadie at a bereavement group and she later helps him after a car crash. Called up by his estranged pastor brother Samuel, Joe goes to Barcelona to be with his terminally sick dad. He sees demons and the number 11, then finds that some evil will occur on 11/11/11... Timothy Gibbs' acting helps to prop up this atmospheric and suspenseful, but slow-moving, Spanish-filmed horror movie. It's well shot by the director of *Saw* 2, 3 and 4, Darren Lynn Bousman, though he doesn't manage a great climax. (Original title: *11-11-11*) DW

▸ Timothy Gibbs, Michael Landes, Wendy Glenn, Benjamin Cook.
▸ *Dir* and *Screenplay* Darren Lynn Bousman, *Pro* Richard Heller, Ferran Monje, Christian Molina etc, *Ph* Joseph White, *Pro Des* Mani Martinez, *Ed* Martin Hunter, *M* Joseph Bishara, *Cos* Toni Martin.

Capacity Pictures/Canonigo Films/Epic Pictures Group-Eagle Films.
90 mins. USA/Spain. 2011. Rel: 6 Apr 2012. Cert. 15.

7 Days in Havana ★★½

Despite occasional connections this compendium piece consists of seven essentially distinct little

Palestinian women protest in Emad Burnat and Guy Davidi's award-winning documentary *5 Broken Cameras.*

tales set in Havana, two of them linked to the Film Festival there. Given that each one has a different director – some very well known (see credits below) – it is surprising to find the film so indifferent. Only Suleiman and Noé, for better or worse, provide a personal signature, but the best piece, Laurent Cantet's modest *The Fountain*, is reserved for the final slot. (Original title: *7 dias en La Habana*) MS

❯ Josh Hutcherson, Nathalia Amore, Emir Kusturica, Elia Suleiman, Daniel Brühl, Vladimir Cruz.
❯ *Dir* Benicio del Toro, Pablo Trapero, Julio Medem, Elia Suleiman, Gaspar Noé, Juan Carlos Tabío and Laurent Cantet, *Pro* Alvaro Longoria and others, *Screenplay* Leonardo Padura, Suleiman, Cantet, Noé, Medem, Trapero etc, *Ph* Daniel Aranyó and Diego Dussuel, *Art Dir* and *Cos* Juan Pedro de Gaspar, *Ed* Various, *M* Xavi Turull.
Full House & Morena Films/Backup Films etc-Soda Pictures.
129 mins. Spain/France/Cuba. 2012. Rel: 6 Jul 2012. Cert. 15.

About Elly ★★★★

Asghar Farhadi made this drama in 2009 before his acclaimed *A Separation* and I actually prefer this piece. It's a compelling study of Iranian attitudes centred on a weekend gathering by the Caspian Sea to which Elly, a teacher from a nursery school, is invited so that she can meet a divorcé. When Elly disappears (they wonder if she has drowned or walked away), there are echoes of *L'avventura* with the focus moving to the responses and actions of the rest of the party.

It's not always easy to tell all the characters apart, but the film is remarkable even so. (Original title: *Darbareye Elly*) MS

❯ Golshifteh Farahani, Taraneh Alidousti, Shabab Hosseini, Merila Zarei, Saber Abar.
❯ *Dir, Screenplay, Art Dir* and *Cos* Asghar Farhadi, *Pro* Farhadi and Mahmoud Razavi, *Ph* Hossein Jafarian, *Ed* Hayedeh Safiyari, *M* Andrea Bauer.
Simaye Mehr and Dreamlab-Axiom Films.
118 mins. France/Iran. 2009. Rel: 14 Sep 2012. Cert. 12A.

Abraham Lincoln: Vampire Hunter ★½

A title as audaciously daft as *Abraham Lincoln: Vampire Hunter* promises much, raising hopes that the movie folk responsible are capable of delivering the gag-fuelled historical fang-fest it suggests. They aren't. A clunky affair that sees Honest Abe (Benjamin Walker) staking vamps in league with the Southern slave states, the film dishes up a couple of decent action sequences but is mainly slo-mo axe slashes and CGI blood geysers. A humourless and fright-free non-event. MJ

❯ Benjamin Walker, Dominic Cooper, Anthony Mackie, Mary Elizabeth Winstead, Rufus Sewell.
❯ *Dir* Timur Bekmambetov, *Pro* Bekmambetov, Tim Burton and Jim Lemley, *Screenplay* Seth Grahame-Smith, from his novel, *Ph* Caleb Deschanel, *Pro Des* François Audouy, *Ed* William Hoy, *M* Henry Jackman, *Cos* Varvara Avdyushko and Carlo Poggioli.
Bazelevs Company/Dune Entertainment/Tim Burton Productions-20th Century Fox.
105 mins. USA. 2012. Rel: 20 June 2012. Cert. 15.

Act of Valour ★

This mindless film about a group of Navy Seals sent to rescue a kidnapped CIA operative comes over more like a recruitment commercial, lavishly produced by Mike McCoy and Scott Waugh. The set-pieces are spectacular but the acting by real-life Navy Seals is inevitably dreadful. There is a lot of gung-ho action accompanied by a sentimental and over-orchestrated score. See it and enlist, or avoid. GS

▶ Rosélyn Sanchez, Nestor Serrano, Emilio Rivera, Jason Cottle, Alex Veadov.
▶ *Dir* and *Pro* Mike McCoy and Scott Waugh, *Screenplay* Kurt Johnstad, *Ph* Shane Hurlbut, *Pro Des* John Zachary, *Ed* Siobhan Prior, Michael Tronick and Waugh, *M* Nathan Furst, *Cos* Erica Clum.

Bandito Brothers-Momentum Pictures.
110 mins. USA. 2012. Rel: 23 Mar 2012. Cert. 15.

Acts of Godfrey ★★

Vic (Iain Robertson) is a rather shy man who is sent by his employers to a motivational course in a country house hotel in order to develop his killer instincts. The course is organised by Godfrey (Simon Callow), who immediately pairs Vic with Mary (Myfanwy Waring)... You have to admire Johnny Daukes' guts to make an entire film in verse, even though the gimmick becomes tiresome by the end. This must also be a milestone in Simon Callow's career, as someone else appears naked rather than him. GS

▶ Simon Callow, Myfanwy Waring, Iain Robertson, Doon McKichan, Harry Enfield, Ian Burfield, Celia Imrie.
▶ *Dir, Screenplay* and *Music* Johnny Daukes, *Pro* Tony Schlesinger, *Ph* Stuart Graham, *Pro Des* Michael Mulligan, *Ed* Gary Dollner, *Cos* Jacky Levy.

Goldcrest-Guerilla Films.
85 mins. UK. 2012. Rel: 27 Jan 2012. Cert. 15.

Family network: Mélanie Laurent and Denis Ménochet in Laurent's charming and credible *The Adopted*.

The Adopted ★★★

The French actress Mélanie Laurent here turns writer-director and makes women central in a story set in Lyons. It's a three-part tale, a family drama with a strong sibling emphasis (Laurent herself plays one of two sisters). More background detail in the writing would have helped to draw us in and this mainstream movie does not eschew sentimentality. Those who most take to the film will probably be women able to identify directly with the leading characters. (Original title: *Les Adoptés*) MS

▶ Denis Ménochet, Marie Denarnaud, Mélanie Laurent, Théodore Maquet-Foucher, Audrey Lamy.
▶ *Dir* Mélanie Laurent, *Pro* Bruno Levy, *Screenplay* Laurent, Morgan Perez and Chris Deslandes, *Ph* Arnaud Potier, *Art Dir* Stanislas Reydellet, *Ed* Guerric Catala, *M* Jonathan Morali and Yann Arnaud, *Cos* Maïra Ramedhan-Levi.

A moveMovie, StudioCanal, TF1 Films Production etc-StudioCanal Limited.
100 mins. France. 2011. Rel: 24 Feb 2012. Cert. 15.

African Cats ★★★★

Shot in Kenya's south-west region over two years, this nature film puts its chief focus on lions and cheetahs. Its glory lies in its visuals: perfectly judged long shots, stunning close-ups and remarkable precision in capturing the essentials at dramatic moments. For the UK print Patrick Stewart narrates and the film is more successful than most in creating a story around animal footage. It's the work of Disneynature [sic]. MS

▶ With Patrick Stewart (narrator).
▶ *Dir* Keith Scholey with Alastair Fothergill, *Pro* Scholey and Alix Tidmarsh, *Screenplay* Scholey and John Truby from a story by Scholey and Owen Newman, *Ph* Newman and Sophie Darlington etc, *Ed* Martin Elsbury, *M* Nicholas Hooper.

A Fothergill/Scholey production-Buena Vista.
89 mins. USA. 2011. Rel: 27 Apr 2012. Cert. U.

Ai Weiwei Never Sorry ★★★½

Filmed from 2008 onwards this documentary is a portrait of the Chinese artist Ai Weiwei, an admirable thorn in the side of the authorities. His story could be more arrestingly told and, perhaps inevitably in a film lasting only 91 minutes, it is less than complete. Nevertheless he emerges honourably as a patriot deeply critical of his country's government, and there are interesting passages to make us ponder when political messages become art and when they remain distinct from it. MS

▶ With Ai Weiwei.
▶ *Dir* and *Ph* Alison Klayman, *Pro* Klayman and

Adam Schlesinger, *Ed* Jennifer Fineran, *M* Ilanlsakov.

United Expression Media/MUSE Film and Television etc-Artificial Eye.
91 mins. USA. 2012. Rel: 10 Aug 2012. Cert. 15.

Albert Nobbs ★★★½

Glenn Close's performance as a woman who lived as a man for 30 years was originally given on stage. Albert is a successful hotel waiter but his ambition is to own a tobacco shop. When house painter Hubert arrives at the hotel, Albert has to share a room and his secret is discovered. Glenn Close does not totally convince as a man, whereas it is truly surprising when Hubert undresses and is revealed, in a remarkable performance, to be Janet McTeer! Pauline Collins as the hotelier, Brendan Gleeson as the doctor and Mia Wasikowska as the apple of Albert's eye all offer fine support in this study of the nature of gender. MHD

▶ Glenn Close, Mia Wasikowska, Aaron Johnson, Janet McTeer, Pauline Collins, Phyllida Law, Brendan Gleeson.
▶ *Dir* Rodrigo Garcia, *Pro* Glenn Close, Bonnie Curtis, Julie Lynn and Alan Moloney, *Screenplay* Close, John Banville and Gabriella Prekop, from a treatment by István Szabó, based on a story by George Moore, *Ph* Michael McDonough, *Pro Des* Patrizia von Brandenstein, *Ed* Steven Weisberg, *M* Brian Byrne, *Cos* Pierre-Yves Gayraud.

Chrysalis Films/Mockingbird Pictures/WestEnd Films/ Parallel Film Productions/Trillian Productions/Morrison Films/Canal +/Irish Film Board-Entertainment One.
113 mins. UK/Ireland/France/USA. 2011. Rel: 27 Apr 2012. Cert. 15.

Alex Cross ★

Tyler Perry takes over from Morgan Freeman as Alex Cross in this third movie instalment of James Patterson's thriller novel saga. *Kiss the Girls* (1997) and *Along Came a Spider* (2001) were considerable successes back in their day, but this doesn't work nearly so well. Perry fails to establish authority or charisma in the character, the acting's generally moderate (thanks mainly to script weaknesses), the yarn is predictable, implausible and rather nasty, and the shaky-cam filming style clumsy. What's Matthew Fox (*Lost*) done to deserve playing the role of Picasso, a vile serial killer who's into torturing and slaying Detroit's rich businessmen? DW

▶ Tyler Perry, Matthew Fox, Edward Burns, Rachel Nichols, Cicely Tyson, Jean Reno.
▶ *Dir* Rob Cohen, *Pro* Bill Block, Steve Bowen, Leopoldo Gout, Paul Hanson, Randal Emett and James Patterson, *Screenplay* Mark Moss and Kerry Williamson, based on James Patterson's novel

Cross, *Ph* Ricardo Della Rosa, *Pro Des* Laura Fox, *Ed* Matt Diezl and Thom Noble, *M* John Debney, *Cos* Abigail Murray.

QED International/Block-Hanson/Emmett-Furla Films/ Envision Entertainment Corporation/James Patterson Entertainment/IAC Productions-Entertainment Film Distributors.
101 mins. USA. 20112. Rel: 30 Nov 2012. Cert. 15.

All in Good Time ★★★★

This engaging remake of *The Family Way*, filmed by the Boulting Brothers in 1966, remains faithful to Bill Naughton's original stage work. It's still the story of a young couple having difficulty in consummating their marriage, told in a manner at once comic and touching. The novelty of this version is that the characters have become Indians living in this country (Ayub Khan Din of *West is West* made the adaptation). If you like the films of Gurinder Chadha, you should enjoy this. MS

▶ Harish Patel, Reece Ritchie, Amara Karan, Meera Syal, Neet Mohan, Shelley King, Hassani Shapi.
▶ *Dir* Nigel Cole, *Pro* Andy Harries and Suzanne Mackie, *Screenplay* Ayub Khan Din, from his play *Rafta Rafta* based on Bill Naughton's play *All in Good Time*, *Ph* David Higgs, *Pro Des* Cristina Casali, *Ed* Michael Parker, *M* Niraj Chag, *Cos* Natalie Ward.

Studio Canal Features/UK Film Council/a Left Bank Pictures production-StudioCanal Limited.
94 mins. UK. 2012. Rel: 11 May 2012. Cert. 12A.

All's Well, Ends Well ★

You have to blame Chinese New Year for the unnecessary release of this lame comedy. Four couples are paired by a dating agency run by Maxine (Gong Linna), a divorcee looking for

Marital masala: Amara Karan and Reece Ritchie in Nigel Cole's All in Good Time.

love – but you can see the outcome a mile off in a series of false endings long before the final credits. Unfortunately the actors raise the volume in their attempts to play farcical comedy, failing miserably. Painful to watch. (Original title: *Baat seng bou hei*) GS

▶ Donnie Yen, Lynn Hung, Mini Yang, Gong Linna, Suet Lam.
▶ *Dir* Hing-Ka Chan, *Pro* Amy Chin and Bak-Ming Wong, *Screenplay* Chan and Janet Chung, *Ph* Man Po Cheung, *Ed* Ka-Fei Chung.
Icon Pictures-Pegasus Motion Pictures.
115 mins. Hong Kong. 2012. Rel: 27 Jan 2012. Cert. 15.

Alps ★★½

This strange film from Greece by Yorgos Lanthimos of *Dogtooth* (2009) takes half its length to reveal what exactly is being done by a group based in a hospital. Deliberately cryptic, they have taken the name of 'Alps'. Clearly the movie is some kind of allegory partly centred on issues of identity but, even when what is going on is revealed, just what it is all meant to signify remains obscure. It's strictly for those who like to puzzle over a puzzle! MS

▶ Aggeliki Papoulia, Aris Servetalis, Johnny Vekris, Ariane Labed, Eftihia Stefanidou.
▶ *Dir* Yorgos Lanthimos, *Pro* Athina Rachel Tsangari and Lanthimos, *Screenplay* Lanthimos and Efthimis Filippou, *Ph* Christos Voudouris, *Pro Des* Anna Georgiadou, *Ed* Yorgos Mavropsaridis, *Cos* Thanos Papastergiou and Vassilia Rozana.
A Haos Film production/ERT etc-Artificial Eye.
94 mins. Greece. 2011. Rel: 9 Nov 2012. Cert. 15.

A light touch: Aggeliki Papoulia in Yorgos Lanthimos' unsettling and potent Alps.

The Amazing Spider-Man ★★★

The likes of Christopher Nolan, Bryan Singer and Joss Whedon have raised the bar so high for the superhero genre that this *Spider-Man* reboot seems less than amazing. The special effects are incredible and Andrew Garfield and Emma Stone bring intelligence to their performances – but we need so much more. If extra time had been allocated to the human interaction between Peter Parker (Garfield) and Gwen Stacy (Stone), then the story and the effects around them would have had more impact. Still, the techno-babble surrounding cross-species genetics might just make you believe a man can spin. JC-W

▶ Andrew Garfield, Emma Stone, Rhys Ifans, Denis Leary, Campbell Scott, Irrfan Khan, Martin Sheen, Sally Field, Chris Zylka, Embeth Davidtz, C Thomas Howell, Stan Lee.
▶ *Dir* Marc Webb, *Pro* Laura Ziskin, Avi Arad and Matt Tolmach, *Screenplay* James Vanderbilt, Alvin Sargent and Steve Kloves, *Ph* John Schwartzman, *Pro Des* J Michael Riva, *Ed* Alan Edward Bell, Michael McCusker and Pietro Scalia, *M* James Horner, *Cos* Kym Barrett.
Columbia Pictures/Laura Ziskin Prods/Marvel Enterprises/Marvel Studios-Sony Releasing.
136 mins. USA. 2012. Rel: 3 July 2012. Cert. 12A.

American Evil ★★★

Co-writer and director Georgina Lightning stars as a Native American woman, haunted by visions, who finds a priest is trying to stop her from learning what really happened at her mother's evil boarding school, back when children could be forced into strict Catholic schools to obliterate their language and culture. This well-meaning suspense drama tackles its serious issues conscientiously, revealing some shocking truths. Even if the script and acting aren't quite up to the big themes, this is a brave and engrossing film. (Original title: *Older Than America*) DW

▶ Georgina Lightning, Bradley Cooper, Jeri Arredondo, Adam Beach. Tantoo Cardinal, Wes Studi.
▶ *Dir* Georgina Lightning, *Pro* Christine K Walker, *Screenplay* Lightning and Walker, *Ph* Shane F Kelly, *Pro Des* Carol Strober, *Ed* Clayton Condit, *M* George S Clinton, *Cos* Tere Duncan.
Older Than America-Tribal Alliance Productions.
102 mins. USA. 2008. Rel: 10 Feb 2012. Cert. 15.

American Pie: Reunion ★★★½

Ten years after their first gross adventure, the friends return to East Great Falls for their high school reunion. Jim (Jason Biggs) and Michelle (Alyson Hannigan) are now married with a child while Finch still longs for Stiffler's mum (Jennifer Coolidge). And Stiffler (Seann William Scott) is as immature as ever... It's good to see these totally unchanged characters get back together and luckily there's more of Eugene Levy this time around; his ingenious pairing with Coolidge is a treat. (Original title: *American Reunion*) GS

▶ Jason Biggs, Alyson Hannigan, Chris Klein, Seann William Scott, Jennifer Coolidge, Eugene Levy, Thomas Ian Nicholas.
▶ *Dir* and *Screenplay* Jon Hurwitz and Hayden Schlossberg, based on characters created by Adam Herz, *Pro* Herz, Craig Perry, Chris More and Warren Zide, *Ph* Daryn Okada, *Pro Des* William Arnold, *Ed* Jeff Betancourt, *M* Lyle Workman, *Cos* Mona May.
Universal Pictures/Practical Pictures/Relativity Media/ Zide-Perry Productions-Universal.
113 mins. USA. 2012. Rel: 2 May 2012. Cert. 15.

Amour ★★★½

He is lovingly concerned, she is declining through dementia: the old couple here are splendidly played by those veteran French actors Jean-Louis Trintignant and Emmanuelle Riva. Isabelle Huppert is superb too as their daughter and Michael Haneke's approach is admirably unsentimental. But the fact is that, whether or not it's due to my age, this is the most depressing film I have ever seen. Its admirers choose not to mention the final scenes which are unnecessarily elusive as to their meaning. MS

▶ Jean-Louis Trintignant, Emmanuelle Riva, Isabelle Huppert, Alexandre Tharaud, William Shimell.
▶ *Dir* and *Screenplay* Michael Haneke, *Pro* Margaret Menegoz, Stefan Arndt, Veit Heiduschka and Michael Katz, *Ph* Darius Khondji, *Art Dir* Jean-Vincent Puzos, *Ed* Monika Willi and Nadine Muse, *Cos* Catherine Leterrier.
Les Films du Losange/X Filme Creative Pool/Bayerischer Rundfunk etc-Artificial Eye.
127 mins. France/Germany/Austria. 2012. Rel: 16 Nov 2012. Cert. 12A.

Angel & Tony ★★★

Perhaps Alix Delaporte needed a co-writer: she is both writer and director here and creates a believable but very unsympathetic character in the conniving Angel. Her past history, and the way in which her relationship with the fisherman Tony develops, become important to the story but without the details convincing us as they should. Another writer might have corrected this. The Normandy coast provides an attractive location and the acting is good. MS

▶ Clotilde Hesme, Grégory Gadebois, Evelyne Didi, Antoine Couleau, Patrick Descamps.
▶ *Dir* and *Screenplay* Alix Delaporte, *Pro* Hélène Cases, *Ph* Claire Mathon, *Art Dir* Hélène Ustaze, *Ed* Louise Decelle, *M* Mathieu Maestracci, *Cos* Bibiane Blondy.
Lionceau Films/Canal+/CinéCinéma etc-Peccadillo Pictures Ltd.
83 mins. France. 2010. Rel: 4 May 2012. Cert. 15.

The Angels' Share ★★★★

Dealing with a young couple in Glasgow (the perfectly cast Paul Brannigan and Siobhan Reilly), this Ken Loach film initially promises to be his best ever. However, the seriousness of their tribulations is put to one side and the film becomes a comedy about a scam at the expense of the whisky trade. This switch puts the work on a lower level than had first appeared, but it's nevertheless immensely engaging. Using real-life whisky expert Charlie MacLean as a whisky expert is a special joy. MS

Love story: The 85-year-old Emmanuelle Riva (embraced by Jean-Louis Trintignant) in her Oscar-nominated performance as Anne, in Michael Haneke's poignant *Amour*.

▶ Paul Brannigan, John Henshaw, Gary Maitland, Jasmin Riggins, William Ruane, Roger Allam, Siobhan Reilly, Charlie MacLean.

▶ *Dir* Ken Loach, *Pro* Rebecca O'Brien, *Screenplay* Paul Laverty, *Ph* Robbie Ryan, *Pro Des* Fergus Clegg, *Ed* Jonathan Morris, *M* George Fenton, *Cos* Carole K. Fraser.

Sixteen Films/Why Not Productions/Wild Bunch/BFI etc-E1 Films.
101 mins. UK/France/Italy 2012. Rel: 1 June 2012. Cert. 15.

Anna Karenina ★★★½

Joe Wright's decision to set this retelling of Tolstoy's classic Russian drama in a theatre proves sadly disruptive. Cast against type as the deceived husband, Jude Law is excellent, while Keira Knightley's Anna is well judged, even if her young lover (Aaron Taylor-Johnson as he is now named) is more toy boy than Russian Count. Production values are admirable, but one regrets it every time that the stage setting reasserts itself. MS

▶ Keira Knightley, Jude Law, Aaron Taylor-Johnson, Kelly Macdonald, Matthew Macfadyen, Domhnall Gleeson, Olivia Williams, Emily Watson.

▶ *Dir* Joe Wright, *Pro* Tim Bevan, Eric Fellner and Paul Webster, *Screenplay* Tom Stoppard, from the novel by Leo Tolstoy, *Ph* Seamus McGarvey, *Pro Des* Sarah Greenwood, *Ed* Melanie Ann Oliver, *M* Dario Marianelli, *Cos* Jacqueline Durran.

Focus Features/a Working Title production-Universal.
130 mins. USA/UK. 2012. Rel: 7 Sep 2012. Cert. 12A.

Anton Corbijn Inside Out ★★

An object lesson in how not to make a film, Klaartje Quirijins' documentary about the Dutch filmmaker Anton Corbijn (*Control*, *The American*), who is also famed as a photographer, seems utterly shapeless. Interviewees go unnamed, key questions are not asked and anyone wanting an insightful portrait of a very private man will not find it here. Being so unrevealing, it seems endless even though it lasts less than 90 minutes. MS

▶ With Anton Corbijn, Bono, Lou Reed, Martin Gore, James Hetfield.

▶ *Dir* Klaartje Quirijins, *Pro* Sandor Verdonk, Gertjan Langeland and others, *Written by* Quirijins and Thomas den Drijver, *Ph* Diderik Evers and Martjin van Broekhuizen, *Ed* Boris Gerrets, *M* Gavin Friday.

A LEV Pictures production/CTM Films/Fastnet Films etc-Momentum Pictures.
85 mins. The Netherlands/Germany/UK/Italy/Sweden. 2012. Rel: 14 Sep 2012. Cert. 15.

Argo ★★★½

Surprisingly successful at the Academy Awards, *Argo* is no more than a well-made thriller, partly based on a real incident concerning the taking hostage of US Embassy staff in Tehran in 1980. When six staff members escape to the Canadian Embassy, CIA man Tony Mendez (Ben Affleck) concocts a plan to return them to the US. This involves inventing a bogus science fiction film

The best bad idea: Ben Affleck (left) poses as a movie producer in his Oscar-winning *Argo*.

called *Argo*, with the six escapees pretending they're scouting for locations. Chris Terrio's screenplay is a sharp mixture of action and suspense coupled with some black humour from Alan Arkin's cynical Hollywood producer. Affleck himself concentrates more on directing the film than his own somewhat subdued performance. If the final chase is not how it really happened, it still makes for exciting cinema. MHD

▶ Ben Affleck, Bryan Cranston, Alan Arkin, John Goodman, Bob Gunton, Chris Mesina, Victor Garber, Tate Donovan, Clea DuVall.
▶ *Dir* Ben Affleck, *Pro* Affleck, George Clooney and Grant Heslov, *Screenplay* Chris Terrio, based on Antonio J Mendez' book *The Master of Disguise*, and Joshuah Bearman's article 'Escape from Tehran', *Ph* Rodrigo Prieto, *Pro Des* Sharon Seymour, *Ed* William Goldenberg, *M* Alexandre Desplat, *Cos* Jacqueline West.

Warner Bros/GK Films/Smokehouse Pictures-Warner Bros. 120 mins. USA. 2012. Rel: 7 Nov 2012. Cert. 15.

Arirang ★★★★

Following a film shoot that nearly killed his lead actress, this represents bad boy Korean director Kim Ki-Duk's first movie since his 2008 breakdown. Named after a local folk song with themes of parting and sorrow, it's a documentary showing him in exile and musing over his current situation. It's a surprisingly compelling portrait of his internal, mental landscape. JC

▶ With Kim Ki-Duk.
▶ *Dir, Pro, Screenplay, Ph, Pro Des, Ed* Kim Ki-Duk.

Kim Ki-Duk Film-Crest International. 100 mins. South Korea. 2011. Rel: 8 June 2012. Cert. 12.

The Assault ★★★★

Julien Leclercq turns the events surrounding the 1994 hijacking of an Air France plane by Algerian jihadists into a thrilling action movie. Showing the work of a SWAT team and all they have to undergo in a day's work, it becomes an absorbing game of cat and mouse between the terrorists and their pursuers. Human interest is centred on SWAT man Thierry (Vincent Elbaz) and his wife Carole (Mélanie Bernier) as the family awaits the outcome of the potentially tragic situation. Leclercq's taut direction and Thierry Pouget's almost monochrome cinematography only add to the general excitement in this outstanding action film. (Original title: *L'Assaut*) MHD

▶ Vincent Elbaz, Grégori Derangère, Mélanie Bernier, Philippe Bas, Aymen Saïdi, Marie Guillard.
▶ *Dir* Julien Leclercq, *Pro* Leclercq and Julien Madon, *Screenplay* Leclercq and Simon Moutairoux, from the book by Roland Môntins and Gilles Cauture, *Ph* Thierry Pouget, *Ed* Mickael Dumontier, Christine

Lucas Navarro and Frédéric Thoraval, *M* Leslie Jones and Louise Ruckaby, *Cos* Muriel Legrand.

Labyrinthe Films/Mars Films/Canal +/CineCinema etc-StudioCanal. 91 mins. France. 2010. Rel: 23 Apr 2012. Cert. 15.

Trigger effect: Aymen Saïdi takes a hostage in Julien Leclercq's true-life *The Assault*.

The Athlete ★★★★

Abebe Bikila was the first African ever to win gold in the Olympics. An Ethiopian soldier and marathon runner, he achieved success in Rome in 1960 and again in Tokyo in 1964. He really put Ethiopia on the sporting map and became a national hero. Sadly, Bikila was involved in a car crash and was confined to a wheelchair for the rest of his short life but not before appearing in the Paralympics. Rasselas Lakew, co-writer and co-director, appears as Bikila in a film that mixes drama with actual Olympics footage. It's a remarkably moving story told with real respect and great affection in a true cinematic style. (Original title: *Atletu*) MHD

▶ Rasselas Lakew, Dag Malmberg, Ruta Gedmintas, Abba Waka Dessalegn.
▶ *Dir* Rasselas Lakew and Davey Frankel, *Pro* Lakew, Frankel and Daryn Welch, *Screenplay* Lakew, Frankel and Mikael Aemiro Awake, *Ph* Toby More, Philip C Pfeiffer, Radoslav Spassov and Rodney Taylor, *Ed* Frankel and Matt Mayer, *M* Christian Meyer.

A V Patchbay/El Atleta/ Instinctive Film/Riot Entertainment etc-Ballpark Film Distributors. 92 mins. USA/Germany/Ethiopia. 2009. Rel: 29 June 2012. Cert. PG.

Aurora ★★★

Again setting his film in Bucharest and this time taking the lead role himself, Cristi Puiu, who made *The Death of Mr. Lazarescu* (2005), confirms his talent. The use of sound and the composition of images show absolute precision. However, we are invited to follow in decidedly minimalist style a man about whom we know very little, and we

Pickin' the blues: Riley B King in Jon Brewer's documentary *B.B. King: The Life of Riley*.

do so for around three hours. His early interest in a gun points to violence ahead and eventually things slot into place, but the story told never seems to justify the time taken to tell it. MS

❯ Cristi Puiu, Clara Voda, Valeria Seciu, Catrinel Dumitrescu, Luminita Gheorghiu.
❯ *Dir* and *Screenplay* Cristi Puiu, *Pro* Anca Puiu and Bobby Paunescu, *Ph* Viorel Sergovici, *Art Dir* Vali Ighigheanu and Andreea Popa, *Ed* Ioachim Stroe, *Cos* Ana Andrei and Monica Florescu.

A Mandragora production/Parisienne de Production/ Bord Cadre Films etc-New Wave Films.
184 mins. Romania/France/Switzerland/Germany. 2010. Rel: 9 Nov 2012. Cert. 12A.

Avengers Assemble ★★★★

While the idea of the Incredible Hulk, Iron Man, Captain America and Thor joining forces to save our planet is, in itself, audacious, the result is better than one might have hoped for. The joy of *Avengers Assemble* is not the flying masonry, toppling skyscrapers or extraterrestrials with halitosis, but the interaction of the characters. Thus, Thor uttereth his discourse in olde English, Captain America talks in WWII slang, Dr Bruce Banner (aka the Hulk) speaks like a normal human being and Iron Man (Tony Stark) chatters away in technobabble. In short, this is popcorn of the highest order – popcorn with an explosion of flavours. (US title: *The Avengers*; aka *Marvel Avengers Assemble*) JC-W

❯ Robert Downey Jr, Chris Evans, Mark Ruffalo, Chris Hemsworth, Scarlett Johansson, Jeremy Renner, Tom Hiddleston, Stellan Skarsgård, Samuel L Jackson, Clark Gregg, Cobie Smulders, Gwyneth Paltrow, Jerzy Skolimowski, Powers Boothe, Jenny Agutter, Harry Dean Stanton, Ashley Johnson.
❯ *Dir* and *Screenplay* Joss Whedon, *Pro* Kevin Feige, *Ph* Seamus McGarvey, *Pro Des* James Chinlund, *Ed* Jeffrey Ford and Lisa Lassek, *M* Alan Silvestri, *Cos* Alexandra Byrne.

Marvel Studios/Paramount Pictures-Walt Disney.
142 mins. USA. 2012. Rel: 26 Apr 2012. Cert. 12A.

B. B. King: The Life of Riley
★★★★

Jon Brewer's illuminating documentary celebrates the life and career of the inimitable BB King from the tender age of ten, when he was forced by circumstance to work as a sharecropper. It is eloquently narrated by Morgan Freeman, who also appears amongst many artists singing their praises to the King of the Blues. A fine tribute to a unique talent. GS

❯ Narrator: Morgan Freeman. With BB King, Bruce Willis, Carlos Santana, Eric Clapton, Bono, Ron Wood, Bonnie Raitt, Bobby Bland, Derek Trucks, Joe Walsh, Leon Russell.
❯ *Dir* Jon Brewer, *Pro* Brewer and Bill Szymczyk, *Ed* Matt Greenham.

Emperor Media.
123 mins. UK 2012. Rel: 15 Oct 2012. Cert. PG.

Babycall ★★★

This psychological thriller from Norway's Pål Sletaune brings to mind Polanski's classic

Repulsion. It concerns a troubled mother plagued by sounds from her babycall of a child seemingly in distress even when her eight-year-old son proves to be sleeping soundly. The twist in the film's tail, if not unexpected, nevertheless raises all sorts of unanswerable questions about what one has seen earlier. But, if that makes the piece less than satisfactory, the lead role is a nicely contrasted triumph for Noomi Rapace, the screen's first and best Lisbeth Salander. MS

‣ Noomi Rapace, Vetle Qvenild Werring, Kristoffer Joner, Stig Amdam, Maria Bock.
‣ *Dir* and *Screenplay* Pål Sletaune, *Pro* Turid Øversveen, *Ph* John Andreas Andersen, *Art Dir* Roger Rosenberg, *Ed* Jon Endre Mørk, *M* Fernando Valazquez, *Cos* Ellen Ystehede.

41/2/a Pandora Film, BOB Film Sweden co-production etc-Soda Pictures.
96 mins. Norway/Germany/Sweden. 2011. Rel: 30 Mar 2012. Cert. 15.

The Babymakers ★

Although capable of crafting such sublime screen idiocy as *Super Troopers* and *Beerfest*, Jay Chandrasekhar slums it as the director and co-star of this lamentable, laugh-free bore. Together with his moronic friends, a regular idiot hires a mentalist robber to bust them into a sperm bank to steal back a deposit he made years earlier – his wife now wants a baby and he's currently firing blanks. As bad as this sounds, it's actually worse, a gross-out caper flick delivered dead on arrival. MJ

‣ Paul Schneider, Olivia Munn, Michael Yurchak, Wood Harris, Jay Chandrasekhar, Kevin Heffernan, Nat Faxon, Sharon Maughan.
‣ *Dir* Jay Chandrasekhar, *Pro* Chandrasekhar, Jason Blum and Brian Kavanaugh-Jones, *Screenplay* Peter Gaulke and Gerry Swallow, *Ph* Franco G DeMarco, *Pro Des* Katie Byron, *Ed* Brad Katz, *M* Edward Shearmur and Georg Brandl Egloff, *Cos* Tricia Gray.

Duck Attack Films/Alliance Films/Automatik Entertainment/IM Global-Millennium Entertainment.
95 mins. USA. 2012. Rel: 28 Sep 2012. Cert. 15.

Barbara ★★★

Christian Petzold's regular leading lady, Nina Hoss, is on great form here in the title role. Barbara is a nurse in a provincial German hospital where she bonds with a colleague (the able Ronald Zehrfeld). Rather late in the day it becomes clear that this is East Germany in the 1980s and Barbara's aim is to escape. But then there's a conflict with what she sees as her duty. This should make for telling drama, but it feels far too set up to convince and the story could have been better told. MS

‣ Nina Hoss, Ronald Zehrfeld, Mark Waschke, Jasna Fritzi Bauer, Rainer Bock
‣ *Dir* and *Screenplay* Christian Petzold, *Pro* Florian Koerner von Gustorf and Michael Weber, *Ph* Hans Fromm, *Art Dir* KD Gruber, *Ed* Bettina Böhler, *M* Stefan Will, *Cos* Anette Guther.

Schramm Film Koerner & Weber in co-production with ZDF and ARTE etc-Soda Pictures.
105 mins. Germany. 2012. Rel: 28 Sep 2012. Cert. 12A.

Barbaric Genius ★★★

Paul Duane's documentary examines the mystery behind John Healy, a Scottish man who spent his twenties on the streets of London in the company of winos and muggers, later becoming a celebrity and a literary phenomenon when his autobiographical novel *The Grass Arena* was published by Faber & Faber. This fascinating film presents Healy as a person of many contradictions but unfortunately we never get to know the real man. GS

‣ With John Healy, Frank Boyle, Dick Fitzgerald, Robert McCrum, Megan Larkin.
‣ *Dir* Paul Duane, *Pro* Duane and Mary Carson, *Ph* Duane, Anthony Dalton, Ben Richards and Joe Edwards, *Ed* Ian De Brí and Colm O'Brien, *M* Leon O'Neill.

Screenworks-Screenworks.
72 mins. Ireland/UK/USA. 2011. Rel: 25 May 2012. Cert. 15.

Battleship ★½

Like *Transformers* this over-long and hollow blockbuster is based on a Hasbro combat game. Lt Alex Hopper (Taylor Kitsch) and his older brother Stone (Alexander Skarsgård) find themselves in the middle of an alien invasion during a naval war games exercise. It's like *Independence Day* at sea, full of patriotism and

Bad medicine: Nina Hoss (left) as *Barbara*.

Before the storm: The remarkable Quvenzhané Wallis in her Oscar-nominated performance as Hushpuppy, in Benh Zeitlin's *Beasts of the Southern Wild.*

American flag-waving and filmed in the style of a glossy Navy commercial. The actors have no chance amid the implausible set-pieces, laughable dialogue, extremely loud sound effects, manipulative score and machine-gun editing. GS

▶ Alexander Skarsgård, Rihanna, Liam Neeson, Taylor Kitsch, Brooklyn Decker, Adam Godley, Hamish Linklater.
▶ *Dir* Peter Berg, *Pro* Berg, Bennett Schneir, Scott Stuber, Duncan Henderson, Brian Goldner and Sarah Aubrey, *Screenplay* Jon Hoeber and Erich Hoeber, *Ph* Tobias A Schliessler, *Pro Des* Neil Spisak, *Ed* Colby Parker Jr, Paul Rubell and Billy Rich, *M* Steve Jablonsky, *Cos* Louise Mingenbach and Kim Tillman.

Universal Pictures/Hasbro/Battleship Delta Productions/ Bluegrass Films/Film 44-Universal Pictures International. 131 mins. USA. 2012. Rel: 11 Apr 2012. Cert. 12A.

Beasts of the Southern Wild ★★★

A *Louisiana Story* never dreamt of by Robert Flaherty, this looks at life through the eyes of its six-year-old heroine (the utterly uncute Quvenzhané Wallis). She and her father are African-Americans living in poverty and caught up in floods. However, this realistic material yields to the presence of imaginary and supposedly threatening prehistoric creatures. Some sort of magic realism may have been intended, but for me the mix doesn't work, although it does for some. In any case it's an honourable and unconventional film even if its eventual optimism seems forced. MS

▶ Quvenzhané Wallis, Dwight Henry, Levy Easterly, Lowell Landes, Pamela Harper, Gina Montana.
▶ *Dir* Benh Zeitlin, *Pro* Dan Janvey, Josh Penn and Michael Gottwald, *Screenplay* Lucy Alibar and Zeitlin, from Alibar's play, *Ph* Ben Richardson, *Pro Des* Alex Digerlando, *Ed* Crockett Doob and Affonso Gonçalves, *M* Dan Romer and Zeitlin, *Cos* Stephani Lewis.

Fox Searchlight Pictures/a Cinereach and Court 13 production etc-Studiocanal Limited. 93 mins. USA. 2012. Rel: 19 Oct 2012. Cert. 12A.

Beauty ★★★½

This gay drama from South Africa is a dark affair. Impressively directed and co-written by Oliver Hermanus and admirably played by lead actor Deon Lotz, this is a work of social criticism. It shows how society's attitudes drive a married man into hiding his homosexuality, resulting eventually in behaviour on his part that is truly repellent. The man in question is seen as a victim, yet his extreme actions encourage us to despise him. The film disturbs but not always in the right way. (Original title: *Skoonheid*) MS

▶ Deon Lotz, Charlie Keegan, Michelle Scott, Albert Maritz, Roeline Daneel, Sue Diepeveen.
▶ *Dir* and *Ed* Oliver Hermanus, *Pro* Didier Costet, *Screenplay* Hermanus and Costet, *Ph* Jamie Ramsay, *Pro Des* J Franz Lewis, *M* Ben Ludik, *Cos* Reza Levy.

A Moonlighting Skoonheid Productions/Equation co-production etc-Peccadillo Pictures Ltd. 105 mins. South Africa/France. 2011. Rel: 20 Apr 2012. Cert. 18.

Beauty and the Beast (3D version) ★★★★★

Disney's 1991 classic dusted off and converted to 3D is a treat. Groundbreaking in its day for its CGI ballroom backgrounds, it could have been art directed with 3D in mind, showing off the format to greater effect than most contemporary movies, animated or otherwise. Nothing that made it good first time around has dated. JC

▶ With the voices of Paige O'Hara, Robby Benson, Richard White, Jerry Orbach, David Ogden Stiers, Angela Lansbury, Bradley Michael Pierce, Jo-Anne Worley.
▶ *Dir* Gary Trousdale and Kirk Wise, *Pro* Don Hahn and John Lasseter (3D version), *Screenplay* Linda Wolverton, from a story by Jeanne-Marie Leprince de Beaumont etc, *Art Dir* Brian McEntee, *Ed* John Carnochan and Bill Wilner, *M* Alan Menken.

Walt Disney Pictures/Walt Disney Feature Animation/ Silver Screen Partners IV-Walt Disney Studios Motion Pictures. 84 mins. USA. 1991. Re-release: 4 May 2012. Cert. U.

Being Elmo ★★★★

Subtitled *A Puppeteer's Journey*, this is the engaging story of Kevin Clash from Baltimore who, having loved *Sesame Street* as a child, would later work for Jim Henson and create the Muppet named Elmo. This warm-hearted film not only records this success story but also stands as a moving tribute to Henson, who died at the early age of 53. The artistry in bringing puppets to individual life is splendidly conveyed. MS

▶ With Kevin Clash, Whoopi Goldberg, Frank Oz, Cheryl Henson, Rosie O'Donnell.
▶ *Dir* Constance Marks with Philip Shane, *Pro* Marks, James Miller and Corinne Lapook, *Written by* and *Ed* Shane and Justin Weinstein, *Ph* Miller, *M* Joel Goodman.

Submarine Deluxe and Constance Marks Productions-Dogwoof.
76 mins. USA. 2011. Rel: 27 Apr 2012. Cert. U.

Bel Ami ★★

Although Robert Pattinson would redeem himself later in *Cosmopolis* [qv], his performance here, playing Guy de Maupassant's anti-hero who makes his way unscrupulously through 1890s Paris, is wooden. The women he lures and uses are well played by Kristin Scott Thomas, Uma Thurman and Christina Ricci, but they are undermined by having to focus on a plank. It doesn't help either that this very French piece is played in English and that the joint directors, noted for their theatre work, show no flair for cinema. MS

▶ Robert Pattinson, Uma Thurman, Kristin Scott Thomas, Christina Ricci, Holliday Grainger.
▶ *Dir* Declan Donnellan and Nick Ormerod, *Pro* Uberto Pasolini, *Screenplay* Rachel Bennette, from the novel by Guy de Maupassant, *Ph* Stefano Falivene, *Pro Des* Attila F Kovacs, *Ed* Masahiro Hirakubo, *M* Lakshman Joseph de Saram and Rachel Portman, *Cos* Odile Dicks-Mireaux.

Redwave Films/19 Entertainment/Protagonist Pictures/Rai Cinema-StudioCanal Limited.
102 mins. UK/Italy. 2012. Rel: 9 March 2012. Cert. 15.

Beloved ★★★½

Featuring songs from Alex Beaupain, Christophe Honoré's film echoes the work of Jacques Demy even to the extent of starring Catherine Deneuve. With a tale by turns romantic and dramatic, it stretches over 50 years or so and finds room for performances from the director Milos Forman and from Deneuve's daughter Chiara Mastroianni. It quite lacks the emotional power of *The Umbrellas of Cherbourg* but it is enjoyable because Honoré and his editor convey their delight in filmmaking. (Original title: *Les Bien-aimés*) MS

▶ Chiara Mastroianni, Catherine Deneuve, Ludivine Sagnier, Louis Garrel, Milos Forman.
▶ *Dir* Christophe Honoré, *Pro* Pascal Caucheteux, *Screenplay* Honoré with the complicity of Adam Thirlwell, *Ph* Rémy Chevrin, *Art Dir* Samuel Deshors, *Ed* Chantal Hymans, *M* Alex Beaupain, *Cos* Pascaline Chavanne.

A Why Not Productions, France 2 Cinéma, Sixteen Films, Negativ co-production etc-New Wave Films.
139 mins. France/UK/Czech Republic 2011. Rel: 11 May 2012. Cert. 15.

Berberian Sound Studio ★★★

This is a daring choice for his second feature by *Katalin Varga*'s Peter Strickland. It concerns a British sound expert (the superb Toby Jones)

Extreme Foley: Toby Jones in Peter Strickland's *Berberian Sound Studio*.

Jaipur japery: Judi Dench enjoys her Indian summer in John Madden's gratifyingly old-fashioned *The Best Exotic Marigold Hotel.*

caught up in making a horror film in 1970s Italy. It's about his mental disintegration when making such a movie and the first half is admirable. Ultimately, though, unlike Haneke's *Funny Games*, it isn't clear what Strickland is trying to say. His film, although it has staunch admirers, ends up both obscure and self-consciously arty. MS

▶ Toby Jones, Cosimo Fusco, Antonio Mancino, Salvatore Li Causi, Fatma Mohamed.
▶ *Dir* and *Screenplay* Peter Strickland, *Pro* Keith Griffiths and Mary Burke, *Ph* Nic Knowland, *Pro Des* Jennifer Kernke, *Ed* Chris Dickens, *M* Broadcast, *Cos* Julian Day, *Supervising Sound Ed* Joakim Sundström.
Film4/UK Film Council/an Illuminations Films & Warp X Production etc-Artificial Eye.
92 mins. UK 2011. Rel: 31 Aug 2012. Cert. 15.

The Best Exotic Marigold Hotel ★★★★

You can't keep an old thespian Dame down – witness Maggie Smith in *Harry Potter* and *Quartet*, and Judi Dench in *Skyfall* and *J. Edgar*. They're back together again in *The Best Exotic Marigold Hotel*, along with other old-timers Bill Nighy, Tom Wilkinson, Penelope Wilton and Ronald Pickup in a tale of Brit pensioners heading for retirement in India... Life is not how they imagined it, however, as they settle into the titular hotel run by young Dev (*Slumdog Millionaire*) Patel. Problems ensue but they don't amount to very much on the sunny side of the street in Jaipur. It's engaging, endearing and entertaining. MHD

▶ Judi Dench, Maggie Smith, Tom Wilkinson, Bill Nighy, Penelope Wilton, Celia Imrie, Ronald Pickup, Dev Patel.
▶ *Dir* John Madden, *Pro* Graham Broadbent and Peter Czernin, *Screenplay* Ol Parker, based on Deborah Moggach's novel *These Foolish Things*, *Ph* Ben Davis, *Pro Des* Alan MacDonald, *Ed* Chris Gill, *M* Thomas Newman, *Cos* Louise Stjernsward.
Blueprint Pictures/Participant Media/ImageNation Abu Dhabi-20th Century Fox.
124 mins. UK/USA/United Arab Emirates. 2011. Rel: 24 Feb 2012. Cert. 12A.

Best Laid Plans ★★★

Set in Nottingham, this powerful Brit drama centres on cash-strapped crook Danny (Stephen Graham), who manipulates Joseph (Adewale Akinnuoye-Agbaje), a giant bruiser with learning difficulties, into illegal cage fights to pay off his debt to a crime lord. Chris Green's script reworks ideas from John Steinbeck's *Of Mice and Men* to considerable effect and without obvious strain or effort. Both actors are outstanding, and so is Maxine Peake as the woman Jo falls for. The film is a skilfully handled nail-biter. DW

▶ Stephen Graham, Adewale Akinnuoye-Agbaje, Lee Ingleby, Maxine Peake, Emma Stansfield, Brad Moore.
▶ *Dir* David Blair, *Pro* Stacey Murray and Bradley Moore, *Screenplay* Chris Green and Jeremy Sheldon, loosely based on John Steinbeck's novel *Of Mice and Men*, *Ph* Ali Asad, *Pro Des* Kristian Milsted, *Ed* Pia Di Ciaula, *M* Robert Lane, *Cos* Rebecca MacManus.

Moli Films/Made Up North Productions/AV Pictures-Vertigo Films.
108 mins. UK. 2012. Rel: 3 Feb 2012. Cert. 15.

Big Boys Gone Bananas!*
★★★★

The title may mislead for this is a serious and involving documentary. Fredrik Gertten follows up his 2009 film *Bananas!**, which was critical of the Dole Food Company regarding their exploitation of Nicaraguan plantation workers. That film was recommended by George Savvides in the 2010-11 edition of this annual and I now recommend this sequel. It covers fresh ground by recording the attempts of Dole to prevent screenings of *Bananas!** and is centred on the right to freedom of speech. MS

▶ With Fredrik Gertten, Margarete Jangård.
▶ *Dir* Fredrik Gertten, *Pro* Margarete Jangård, *Ph* Various, *Ed* Jesper Osmund and Benjamin Binderup, *M* Conny Malmqvist and Dan 'Gisen' Malmquist.

WG Film/SVT/Film i Skåne etc-Dogwoof.
90 mins. Sweden. 2012. Rel: 21 Sep 2012. No Cert.

Big Miracle ★★★

In this likable film inspired by a true story, Drew Barrymore plays an animal lover activist who starts a campaign to save a family of three whales trapped in Alaska. She joins a small-town reporter (John Krasinski) and the race against time begins before the Arctic Circle ice freezes around the whales... It's a touching film, perhaps a bit over-long, and provides good family entertainment. GS

▶ Drew Barrymore, John Krasinki, Kristen Bell, Vinessa Shaw, Ted Danson, Kathy Baker, Dermot Mulroney.
▶ *Dir* Ken Kwapsis, *Pro* Eric Felner, Tim Bevan, Steve Golin, Michael Sugar and Liza Chasin, *Screenplay* Jack Amiel and Michael Begler, based on the book *Freeing the Whales* by Tom Rose, *Ph* John Bailey,

Pro Des Nelson Coates, *Ed* Cara Silverman, *M* Cliff Eidelman, *Cos* Shay Cunliffe.

Working Title Films/Anonymous Content-Universal Pictures.
107 mins. UK/USA. 2012. Rel: 10 Feb 2012. Cert. PG.

Bill Cunningham New York
★★★★

Arguably better suited to TV than to cinema presentation, this is nevertheless a telling portrait of a fascinating man, the photographer Bill Cunningham, now an octogenarian. Be his work connected with fashion or with the social scene, he is a New York character in his own right. A very private person, Cunningham may leave you wanting to know more, but he is as individual a figure as Dame Edith Sitwell and his sheer joy in his work is wonderfully conveyed. MS

▶ With Bill Cunningham, Anna Wintour, Tom Wolfe.
▶ *Dir* Richard Press, *Pro* Philip Gefter, *Ph* Tony Cenicola and Press, *Ed* Ryan Denmark, *Ph Animation* Keira Alexandra.

The New York Times/First Thought Films-Dogwoof.
84 mins. USA. 2010. Rel: 16 Mar 2012. Cert. 12A.

The Bird ★★½

The setting is Bordeaux and the talented Sandrine Kiberlain is at the centre of this minimalist piece about a loner so withdrawn that it seems unlikely when an admirer wants to give her a new life. What brought about this extreme state is only suggested while, in contrast, the symbolism of a bird trapped in the wall of her apartment but needing to escape could not be more heavy-handed. Despite Kiberlain's valiant efforts, watching this film is something of an endurance test. (Original title: *L'Oiseau*) MS

▶ Sandrine Kiberlain, Clément Sibony, Bruno Todeschini, Serge Riaboukine.

Nottingham mice: Stephen Graham and Adewale Akinnuoye-Agbaje in David Blair's *Best Laid Plans*, a loose adaptation of Steinbeck's *Of Mice and Men*.

Torrents of Arabia: Antonio Banderas in Jean-Jacques Annaud's *Black Gold*.

▶ *Dir* Yves Caumon, *Pro* Bertrand Gore, *Screenplay* Caumon with Marc Wels, *Ph* Céline Bozon, *Art Dir* Sophie Reynaud-Malouf, *Ed* Sylvie Fauthoux, *M* Thierry Machuel, *Cos* Marie Le Garrec.

A Blue Monday Productions/Arte France Cinéma co-production etc-Picturehouse.
94 mins. France. 2011. Rel: 17 Aug 2012. Cert. 12A.

Black Gold ★★★★

Here's a guilty pleasure! Poorly received by the critics, Jean-Jacques Annaud's film is an adventure tale set in the first half of the 20th century that turns on the exploitation of oil in the Arabian Peninsula. Instead of being a serious, intelligent treatment, this movie exists in a time warp, taking me back to my youthful cinema-going in the 1950s. It looks great on the big screen and both Mark Strong and Freida Pinto do well by it, but it's nostalgia not quality that wins the day. MS

▶ Tahar Rahim, Antonio Banderas, Mark Strong, Freida Pinto, Riz Ahmed, Liya Kebede.
▶ *Dir* Jean-Jacques Annaud, *Pro* Tarak Ben Ammar, *Screenplay* Menno Meyjes, based on Hans Ruesch's novel *The Great Thirst* as adapted by Annaud and Alain Godard, *Ph* Jean-Marie Dreujou, *Pro Des* Pierre Quefféléan, *Ed* Herve Schneid, *M* James Horner, *Cos* Fabio Perrone.

A Quinta Communications, Prima TV, Carthago Films and France 2 Cinéma co-production etc-Warner Bros.
130 mins. France/Italy/Qatar. 2011. Rel: 24 Feb 2012. Cert. 12A.

Blackthorn ★★

Popular myth would have it that Butch Cassidy and the Sundance Kid died in a hail of bullets – à la the end of George Roy Hill's classic 1969 Western. However, there's no hard evidence to support this conclusion and here Butch re-emerges as James Blackthorn, a grey-haired old man shacked up in Bolivia with a native woman half his age… As Blackthorn, Sam Shepard has the grizzled look of an old-timer with a past but has none of the inner unpredictability of Clint Eastwood – or the charm of Paul Newman. The main trouble is that the film relies too heavily on the legend without a decent enough story to hold the interest. JC-W

▶ Sam Shepard, Eduardo Noriega, Stephen Rea, Magaly Solier, Nikolaj Coster-Waldau, Padraic Delaney, Dominique McElligott.
▶ *Dir* Mateo Gil, *Pro* Ibón Cormenzana, Andrés Santana, Jan Pace and Paolo Agazzi, *Screenplay* Miguel Barros, *Ph* Juan A. Ruiz Anchía, *Pro Des* Juan Pedro De Gaspar, *Ed* David Gallart, *M* Lucio Godoy, *Cos* Clara Bilbao.

Ariane Mararía Films/Arcadia Motion Pictures/Quickfire Films/Nix Films/Eter Pictures/Manto Films/Canal+ España etc-Chelsea Films.
102 mins. Spain/USA/Bolivia/France. 2011. Rel: 13 Apr 2012. Cert. 15.

Blank City ★★★★

A film about films, Céline Danhier's debut documentary has the advantage of covering unfamiliar territory. It's an able, straightforward piece about the New York filmmakers of the 1970s such as Amos Poe, Lizzie Borden and Bette Gordon. Jim Jarmusch, who started out there in what was once called the 'No Wave', is one of the best speakers on hand and the film charts well an almost forgotten corner of American cinema. MS

❯ With Jim Jarmusch, Richard Kern, Nick Zedd, Amos Poe, John Lurie, Lydia Lunch, Deborah Harry.
❯ *Dir* Celine Danhier, *Pro* Aviva Wishnow and Vanessa Roworth, *Ph* Ryo Murakami and Peter Szollosi, *Ed* Roworth, *M* Ecce Homo.

A Pure Fragment production/Submarine Entertainment-E2 Films.
94 mins. USA. 2010. Rel: 2 Mar 2012. No Cert.

Blood Car ★★★

Made in Atlanta Georgia, this surprisingly entertaining triple-award-winning black comedy is set the day after tomorrow, when petrol's so dear other fuels are needed. Needs must… One guy, elementary school teacher Archie Andrews (Mike Brune), comes up with his own answer; yes, human blood, I'm afraid. So he goes on a killing spree. Made for next to nothing ($25,000), it comes up with the goods, with a crazy mix of laughs, gore and social satire tastily stirred. Anna Chlumsky (from *My Girl*) co-stars. DW

❯ Mike Brune, Anna Chlumsky, Katie Rowlett, Mat Hutchinson, Marla Malcolm.
❯ *Dir* Alex Orr, *Pro* Orr, Adam Pinney and Chris Antignane, *Screenplay* Orr and Pinney, from a story by them and Hugh Braselton, *Ph* Pinney, *Pro Des* Robert Paraguassu, *Ed* Pinney and Jon Swindall, *Sound Designer* Mark Clark, *Cos* Stephanie Aylworth.

FWW Films/Fake Wood Wallpaper-Left Films.
76 mins. USA. 2007. Rel: 24 Feb 2012. Cert. 18.

Bombay Beach ★★★½

The title refers to a now forlorn resort in California beside the expanse of water known as the Salton Sea. The photographer and visual artist Alma Har'el is the filmmaker and her interest is in the people there, especially in three males. There's a child who is probably bipolar, an articulate loner in his eighties and a young man escaping from a criminal background in South Central Los Angeles. Some effects seem contrived and the first half feels haphazard, but this uncondescending piece does become involving. MS

❯ With Dorran 'Red' Forgy, Mike, Sarah and Benny Parrish, CeeJay Thompson.
❯ *Dir* and *Ph* Alma Har'el, *Pro* Har'el and Boaz Yakin, *Ed* Joe Lindquist and Har'el, *M* Zach Condon.

Bombay Films Inc.-Dogwoof.
80 mins. USA. 2011. Rel: 3 Feb 2012. No Cert.

Bonsai ★★★

Based on a novel said to be full of metaphors and aphorisms, this film is something of an oddity but strongly stamped with the flavour of Santiago de Chile. There we encounter a writer finding material in a past romance and the film switches back and forth between the present and what happened eight years earlier. There's insufficient detail for us to really care about the love story, but the film's humour is often engaging and it's one of a kind. It is subtitled *A Story of Love, Books and Plants*. MS

❯ Diego Noguera, Natalia Galgani, Trinidad González, Hugo Medina, Gabriela Arancibia.
❯ *Dir* and *Screenplay* (from the novel by Alejandro Zambra) Cristián Jiménez, *Pro* Bruno Bettati, Nadia Turincev and Julie Gayet, *Ph* Inti Briones, *Art Dir* Jorge Zambrano, *Ed* Soledad Salfate, *M* Caroline Chaspoul and Eduardo Henríquez, *Cos* Mary Ann Smith.

Jirafa (Valdivia)/Rouge International (Paris)/Rizoma (Buenos Aires)/Ukbar Filmes (Lisbon) etc-Network Releasing.

A dry dream: A scene from Alma Har'el's documentary *Bombay Beach*.

96 mins. Chile/France/Argentina/Portugal. 2011.
Rel: 30 Mar 2012. Cert. 15.

Booked Out ★★★½

Mirren Burke stars as Polaroid-fanatic artist Ailidh, who lives in a quaint London apartment block. Spying on him for months, Ailidh develops a crush on boy-next-door Jacob and decides to find out more about him. Rollo Weeks plays Jacob, the redoubtable Sylvia Syms plays crazy old Mrs Nicholls, a widow who thinks her husband is still alive, while Claire Garvey is Jacqueline, a mystery woman Jacob visits daily. This could be a thriller movie set-up, but it turns out to be a lovely, charming life-affirmer. All four actors are cracking, the script's deliciously bittersweet and the film's a well-honed delight. DW

▶ Mirren Burke, Rollo Weeks, Claire Garvey, Sylvia Syms, Gabriela Montaraz.
▶ *Dir* and *Screenplay* Bryan O'Neil, *Pro* Sam Alani, *Ph* Jordan Cushing, *Pro Des* Sara Ranieri, *Ed* Faisel N Butt and Tom Werber, *M* Mark West and Derek Yau, *Cos* Sophie Howard.
BON Productions/Balagan Productions/Salani Films-Screen Projex.
86 mins. UK. 2011. Rel: 9 Mar 2012. Cert. 12A.

The Bourne Legacy ★★★★

The Bourne Legacy is as different from *The Bourne Ultimatum* as *Prometheus* is from *Aliens*. It was directed by Tony Gilroy, who is not in the business of delivering simplistic action scenarios. This is a cerebral take on the Bourne programme and has less to do with the central protagonist-on-the-run (Jeremy Renner) than with a slew of other characters. There's a lot of exposition and it's frighteningly up-to-date stuff, reflecting the real research going on in laboratories around the world. So if the film is not as exhilarating as *Supremacy*

Bourne Tomorrow: Jeremy Renner and Rachel Weisz add credibility to Tony Gilroy's thoroughly gripping *The Bourne Legacy.*

or *Ultimatum*, it's a more measured and intelligent ride and a thoroughly gripping one. JC-W

▶ Jeremy Renner, Rachel Weisz, Edward Norton, Albert Finney, Joan Allen, Stacy Keach, Oscar Isaac, Scott Glenn, Dennis Boutsikaris, David Strathairn, Donna Murphy, Željko Ivanek, Elizabeth Marvel, Paddy Considine.
▶ *Dir* Tony Gilroy, *Pro* Frank Marshall and Patrick Crowley, *Screenplay* Tony Gilroy and Dan Gilroy, *Ph* Robert Elswit, *Pro Des* Kevin Thompson, *Ed* John Gilroy, *M* James Newton Howard, *Cos* Shay Cunliffe.
Universal/Relativity Media/Kennedy/Marshall/Captivate Entertainment- Universal.
134 mins. USA. 2012. Rel: 13 Aug 2012. Cert. 12A.

Boxing Day ★★½

This is Bernard Rose's third feature derived from Tolstoy but, despite retaining the services of Danny Huston, he's not repeating himself. Relocated to modern America, this tale of a capitalist entrepreneur feeding off property deals is almost a two-hander featuring him and his driver. Unlike its predecessors, this is minimalist cinema so stretched out as to become boring and with a redemptive finale which, alas, comes across as glib and sentimental. The actors do their best, but in vain. MS

▶ Danny Huston, Matthew Jacobs, Edie Dakota, Lisa Enos, Jo Farkas, Julie Marcus, Lyne Renee.
▶ *Dir, Screenplay* (based on Tolstoy's novella *Master and Man*), *Ph* and *Ed* Bernard Rose, *Pro* Luc Roeg and Naomi Despres, *M* Rose and Nigel Holland.
BFI/an Independent/Giant Door production/LipSync Productions-Independent Distribution.
94 mins. UK/USA. 2012. Rel: 21 Dec 2012. Cert. 15.

Brave 3D ★★★½

Technically admirable, this Pixar production from Disney is an animation work which opts for the full wide screen and in so doing gloriously shows off its setting, the Scottish Highlands. It's notable too for featuring not a hero but a feisty heroine, a princess rebelling against the life being laid down for her. Among the voice cast Emma Thompson is ideal as the Queen but, with a spell turning her into a bear, the film's second half gets bogged down in a less engaging kind of fantasy world. MS

▶ With the voices of Kelly Macdonald, Billy Connolly, Emma Thompson, Julie Walters, Robbie Coltrane, Kevin McKidd.
▶ *Dir* Mark Andrews and Brenda Chapman, *Pro* Katherine Sarafian, *Screenplay* Andrews, Steve Purcell, Chapman and Irene Mecchi, from Chapman's story, *Ph* Robert Anderson and Danielle Feinberg, *Pro Des* Steve Pilcher, *Ed* Nicholas C Smith, *M* Patrick Doyle, *Supervising Animators* Alan Barillaro and Steven Clay Hunter.

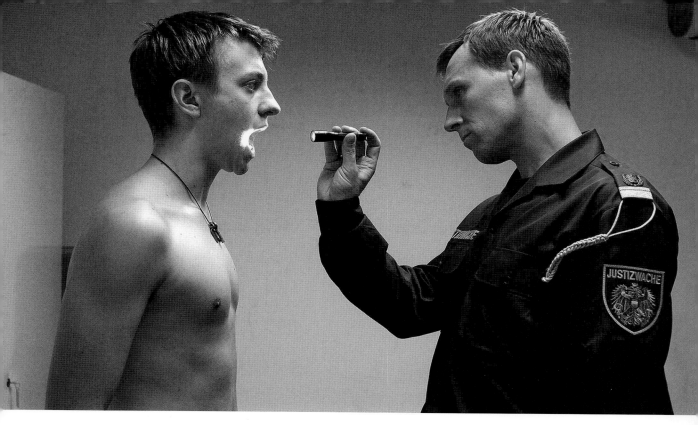

Disney/a Pixar Animation Studios film-Buena Vista.
100 mins. USA. 2012. Rel: 13 Aug 2012. Cert. PG.

Breathing ★★★★★

This striking debut as writer and director by the
actor Karl Markovics also benefits from superb
photography. Eighteen-year-old Thomas Schubert
is perfect as a youth living in a juvenile detention
centre but encouraged to find work which, if
properly done, may aid his release. This is an
understated work and haunting for that very
reason, although it may be too minimalistic to
appeal to all. But, as we learn something of the
youth's past and come to care about his future,
this admirable film invites us to sympathise with
people regardless of their weaknesses. (Original
title: *Atmen*) MS

❧ Thomas Schubert, Karin Lischka, Georg Friedrich,
Gerhard Liebmann, Elena Dörfler.
❧ *Dir* and *Screenplay* Karl Markovics, *Pro* Dieter
Pochlatko and Nikolaus Wisiak, *Ph* Martin Gschlacht,
Pro Des Isodor Wimmer, *Ed* Alarich Lenz, *M* Herbert
Tucmandl, *Cos* Caterina Czepek.
**An epo-film Prodktionsgesellschaft mbH/Wien-Graz
production/ORF Film etc-Verve Pictures.**
94 mins. Austria. 2011. Rel: 20 Apr 2012. Cert. 15.

Breaking Wind Part 1 ★

Here is another spoof on the Twilight Saga that
makes *Vampires Suck* look like a masterpiece. It is
a truly abysmal film with no redeeming features
whatsoever; for a supposed comedy it fails to
raise even a smile. The obese and always shirtless
Jacob (Frank Pacheco) has no desire for Bella
(Heather Ann Davis) – he is more interested in
eating or farting, or perhaps doing both at the
same time. Avoid like the plague! (Original title:
Breaking Wind) GS

❧ Heather Ann Davis, Eric Callero, Frank Pacheco,
Danny Trejo.
❧ *Dir* and *Screenplay* Craig Moss, *Pro* Moss, Amy
Jarvela and Bernie Gewissler, *Ph* Rudy Harbon,
Pro Des Russell M Jaeger, *Ed* Austin Michael Scott,
M Todd Haberman, *Cos* Ariyela Wald-Cohain.
Primary Pictures-Lionsgate.
79 mins. USA. 2011. Rel: 30 Mar 2012. Cert. 15.

The Brooklyn Brothers Beat
the Best ★★½

First-time writer-director Ryan O'Nan also plays
Alex, a struggling singer-songwriter who hits
rock bottom after his girlfriend dumps him; as
if that wasn't enough, his boss fires him. But his
luck changes when Jim (Michael Weston) enters
his life, an eccentric and self-proclaimed musical
revolutionary who promises Alex a country tour
as part of a duo. This is a likable and original
film but lacks credibility, despite the decent
performances. GS

❧ Ryan O'Nan, Michael Weston, Arielle Kebel,
Andrew McCarthy, Christopher McDonald, Wilmer
Valderrama.
❧ *Dir* and *Screenplay* Ryan O'Nan, *Pro* Jason
Michael Berman and Kwesi Collison, *Ph* Gavin
Kelly, *Pro Des* Ola Maslik, *Ed* Annette Davey, *M* Rob
Simonsen, *Cos* Derek Sullivan.

Naked and the
dead: Thomas
Schubert (left) in
Karl Markovics'
memorable
Breathing.

Brooklyn Brothers 5/Character Brigade/Taggart Productions/Tide Rock Films-Signature Entertainment. 98 mins. USA. 2011. Rel: 20 July 2012. Cert. 15.

Buck ★★★★

Buckskin Bannaman, the subject of this appealing documentary, was an adviser on Robert Redford's movie *The Horse Whisperer*. Cindy Meehl's film looks at his work and his life as he travels America to give classes in the control of horses, how to discipline them with love and understanding. His belief in this grew out of his own sufferings in childhood, adding to the interest of a thoroughly worthwhile film about a man one comes to admire. MS

▶ With Buck Bannaman, Robert Redford, Mary Bannaman, Reata Bannaman.
▶ *Dir* Cindy Meehl, *Pro* Julie Goldman, *Ph* Guy Mossman and Luke Geissbühler, *Ed* Toby Shimin, *M* David Robbins.

Cedar Creek Productions/Motto Pictures/Back Allie Productions-Revolver Entertainment. 89 mins. USA 2011. Rel: 27 Apr 2012. Cert. PG.

The Cabin in the Woods ★★★½

From the people who brought you *Buffy the Vampire Slayer* (Drew Goddard and Joss Whedon) comes a contemporary and even spookier variation on the old dark house theme, only here it's an old dark cabin stuck out among the trees. Five students book into the holiday home from Hell with its two-way mirrored bedroom and weird artefacts in the cellar. But, unbeknown to them, they are being watched by two strange men... Think *Evil Dead* meets *The Truman Show* with a touch of *Friday the 13th* plus laughs thrown in for good measure. Kristen Connolly, Chris Hemsworth and their young friends put up a brave fight in this stalk and slash mixture of horror and humour. MHD

▶ Kristen Connolly. Chris Hemsworth, Anna Hutchison, Fran Kranz, Jesse Williams, Richard Jenkins, Bradley Whitford, Sigourney Weaver.
▶ *Dir* and *Pro* Drew Goddard, *Screenplay* Goddard and Joss Whedon, *Ph* Peter Deming, *Pro Des* Martin Whist, *Ed* Lisa Lassek, *M* David Julyan, *Cos* Shawna Trpcic.

Lionsgate/Mutant Enemy-Lionsgate. 95 mins. USA. 2011. Rel: 13 Apr 2012. Cert. 15.

Café de Flore ★

The two plot-lines in this film, one set in contemporary Montreal and the other in Paris in 1969, eventually link up – but it will only make sense if you believe in reincarnation and by that stage you won't care anyway. The film cuts back and forth irritatingly between a devoted mother with a Down's Syndrome child and a rich man torn between wife and mistress. In the process the film strikes me as being as preposterous as it is self-indulgent. MS

▶ Vanessa Paradis, Kevin Parent, Marin Gerrier, Alice Dubois, Hélène Florent. Evelyne Brochu.
▶ *Dir*, *Screenplay* and *Ed* Jean-Marc Vallée, *Pro* Pierre Even and Marie-Claude Poulin, *Ph* Pierre Cottereau, *Art Dir* Florence Babin-Beaudry and Emmanuelle Pucci, *Cos* Ginette Magny and Emmanuelle Youchnovski.

Alliance Vivafilm/an Item 7, Monkey Pack Films, Crazy Films co-production etc-Momentum Pictures. 121 mins. Canada/France. 2011. Rel: 11 May 2012. Cert. 15.

Call Me Kuchu ★★★★

This is a film that could well move you both to tears and to anger. In Uganda 'kuchu' is a term applied to people who are lesbian, gay, bisexual or transgender and this documentary features David Kato, the first openly gay man in that country. He paid for it with his life and the film provides a devastating look at homophobia fuelled by government bills, inflammatory publications and evangelical support (in which latter context Bishop Senyonjo, in contrast, represents the voice of sanity and of true religion). Recommended. MS

▶ With David Kato, Gilles Muame, Bishop Senyonjo.
▶ *Dir* and *Pro* Katherine Fairfax Wright and Malika Zouhali-Worrall, *Ph* and *Ed* Wright, *M* Jon Mandabach.

Chicken & Egg Pictures etc-Dogwoof. 87 mins. USA/Ireland/UK. 2012. Rel: 2 Nov 2012. Cert. 12A.

Cabin frenzy: Fran Kranz in Drew Goddard's fun and sadistic *The Cabin in the Woods.*

Closet call: A scene from Katherine Fairfax Wright and Malika Zouhali-Worrall's daring documentary *Call Me Kuchu*.

The Campaign ★★

A lightly seasoned tale of political shenanigans from comedy everyman Jay Roach, this is hit-and-miss, middle-of-the-road stuff with a non-partisan approach that prevents it from achieving any edge. That said, there are some decent gags along the way, and fun, if familiar, performances from Will Ferrell and Zach Galifianakis as wildly different rivals on the campaign trail. The former's a tactless, ruthless son of a bitch, the latter a clueless oddball, so no surprises there. Or indeed, anywhere else. MJ

▶ Will Ferrell, Zack Galifianakis, Brian Cox, Dan Aykroyd, Dylan McDermott, Jason Sudeikis, John Lithgow, Katherine LaNasa, Sarah Baker.

▶ *Dir* Jay Roach, *Pro* Roach, Ferrell, Galifianakis and Adam McKay, *Screenplay* Chris Henchy and Shawn Harwell, from a story by them and McKay, *Ph* Jim Denault, *Pro Des* Michael Corenblith, *Ed* Craig Alpert and Jon Poll, *M* Theodore Shapiro, *Cos* Daniel Orlandi.

Everyman Pictures/Gary Sanchez Productions-Warner Bros.
85 mins. USA. 2012. Rel: 28 Sep 2012. Cert. 15.

Carancho ★★★½

Pablo Trapero's film, the title of which translates as 'The Vulture', is a tough drama set in Buenos Aires and splendidly acted by Ricardo Darin and Martina Gusmán. Darin plays a lawyer caught up in crime and Gusmán is a trainee doctor with a drug problem of her own who aids emergency services. They meet at the scene of a street accident and fall in love, but fate is against them.

It's a good film somewhat spoilt for me by the fashionably contrived and exaggerated climax. MS

▶ Ricardo Darín, Martina Gusmán, Carlos Weber, José Luis Arias, Gabriel Almirón.
▶ *Dir* and *Pro* Pablo Trapero, *Screenplay* Alejandro Fadel, Martín Mauregui, Santiago Mitre and Trapero, *Ph* Julián Apezteguia, *Art Dir* Mercedes Alfonsín, *Ed* Ezequiel Borovinsky and Trapero, *Cos* Marisa Urruti.

Matanza Cine/Finecut/Patagonik/Ad Vitam/L90
Producciones etc-Axiom Films Limited.
107 mins. Argentina/South Korea/France/Chile. 2010.
Rel: 2 Mar 2012. Cert. 12A.

Carnage ★★

A sell-out success on stage, Yasmina Reza's comedy was re-written for the screen by her and director Roman Polanski. Relocating from Paris to New York, it deals with two sets of parents at odds on account of a playground incident in which one son hit another. A storm in a beaker, perhaps, but the grown-ups will not let it pass. Instead they bicker as more recriminations come out into the open. It's all highly unbelievable and, do what they may, the cast of Christoph Waltz, Jodie Foster, Kate Winslet and John C Reilly just cannot resuscitate the script to anything approaching real life. A major disappointment from Polanski. MHD

▶ Jodie Foster, Kate Winslet, Christoph Waltz, John C Reilly, Elvis Polanski, Ethan Longstreet.
▶ *Dir* Roman Polanski, *Pro* Said Ben Said, *Screenplay* Polanski and Yasmina Reza, from Reza's play *Le Dieu du*

Double-barrelled laughs? Diego Luna goes for it in Matt Piedmont's *Casa de mi Padre*.

carnage, as translated by Michael Katims, *Ph* Pawel Edelman, *Pro Des* Dean Tavoularis, *Ed* Herve de Luze, *M* Alexandre Desplat, *Cos* Milena Canonero.

SBS Productions/Constantin Film Produktion/SPI Flm Studio/France 2 Cinéma/Canal +/CinéCinéma/France Télévisions/Wild Bunch/Polish Institute etc-StudioCanal. 80 mins. USA. 2011. Rel: 3 Feb 2012. Cert. 15.

Casa de mi Padre ★★★½

Prodigal son and corrupt drug dealer Raul (Diego Luna), along with his beautiful fiancée Sonia (Genesis Rodriguez), returns to his father's Mexican ranch and soon puts everyone's life in jeopardy. But his older brother Armando (Will Ferrell) is determined to protect the family... The dialogue of this delicious pastiche of Spaghetti Westerns is in Spanish and the thunderous score never misses an opportunity to highlight a dramatic effect. It's very funny and Ferrell is in good form as a hot-blooded Mexican. GS

▶ Will Ferrell, Gael García Bernal, Diego Luna, Genesis Rodriguez, Pedro Armendáriz Jr, Louis Carazo.
▶ *Dir* Matt Piedmont, *Pro* Ferrell, Adam McKay, Jessica Elbaum, Emilio Diez Barroso, Kevin J Messick, Darlene Caamano Loquet, *Screenplay* Andrew Steele, *Ph* Ramsey Nickell, *Pro Des* Kevin Kavanaugh, *Ed* David Trachtenberg, *M* Andrew Feltenstein and John Nau, *Cos* Trayce Gigi Field and Marylou Lim.
NALA Films/Gary Sanchez Productions-StudioCanal. 84 mins. USA. 2012. Rel: 8 June 2012. Cert. 15.

A Cat in Paris ★★★½

This French animation is amiable but unexceptional. Released in both dubbed and subtitled versions, this is a Parisian tale about a burglar whose night-time assistant is a cat. Ironically the cat belongs to Jeanne, a police commissioner. Widowed by the film's gang leader villain, Jeanne has a seven-year-old daughter who becomes attached to the cat, Dino. The drawing style is short on charm, but this unusual piece carries pleasing echoes of such contrasted movies as *To Catch a Thief* and *King Kong*. (Original title: *Une Vie de chat*) MS

▶ With the voices in English of Mark Irons, Sara Vertongen, Jerry Killick.
▶ *Dir* Alain Gagnol and Jean-Loup Felicioli, *Pro* Jacques-Rémy Girerd, *Screenplay* Gagnol and Girerd, *Ed* Hervé Guichard, *M* Serge Besset, *Animation Supervisor & Graphic Design* Felicioli.
Folimage Features/Lunanime/Digit Anima/France 3 Cinéma etc-Soda Pictures. 65 mins. France/Belgium 2010. Rel: 6 Apr 2012. Cert. PG.

Celeste and Jesse Forever ★★★

This comedy has a tone of its own. Unusually it features a couple on the point of divorce, although their differences don't prevent them from remaining best friends. As each pursues other prospects and Jesse finds that a passing encounter has led to pregnancy, we sense that it's the couple, Celeste and Jesse, who really belong together. Their rapport is well suggested, but their behaviour is such that they are on the borderline between being sympathetic and irritating. How you feel about them will be crucial to your response to the film. MS

▸ Rashida Jones, Andy Samberg, Chris Messina, Ari Gaynor, Will McCormack, Elijah Wood, Emma Roberts.
▸ *Dir* Lee Toland Krieger, *Pro* Lee Nelson, Jennifer Todd and Suzanne Todd, *Screenplay* Rashida Jones and Will McCormack, *Ph* David Lanzenberg, *Pro Des* Ian Phillips, *Ed* Yana Gorskaya, *M* Sunny Levine and Zach Cowie, *Cos* Julia Caston.

Envision Media Arts/a Team Todd production-BuenaVista.
92 mins. USA. 2012. Rel: 7 Dec 2012. Cert. 15.

Charlie Casanova ★

Nouveau riche sociopath Charlie (Emmett Scanlan) is prepared to kill on impulse and uses playing cards to determine his actions after he kills a working class girl in a hit and run... Scanlan injects enough energy into his loathsome character but, unlike Malcolm McDowell in *A Clockwork Orange* (a film the producers want theirs to be compared with), he lacks any charisma whatsoever. Writer-director Terry McMahon tries hard to be extra controversial but this deeply unpleasant project leaves a bad taste in the mouth. GS

▸ Emmett Scanlan, Damien Hannaway, Ruth McIntyre, Tony Murphy, Valeria Bandino, Thomas Farrell, Tommy O'Neil.
▸ *Dir, Pro* and *Screenplay* Terry McMahon, *Ph* Eoin Macken, *Ed* Tony Kearns, *M* Mark Ivan O'Gorman, *Cos* Anouk Sablayrolles.

Source Productions-StudioCanal.
94 mins. Ireland. 2010. Rel: 11 May 2012. Cert. 18.

Chasing Ice ★★★★

This is serious stuff. Jeff Orlowski's documentary evidencing climate change features the photographer James Balog. It was Balog who felt that the case for it needed to be proved visually rather than statistically and set up cameras in the Arctic to record the effects on glaciers. He wanted the public to be grabbed in the gut and these pictures – not least when featuring time-lapse images concentrating years and months – do just that. MS

▸ With James Balog, Louie Psihoyos, Adam LeWinter, Jeff Orlowski. Suzanne Balog.
▸ *Dir* and *Ph* Jeff Orlowski, *Pro* Orlowski, Paula DuPré Pesmen and Jerry Aronson, *Written by* Mark Monroe, *Ed* Davis Coombe, *M* J Ralph.

Submarine Deluxe/an Exposure production/Diamond Docs-Dogwoof.
80 mins. USA. 2012. Rel: 14 Dec 2012. Cert. 12A.

Chernobyl Diaries ★★

For a horror film, the idea behind *Chernobyl Diaries* is a rather ingenious, if ghoulish, one. However, the four credited scriptwriters have failed to come up with a decent story to hang it on. Four attractive American tourists are on a Eurotrip bound for Moscow, when they are persuaded to dabble in a bit of "extreme tourism" while in Kiev... First-time director Brad Parker exhibits a commendable command of his medium and there are good performances from the principals, particularly Devin Kelley as an independent spirit with a camera. But after the promising set-up, the film loses momentum and ends up going nowhere. JC-W

▸ Ingrid Bolsø Berdal, Dimitri Diatchenko, Olivia Taylor Dudley, Devin Kelley, Jesse McCartney, Nathan Phillips, Jonathan Sadowski.
▸ *Dir* Brad Parker, *Pro* Parker, Oren Peli and Brian Witten, *Screenplay* Peli, Carey Van Dyke, Shane Van Dyke and Martin Solibakke, *Ph* Morten Søborg, *Pro Des* Aleksandar Denic, *Ed* Stan Stalfas, *M* Diego Stocco, *Cos* Momirka Bailovic.

Alcon Entertainment/FilmNation Entertainment-StudioCanal.
87 mins. USA. 2012. Rel: 22 June 2012. Cert. 15.

Chronicle ★★★★

As a narrative device, the 'video diary' has been used with varying degrees of success. But, let's face it, it's the cinematic equivalent of a doctor's scrawl in place of a gorgeous piece of calligraphy. And it's cheap. However, the screenwriter Max Landis (son of John) and debutant director Josh Trank have come up with a story worthy of the gimmick. After three teenagers find themselves endowed with telekinetic powers, they record their every move as their abilities increase. Moreover, the three leads not only display winning personalities but are believable as well. Indeed, you'll believe a geek can fly. JC-W

▸ Dane DeHaan, Alex Russell, Michael B Jordan, Michael Kelly, Ashley Hinshaw, Bo Petersen.

Moving diaries: Dane DeHaan in Josh Trank's wholly engaging *Chronicle.*

▶ *Dir* Josh Trank, *Pro* John Davis and Adam Schroeder, *Screenplay* Max Landis, from a story by Landis and Trank, *Ph* Matthew Jensen, *Pro Des* Stephen Altman, *Ed* Elliot Greenberg, *Cos* Diana Cilliers.

Davis Entertainment/Dune Entertainment-Twentieth Century Fox.
83 mins. USA/UK. 2012. Rel: 1 Feb 2012. Cert. 12A.

Cinema Komunisto ★★★

Yugoslavia's President Tito was a film buff who saw cinema as a means of propaganda. The state-built Avala Film Studios brought in much-needed currency when it gained international weight, but no less significantly its films celebrated the wartime partisans and Tito himself. (Richard Burton, no less, played him there in 1972.) Mila Turajlic's documentary lacks drive but, in dealing with unfamiliar territory albeit involving undistinguished films, it does see Tito's cinema as a metaphor for the way in which he held the country together. MS

▶ With Leka Konstantinovic, Gile Djuric, Bata Zivojinovic
▶ *Dir* and *Written by* Mila Turajlic, *Pro* Dragan Pesikan, Turajlic and others, *Ph* Goran Kovacevic, *Ed* Aleksandra Milovanovic, *M* Nemanja Mosurovic.

Dribbling Pictures/3K Productions/Intermedia Network etc-E2 Films.
101 mins. Serbia/The Netherlands/Greece. 2010. Rel: 23 Nov 2012. Cert. PG.

Circumstance ★★★½

Sapphic sedition: Nikohl Boosheri and Sarah Kazemy in Maryam Keshavarz's *Circumstance*.

Made by an Iranian living in America, Maryam Keshavarz, this is nevertheless set in Tehran. Concentrating largely on young people and with a lesbian relationship at its centre, this offers a view of Iran today very different from what we usually see. Not everything works as smoothly

as it might, but the acting is good and the film is undoubtedly deeply felt. The gay and lesbian issues highlight a social critique founded on the need for personal freedom. MS

▶ Nikohl Boosheri, Sarah Kazemy, Reza Sixo Safai, Sina Amedson, Keon Mohajeri, Soheil Parsa.
▶ *Dir* and *Screenplay* Maryam Keshavarz, *Pro* Karin Chien, Keshavarz and Melissa M Lee, *Ph* Brian Rigney Hubbard, *Pro Des* Natacha Kalfayan, *Ed* Andrea Chignoli, *M* Gingger Shankar, *Cos* Lamia Choucair.

Participant Media/Marrakesh Films/A Space Between/ Bago Pictures/Neon Productions etc-Peccadillo Pictures Ltd.
102 mins. USA/The Netherlands/France/Morocco/Hong Kong. 2011. Rel: 24 Aug 2012. Cert. 15.

Cleanskin ★½

Secret service agent Ewan (Sean Bean) goes undercover to become the bodyguard of a small-time London arms dealer in order to discover who he's selling Semtex to... This is an improvement on Hadi Hajaig's previous film *Puritan*, but again it is almost impossible to care about any of his thinly sketched and unsympathetic characters. It's predictable, very routine and not very exciting. GS

▶ Sean Bean, Charlotte Rampling, Abhin Galeya, Tom Burke, Tuppence Middleton, James Fox, Michelle Ryan, Peter Polycarpou.
▶ *Dir, Pro, Screenplay* and *Ed* Hadi Hajaig, *Ph* Ian Howes, *Pro Des* Stephane Collonge and Humphrey Jaeger, *M* Simon Lambros, *Cos* Maja Meschede.

The UK Film Studio-Warner Brothers Pictures.
108 mins. UK. 2012. Rel: 9 Mar 2012. Cert. 15.

Cloclo ★★★½

Claude François probably doesn't mean much to British music audiences of the 1960s, brought up on Cliff Richard, Tom Jones and The Beatles, even though the successful French singer-songwriter (known as Cloclo) has been compared to all three. Popular mainly in Europe, when he was about to venture to the US he electrocuted himself in his bath, aged 39. He covered many American pop songs but is best remembered for writing 'Comme d'habitude', which Paul Anka rewrote as 'My Way'. Florent-Emilio Siri's film spares us none of the unsavoury, controlling side of the entertainer, including his womanising, in a terrific performance by lookalike actor Jérémie Renier. MHD

▶ Jérémie Renier, Benoît Magimel, Monica Scattini, Joséphine Japy, Robert Knepper.
▶ *Dir* Florent-Emilio Siri, *Pro* Jean-Baptiste Dupont and Cyril Colbeau-Justin, *Screenplay* Siri and Julien Rappeneau, *Ph* Giovanni Fiore Coltellacci, *Pro Des* Philippe Chiffre, *Ed* Oliver Gajan, *M* Alexandre Desplat, *Cos* Mimi Lempicka.

LGM Cinéma/Flèche Productions/StudioCanal/TFI Films
Production/Canal +/Ciné +/Coficup/Backup Films
etc-StudioCanal.
148 mins. France/Belgium. 2012. Rel: 22 June 2012.
Cert. 12A.

Clone ★★★★

This SF art film was first screened at the 2010
London Film Festival under the title *Womb*. It
tells the story of Rebecca (Eva Green), a young
woman who goes against her better judgment
when she decides to clone her beloved husband
after he dies in a tragic accident. Director
Benedek Fliegauf shoots this intriguing story
like an Ingmar Bergman film, with superb
cinematography of a beautiful, isolated coastal
landscape. Green is excellent and so is Matt
Smith in the dual roles of husband and son.
(Original title: *Womb*) GS

▶ Eva Green, Matt Smith, Lesley Manville, Peter
Wight, Ella Smith.
▶ *Dir* and *Screenplay* Benedek Fliegauf, *Pro* Roman
Paul, András Muhi and Gerhard Meixner, *Ph* Péter
Szatmári, *Pro Des* Erwin Prib, *Ed* Xavier Box, *M* Max
Richter, *Cos* Mariano Tufano.

Razor Film Produktion GmbH/Asap Films/Boje Buck
Produktion/ZDF-Arte/arte France Cinéma/Inforg
Stúdió-Arrow Films.
111 mins. Germany/Hungary/France. 2010. Rel: 4 May
2012. No Cert.

Cockneys vs Zombies ★★★★

Accidentally unlocked in the East End by some
builders, an old vault unleashes a troop of
starving zombies. Meanwhile a group of unlikely
bank robbers attempt a heist in order to save a
nursery from redevelopment. This is the most fun
zombie film since *Shaun of the Dead*. It's also good
to see actors of a certain age, including Honor
Blackman, kick ass like there's no tomorrow. GS

▶ Georgia King, Michelle Ryan, Honor Blackman,
Rasmus Hardiker, Alan Ford, Richard Briers, Harry
Treadaway, Georgina Hale.
▶ *Dir* Matthias Hoene, *Pro* Hoene, Mark Lane and
James Harris, *Screenplay* Lucas Roche and James
Moran, from an idea by Hoene, *Ph* Daniel Bronks,
Pro Des Matthew Button, *Ed* Neil Farrell and John
Palmer, *M* Jody Jenkins, *Cos* Matthew Price.

Limelight/Molinaire/Tea Shop & Film Company-
StudioCanal.
88 mins. UK. 2012. Rel: 31 Aug 2012. Cert. 15.

Code Name: Geronimo ★★

In recent history there can be few more significant
moments in the global calendar: where were you
when Osama bin Laden was shot? One might
have hoped for something classically intense
and illuminating from a film version, but John
Stockwell, former teen actor and current B-movie
director, brings an almost corporate proficiency
to this world-changing story. Thus, the screen is
littered with pointless dates, top brass stereotypes
populate the boardrooms of Langley and Fort
Bragg, and the Navy Seals look like vaguely
human avatars from a video game. JC-W

▶ Cam Gigandet, Anson Mount, Freddy Rodríguez,
Xzibit, Kathleen Robertson, Robert Knepper, William
Fichtner.

East End Z: Harry
Treadaway defends
his turf in Matthias
Hoene's *Cockneys
vs Zombies*.

Cavill's caveat: Henry Cavill dictates his terms in Mabrouk El Mechri's *The Cold Light of Day*.

The Cold Light of Day ★★★½

When business consultant Will (Henry Cavill) heads for a boating holiday with his family in Spain, he gets a raw deal from his father (Bruce Willis), who claims to be a cultural attaché. Having gone ashore in Alicante, Will returns to the yacht to find mum, dad, brother and his girlfriend gone. He is warned that, unless a missing briefcase is returned immediately, Will may himself be for the chop. It turns out that dad is actually a CIA agent, not an attaché, with or without briefcase, and that his boss (Sigourney Weaver) will stop at nothing to get it. This is moderately exciting tosh that holds its intrigue long enough to be watchable, with Cavill getting in some action training for the next *Superman* movie. MHD

▶ Henry Cavill, Bruce Willis, Sigourney Weaver, Caroline Goodall, Rafi Gavron, Emma Hamilton, Jim Piddock, Paloma Bloyd, Colm Meaney, Verónica Echegui.
▶ *Dir* Mabrouk El Mechri, *Pro* Mark D Evans and Trevor Macy, *Screenplay* Scott Wiper and John Petro, *Ph* Remi Adefarasin, *Pro Des* Benjamin Fernández, *Ed* Valerio Bonelli, *M* Lucas Vidal, *Cos* Bina Daigeler.

Summit Entertainment/Intrepid Pictures/Galavis Film/Picture Machine/Film Rites/Fria Luz Del Dia A.I.E.-Entertainment One.
93 mins. USA. 2012. Rel: 6 Apr 2012. Cert. 12A.

▶ *Dir* John Stockwell, *Pro* Nicolas Chartier, Zev Foreman and Tony Mark, *Screenplay* Kendall Lampkin, *Ph* Peter Holland, *Pro Des* Guy Barnes, *Ed* Ben Callahan, *M* Paul Haslinger, *Cos* Miye Matsumoto.
Voltage Pictures/The Weinstein Company-StudioCanal.
99 mins. USA. 2012. Rel: 14 Dec 2012. Cert. 15.

Comes a Bright Day ★★

Ambitious bellboy Sam (Craig Roberts) falls head over heels when he sets eyes on Mary Bright (Imogen Poots) at his local café. But when he follows her into the jewellery shop where she works, he is taken hostage by thieves, along with Mary and the shop owner (Timothy Spall). Writer-director Simon Aboud's uninspired film adds nothing new to an over-familiar premise, and even the usually reliable Spall looks uncomfortable. However, Roberts, so good in *Submarine*, gives another persuasive performance. GS

▶ Craig Roberts, Imogen Poots, Kevin McKidd, Timothy Spall, Geoff Bell.
▶ *Dir* and *Screenplay* Simon Aboud, *Pro* Christine Alderson, *Ph* John Lynch, *Pro Des* Ricky Eyres, *Ed* Gavin Buckley, *M* Joel Cadbury, Paul Stoney and Melissa Parmenter, *Cos* Ian Fulcher.

Ipso Facto Films/Matador Pictures/Smudge Films/Cinema Six etc-Ipso Facto Films.
91 mins. UK. 2012. Rel: 13 July 2012. Cert. 15.

Confession of a Child of the Century ★

Sylvie Verheyde's adaptation of de Musset's novel takes place after the Napoleonic Wars and follows the adventures of Octave (Pete Doherty), a heartbroken young man who believes he has found a new love when he meets Brigitte (Charlotte Gainsbourg) in the French countryside. Doherty is simply unwatchable as the spoilt and ineffectual lover and delivers a truly abysmal performance. His narration is incomprehensible and he almost manages to reduce the usually excellent Gainsbourg to his level. GS

▶ Charlotte Gainsbourg, Pete Doherty, August Diehl, Lily Cole, Volker Bruch.
▶ *Dir* and *Screenplay* Sylvie Verheyde, based on Alfred de Musset's novel *La Confession d'un enfant du siècle*, *Pro* Bruno Berthemy, *Ph* Nicolas Gaurin, *Pro Des* Thomas Grézaud, *Ed* Cristel Dewynter, *Cos* Esther Walz.

Les Films du Veyrier/Integral Films/Warp Films/arte France Cinéma/Wild Bunch/Canal+/Procirep/Angoa etc-Soda Pictures.
120 mins. France/Germany/UK. 2012. Rel: 7 Dec 2012. Cert. 15.

Contraband ★★★

Chris Farraday used to be a helluva smuggler. But now he's settled down and is running his own alarm installation business in New Orleans. Then his brother-in-law falls foul of a local hoodlum and Chris is forced to complete one last job – in Panama City… If *Contraband* is an above-average thriller, it's because of the original premise, translated from the 2008 Icelandic movie *Reykjavík-Rotterdam*. The star of the latter takes over the directorial reins here and fashions a gritty, hard-hitting affair with a fascinating insight into smuggling techniques. If only he had given us more of the inside dope and less of the gun battles and car chases. JC-W

➤ Mark Wahlberg, Kate Beckinsale, Ben Foster, Giovanni Ribisi, Lukas Haas, Caleb Landry Jones, Diego Luna, JK Simmons, David O'Hara.
➤ *Dir* Baltasar Kormákur, *Pro* Kormákur, Tim Bevan, Eric Fellner, Stephen Levinson and Mark Wahlberg, *Screenplay* Aaron Guzikowski, *Ph* Barry Ackroyd, *Pro Des* Tony Fanning, *Ed* Elísabet Ronaldsdóttir, *M* Clinton Shorter, *Cos* Jenny Eagan.

Relativity Media/Working Title/Blueeyes Prods/Leverage/StudioCanal-Universal.
109 mins. USA/UK/France. 2012. Rel: 16 Mar 2012. Cert. 15.

Coriolanus ★★★★

An unlikely film subject, perhaps, but first-time director Ralph Fiennes succeeds by updating the Shakespeare text (courtesy of screenwriter John Logan) to modern-day Serbia and its war-torn landscape – but set in "a place calling itself Rome." Fiennes also plays the title role of the General who turns against his people to become Consul but sides with one of his enemies, Tullus Aufidius (Gerard Butler), in a piece that mirrors the actions of today's political leaders. Coriolanus' mother Volumnia (Vanessa Redgrave)

is the power behind the throne. A formidable mixture of Serbian and British actors, including Brian Cox, Paul Jesson and James Nesbitt, lend weight to a rigorous project. MHD

➤ Ralph Fiennes, Gerard Butler, Vanessa Redgrave, Brian Cox, Jessica Chastain, Paul Jesson, James Nesbitt, John Kani, Jon Snow.
➤ *Dir* Ralph Fiennes, *Pro* Fiennes, John Logan, Gabrielle Tana, Julia Taylor-Stanley, Colin Vaines, *Screenplay* John Logan, based on William Shakespeare's play, *Ph* Barry Ackroyd, *Pro Des* Ricky Eyres, *Ed* Nicolas Gaster, *M* Ilan Eshkeri, *Cos* Bojana Nitkovic.

Icon Entertainment International/BBC Films/Hermetof Pictures/Lip Sync Productions LLP/Artemis Films etc-Lionsgate.
123 mins. UK. 2011. Rel: 20 Jan 2012. Cert. 15.

Corman's World: Exploits of a Hollywood Rebel ★★★

With his record for fostering future stars and young directors who would later achieve distinction, Roger Corman would be a key figure in American cinema even if he had not made classics of his own. But he was also the king of trashy exploitation. Here filmmaker Alex Stapleton gives him an easy ride: she relishes the schlock and never asks questions that would make us understand this two-sided man better. The film may entertain but it can only be seen as a lost opportunity. MS

Too noble for the world: Jessica Chastain as Virgilia and Ralph Fiennes as *Coriolanus*.

▶ With Roger Corman, Robert De Niro, Martin
Scorsese, Quentin Tarantino, Paul WS Anderson.
▶ *Dir* Alex Stapleton, *Pro* Stone Douglass, Mickey
Barold, Stapleton and others, *Ph* Patrick Simpson,
Ed Victor Livingston and Philip Owens, *M* Air.

**A&E Indiefilms/a Far Hills/Stick N Stone production/
Gallant Films-104 Films.
86 mins. USA. 2011. Rel: 21 Feb 2012. Cert. 15.**

Corpo celeste ★★

Alice Rohrwacher's film can't sustain its feature
length, being essentially just an anecdote
about a young girl rebelling against a Catholic
upbringing. Aiming at both comedy and drama
in turn, this very Italian tale is sadly inadequate
in both modes. Although probably fuelled by
anger on Rohrwacher's part, her film fails to work
either as satirical comedy or as involving drama:
it's just nothing very much at all. MS

▶ Yile Vianello, Salvatore Cantalupo, Pasqualina
Scuncia, Anita Caprioli, Maria Trunfio.
▶ *Dir* and *Screenplay* Alice Rohrwacher, *Pro* Carlo
Cresto-Dina, Jacques Bidou, Marianne Dumoulin
and Tiziana Soudani, *Ph* Hélène Louvart, *Art Dir* Luca
Servino, *Ed* Marco Spoletini, *Cos* Loredana Buscemi.

**Rai Cinema/a Tempesta, JBA Production, AMKA Films
Productions production etc-Artificial Eye.
99 mins. Italy/France/Switzerland 2011.
Rel: 30 Mar 2012. Cert. U.**

Cosmopolis ★★★

Studiously intellectual in its appeal, this adaptation
of Don DeLillo's novel of 2003 gains from the fact
that the book foreshadowed the financial crisis of
2008. With dialogue as stylised as Pinter's, it covers
one day and is mainly set inside the limousine
of a financier (Robert Pattinson of all people).
Capitalism may be under attack, but it's too far
removed from naturalism to satisfy except when
it comes to the technical aspects – the direction
of David Cronenberg and the photography by
Peter Suschitzky have real distinction. MS

▶ Robert Pattinson, Juliette Binoche, Samantha
Morton, Paul Giamatti, Sarah Gadon, Mathieu
Amalric, Emily Hampshire, Kevin Durand.
▶ *Dir* and *Screenplay* (from the novel by Don DeLillo)
David Cronenberg, *Pro* Paulo Branco and Martin Katz,
Ph Peter Suschitzky, *Pro Des* Arv Grewal, *Ed* Ronald
Sanders, *M* Howard Shore, *Cos* Denise Cronenberg.

**Alfama Films/Prospero Pictures production/France 2
Cinéma etc-E1 Films.
109 mins. Canada/France/Portugal/Italy. 2012.
Rel: 15 June 2012. Cert. 15.**

Cross of Honour ★★★

In this World War II true story three German and
two British pilots find refuge in a remote cabin in
the Norwegian wilderness after their aircrafts crash

in the snow. And they must join forces in order to survive... This is a gripping story of friendship and survival atmospherically directed by Petter Næss. Rupert Grint is effective as Smith, the prejudiced Liverpudlian, and so is David Kross as the wounded German. The characters occasionally sink into stereotypes but overall this is an engaging film. (Original title: *Into the White*) GS

▶ Florian Lukas, Lachlan Nieboer, Rupert Grint, Kim Haugen, Stig Henrik Hoff, David Kross.
▶ *Dir* Petter Næss, *Pro* Valerie Saunders and Peter Aalbæck Jensen, *Screenplay* Næss, Dave Mango and Ole Meldgaard, *Ph* Daniel Voldheim *Pro Des* Udo Kramer, *Ed* Frida Eggum Michaelsen, *Cos* Steffi Bruhn.
Zentropa International Norway/Zentropa International Sweden/Trollhätten Film AB/Eurimages –Magnolia Pictures. 100 mins. Norway/Sweden. 2012. Rel: 28 Sep 2012. Cert. 15.

Damsels in Distress ★★

Still failing to match *Metropolitan* (1990), Whit Stillman now comes up with a college tale in which the males are boorish morons while the females adopt an insufferable air of superiority. The one female student who rightly criticises the others rather fades away. In any case the cast is largely lacklustre and any wit loses out because Stillman's attitude to his characters is patronising and condescending. A Gershwin song aids the ending until it's followed by a second, inferior number. MS

▶ Greta Gerwig, Adam Brody, Analeigh Tipton, Hugo Becker, Megalyn Echikunwoke, Ryan Metcalf.

▶ *Dir* and *Screenplay* Whit Stillman, *Pro* Stillman, Martin Shafer and Liz Glotzer, *Ph* Doug Emmett, *Pro Des* Elizabeth J Jones, *Ed* Andrew Hafitz, *M* Mark Suozzo and Adam Schlesinger, *Cos* Ciera Wells.
Westerly Films/a Steeplechase-Analytic production etc-Sony. 99 mins. USA. 2011. Rel: 27 Apr 2012. Cert. 15.

A Dangerous Method ★★★½

David Cronenberg's film covers the work of psychoanalysts Sigmund Freud (Viggo Mortensen) and Carl Jung (Michael Fassbender) and patient Sabina Spielrein (Keira Knightley), who arrives at Jung's clinic in a state of high excitement but emerges with enough self-knowledge to become a psychiatrist herself. Freud's idea is to help the patient understand herself, whereas Jung believes in striving to make the subject achieve in areas they wouldn't understand without therapy – but not without Jung bedding Spielrein first. Is this a failure in medical ethics or just a vital part of the treatment? Mortensen and Fassbender hammer it out with credibility while Knightley gives a selfless portrait of a woman at her wits' end. MHD

▶ Keira Knightley, Viggo Mortensen, Michael Fassbender, Vincent Cassel, Sarah Gadon.
▶ *Dir* David Cronenberg, *Pro* Jeremy Thomas, *Screenplay* Christopher Hampton, based on his play *The Talking Cure* and John Kerr's Book *A Most Dangerous Method*, *Ph* Peter Suschitzky, *Pro Des* James McAteer, *Ed* Ronald Sanders, *M* Howard Shore, *Cos* Denise Cronenberg.

Mindful things: Michael Fassbender as Jung and Viggo Mortensen as Freud in David Cronenberg's *A Dangerous Method*.

Recorded Picture Company/Lago Film/Prospero Pictures/ Talking Cure Productions/Téléfilm Canada etc-Lionsgate. 99 mins. UK/Germany/Canada/Switzerland. 2011. Rel: 10 Feb 2012. Cert. 15.

Dark Horse ★★★

Sad to say, the splendidly idiosyncratic writer-director Todd Solondz is off form here. Where the superb *Life During Wartime* (2009) was an ensemble piece, this has at its centre a man in his thirties (Jordan Gelber) still living with his parents. Is he a sad sack hero or something more disturbing? Later scenes in the film may be real or imaginary, but the conclusion works neither as black comedy nor as tragic denouement. It's still utterly individual, though, despite being disappointing. MS

❯ Jordan Gelber, Selma Blair, Mia Farrow, Christopher Walken, Justin Bartha, Donna Murphy.
❯ *Dir* and *Screenplay* Todd Solondz, *Pro* Ted Hope and Derrick Tseng, *Ph* Andrij Parekh, *Pro Des* Alex DiGerlando, *Ed* Kevin Messman, *Cos* Kurt and Bart.

Goldcrest Films/a Double Hope production-Axiom Films Limited.
86 mins. USA. 2011. Rel: 29 June 2012. Cert. 15.

The Dark Knight Rises ★★½

One might think that the aim of a $250 million comic-strip blockbuster was to thrill, amaze, excite or amuse, or a combination of all four. *The Dark Knight Rises*, the supposed conclusion to Christopher Nolan's remarkable trilogy, achieves other things: to baffle, bemuse, frustrate and infuriate. The best thing about it is the recycled music of Hans Zimmer – even as it drowns out the dialogue it at least propels the action forward. The film remains impressive in its visual sweep, even though there are none of the set-pieces that made *The Dark Knight* so special. JC-W

❯ Christian Bale, Michael Caine, Gary Oldman, Anne Hathaway, Tom Hardy, Marion Cotillard, Joseph Gordon-Levitt, Morgan Freeman, Juno

Temple, Aidan Gillen, Matthew Modine, Tom Conti, Ben Mendelsohn, Chris Ellis, William Devane, Liam Neeson, Cillian Murphy.
❯ *Dir* Christopher Nolan, *Pro* Emma Thomas, Christopher Nolan and Charles Roven, *Screenplay* Jonathan Nolan and Christopher Nolan, *Ph* Wally Pfister, *Pro Des* Nathan Crowley and Kevin Kavanaugh, *Ed* Lee Smith, *M* Hans Zimmer, *Cos* Lindy Hemming.

Warner Bros/DC Entertainment/Legendary Pictures/ Syncopy-Warner Bros.
164 mins. USA/UK. 2012. Rel: 20 July 2012. Cert. 12A.

Dark Shadows ★★★

A family saga with vampires, Tim Burton's film is an affectionately humorous take on the TV series popular in the 1960s. Johnny Depp is an 18th century werewolf resurfacing in 1972 to support his family and to defeat the still-living woman whose curse born of thwarted love brought him to this state. His is a highly original creation and memorable, but the film itself becomes overblown and the plot silly; Burton would be on much firmer ground with *Frankenweenie* [qv]. MS

❯ Johnny Depp, Michelle Pfeiffer, Helena Bonham Carter, Eva Green, Jackie Earle Haley, Bella Heathcote, Jonny Lee Miller, Chloë Grace Moretz, Christopher Lee, Alice Cooper.
❯ *Dir* Tim Burton, *Pro* Richard D Zanuck, Graham King, Johnny Depp and others, *Screenplay* Seth Grahame-Smith, from a story by him and John August based on the TV series created by Dan Curtis, *Ph* Bruno Delbonnel, *Pro Des* Rick Heinrichs, *Ed* Chris Lebenzon, *M* Danny Elfman, *Cos* Colleen Atwood.

Warner Bros. Pictures/an Infinitum Nihil/GK Films/ Zanuck Company production etc-Warner Bros.
113 mins. USA. 2012. Rel: 11 May 2012. Cert. 12A.

Dark Tide ★½

The sexy pairing of Halle Berry and Olivier Martinez as ex-lovers brought together for this shark adventure set in South Africa may sound good on paper, but the zero chemistry between them and the clunky dialogue make this a very dull affair. And then there is the arrival of the loathsome English businessman William Brady (an OTT Ralph Brown), who, hiring Berry's boat and her crew, demands to swim with the sharks. Well, not surprisingly, he gets what he deserves – but not soon enough. GS

❯ Halle Berry, Olivier Martinez, Ralph Brown, Mark Elderkin, Luke Tyler.
❯ *Dir* John Stockwell, *Pro* Matthew E Chausse and Jeanette Buerling, *Screenplay* Ronnie Christensen and Amy Sorlie, from a story by Sorlie, *Ph* Jean-François Hensgens, *Pro Des* Tom Hannam, *Ed* Ben Callahan and Andrew MacRitchie, *M* Mark Sayfritz, *Cos* Moira Anne Meyer.

Shadow play: Helena Bonham Carter (far left), Eva Green (third left), Chloë Grace Moretz (left of Depp), Johnny Depp (centre), Jackie Earle Haley, Jonny Lee Miller and Michelle Pfeiffer in Tim Burton's *Dark Shadows*.

Magnet Media Productions/Mirabelle Pictures/Film Afrika Worldwide/Lypsync Productions/Social Capital-Wrekin Hill Entertainment.
94 mins. USA/South Africa. 2012. Rel: 19 Oct 2012. Cert. 15.

The Darkest Hour 3D ★★

Chris Gorak's futuristic thriller looks spectacular in 3D but is let down by a one-dimensional script and inept dialogue. Five young people (four Americans) find themselves in the middle of a deserted Moscow after a devastating alien attack. The aliens are made of electromagnetic wave energy and only something electrical makes them visible. It is a creepy premise with some impressive set-pieces, but the unexplored characters and clumsy scenario fail to engage. GS

▶ Emile Hirsch, Olivia Thirlby, Max Minghella, Rachael Taylor.
▶ Dir Chris Gorak, Pro Timur Bekmambetov and Tom Jacobson, Screenplay Jon Spaihts, from a story by Spaihts, Leslie Bohem and MT Ahern, Ph Scott Kevan, Pro Des Valeri Viktorov, Ed Priscilla Nedd-Friendly and Fernando Villena, M Tyler Bates, Cos Varvara Avdyushko.

Regency Enterprises/Summit Entertainment/New Regency Pictures/Jacobson Company/Bazelevs-Twentieth Century Fox.
89 mins. USA/Russia. 2011. Rel: 13 Jan 2012. Cert. 12A.

Dead Europe ★★½

Athens, Paris and Budapest are the ports of call when a son raised in Australia takes his father's ashes back to Greece for dispersal. During the trip horrifying family secrets are revealed. However, on screen the narrative plays like a mystery tale, sidestepping into a ghost story featuring a family curse before it proves to be an allegory about inhumanity in Europe. It's ambitious but it never coheres satisfactorily, in contrast to that other look at the past haunting the present, 2010's Incendies. MS

▶ Ewen Leslie, Kodi Smit-McPhee, Marton Csokas, Jean-François Balmer, Françoise Lebrun.
▶ Dir Tony Krawitz, Pro Emile Sherman, Iain Canning and Liz Watts, Screenplay Louise Fox, from the novel by Christos Tsiolkas, Ph Germain McMicking, Pro Des Fiona Crombie, Ed Alexandre de Franceschi and Scott Gray, M Jed Kurzel, Cos Emily Seresin.

Screen Australia/a See-Saw Films production/Porchlight Films etc-Momentum Pictures.
84 mins. Australia/UK. 2012. Rel: 14 Dec 2012. Cert. 18.

The Descendants ★★★★

Alexander Payne's delayed follow-up to his 2004 hit Sideways is set in Hawaii. George Clooney plays a workaholic lawyer who, when a boating accident puts his wife into a coma, has to face up to two things: the need to look after his children and the fact that his neglect of his wife led her into an affair with a married man. Full marks to the casting director here, and also to the writers for a screenplay which successfully injects humour into the drama. The conclusion could be more succinct, but Clooney has rarely been better. MS

▶ George Clooney, Shailene Woodley, Beau Bridges, Robert Forster, Judy Greer, Matthew Lillard.
▶ Dir Alexander Payne, Pro Jim Burke, Payne and Jim

Family business: George Clooney with Shailene Woodley in Alexander Payne's Oscar-winning The Descendants.

Taylor, *Screenplay* Payne, Nat Faxon and Jim Rash, from the novel by Kaui Hart Hemmings, *Ph* Phedon Papamichael, *Pro Des* Jane Ann Stewart, *Ed* Kevin Tent, *Cos* Wendy Chuck.

Fox Searchlight Pictures/an Ad Hominem Enterprises production etc-20th Century Fox.
115 mins. USA/UK. 2011. Rel: 27 Jan 2012. Cert. 15.

The Decoy Bride ★★

In order to avoid the press, American film star Lara Tyler (Alice Eve) switches the location of her marriage to English author James Arber (David Tennant). But when notorious paparazzo Marco (Federico Castelluccio) tracks them to the remote Scottish island of Hegg, their only hope of escaping his lens is to use a decoy bride... This could have been a strong satire on the gutter press and human greed but it's let down by an underdeveloped and sluggish script. GS

❯ Kelly Macdonald, David Tennant, Alice Eve, James Fleet, Michael Urie, Dylan Moran, Sally Phillips, Hamish Clark, Federico Castellucio.
❯ *Dir* Sheree Folkson, *Pro* Douglas Rae, Robert Bernstein and Paul Ritchie, *Screenplay* Sally Phillips and Neil Jaworski, from a story by Phillips, *Ph* Nanu Segal, *Pro Des* Alison Dominitz, *Ed* Daniel Farrell, *M* Julian Nott, *Cos* Louise Allen.

Isle of Man Film/Cinema NX/Ecosse Films/Scottish Screen-Cinema NX.
89 mins. UK. 2011. Rel: 9 Mar 2012. Cert. 12A.

Delicacy ★★★★

Underrated by many, this is an excellent vehicle for Audrey Tautou which should certainly please her fans. She plays Nathalie who, grieving for a dead lover, encounters at work a Swede named Markus (François Damiens). That Markus, who is attracted to her, is far removed from the usual image of an engaging wooer is part of the humour and charm here (Damiens is excellent). This is an adroit example of popular cinema which shows Tautou to advantage. (Original title: *La Délicatesse*) MS

❯ Audrey Tautou, François Damiens, Bruno Todeschini, Pio Marmaï, Mélanie Bernier.
❯ *Dir* David and Stéphane Foenkinos, *Pro* Xavier Rigault and Marc-Antoine Robert, *Screenplay* David Foenkinos, from his novel *La Délicatesse*, *Ph* Rémy Chevrin, *Set Des* Maamar Ech-Cheikh, *Ed* Virginie Bruant, *Cos* Emmanuelle Youchnovski.

A 2.4.7. Films, StudioCanal, France 2 Cinéma co-production etc-StudioCanal Limited.
109 mins. France/Belgium. 2011. Rel: 13 Apr 2012. Cert. 12A.

Detachment ★★★½

Like his earlier *American History X* (1999), Tony Kaye's third feature is explosive and bitter – here his target is school life in America today with kids out of control and apathetic. Adrien Brody holds the centre as a teacher, but in characteristic Kaye style the film is sometimes hysterical. If it descends into melodrama it is at least his own kind of melodrama, and it never bores. MS

❯ Adrien Brody, Betty Kaye, Marcia Gay Harden, Lucy Liu, James Caan, Blythe Danner, Sami Gayle, Christina Hendricks, William Petersen, Tim Blake Nelson, Bryan Cranston.
❯ *Dir* and *Ph* Tony Kaye, *Pro* Austin Stark, Benji Kohn, Bingo Gubelmann and others, *Screenplay* Carl Lund, *Pro Des* Jade Healy, *Ed* Peter Goddard, *M* The Newton Brothers, *Cos* Wendy Schecter.

Tribeca Film/a Paper Street Films presentation/ Kingsgate Films etc-G2 Pictures.
98 mins. USA. 2011. Rel: 13 July 2012. Cert. 15.

Deviation ★

This is another dreadful film starring the ubiquitous Danny Dyer, who seems determined to ruin his once promising career. He plays Frank Norton, a psychotic murderer who, after he escapes from Broadmoor Hospital, takes as a hostage Amber (Anna Walton), a young nurse desperate to get back home to her daughter. However, he is forced into a nightmare drive across London... The script never rings true and the actors struggle to inhabit their characters. GS

❯ Danny Dyer, Anna Walton, James Doherty, Roy Smiles, David Fynn, Ben Wigzell.
❯ *Dir* and *Screenplay* JK Amalou, *Pro* Amalou and Lara Greenway, *Ph* Ollie Downey, *Pro Des* Chloe Brady, *Ed* St John O'Rorke, *M* Fryars, *Cos* Emma Harding.

Silver Leaf Pictures-Revolver Entertainment.
90 mins. UK. 2012. Rel: 24 Feb 2012. Cert. 15.

School matters: Lucy Liu and Blythe Danner in Tony Kaye's *Detachment*.

The Devil Inside ★★

Isabella (Fernanda Andrade) travels to Italy to see her mother Maria Rossi (Suzan Crowley), who has been locked away in the Centrino Hospital for the criminally insane for brutally killing three men during an exorcism 20 years earlier. There are a few shocking moments here, like a scene at a christening, but overall the faux-documentary style, which has been done to death in recent years, has lost all impact. GS

▶ Fernanda Andrade, Simon Quarterman, Evan Helmuth, Suzan Crowley, Lelia Goldoni.
▶ *Dir* William Brent Bell, *Pro* Matthew Peterman and Morris Paulson, *Screenplay* Bell and Peterman, *Ph* Gonzalo Arnat, *Pro Des* Tony DeMille, *Ed* Bell and Timothy Mirkovich, *M* Brent Detar and Ben Romans, *Cos* Terri Prescott.
Prototype-United Pictures International.
83 mins. USA. 2012. Rel: 16 Mar 2012. Cert. 15.

Diana Vreeland: The Eye Has to Travel ★★★★

You don't need to be interested in fashion to relish this documentary since Diana Vreeland (1903-89), a key figure at *Harper's Bazaar* and *Vogue*, was almost as idiosyncratic as Dame Edith Sitwell. This film (from a director married to her grandson) avoids hagiography to bring us a picture of a formidable, even frightening woman who was her own creation. Drawing on interviews she gave to George Plimpton, a truly fascinating portrait emerges of a woman who undoubtedly deserved to be considered an artist. MS

▶ With Diana Vreeland, Angelica Huston, Ali MacGraw, David Bailey, Joel Schumacher.
▶ *Dir* and *Pro* Lisa Immordino Vreeland with Bent-Jorgen Perlmutt and Frederic Tcheng, *Written by* Vreeland, Perlmutt and Tcheng, *Ph* Cristobal Zanartu, *Ed* Perlmutt and Tcheng, *M* Paul Cantelon.
A Gloss Studio presentation/a Mago Media production-StudioCanal Limited.
86 mins. USA. 2011. Rel: 21 Sep 2012. Cert. PG.

Diary of a Wimpy Kid: Dog Days ★★★½

Greg (Zachary Gordon) looks forward to the summer holidays but all his plans go wrong. His friendship with Rowley (Robert Capron) is on the verge of collapse, but his relationship with Rodrick (Devon Bostick), his brother and main tormentor, miraculously improves. The success of this family-friendly franchise lies in the spot-on casting. Gordon and Capron continue to share endearing screen chemistry while Steve Zahn and Rachael Harris add just the right eccentricity as Greg's likable parents. GS

Harpers bizarre: A scene from Lisa Immordino Vreeland and Bent-Jorgen Perlmutt's *Diana Vreeland: The Eye Has to Travel.*

> Zachary Gordon, Steve Zahn, Robert Capron, Rachael Harris, Devon Bostick.
> *Dir* David Bowers, *Pro* Nina Jacobson and Brad Simpson, *Screenplay* Maya Forbes and Wallace Wolodarsky, based on Jeff Kinney's books *The Last Straw* and *Dog Days*, *Ph* Anthony B Richmond, *Pro Des* Brent Thomas, *Ed* Troy Takaki, *M* Edward Shearmur, *Cos* Monique Prudhomme.

Twentieth Century Fox Film Corporation/Dune Entertainment/Fox 2000 Pictures/Color Force/TCF Vancouver Productions-20th Century Fox.
94 mins. USA/Canada. 2012. Rel: 3 Aug 2012. Cert. U.

The Dictator ★★★

Admiral General Hafez Aladeen lives in a spectacular palace, can bed all the women he wants and enjoys an autonomy greater than any leader on the planet. Yet all he really wants is somebody to cuddle every night… Since becoming a global brand, Sacha Baron Cohen has had to adjust his mode of offensiveness. So no longer are unsuspecting politicians, Kazakhstanis or Pamela Anderson the butt of his jokes, but the oil-rich, God-fearing tyrants of the Middle East. There are a few laughs – and a larger number of groans – but maybe this time the satirist has tackled too many themes for this to reach the cult status of a *Borat*. JC-W

> Sacha Baron Cohen, Anna Faris, Ben Kingsley,

Camel tow: Sacha Baron Cohen takes on New York in Larry Charles' smutty, disturbing and occasionally very funny *The Dictator*.

Jason Mantzoukas, Chris Elliott, Fred Armisen, JB Smoove, Megan Fox, John C Reilly, Garry Shandling, Edward Norton.
> *Dir* Larry Charles, *Pro* Sacha Baron Cohen, Alec Berg, Jeff Schaffer, David Mandel, Anthony Hines and Scott Rudin, *Screenplay* Cohen, *Ph* Lawrence Sher, *Pro Des* Victor Kempster, *Ed* Greg Hayden and Eric Kissack, *M* Erran Baron Cohen, *Cos* Jeffrey Kurland.

Four by Two Films-Paramount.
83 mins. USA. 2012. Rel: 16 May 2012. Cert. 15.

The Dinosaur Project ★★½

This shaky-cam 'found footage' outing owes a lot to *Jurassic Park III*, *Cloverfield* and TV's *Walking with Dinosaurs*. Explorer Richard Dillane leads an expedition to the Congo jungle (filmed in South Africa) to find a water creature and has to deal with his geeky stowaway son (Matt Kane), a helicopter crash and a colony of dinosaurs. The movie is worthwhile, just, for the fantastic CGI dinos but the rough acting and clichéd story let it down. Not bad, but lacks bite. DW

> Richard Dillane, Natasha Loring, Matt Kane, Peter Brooke, Abena Ayevor.
> *Dir* Sid Bennett, *Pro* Nick Hill, *Screenplay* Bennett and Jay Basu, from a story by Bennett and Tom Pridham, *Ph* Pridham, *Pro Des* Franz Lewis, *Ed* Ben Lester, *M* Richard Blair-Oliphant, *Cos* Joanne Walter.

Moonlighting Films-StudioCanal.
83 mins. UK. 2012. Rel: 10 Aug 2012. Cert. 12A.

Dinotasia ★½

This odd project about the Cretaceous Age is treading on David Attenborough's territory but without his sophistication and skill. It is a mixture of animated action, creature modelling, drawings and location photography. Even the distinctive narration of Werner Herzog can't rescue this dull film. Only a segment in which a mother pterodactyl pushes her youngsters out of the nest in order to fend for themselves is vaguely interesting. GS

❧ With Werner Herzog (narrator).
❧ *Dir* and *Written by* David Krentz and Erik Nelson, *Pro* Nelson, *Ph* Christopher Popp, *M* Mark Leggett.
Picturehouse Entertainment-Picturehouse Entertainment.
83 mins. USA. 2012. Rel: 4 May 2012. Cert. PG.

The Divide ★★

Eight strangers seek refuge in the basement of their apartment building after a nuclear attack on New York. They soon realise that there is no escape from this living hell and only the fittest may be able to survive. The opening is similar to *The Darkest Hour* but this is a much nastier affair. It is atmospherically shot but the problem is that the characters are loathsome from the word go and there is no room for development before the action falls into the *Lord of the Flies* category. GS

❧ Lauren German, Michael Biehn, Milo Ventimiglia, Michael Eklund, Rosanna Arquette, Courtney B Vance, Iván González, Ashton Holmes.
❧ *Dir* Xavier Gens, *Pro* Ross M Dinerstein, Juliette Hagopian, Daryn Welch Nathaniel Rollo, *Screenplay* Karl Mueller and Eron Sheean, *Ph* Lauren Barès, *Pro Des* Tony Noble, *Ed* Carlo Rizzi, *M* Jean-Pierre Taieb, *Cos* Mary Hyde-Kerr.
Instinctive Film/Preferred Content/Ink Connection etc-Momentum Pictures.
122 mins. Germany/Canada/USA. 2011.
Rel: 20 Apr 2012. Cert. 18.

Dr Seuss's The Lorax ★★½

The 1970s book by Dr Seuss had an ecological point about preservation over consumption in its tale of the Onceler, an outcast hermit who lives alone because he let everything organic be destroyed. Thus everything in Thneedville, including all the trees, flowers and grass, is fake. There is no good air except that which is sold in bottles. Young Ted (voiced by Zac Efron) decides to go out of town in search of a real tree to impress his girlfriend Audrey (Taylor Swift). First he has to find the Lorax (Danny DeVito), a friendly, furry creature who hugs trees and

Future fear: Karl Urban metes out his justice in Pete Travis' lean and graphic *Dredd*.

tries to preserve them. The animation is OK but the general feeling is one of tiredness, and it's unlikely to appeal to children. MHD

❧ With the voices of Danny DeVito, Ed Helms, Rob Riggle, Zac Efron, Taylor Swift, Betty White, Jenny Slate.
❧ *Dir* Chris Renaud and Kyle Balda, *Pro* Janet Healey and Chris Meledandri, *Screenplay* Ken Dorio and Cinco Paul, from the book by Dr Seuss, *Pro Des* Yarrow Cheney, *Ed* Claire Dodgson, Steven Liu and Ken Schretzmann, *M* John Powell.
Universal Pictures/Illumination Entertainment-Universal Pictures.
86 mins. USA. 2012. Rel: 27 July 2012. Cert. U.

Dredd ★★★

The last time Judge Dredd passed judgment on the cinema screen, it was Sylvester Stallone in the black and red helmet. But just as Arnie's camp antics in *Total Recall* were given a sober re-think in the recent remake, so this re-boot trims all the comic-book fat from Sly's 1995 turn. While dystopian futures are becoming a tad omnipresent, this one is given some vertiginous aerial perspectives (in 3D), along with some astonishingly graphic slo-mo, close-up, multi-dimensional slaughter. There's not a lot of humanity, and Karl Urban (Dredd) and Olivia Thirlby don't attempt much acting, but it's a visually gripping ride. JC-W

❧ Karl Urban, Olivia Thirlby, Lena Headey, Wood Harris, Domhnall Gleeson.
❧ *Dir* Pete Travis, *Pro* Alex Garland, Andrew Macdonald and Allon Reich, *Screenplay* Garland, *Ph* Anthony Dod Mantle, *Pro Des* Mark Digby, *Ed* Mark Eckersley, *M* Paul Leonard-Morgan, *Cos* Diana Cilliers and Michael O'Connor.
DNA Films/IM Global/Peach Trees/Reliance Big Entertainment/Reliance Big Pictures/Rena Film-Entertainment Film Distributors.
95 mins. UK/USA/India/South Africa. 2012.
Rel: 7 Sep 2012. Cert. 18.

Eames: The Architect and the Painter ★★★★

This is a thoroughly able look back at the careers of husband and wife team Charles and Ray Eames who were key figures in design after the Second World War as well as being filmmakers. Charles overshadowed his wife, but that is partly a reflection of the times they lived in and to its credit this sympathetic, fair-minded film avoids hagiography. Ultimately one comes to see it as a successful portrait of two very striking individuals. MS

▶ With Jeannine Oppewall, Gordon Ashby, Paul Schrader, James Franco (narrator).
▶ *Dir* and *Pro* Jason Cohn and Bill Jersey, *Narration written by* Cohn, *Ph* Various, *Ed* Don Bernier, *M* Michael Bacon.

Quest Productions/Bread and Butter Films etc-Soda Pictures.
85 mins. USA. 2011. Rel: 3 Aug 2012. Cert. 12A.

East End Babylon ★★

This over-long documentary explores the birth and brief success of the 1970s punk rock group Cockney Rejects, which was the first band to combine rock 'n' roll with football; they are vociferous West Ham United supporters. Three members of the group are interviewed at length, especially Jeff 'Stinky' Turner, who certainly has the gift of the gab but is rather too pleased with himself and never shuts up. Even his mother appears, though she does add another dimension to the film, touching on life in the East End after the war. It's interesting but repetitive and over-explanatory. GS

▶ With Cockney Rejects, Jeff Turner, Mick Geggus, Vince Riordan, Jeff Geggus, Gary Bushell, Stephen H Harmer.
▶ *Dir* Richard England, *Associate Pro* George

Grand designs: Jason Cohn and Bill Jersey examine the architecture and chairs of Charles and Ray Eames in their Peabody-winning Eames: The Architect and the Painter.

Hencken, Stephen Malit and Karen Janody, *Screenplay* England and Mick Geggus, *Ph* Steve Organ, *Art Dir* Tadeus Blower, *Ed* Henry Stein, *M* Dave Edwards, Mick Geggus and Phil Zackarias.

Cadiz Music Ltd-Universal Music.
101 mins. UK. 2012. Rel: 8 Nov 2012. Cert. 18.

Edge ★★½

Made before *Dreams of a Life* (2011), which aroused interest in the work of Carol Morley, *Edge* shows her weaknesses as a writer. Here she tries to create a drama that features a group of unhappy people staying in a hotel on the Sussex coast. Morley is good at conveying mood, but the various plot lines, which at times become interlinked, are so unpersuasive that the cast are at a serious disadvantage. This is a particular shame since that undervalued actress Marjorie Yates gives a valiant performance. MS

▶ Maxine Peake, Paul Hilton, Joe Dempsie, Nichola Burley, Julie T Wallace, Ania Wendzikowska, Marjorie Yates.
▶ *Dir* and *Screenplay* Carol Morley, *Pro* Cairo Cannon, *Ph* Mary Farbrother, *Pro Des* Chris Richmond, *Ed* Fiona DeSouza, *M* Ivor Talbot.

Cannon and Morley Productions/Genesis Entertainment-Dogwoof.
93 mins. UK. 2010. Rel: 13 Apr 2012. Cert. 15.

El Bulli: Cooking in Progress ★★★½

This is a curious but absorbing documentary about, arguably, one of the best and most exclusive restaurants in the world, Ferran Adrià's El Bulli in Catalonia, Spain. Every year the restaurant closes for six months while the Chef-Patron and his staff repair to their Barcelona HQ, experimenting with food and inventing new dishes for the next season. It's all very scientific and more like a laboratory than a kitchen. There's a definite coldness about the ingenuity of these technicians searching for something new just for the sake of it, rather than coming up with a tasty, nourishing and lip-smackingly enjoyable bill of fare. MHD

▶ With Ferran Adrià, Oriol Castro, Eduard Zatruch, Eugeni De Diego, Aitor Loza
▶ *Dir* Gereon Wetzel, *Pro* Ingo Fliess, Petra Felber and Jutta Krug, from a concept by Wetzel and Anna Gnesti Rosell, *Ph* Josef Mayerhofer, *Ed* Anja Pohl, *M* Stephan Dietheim.

If... Productions/Bayerischer Rundfunk/Westdeutscher Rundfunk-Artificial Eye.
108 mins. Germany. 2011. Rel: 27 July 2012. Cert. 12A.

Electric Man ★★★½

Good-natured and chucklesome little Scottish low-budget caper about nerdy comic bookshop owners

Jazz and Wolf (Toby Manley, Mark McKirdy), who think a rare comic is the answer to their cash problems. But there are other folk who want to get hold of the incredibly rare first edition of *Electric Man*... Wittily written, smartly handled and funny, with engaging performances all round, it's a success. Edinburgh is nicely used as a background. DW

▶ Toby Manley, Mark McKirdy, Derek Dick (Fish), Jennifer Ewing, Mark McDonnell, Emily Lockwood and Andre Vincent.
▶ *Dir* David Barras, *Pro* Ellen-Raisa Jackson, *Screenplay* Barras and Scott MacKay, *Ph* Rich Steel, *Pro Des* Marianne Gallagher, *Visual Effects* Charlotte Rodenstedt, *Animation* Andrew Murchie, Susanna Murphy, *M* Blair Mowat.
Dugbus Ltd.
100 mins. UK. 2012. Rel: 29 Nov 2012. Cert. 12A.

Electrick Children ★★★½

Julia Garner shines as Rachel, a 15-year-old girl from a Mormon community who becomes pregnant. She believes it's an immaculate conception via a singer on a music cassette, but her parents think it's an appalling sin and quickly arrange a marriage for her. However, she steals her family's truck and drives to Las Vegas to find the singer. This quirky, touching, expertly handled story has charismatic acting from Billy Zane and Cynthia Watros as Rachel's parents, Rory Culkin as the goofy band member who helps her, and Liam Aiken as her older brother who tags along to prove he wasn't her lover. DW

▶ Julia Garner, Rory Culkin, Liam Aiken, Bill Sage, Cynthia Watros, Billy Zane.
▶ *Dir* and *Screenplay* Rebecca Thomas, *Pro* Richard Neustadter and Jessica Caldwell, *Ph* Mattias Troelstrup, *Pro Des* Elizabeth Van Dam, *Ed* Jennifer Lilly, *M* Eric Colvin, *Cos* Stacey Berman.
Live Wire Films-Revolver Entertainment.
96 mins. USA. 2012. Rel: 13 July 2012. Cert. 15.

Elena ★★★★★

Elena and Vladimir, an ageing wedded couple, are both on their second marriages with their own families. Elena has a poor, worthless, sponging son with wife and children, whereas the well-off Vladimir has a single, estranged daughter. Elena wants Vladimir to support her grandson through university but he says he married *her*, not her children. When Vladimir has a heart attack, he makes a decision about his will, but life and death are not as simple as that... Andrey Zvyagintsev's cool, measured film is a brilliant study of family relationships with a superb central performance by Nadezhda Markina in an altogether unbeatably fine cast. MHD

▶ Nadezhda Markina, Andrey Smirnov, Elena Lyadova, Aleksey Rozin, Evgeniya Knushkina.
▶ *Dir* Andrey Zvyagintsev, *Pro* Aleksandr Rodnianskiy, *Screenplay* Zvyagintsev and Oleg Negin, *Ph* Mikhail Krichman, *Art Dir* Andrey Ponkratov, *Ed* Anna Mass, *M* Philip Glass.
Non-Stop Productions-New Wave Films.
109 mins. Russia. 2011. Rel: 26 Oct 2012. Cert. 12.

Elfie Hopkins ★½

Ryan Andrews' disappointing debut follows the story of Elfie (Jaime Winstone), a stubborn young

Class act: Nadezhda Markina (right, with baby) in Andrey Zvyagintsev's *Elena.*

Discreet charm: Malgoska Szumowska (left) directs Juliette Binoche in her personal and haunting *Elles*.

woman determined to solve the mystery behind the disappearance of some fellow villagers. She suspects her new neighbours but no one believes her apart from her best friend Dylan (Aneurin Barnard). Winstone is usually a good character actress but in this misjudged thriller she is unable to make an impact. Barnard – so good in *Hunky Dory* – is wasted. GS

▶ Ray Winstone, Jaime Winstone, Rupert Evans, Kimberley Nixon, Steven Mackintosh, Aneurin Barnard, Will Payne.
▶ *Dir* Ryan Andrews, *Pro* Andrews, Riyad Barmania, Jonathan Sothcott, Michael Wiggs, Billy Murray and Steve Matthews, *Screenplay* Andrews and Barmania, *Ph* Tobia Sempi, *Pro Des* Tim Dickel, *Ed* Peter Hollywood, *M* Jordan Andrews, *Cos* Sian Jenkins.

Black and Blue Films/Size 9 Productions/Tweed Films-Kaleidoscope.
89 mins. UK. 2012. Rel: 20 Apr 2012. Cert. 15.

Elles ★★★

Made in Paris by a Polish director, Malgoska Szumowska, this tells of a journalist (Juliette Binoche) who, when investigating students who readily support themselves through prostitution, comes to question attitudes in her own family where outwardly bourgeois conformity hides sexual deceits. Binoche is excellent, but the film plays up sex scenes even as it criticises pornography. Indeed its tone is such that even listening to Beethoven's Seventh Symphony asks to be taken as a sign of hypocritical bourgeois behaviour! MS

▶ Juliette Binoche, Anaïs Demoustier, Joanna Kulig, Krystyna Janda, Louis-Do de Lencquesaing.
▶ *Dir* Malgoska Szumowska, *Pro* Marianne Slot, *Screenplay* Tine Byrckel and Szumowska, *Ph* Michal Englart, *Art Dir* Pauline Bourdon, *Ed* Françoise Tourmen and Jacek Drosio, *M* Pawel Mykietyn, *Cos* Katarzyna Lewinska.

Slot Machine/Zentropa International Poland/Zentropa International Köln etc-Artificial Eye
99 mins. France/Poland/Germany. 2011. Rel: 20 Apr 2012. Cert. 18.

The Emperor and the White Snake ★★★

A thousand-year-old white snake demon assumes female human form to make a herbalist fall in love with and marry her. But Jet Li's demon-hunting monk wants to send her back to the demon realm. The plot also includes talking mice! Ching Siu-Tung's film sources Chinese mythology, relies too much on computer effects work and weepy romantic drama trappings, yet nevertheless manages some impressive intermittent action. Also known, more appropriately, as *The Sorcerer and the White Snake*. (Original title: *Bai she chuan shuo*) JC

▶ Jet Li, Shengyi Huang, Raymond Lam, Charlene Choi, Zhang Wen, Vivian Hsu.
▶ *Dir* Ching Siu-Tung, *Pro* Po Chu Chui, *Screenplay* Charcoal Tan, Tsang Kan Cheung and Szeto Cheuk Hon, *Ph* Kwok-Man Keung, *Ed* Angie Lam, *M* Mark Lui, *Cos* William Chang.

Juli Entertainment Media-Metrodome Distribution.
100 mins. China. 2011. Rel: 30 Mar 2012. Cert. 12.

End of Watch ★★★★

Cop movies, especially actioners set within the province of the LAPD, are hardly original Hollywood fodder. What separates *End of Watch* from more recent outings is that the principal grunts, Brian Taylor (Jake Gyllenhaal) and Mike Zavala (Michael Peña), are actually decent guys. Played out as a diary of their lives (there are cameras everywhere), the film succeeds in building a convincing chemistry between the two officers. Furthermore, the edgy camerawork adds considerable suspense to the action sequences, many of which are acutely thrilling stuff. But it's the edgy, profanity-streaked performances that ultimately distinguish this policier. JC-W

▶ Jake Gyllenhaal, Michael Peña, Anna Kendrick, America Ferrera, Cody Horn, Natalie Martinez, Frank Grillo.
▶ *Dir* and *Screenplay* David Ayer, *Pro* Ayer, Matt Jackson, John Lesher, Jillian Longnecker, Alex Ott and Ian Watermeier, *Ph* Roman Vasyanov, *Pro Des* Devorah Herbert, *Ed* Dody Dorn, *M* David Sardy, *Cos* Mary Claire Hannan.
Exclusive Media Group/Emmett/Furla Films/Hedge Fund Film Partners/Crave Films-StudioCanal.
108 mins. USA. 2012. Rel: 23 Nov 2012. Cert. 15.

English Vinglish ★★★½

Hard-working Indian housewife Shashi (Bollywood star Sridevi) is made to feel insecure by her family because of her lack of English. But when she travels to New York for a wedding she secretly enrols on a crash course. All the stereotypes are in her class, from the gay teacher to the French chef. The situation is not dissimilar to the British TV sitcom *Mind Your Language* but done in an endearing and unashamedly sentimental way. A real crowd-pleaser, despite the silly title. GS

▶ Sridevi, Adil Hussain, Mehdi Nebbou, Priya Anand, Sujatha Kumar.
▶ *Dir* and *Screenplay* Gauri Shinde, *Pro* Sunil Lulla, Rakesh Jhunjhunwala, R. Balki and R Jamani, *Ph* Laxman Utekar, *Pro Des* Mustafa Stationwala, *Ed* Hemanti Sarkar, *M* Amit Tivedi, *Cos* Vera Chow.
Curbside Films/Eros International/Hope Productions-Eros International.
134 mins. India. 2012. Rel: 5 Oct 2012. Cert. PG.

Even the Rain ★★★½

Just what Icíar Bollaín can achieve as a filmmaker was shown in her 2003 masterpiece *Take My Eyes*. Here, however, very promising material ultimately leads in Paul Laverty's screenplay to an unconvincing climax. Until then the film draws a fascinating parallel between contemporary filmmakers in Bolivia behaving unscrupulously and the events depicted in their movie, which concerns the treatment of the native peoples after Columbus landed. Even if there are decided weaknesses here, *Even the Rain* is never less than an interesting film. (Original title: *También la lluvia*) MS

▶ Luis Tosar, Gael García Bernal, Juan Carlos Aduviri, Karra Elejalde, Raúl Arévalo.
▶ *Dir* Icíar Bollaín, *Pro* Juan Gordon, *Screenplay* Paul Laverty, *Ph* Alex Catalán, *Art Dir* Juan Pedro de Gaspar, *Ed* Angel Hernández Zoido, *M* Alberto Iglesias, *Cos* Sonia Grande.
A Morena Films production/Mandarin Cinema/Vaca Films etc-Dogwoof.

Juan Carlos Aduviri in Icíar Bollaín's ingenious, incendiary and beautiful *Even the Rain.*

103 mins. Spain/Mexico/France. 2010. Rel: 18 May 2012. Cert. 15.

Everything or Nothing: The Untold Story of 007 ★★★

Detailing the tempestuous times of the Bond franchise rather than focusing on the films themselves, this revealing documentary sheds light on the lives of the men who devoted their lives to 007: melancholic author Ian Fleming and force-of-nature producers Albert R Broccoli and Harry Saltzman. A story of stormy relationships with candid contributions from family, friends, stars and behind-the-scenes legends, it's a tale of the toll a franchise can take on a person, with thrilling, untamed asides from the scene-stealing George Lazenby. MJ

❧ With Barbara Broccoli, Daniel Craig, Pierce Brosnan, Timothy Dalton, Judi Dench, Lewis Gilbert, George Lazenby, Christopher Lee, Sam Mendes, Roger Moore, Michael G Wilson, Ken Adam, Maud Adams etc.
❧ *Dir* Stevan Riley, *Pro* Simon Chinn and John Battsek, *Screenplay* Riley and Peter Etedgui, *Ph* Richard Numeroff, *Pro Des* Erik Rehl, *Ed* Claire Ferguson.

Paradise Pictures/Red Box Films-Sony Pictures Releasing. 98 mins. UK. 2012. Rel: 5 Oct 2012. Cert. 12A.

Excision ★★½

Rampant teenage hormones collide with bloody body horror in this macabre, cultish effort from feature first-timer Richard Bates Jr. A creepy, kooky, spotty, dotty student (AnnaLynne McCord) dreams of sex, death and surgery. Eager to earn the approval of the cruel, cold control freak she calls mom (Traci Lords), a mad plan is hatched and mentalism ensues. For the most part calmly peculiar with disquieting gory stylings and batty erotic dream sequences, this is a strange, minor movie with a pair of intense central performances and pleasing cameos from the likes of John Waters and Malcolm McDowell. MJ

❧ AnnaLynne McCord, Traci Lords, Ariel Winter, Roger Bart, Malcolm McDowell, Marlee Matlin, Ray Wise, John Waters, Matthew Gray Gubler, Jeremy Sumpter.
❧ *Dir* and *Screenplay* Richard Bates Jr, *Pro* Dylan Hale Lewis, *Ph* Itay Gross, *Pro Des* Armen Ra, *Ed* Steve Ansell and Yvonne Valdez, *M* Steve Damstra II and Mads Heldtberg, *Cos* Anthony Tran.

BXR Productions-Monster Pictures. 81 mins. USA. 2012. Rel: 2 Nov 2012. Cert. 18.

Exit Humanity ★★★

We're in the aftermath of the American Civil War and in undead territory for this unusual, serious-minded Canadian-made horror. Mark Gibson stars as hero Edward Young, a Confederate veteran who finds a plague of zombies has broken out and has to put both his wife and

Dream life: AnnaLynne McCord in Richard Bates Jr's gruesome (and unusual) *Excision*.

When you need an orthodontist... Mark Gibson (right) gets professional in John Geddes' *Exit Humanity*.

son out of their misery. He falls in with new companions, who are soon under threat. Brian Cox narrates in chapters from the hero's journal and Dee Wallace (Healer), Bill Moseley (General) and Stephen McHattie (Doctor) provide strong cameos. The film's a tad slow and long, but makes up for it by being well crafted, intelligent and atmospheric. DW

▶ Brian Cox, Mark Gibson, Dee Wallace, Bill Moseley, Stephen McHattie.
▶ *Dir, Screenplay* and *Ed* John Geddes, *Pro* Geddes, Jessie T Cook, Matt Wiele and Cody Calahan, *Ph* Brendan Uegama, *Pro Des* Jason David Brown, *M* Jeff Graville, Nate Kreiswirth and Ben Nudds, *Cos* Alex Brown.

Foresight Features-Metrodome Distribution.
114 mins. Canada. 2011. Rel: 29 June 2012. Cert. 15.

The Expendables 2 ★½

The first *Expendables* was a cringe-worthy display of ego over artistry. It was also mindless, witless and offensive. The follow-up, which mixes and matches new and old blood, is little better, being a formulaic, illogical, predictable and messy affair. All noise and no bang. Watching it is like unwrapping a faded piece of memorabilia and discovering that the lines you once cherished weren't actually that funny in the first place. And for every embarrassing cameo, there is an uneven bit of cinematography and an excruciating piece of dialogue; eg, Statham: "I now pronounce you man and knife." JC-W

▶ Sylvester Stallone, Jason Statham, Jet Li, Dolph Lundgren, Chuck Norris, Terry Crews, Randy Couture, Liam Hemsworth, Jean-Claude Van Damme, Bruce Willis, Arnold Schwarzenegger, Yu Nan, Scott Adkins, Amanda Ooms.
▶ *Dir* Simon West, *Pro* Avi Lerner, Danny Lerner, Kevin King Templeton and Les Weldon, *Screenplay* Richard Wenk and Sylvester Stallone, *Ph* Shelly Johnson, *Pro Des* Paul Cross, *Ed* Todd E Miller, *M* Brian Tyler, *Cos* Lizz Wolf.

Millennium Films/Nu Image-Lionsgate.
102 mins. USA. 2012. Rel: 16 Aug 2012. Cert. 15.

Extremely Loud & Incredibly Close ★★½

An earlier adaptation from Jonathan Safran Foer (2005's *Everything is Illuminated*) was sadly underrated, but here the general dismissal of Stephen Daldry's film was all too apt. Over-literary dialogue and mawkish sentimentality mark this portrayal of events consequent on the tragedy of 9/11, which in any case leads to a plot twist of startling absurdity. Only Max von Sydow emerges with dignity, although as ever the colour photography by Chris Menges is impeccable. MS

▶ Sandra Bullock, Thomas Horn, Tom Hanks, Max von Sydow, Viola Davis, John Goodman, Jeffrey Wright, Zoe Caldwell.
▶ *Dir* Stephen Daldry, *Pro* Scott Rudin, *Screenplay* Eric Roth, from the novel by Jonathan Safran Foer, *Ph* Chris Menges, *Pro Des* KK Barrett, *Ed* Claire Simpson, *M* Alexandre Desplat, *Cos* Ann Roth.

Warner Bros. Pictures-Warner Bros.
129 mins. USA. 2011. Rel: 17 Feb 2012. Cert. 12A.

F Type ★★★

The 'type' in question is the form of solitary confinement introduced in Turkish prisons in 2000. It did not go down well. Inmates across the country banded together for a fast 'to the death' and in the ensuing backlash 32 died and hundreds were injured. Such was the social impact that *F Type* is one of three films on the subject. Weaving together nine different stories from some of Turkey's most celebrated filmmakers, the style is a bit didactic but not without a good deal of power, compassion and even some dark humour. (Original title: *F tipi film*) CB

▶ Ezel Akay, Erkan Can, Derya Durmaz, Firat Taniş, Tansu Biçer, Gizem Soysaldi, Civan Canova.
▶ *Dir* and *Written by* Ezel Akay, Mehmet Ilker Altinay,

Magical mystery: Dominique Abel, Bruno Romy and Fiona Gordon in their self-written and -directed *The Fairy*.

Aydin Bulut, Hüseyin Karabey, Sirri Sürreya Önder, Bariş Pirhasan, Reis Çelik and Vedat Özdemir and the Grup Yorum Collective, *Pro* and *M* Grup Yorum, *Ed* Ismail 'Niko' Canlisoy and Gürcan Cansever.

Idil Kultur Merkezi Company-Grup Yorum Collective. 118 mins. Turkey. 2012. Rel: 28 Dec 2012. No Cert.

The Fairy ★★★½

Dominique Abel and Fiona Gordon, who star in their own films, are an acquired taste. This follow-up to *Rumba* (2008) confirms it. Although their work contains echoes of Tati and Keaton, some find their comedies irritatingly silly. Those who do won't be won over by this tale of a fairy (Gordon) who disrupts the life of a night porter in Le Havre (Abel). Personally I'm not completely sold, but I do warm to their idiosyncratic humour of which this is a characteristic example. (Original title: *La Fée*) MS

▶ Dominique Abel, Fiona Gordon, Philippe Martz, Bruno Romy.
▶ *Dir* and *Screenplay* Dominique Abel, Fiona Gordon and Bruno Romy, *Pro* Nathanaël Karmitz, Charles Gillibert and Abel & Gordon, *Ph* Claire Childéric, *Art Dir* Nicolas Girault, *Ed* Sandrine Deegen, *Cos* Claire Dubien.

MK2/Courage mon amour/France 3 Cinéma etc-Verve Pictures Ltd. 94 mins. France/Belgium. 2011. Rel: 29 June 2012. Cert. PG.

False Trail ★★★½

Dysfunctional families prove to be at the heart of this piece although it starts out as a conventional police procedural. The setting is northern Sweden, where a CID man from Stockholm with local connections arrives to investigate the disappearance of a young woman thought to be a murder victim. The screenplay lacks the depth to make the family tragedy telling, but as a crime story it's competently done even if it seems unnecessarily long. (Original title: *Jägarna 2*) MS

▶ Rolf Lassgård, Peter Stormare, Annika Nordin, Kim Tjernström, Eero Milonoff.
▶ *Dir* Kjell Sundvall, *Pro* Peter Possne, Bjorn Carlström and Per Janérus, *Screenplay* Carlström and Stefan Thunberg, *Ph* Jallo Faber, *Pro Des* Bengt Fröderberg, *Ed* Mattias Morheden, *M* Johan Söderqvist, *Cos* Karin Sundvall.

Sonet Film/Harmonica Films/The Chimney Pot/Comax film etc.-Arrow Films. 127 mins. Sweden/Norway. 2011. Rel: 14 Dec 2012. Cert. 15.

A Fantastic Fear of Everything ★

Jack (Simon Pegg) is a crime novelist with a paranoid fear of being murdered, but when he bravely fights his demons and leaves his home for the laundrette he finds himself in the middle of another fearful environment... Crispian Mills and Chris Hopewell's irritatingly repetitive film begins as a claustrophobic tale about one man's fragile mind before sinking into a mishmash of ideas. A cringe-worthy experience and one of the worst films of the year. GS

▶ Simon Pegg, Clare Higgins, Amara Karan, Paul Freeman, Kerry Shale, Sheridan Smith, Alan Drake.

▶ *Dir* Crispian Mills and Chris Hopewell, *Pro* Geraldine Patten, *Screenplay* Mills, *Ph* Simon Chaudoir, *Pro Des* Hopewell, *Ed* Dan Roberts, *M* Michael Price, *Cos* Lou Foley.

Indomina Productions/Pinewood Studios/Keel Films-Universal Pictures International.
100 mins. UK. 2012. Rel: 8 June 2012. Cert. 15.

Fast Girls ★★★½

Fast Girls is the story of two rival sprinters in the 200-metre relay for the 2011 World Athletic Championships in London. Shania Andrews (Lenora Crichlow) is mixed race, gorgeous and naturally fast. Lisa Temple (Lily James) is blonde, gorgeous and ferociously dedicated. The script is pretty mechanical, but the performances are so winning, the emotional buttons so adroitly tweaked and the soundtrack so rousing that it's all rather hard to resist. It raises the term 'feel good' to a whole new level. JC-W

▶ Lenora Crichlow, Lily James, Bradley James, Noel Clarke, Lorraine Burroughs, Phil Davis, Rupert Graves, Emma Fielding.
▶ *Dir* Regan Hall, *Pro* Damian Jones, *Screenplay* Jay Basu, Roy Williams and Noel Clarke, *Ph* John Lynch, *Pro Des* David Bryan, *Ed* Lewis Albrow, *M* Richard Canavan, *Cos* Andy Blake and Miss Molly.

Aegis Film Fund/DJ Films/StudioCanal-StudioCanal.
90 mins. UK. 2012. Rel: 15 June 2012. Cert. 12A.

Faust ★★★½

Whether you regard this as a treatment of Goethe's *Faust* or as a response to it, Alexander Sokurov's film is for better or worse a daunting piece. His approach has the quality of being vigorous and intellectual, but what is intended by some of the variations on the original is at times unclear. This Faust seems less concerned with regaining youthful sexual ardour than with the question of whether or not the existence of evil is also evidence for the existence of God: if there is a soul where is it located? In a good cast Isolda Dychauk's Magarete is very sympathetic, and at least one scene between her and Faust is nothing less than great. MS

▶ Johannes Zeiler, Anton Adasinskiy, Isolda Dychauk, Georg Friedrich, Hanna Schygulla.
▶ *Dir* Alexander Sokurov, *Pro* and *M* Andrey Sigle, *Screenplay* Sokurov and Marina Koreneva, freely adapted from Goethe, *Ph* Bruno Delbonnel, *Art Dir* Elena Zhukova, *Ed* Jörg Hauschild, *Cos* Lidia Krukova.

Proline-Film, St. Petersburg etc-Artificial Eye.
139 mins. Russia. 2011. Rel: 11 May 2012. Cert. 15.

A Few Best Men ★★

Brit groom Xavier Samuel travels to Australia with his three best men, Kris Marshall, Kevin Bishop and Tim Draxl. They cause a lot of problems before he gets hitched to Oz gal Laura Brent. There are a few good laughs along the way, but this comedy from the director of *Priscilla* could have been a whole lot funnier. The likable actors are game for a laugh and just fine when Dean Craig's script supports them, but they're struggling in some desperately unfunny sequences and with too many duff lines. Olivia Newton-John scores a hit as the bride's raunchy mother. DW

▶ Laura Brent, Xavier Samuel, Kris Marshall, Olivia Newton-John, Kevin Bishop, Tim Draxl, Rebel Wilson, Steve Le Marquand, Elizabeth Debicki, Solveig Walking.
▶ *Dir* Stephan Elliott, *Pro* Share Stallings, Laurence Malkin, Antonia Barnard and Gary Hamilton, *Screenplay* Dean Craig, *Ph* Stephen F Windon, *Pro Des* George Liddle, *Ed* Sue Blainey, *M* Guy Gross, *Cos* Lizzy Gardiner.

Screen Australia/Quickfire Films/Screen NSW/Parabolic Pictures/Stableway
Entertainment etc-Walt Disney Studios Motion Pictures.
97 mins. Australia/UK. 2011. Rel: 31 Aug 2012. Cert. 15.

First ★★½

The official documentary film of the 2012 London Olympics takes the safe but slightly dull route of following the mixed-fortune 'journeys' of 12 first-time Olympians from around the world. With the impossible task of compressing two weeks into 108 minutes, it all goes exactly as you would expect, with triumph competing against heartbreak in montage and slo-mo, against a pop soundtrack. The best moments belong to British cyclist Laura Trott, South African swimmer Chad Le Closs and Kenyan athlete David Rudisha. A lovingly made record. DW

▶ With Usain Bolt, Tom Daley, Michael Phelps, Oscar Pistorius, John Orozco, Heena Sidhu, David Rudisha, Chad Le Closs, Laura Trott etc.
▶ *Dir*, *Pro* and *Written by* Caroline Rowland, *Ed* Sim

Soul story: Johannes Zeiler as *Faust* and Isolda Dychauk as Margarete in Alexander Sokurov's adaptation.

Evan-Jones, Chris Petcher and Alan Levy, *M* Sacha Puttnam.

Mango Films/Southern Cross Cameras/Zen HQ Films-Revolver Distribution.
108 mins. UK. 2012. Rel: 23 Nov 2012. Cert 12A.

The Five-Year Engagement ★★★

Tom Solomon (Jason Segel) proposes to Violet Barnes (Emily Blunt) on New Year's Eve – exactly a year after they met. But their wedding plans are put on hold when Violet receives an opportunity to work at the University of Michigan... There are no surprises in this amiable film but it works thanks to the winning chemistry between the two leads. Also effective are Rhys Ifans as Violet's pompous boss and Jacki Weaver as her mother, desperate to see her daughter married before the grandparents die. GS

▶ Jason Segel, Emily Blunt, Chris Pratt, Rhys Ifans, Alison Brie, Jacki Weaver, Jim Piddock. Jane Carr.
▶ *Dir* Nicholas Stoller, *Pro* Stoller, Rodney Rothman and Judd Apatow, *Screenplay* Stoller and Jason Segel, *Ph* Javier Agirresarobe, *Pro Des* Julie Berghof, *Ed* William Kerr and Peck Prior, *M* Michael Andrews, *Cos* Lesa Evans.

Apatow Productions/Relativity Media-Universal Pictures International.
124 mins. USA. 2012. Rel: 22 June 2012. Cert. 15.

The Flowers of War ★★★

As one would expect of China's veteran director Yimou Zhang, this is a well-made film. However, it follows the brilliant *City of Life and Death* and the often striking *City of War: The Story of John Rabe* in portraying the tragic loss of life in 1937 when the Japanese army occupied Nanjing. This version is by far the most commercial with its deliberately sentimental approach, and consequently it comes in a poor third. But, if this treatment is what you prefer, it is undeniably handled with great competence and finds a lead role for Christian Bale. (Original title: *Jin ling shi san chai*) MS

▶ Christian Bale, Ni Ni, Xinyi Zhang, Tianyuan Huang, Atsurô Watabe, Doudou Zhang.
▶ *Dir* Yimou Zhang, *Pro* Weiping Zhang and others, *Screenplay* Heng Liu, from the novel by Geling Yan, *Ph* Xiaoding Zhao, *Pro Des* Yohei Taneda, *Ed* Peicong Meng, *M* Qigang Chen, *Cos* William Chang and Graciela Mazón.

Beijing New Picture Film Company/EDKO Film/New Picture Company etc-Revolver Entertainment.
146 mins. China/Hong Kong. 2011. Rel: 3 Aug 2012. Cert. 15.

Flying Swords of Dragon Gate ★★★

Defying his age, Jet Li gives a spirited performance as General Zhao, a bandit who hunts down corrupt government officials in Tsui Hark's complexly plotted historical adventure sequel to his 1992 *New Dragon Gate Inn*. Here heroes tackle villains before a sandstorm descends on the small desert inn. There are some brilliant set-pieces in this dazzling Hong Kong movie, but the awesome fight inside a hurricane is the clear highlight. Some of the plotting and a little bit of CGI disappoint, but the 3D visuals and action are amazing, while the '90s-style wire work and stunts still astonish. (Original title: *Long men fei jia*) DW

▶ Jet Li, Zhou Xun, Chen Kun, Kwai Lun-mei, Louis Fan, Wu Wai Lap, Mavis Fan.
▶ *Dir* and *Screenplay* Tsui Hark, *Pro* Tsui, Jeffrey Chan and Nansun Shi, *Ph* Sung Fai Choi, *Pro Des* Chung Man Yee, *Ed* Chi Wai Yau, *M* Xin Gu, Wai Lap Wu and Han Chiang Li, *Cos* Chung Man Yee and Hsuan-wu Lai.

Bona International Film Group/ Beijing Lianzi Group/ China Film Group/Shanda Pictures/Shineshow etc-Distribution Workshop.
122 mins. China. 2011. Rel: 19 Oct 2012. Cert. 15.

For a Good Time, Call... ★★★

Conservative Lauren Miller and adventurous Ari Graynor fell out a while ago and hate each other. But, brought together by gay friend Justin Long, they reluctantly agree to share a luxury apartment to save costs. Then the idea of running a phone sex line turns them into new best friends. This female *Odd Couple*-style buddy movie is quite rude (it's an 18) but thankfully a lot funnier and sweeter than it sounds, thanks to the two star performances and a gag-heavy script. Miller's real husband Seth Rogen has a funny cameo, and so does Kevin Smith. DW

Putting up a fight: Gwei Lun-Mei gets on top of things in *Flying Swords of Dragon Gate*.

Lauren Miller, James Wolk, Ari Graynor, Justin Long, Mimi Rogers, Nia Vardalos, Mark Webber, Sugar Lynn Beard, Seth Rogen, Kevin Smith.
▶ *Dir* Jamie Travis, *Pro* Lauren Miller, Katie Anne Naylon, Jenny Hinkey, Jen Weinbaum and Josh Kesselman, *Screenplay* Miller and Naylon, *Ph* James Laxton, *Pro Des* Sue Tebbutt, *Ed* Evan Henke, *M* John Swihart, *Cos* Maya Lieberman.

AdScott Pictures-Universal Pictures.
85 mins. USA. 2012. Rel: 2 Nov 2012. Cert. 18.

The Forgiveness of Blood ★★★½

Joshua Marston is a talented, humane filmmaker as he proved in 2004 with *Maria Full of Grace*. This successor is again a subtitled work. The setting now is Albania and the theme is the cost to families of feuds affecting more than one generation, as encouraged by Balkan tradition. It's interesting and sympathetic, but unlike its predecessor it seriously lacks intensity – partly perhaps because the lead actor is a non-professional without the experience to make the audience fully identify with his character's emotions. (Original title: *La faida*) MS

▶ Tristan Halilaj, Sindi Laçej, Refet Abazi, Luan Jaha, Ilire Vinca Çelaj, Veton Osmani.
▶ *Dir* Joshua Marston, *Pro* Paul Mezey, *Screenplay* Marston and Andamion Murataj, *Ph* Rob Hardy, *Pro Des* Tommaso Ortino, *Ed* Malcolm Jamieson, *M* Jacobo Lieberman and Leonardo Heiblum, *Cos* Emir Turkeshi.

Fandango Portobello/a Journeyman Pictures production etc.-Soda Pictures.
110 mins. Italy/Denmark/USA/Albania. 2010.
Rel: 10 Aug 2012. Cert. 12A.

Four Horsemen ★★★★

Ross Ashcroft's well-researched documentary about the global economic crisis brings new insight into why the current system has failed. The Four Horsemen of the Apocalypse are still causing havoc around the world and continue to exploit those who are struggling to survive. Organised crime is thriving while the earth's natural resources are in danger of extinction. This film is bleak and depressing, and possibly preaching to the converted, but still needs to be seen. GS

▶ Noam Chomsky, Joseph Stiglitz, Herman Daly, Max Keiser, Camilla Batmanghelidjh.
▶ *Dir* Ross Ashcroft, *Pro* Ross & Megan Ashcroft and Jason Whitmore, *Screenplay* Ashcroft and Dominic Frisby, *Ph* Aladin Hasic and Claudio Napoli, *Ed* Simon Modery, *M* Andrew Hewitt, *Animator* Pola Gruszka.

Motherlode-Guerilla Films.
97 mins. UK. 2012. Rel: 14 Mar 2012. Cert. E.

Frankenweenie ★★★★½

Tim Burton is at his best in this most personal of films. It uses stop-motion animation with puppets and works a treat in 3D and black and white. In effect its story is both an autobiographical

Corpse pride: Sparky barks another day in Tim Burton's *Frankenweenie*.

A nasty occupation: Michael Lonsdale and Christopher Buccholz (son of Horst) in Ismaël Ferroukhi's Free Men.

study of a child regarded as an outsider and a re-working of the Frankenstein myth in which Victor Frankenstein is a modern-day child. The grand finale is more obvious with its build-up featuring various monsters, but everything else is utterly individual and deeply felt. MS

▶ With the voices of Charlie Tahan, Martin Short, Martin Landau, Winona Ryder, Catherine O'Hara.
▶ *Dir* Tim Burton, *Pro* Burton and Allison Abbate, *Screenplay* John August, from a screenplay by Lenny Ripp based on an idea by Burton, *Ph* Peter Sorg, *Pro Des* Rick Heinrichs, *Ed* Chris Lebenzon and Mark Solomon, *M* Danny Elfman, *Puppet Des* MacKinnon & Saunders, *Animation Dir* Trey Thomas.
Disney-Buena Vista.
87 mins. USA. 2012. Rel: 17 Oct 2012. Cert. PG.

Free Men ★★★★★

From that deeply humane director Ismaël Ferroukhi, who gave us *Le Grand Voyage* (2004), comes this film set in Paris in 1942. The German occupation has featured in many films before, but Ferroukhi has a new tale to tell and it's rooted in fact. It concerns the help given by the Paris mosque to members of the underground and to Jews in danger. The common humanity that brought this about makes *Free Men* an historical work with a message for today. In a fine cast Michael Lonsdale is outstanding. (Original title: *Les Hommes libres*) MS

▶ Tahar Rahim, Michael Lonsdale, Mahmoud Shalaby, Lubna Azabal, Farid Larbi.

▶ *Dir* Ismaël Ferroukhi, *Pro* Fabienne Vonier, *Screenplay* Ferroukhi and Alain-Michel Blanc, *Ph* Jérôme Alméras, *Art Dir* Thierry François, *Ed* Annette Dutertre, *M* Armand Amar, *Cos* Virginie Montel.
Pyramide Productions/France 3 Cinéma etc-Artificial Eye.
99 mins. France. 2011. Rel: 25 May 2012. Cert. 12A.

Friends with Kids ★★

Jason and Julie are best friends and both want a child. However, neither relishes all the mess that comes with marriage. So they decide to conceive a child together and move on with their own romantic lives… The surprising thing about this 'high concept' romantic comedy is that it's from the keyboard of Jennifer Westfeldt, she who wrote the insightful and gut-bustingly funny *Kissing Jessica Stein*. This time she takes the directorial reins herself and coats her tale of adult frustrations and misunderstanding with a formulaic gloss indebted to everybody from Woody Allen to Rob Reiner. What a pity. JC-W

▶ Adam Scott, Jennifer Westfeldt, Jon Hamm, Kristen Wiig, Maya Rudolph, Chris O'Dowd, Megan Fox, Edward Burns.
▶ *Dir* Jennifer Westfeldt, *Pro* Westfeldt, Riza Aziz, Joey McFarland, Joshua Astrachan, Jake Kasdan and Jon Hamm, *Screenplay* Westfeldt, *Ph* William Rexer II, *Pro Des* Ray Kluga, *Ed* Tara Timpone, *M* Marcelo Zarvos and The 88, *Cos* Melissa Bruning.
Red Granite Pictures/Points West Pictures/Locomotive-Lionsgate.
107 mins. USA. 2011. Rel: 29 June 2012. Cert. 15.

Fun Size ★★★

Teenager Wren (played by the appealing Victoria Justice) loses her little brother (Jackson Nicoll), whom she's supposed to be babysitting at Halloween while their widowed mom (Chelsea Handler) is out partying with a 26-year-old nerd. Wren, her best friend (Jane Levy) and a couple of boys spend the night looking for the kid. More fun than you'd think, it's a bit offbeat and raunchy for a Nickelodeon film. The amusing script doesn't always take the obvious route and the performances spark it up nicely. DW

❧ Victoria Justice, Jane Levy, Jackson Nicoll, Thomas McDonell, Thomas Mann, Johnny Knoxville, Chelsea Handler, Josh Pence.
❧ *Dir* Josh Schwartz, *Pro* Schwartz, Stephanie Savage, David Kanter and Bard Dorros, *Screenplay* Max Werner, *Ph* Yaron Orbach, *Pro Des* Mark White, *Ed* Michael L Sale, *M* Deborah Lurie, *Cos* Eric Daman.

Paramount Pictures/Nickelodeon Movies/Fake Empire Productions/Anonymous Content-Paramount Pictures.
86 mins. USA. 2012. Rel: 29 Oct 2012. Cert. 12A.

Fury ★★★

Foley (Samuel L Jackson) wants a clean start when he gets released from a 25-year prison stretch. Things look bright when he meets Iris (Ruth Negga), a fragile young woman, but then the crooked Ethan (Luke Kirby), son of his former partner, has other plans for him... Jackson is always good value and shares a terrific chemistry with the lovely Negga. The other supporting performances are less convincing but thankfully Negga's strong presence makes the story work. (Original title: *The Samaritan*) GS

❧ Samuel L Jackson, Luke Kirby, Ruth Negga, Tom Wilkinson, Gil Bellows, Aaron Poole.
❧ *Dir* David Weaver, *Pro* Suzanne Cheriton, Tony Wosk and Andras Hamori, *Screenplay* Weaver and Elan Mastai, *Ph* François Dagenais, *Pro Des* Matthew Davies, *Ed* Geoff Ashenhurst, *M* Todor Kobakov and David Whalen, *Cos* Patrick Antosh.

H2O Motion Pictures/2262730 Ontario/Quickfire Films/ Middle Child Films Inc- Entertainment One.
90 mins. Canada. 2012. Rel: Apr 20 2012. Cert. 18.

Gambit ★★★★

Lightweight and even silly at times, this new adaptation of the story told originally in the 1966 movie of the same title is a guilty pleasure (many critics hated it). But this tale of con games and robbery, more comedy than thriller, is utterly unpretentious and admirably succinct (more so than the Ronald Neame version), while the screenplay by the Coen brothers is on firmer ground than their disastrous adaptation of *The Ladykillers*. Forgettable though it is, it's well played, looks good and has a music score which echoes the theme from *The Pink Panther*. MS

❧ Colin Firth, Cameron Diaz, Alan Rickman, Tom Courtenay, Stanley Tucci, Julian Rhind-Tutt.
❧ *Dir* Michael Hoffman, *Pro* Mike Lobell, Adam Ripp and Rob Paris, *Screenplay* Joel and Ethan Coen, from the short story by Sidney Carroll, *Ph* Florian Ballhaus, *Pro Des* Stuart Craig, *Ed* Paul Tothill, *M* Rolfe Kent, *Cos* Jenny Beavan.

CBS Films/Crime Scene Pictures/ArtPhyl etc-Momentum Pictures.
89 mins. UK/USA. 2012. Rel: 23 Nov 2012. Cert. 12A.

Ghost Rider: Spirit of Vengeance 3D ★

In this dull sequel Nicolas Cage returns as Johnny Blaze – the character from the Marvel comic. In the original, Blaze became Ghost Rider when he made a deal with the Devil, but now he must save a young boy from the Devil himself (Ciaran Hinds). This is a huge 'achievement' from the makers of this misconceived franchise – they have managed to deliver an even worse film than the original, and that's saying something. GS

❧ Nicolas Cage, Ciaran Hinds, Idris Elba, Anthony Head, Christopher Lambert, Johnny Whitworth, Fergus Riordan.
❧ *Dir* Mark Neveldine and Brian Taylor, *Pro* Stephen Paul, Avi Arad, Ashok Amritraj and Michael De Luca, *Screenplay* Scott M Gimple, Seth Hoffman and David S. Goyer, from a story by Goyer, *Ph* Brandon Trost, *Pro Des* Kevin Phipps, *Ed* Brian Berdan, *M* David Sardy, *Cos* Bojana Niktovic.

Columbia Pictures/Hyde Park Entertainment/Marvel Entertainment/Crystal Sky Pictures/Michael De Luca/ Imagenation Abu Dhabi-Entertainment One.
95 mins USA/United Arab Emirates. 2011.
Rel: 17 Feb 2012. Cert. 12A.

The Giants ★★★

Three teenagers, two neglected brothers and a loner, bond and experience a series

The art of farce: Alan Rickman and Cameron Diaz in Michael Hoffman's *Gambit*.

of adventures and misadventures – this in a setting which, with prominent river scenes, is exquisitely photographed by Jean-Paul de Zaetijd. The Belgian director Bouli Lanners obtains wonderfully natural performances, but a first half offering understated drama beneath a sometimes comic surface gives way to a pretentious metaphor about journeying through life and it all ends up indeterminately. (Original title: *Les Géants*) MS

▶ Zacherie Chasseriaud, Paul Bartel, Martin Nissen, Karim Lecloux, Marthe Keller.
▶ *Dir* Bouli Lanners, *Pro* Jacques-Henri and Olivier Bronckart, Simon Arnal and others, *Screenplay* Lanners and Elise Ancion, *Ph* Jean-Paul de Zaetijd, *Art Dir* Paul Rouschop, *Ed* Ewin Ryckaert, *M* The Bony King of Nowhere, *Cos* Ancion.

Versus Production/Haut et Court/Samsa Film etc-Artificial Eye.
84 mins. Belgium/France/Luxembourg. 2011. Rel: 13 July 2012. Cert. 15.

Ginger and Rosa ★★★

Two girls have been inseparable friends all their lives, having been born on the same day in 1945 at the same hospital. Now, in 1962, they feel threatened by the Cold War and the impending Cuban Missile Crisis. While Ginger (Elle Fanning) wants to protest against nuclear war, Rosa (Alice Englert) is preoccupied with boyfriends, including a relationship with Ginger's father Roland (Alessandro Nivola). Sally Potter's film is a complex study of the angst of teenage girls and their faltering steps towards adulthood. The two

leads are exceptional and the starry supporting cast add weight, but Potter's screenplay eventually loses its way and lacks full credibility. MHD

▶ Elle Fanning, Alice Englert, Alessandro Nivola, Christina Hendricks, Timothy Spall, Oliver Platt, Jodhi May, Annette Benning.
▶ *Dir* and *Screenplay* Sally Potter, *Pro* Andrew Litvin and Christopher Sheppard, *Ph* Robbie Ryan, *Pro Des* Carlos Conti, *Ed* Anders Refn, *Cos* Holly Waddington.

BBC Films/British Film Institute/Adventure Pictures/Media House Capital/Det Danske Filminstitut-Artificial Eye.
90 mins. UK/Denmark/Canada/Croatia. 2012. Rel: 19 Oct 2012. Cert. 12A.

Girl Model ★★★

This documentary features former model Ashley Arbaugh, who took to scouting for young girls suitable for model work overseas, and a 13-year-old taken from Siberia to Tokyo under a contract of this kind. The film reveals the exploitation involved, the sexualisation of these girls and the risk of prostitution when what has been promised proves illusory. All this is worth airing, but a more forceful approach would have been preferable and even at 78 minutes it feels over-extended. MS

▶ With Ashley Arbaugh, Nadya Vall, Tigran Khachatrian.
▶ *Dir*, *Ph* and *Ed* David Redmon and A Sabin, *Consulting Pro* Marcy and Robert Garriott, *M* Matthew Dougherty and Eric Taxier.

Carnivalesque Films/American Documentary etc-Dogwoof.
77 mins. USA/Canada 2011. Rel: 10 Feb 2012. No Cert.

Glastonbury the Movie (In Flashback) ★★★★

This is a reworking by Robin Mahoney of the film that he made from footage shot at the Glastonbury Music Festival in 1993. I didn't see the original, but what emerges now is a historical document which gives new insights into the period through being viewed from the vantage point of 2012. It's also genuinely cinematic and as much a work of social history as it is a concert movie from a past age. MS

▶ With Stereo MCs, The Orb, Dexter Fletcher, Charlie Creed-Miles, The Lemonheads, The Verve.
▶ *Dir* Robin Mahoney, *Pro* Mahoney and others, *Ph* Aubrey Fagon, Mahoney and Michael Sarne, *Ed* Mahoney and Matthew Salkeld.

November Films.
91 mins. UK. 2012. Rel: 29 June 2012. Cert. 12A.

God Bless America ★★★★

Bobcat Goldthwait, he of 2006's *Sleeping Dogs*, is back on outrageous form with this black comedy. A loner is dismayed by life in America today, as epitomised by witless, exploitative yet adored TV shows, and he decides to kill off some of the worst offenders. The jokey tone of this social critique may mean that Goldthwait is having his cake and eating it. Nevertheless, lead actor Joel Murray triumphs in a role ideal for Paul Giamatti or William H Macy and you warm to a film in which, if Woody Allen is not safe from being savaged, neither is *Juno*'s Diablo Cody. MS

▶ Joel Murray, Tara Lynne Barr, Melinda Page Hamilton, Mackenzie Brooke Smith.
▶ *Dir* and *Screenplay* Bobcat Goldthwait, *Pro* Sean McKittrick and Jeff Culotta, *Ph* Bradley Stonesifer, *Pro Des* Natalie Sanfilippo, *Ed* Jason Stewart and David Hopper, *M* Matt Kollar, *Cos* Sarah de Sa Rego.

Darko Entertainment/Jerkschool Productions-StudioCanal Ltd.
104 mins. USA. 2011. Rel: 4 July 2012. Cert. 15.

Gone ★★½

Waitress Jill (Amanda Seyfried) is still recovering from being kidnapped in the woods. She revisits the site hoping to find clues to her kidnapper's whereabouts. Arriving home one day, she finds that her sister Molly (Emily Wickersham) has gone missing and believes that her kidnapper has taken Molly, thinking she was Jill. The police don't believe her story, so she sets out to find Molly before the kidnapper does to her what he didn't do to Jill. This is standard thriller fare that's high on plot and low on thrills, but it passes the time well enough. MHD

▶ Amanda Seyfried, Daniel Sunjata, Jennifer Carpenter, Sebastian Stan, Emily Wickersham, Wes Bentley, Michael Paré.
▶ *Dir* Heitor Dhalia, *Pro* Sidney Kimmel, Dan Abrams, Chris Salvaterra, Tom Rosenberg and Gary Lucchesi, *Screenplay* Allison Burnett, *Ph* Michael Grady, *Pro Des* Charisse Cardenas, *Ed* John Axelrad, *M* David Buckley, *Cos* Lindsay Ann McKay.

Summit Entertainment/Sidney Kimmel Entertainment/Lakeshore Entertainment-Summit Entertainment.
94 mins. USA. 2012. Rel: 20 Apr 2011. Cert. 15.

All fired up: Joel Murray and Tara Lynne Barr in Bobcat Goldthwait's *God Bless America*.

Goodbye First Love ★★★

The first love depicted in Mia Hansen-Løve's film is that of a 15-year-old in Paris, Camille (Lola Créton). Attracted by an older boy, she sees their romance as destined to last forever but he does not. Yet even when Camille finds another relationship she cannot readily put aside her earlier feelings. This is one of those films which will be involving for those who identify with the central character. I, however, remained a distant observer, believing in these people but not feeling for them. (Original title: *Un Amour de jeunesse*) MS

❧ Lola Créton, Sebastian Urzendowsky, Magne-Håvard Brekke, Valérie Bonneton.
❧ *Dir* and *Screenplay* Mia Hansen-Løve, *Pro* Philippe Martin and David Thion, *Ph* Stéphane Fontaine, *Art Dir* Mathieu Menut and Charlotte de Cadville, *Ed* Marion Monnier, *Cos* Bethsabée Dreyfus.

Les Films Pelléas/Razor Film/ARTE France Cinéma etc-Artificial Eye.
111 mins. France/Germany 2011. Rel: 4 May 2012. Cert. 15.

Goon ★★★

Doug Glatt (Seann William Scott) is a thuggish bouncer who has the ability to beat up almost everyone at the drop of a hat. His violent nature impresses a sports coach who immediately signs him up for his failing ice hockey team. But soon Doug finds his match in Ross (Liev Schreiber), a notoriously violent player on the opposite team... The gags come thick and fast in this crude comedy, which is based on a true story, while Scott is in his element as the foolish but likable antihero. GS

❧ Seann William Scott, Liev Schreiber, Jay Baruchel, Alison Pill, Kim Coates,
❧ *Dir* Michael Dowse, *Pro* Jay Baruchel, André Rouleau, David Gross, Don Carmody and Ian Dimerman, *Screenplay* Baruchel and Evan Goldberg, from the book by Adam Frattasio and Doug Smith, *Ph* Bobby Shore, *Pro Des* Gord Wilding, *Ed* Reginald Harkema, *M* Ramachandra Borcar, *Cos* Heather Neale.

No Trace Camping/Caramel Film/Inferno Pictures Inc/ Don Carmody Productions-Eagle Films.
92 mins. USA/Canada. 2011. Rel: 6 Jan 2012. Cert. 15.

The Gospel of Us ★★★

Easter 2011 saw the staging of a passion play in Port Talbot which treated the town as its stage. The event was filmed and this is the result. Dave McKean's record of it is cinematic, but he adopts an almost avant-garde approach to a complex work which seeks to relate Christ to present day Britain. It's a highly stylised and demanding piece, but Michael Sheen's Christ figure, simply called The Teacher, is often remarkable. MS

❧ Michael Sheen, Matthew Aubrey, David Davies, Nigel Barrett, Di Botcher, Francine Morgan, Darren Lawrence.

Dir, *Ed* and *Pro Des* Dave McKean, *Theatrical Performance Dir* Bill Mitchell and Michael Sheen, *Pro* Eryl Huw Phillips, *Screenplay* Owen Sheers and McKean, from a story by Sheen and Sheers, *Ph* Various, *M* McKean and Ashley Slater, *Cos* Myrridin Wannell and Sue Hill.

The Film Agency for Wales/National Theatre Wales/ Wildworks/a Rondo Media film etc-Soda Pictures. 120 mins. UK 2012. Rel: 13 Apr 2012. Cert. 12A.

Grabbers ★★★

A meteor lands off the Irish coast, spewing bloodsucking aliens onto a nearby island, and two Garda policemen come together to tackle the situation. This mayhem-packed horror parody motors almost entirely on the lovely performances of Richard Coyle and Ruth Bradley, who share some of the best screen chemistry in ages. Russell Tovey also does well as the boffin who tries to help out, so it's sad when his part vanishes. The alien effects are not too bad for a low-budget movie, making this a very likable, hugely amusing piece of nonsense. DW

➤ Richard Coyle, Ruth Bradley, Russell Tovey, Lalor Roddy, David Pearse, Bronah Gallagher, Ned Dennehy, Stuart Graham.
➤ *Dir* Jon Wright, *Pro* James Martin, Piers Tempest, Martina Niland, Kate Myers, Edouardo Levy and Tracy Brimm, *Screenplay* Kevin Lehane, *Ph* Trevor Forrest, *Pro Des* Tom McCullagh, *Ed* Matt Platts-Mills, *M* Christian Henson, *Cos* Hazel Webb-Crozier.

Forward Films/Samson Films/Limelight/High Treason Productions/Irish Film Board/Nvizible-Sony Pictures Releasing. 94 mins. UK/Ireland. 2012. Rel: 26 Dec 2012. Cert. 15.

Grassroots ★★★

This is a film of two halves. The first is an engaging tale of two youngsters in Seattle who unexpectedly prove successful in challenging the incumbent in the City Council elections of 2001. This is well played and amusing, but the factual basis has resulted in a second half which is weighed down by harsh reality (9/11 intrudes) and by a change of tone which turns the incumbent into a friendly figure instead of the man we want to hate. MS

➤ Jason Biggs, Joel David Moore, Lauren Ambrose, Cedric the Entertainer, Tom Arnold.
➤ *Dir* Stephen Gyllenhaal, *Pro* Peggy Rajski, Michael Huffington and others, *Screenplay* Justin Rhodes and Gyllenhaal, based on Phil Campbell's book *Zioncheck for President: A True Story of Idealism and Madness in American Politics*, *Ph* Sean Porter, *Pro Des* Laurie Hicks, *Ed* Neil Mandelberg, *M* Nick Urata, *Cos* Ron Leamon.

An MRB Productions film/Votiv Films/Lanai Productions-Intandem Films. 98 mins. USA. 2012. Rel: 9 Nov 2012. Cert. 15.

Grave Encounters ★★★

There's a ghost-hunting reality show on TV. For their sixth episode, smug host Lance Preston (Sean Rogerson), his camera crew and 'experts' lock themselves for the night into an old psychiatric hospital to see if it's haunted. Actually, it's alive with the ghosts of the one-time inmates, who chase them down a maze of halls and corridors. After a long, slow but suspenseful build-up, there's plenty of terrifying scary stuff.

Atlantic Rim: Ruth Bradley, Richard Coyle and Russell Tovey in Jon Wright's *Grabbers*.

Even if the set-up and 'found footage' filming are over-familiar (think *Paranormal Activity*, *Session 9* and *The Blair Witch Project*), the plot does take enough new twists and turns. DW

❧ Ben Wilkinson, Sean Rogerson, Ashleigh Gryzko, Mackenzie Gray, Juan Riedinger, Merwin Mondesir.
❧ *Dir, Screenplay* and *Ed* The Vicious Brothers, *Pro* Shawn Angelski, *Ph* Tony Mirza, *Pro Des* Paul McCulloch, *M* Quynne Craddock, *Cos* Natalie Simon.

Digital Interference Productions/Twin Engine Films/ Darclight Films-Metrodome Distribution.
92 mins. Canada. 2011. Rel: 20 Apr 2012. Cert. 15.

Great Expectations ★★★

The rating here may be modest, but for anyone who admires David Lean's classic of 1946 this fresh adaptation of Dickens' novel is instantly disposable. London may look dirtier and more authentic under Mike Newell's direction, but that's hardly relevant when you are missing the definitive presence of such artists as Jean Simmons, Alec Guinness, Martita Hunt and Francis L Sullivan. Ralph Fiennes (Magwitch) and Jason Flemyng (Joe Gargery) succeed best in shaking off comparisons. MS

❧ Jeremy Irvine, Helena Bonham Carter, Ralph Fiennes, Holliday Grainger, Robbie Coltrane, Jason Flemyng, Ewen Bremner, Sally Hawkins, Olly Alexander, David Walliams, Toby Irvine, Helena Barlow.
❧ *Dir* Mike Newell, *Pro* Stephen Woolley, Elizabeth Karlsen and others, *Screenplay* David Nicholls, from the novel by Charles Dickens, *Ph* John Mathieson, *Pro Des* Jim Clay, *Ed* Tariq Anwar, *M* Richard Hartley, *Cos* Beatrix Aruna Pasztor.

BFI/BBC Films/Unison Films/HanWay Films/LipSynch productions/Number 9 Films etc-Lionsgate UK.
129 mins. UK/France/USA. 2012. Rel: 30 Nov 2012. Cert. 12A.

The Nun's Story: Sabrina Lechêne and Julie Sokolowski in Bruno Dumont's *Hadewijch*.

The Grey ★★

The Grey tries hard to be better than the genre film it is. The story of seven men living on their wits in the Alaskan wilderness, the film makes the most of its snow-swept setting and punctuates the narrative with philosophical interludes. But we never come to care about these men nor thrill at their various perils. Stalked by a pack of animatronic (and very noisy) wolves, the men bicker in clichés and not one of them emerges as a human being. Liam Neeson, as the alpha male of the group, constantly muses on cosier, more romantic times, but this device eventually becomes an irritant. JC-W

❧ Liam Neeson, Frank Grillo, Dermot Mulroney, Dallas Roberts, Joe Anderson, Nonso Anozie.
❧ *Dir* Joe Carnahan, *Pro* Carnahan, Jules Daly, Ridley Scott and Mickey Liddell, *Screenplay* Carnahan and Ian MacKenzie Jeffers, *Ph* Masanobu Takayanagi, *Pro Des* John Willett, *Ed* Roger Barton and Jason Hellmann, *M* Marc Streitenfeld, *Cos* Courtney Daniel.

Open Road Films/Inferno Distribution/LD Entertainment/Scott Free/Chambara Pictures-Entertainment.
117 mins. USA. 2011. Rel: 27 Jan 2012. Cert. 15.

Hadewijch ★★½

Bruno Dumont's religious drama is his most Bressonian work to date. It concerns Celine, a novitiate who takes the name of Hadewijch on entering a convent but who is sent back into the world when her sense of personal mission is seen as too extreme. The ensuing drama links Catholic and Muslim issues and involves terrorists planning to explode a bomb in Paris. But what one is meant to make of it all remained for me an exasperatingly open question. A Catholic audience may more readily find answers here. MS

❧ Julie Sokolowski, Karl Sarafidis, Yassine Salime, David Dewaele, Brigitte Mayeux-Clerget.
❧ *Dir* and *Screenplay* Bruno Dumont, *Pro* Jean Brehat and Rachid Bouchareb, *Ph* Yves Cape, *Art Dir* Jean Marc Tran Tan Ba, *Ed* Guy Lecorne, *Cos* Annie Morel-Paris and Alexandra Charles.

3B Productions/Arte France Cinéma/ZDF etc-New Wave Films.
105 mins. France/Germany. 2009. Rel: 17 Feb 2012. Cert. 12A.

Happy Happy ★★★½

Agnes Kittelsen is a delight as optimistic teacher Agnes in this deliciously oddball comedy drama, Grand Jury prize-winner at Sundance in 2011 and Norway's Best Foreign Language Film entry at the Academy Awards the following year. Agnes has a closeted gay husband and a nasty son, so she's happy when new tenants arrive at

the neighbouring house, and happier still when she starts an affair with the couple's husband (Henrik Rafaelson, who won a Best Actor award in Norway). Good humour and despair are profitably explored in this ideally acted, quirkily amusing film. (Original title: *Sykt lykkelig*) DW

▶ Agnes Kittelsen, Henrik Rafaelsen, Maibritt Saerens, Oskar Hernæs Brandsø, Ram Shihab Ebedy, Heine Totland.
▶ *Dir* Anne Sewitsky, *Pro* Synnøve Hørsdal, *Screenplay* Ragnhild Tronvoll, *Ph* Anna Myking, *Pro Des* Camilla Lindbråten, *Ed* Christoffer Heie, *M* Stein Berge Svendsen, *Cos* Ellen Dæhli Ystehede.
Naipo Film-Magnolia Pictures.
85 mins. Norway. 2010. Rel: 16 Nov 2012. Cert. 15.

Hara-kiri Death of a Samurai 3D ★★★★

In *13 Assassins* (2010) Miike Takashi offered us an excellent remake of a little-known Japanese samurai film. Here he provides a new version of a classic period piece, Kobayashi's *Hara-kiri* of 1962. He adds 3D, adequately but hardly memorably, to this subtle tale of class, honour and betrayal set in 17th century Japan. The finale resorts to extravagant action, but this distinguished work continues to provide acute social criticism and plays as a tragedy of almost Lear-like intensity. (Original title: *Ichimei*) MS

▶ Ichikawa Ebizo, Eita, Mitsushima Hikari, Takenaka Naoto, Yakusho Koji, Hira Takehiro.

▶ *Dir* Miike Takashi, *Pro* Nakazawa Toshiaki, Jeremy Thomas and others, *Screenplay* Yamagishi Kikumi, from Takiguchi Yasuhiko's story *Ibun ronin ki*, *Ph* Nobuyasu Kita, *Art Dir* Hayashida Yuji, *Ed* Yamashita Kenji, *M* Sakamoto Ryuichi, *Cos* Kurosawa Kazuko.
Sedic International/Dentsu/Shochiku/Kodansha/OLM etc-Revolver Entertainment.
127 mins. Japan/UK. 2011. Rel: 4 May 2012. Cert. 18.

Hard Boiled Sweets ★★

Flavourful *Lock Stock*-style crime thriller with Paul Freeman as Southend crime boss Shrewd Eddie and Peter Wight as the ill-named Jimmy the Gent, the London mobster coming to collect his 'rent'. Soon several teams of crooks are out to steal the suitcase with £1 million in cash. With the script veering between parody and thriller, the characters, plot and dialogue tend towards caricature, cliché and stereotype. But the film is busy, fast-moving and stylishly shot on eye-catching locations and the actors do well with what they're offered. DW

▶ Philip Barantini, Elizabeth Berrington, Adrian Bower, Paul Freeman, Peter Wight, Ian Hart, Laura Greenwood, Liz May Brice, Danny Sapani, Scott Williams.
▶ *Dir* and *Screenplay* David LG Hughes, *Pro* Hughes, Demelza Jones, Michael Riley and Lara Greenway, *Ph* Sara Deane, *Pro Des* Chloe Brady, *Ed* Lloyd George, *M* Tom Morrison, *Cos* Charmaine Parram.
Fatal Black-Universal Pictures.
84 mins. UK. 2012. Rel: 9 Mar 2012. Cert. 15.

Sedentary Samurai: Ichikawa Ebizo in Miike Takashi's *Hara-Kiri: Death of a Samurai.*

Beach slap: Gina Carano and Ewan McGregor tussle in Steven Soderbergh's *Haywire*.

Harold's Going Stiff ★★★

Stan Rowe is OAP Harold Gimble in this original and enjoyable horror mockumentary. Sarah Spencer is his nurse, a cheery care worker who helps him with his stiffness, the onset of rigour disease that ultimately turns sufferers into zombies. But three vigilantes with baseball bats are on the loose outside… Writer-director Keith Wright needed a bigger budget and more filming time (he made this in nine days) but let his imagination soar anyway. It looks good, is original and enjoyable, tells a decent story, and the two stars are fun. DW

❯ Stan Rowe, Sarah Spencer, Andy Pandini, Phil Gascoyne, Lee Thompson, Richard Harrison, Liz Simmons.
❯ *Dir, Ed, Ph* and *Screenplay* Keith Wright, *Pro* Richard Guy, *Pro Des* Anna Pamplin, *M* Tom Kane.
FrissonFilm-High Fliers Distribution.
77 mins. UK. 2011. Rel: 7 Aug 2012. Cert. 15.

The Harsh Light of Day ★★★

Best-selling occult author Daniel Shergold (Daniel Richardson) has his house broken into by intruders who assault him and leave his wife for dead. Left paralysed, he is mourning his loss when a stranger, Infurnari (Giles Alderson), arrives with the means for getting revenge. He makes a Faustian pact with the man who, it transpires, is a vampire. A quick bite gives Daniel special powers including a talent for locating his intruders. Yes, it is another vampire movie but with a twist… Oliver S Milburn's screenwriting and directing debut is a cut above the norm while his cast members acquit themselves with a certain dash. MHD

❯ Daniel Richardson, Giles Alderson, Sophie Linfield, Niki Felstead, Paul Jacques.
❯ *Dir* and *Screenplay* Oliver S Milburn, *Pro* Emma Biggins, *Ph* Samuel Stewart, *Pro Des* Kate Suzanne Hunter and Sophie Razgui-Cottle, *Ed* David Spragg, *M* Jeremy Howard, *Cos* Nina Bertolone.
Corona Pictures/Multistory Films-Left Films.
79 mins. UK. 2012. Rel: 8 June 2012. Cert. 18.

Haywire ★★½

Steven Soderbergh's films are always technically adroit and cover a wide range, but why he wanted to make this spy thriller set largely in Dublin I can't imagine. Gina Carano, known for martial arts, rightly gets top billing as the tough girl heroine, once a marine. But otherwise there's no individuality in this utterly improbable action piece which, with the volume up to '10', comes across as a tasteless celebration of violence unredeemable by its starry cast. MS

❯ Gina Carano, Michael Fassbender, Ewan McGregor, Antonio Banderas, Michael Douglas.
❯ *Dir* Steven Soderbergh, *Pro* Gregory Jacobs, *Screenplay* Lem Dobbs, *Ph* Peter Andrews (ie, Soderbergh), *Pro Des* Howard Cummings, *Ed* Mary Ann Bernard (ie, Soderbergh), *M* David Holmes, *Cos* Shoshana Rubin.
Relativity/Bord Scannán na hÉireann/The Irish Film Board etc-Momentum Pictures.
93 mins. USA/Ireland. 2011. Rel: 18 Jan 2012. Cert. 15.

Headhunters ★★★½

Based on the best-selling novel by Jo Nesbø, *Headhunters* is arguably the most stylish thriller to reach the cinema this year. Well plotted and constructed, it hits the screen running in a non-stop frisson of action. Norwegian corporate headhunter Roger Brown (Aksel Hennie) has a successful daytime career which doesn't stop him from pursuing extramural activities as an art thief, stealing collections from his wealthy clients. He meets his match in Clas Greve (Nikolaj Coster-Waldau) when he attempts to lift a priceless Rubens painting. Roles are switched and the headhunter becomes the hunted in this absorbing chase movie. Director Morten Tyldum screws every last ounce of excitement from his excellent cast. (Original title: *Hodejegerne*) MHD

❧ Aksel Hennie, Nikolaj Coster-Waldau, Synnove Macødy Lund, Julie Ølgaard, Eivind Sander.
❧ *Dir* Mortem Tyldum, *Pro* Marianne Gray and Asle Vatn, *Screenplay* Lars Gudmestad and Ulf Ryberg, based on the novel by Jo Nesbø, *Ph* John Andreas Andersen, *Pro Des* Nina Bjerch Andresen, *Ed* Vidar Flataukan, *M* Trond Bjerknes and Jeppe Kaas, *Cos* Karen Fabritius Gram.
Yellow Bird Films/Nordisk Film/Friland/ARD Degeto Film-Momentum Pictures.
100 mins. Norway/Germany. 2011. Rel: 6 Apr 2012. Cert. 15.

Hello Quo ★★★½

Considering the global standing of Status Quo, it's kind of ridiculous that this is the first film on them. The Quo need little introduction (they've had more chart hits than any other rock band in history) and for their fans this 152-minute documentary should do the trick. An epic combination of archive film, new interviews and concert footage through the ages, *Hello Quo* is just as engaging as its subject matter, which is a good thing. However, the movie's length might test the patience of those less enamoured. CB

❧ With Francis Rossi, Rick Parfitt, Alan Lancaster, John Coghlan, Steve Diggle, John Edwards, Noddy Holder, Jeff Lynne, Brian May, Cliff Richard.
❧ *Dir* Alan G Parker, *Pro* Alexa Morris, *Ph* Dave Meehan.
Hello Quo Movie-Anchor Bay Entertainment.
152 mins. UK. 2012. Rel: 22 Oct 2012. Cert. 15.

Here Comes the Boom ★★

Kevin James is moderately amusing in this modest, inoffensive, feel-good sports comedy, playing a jaded biology teacher inspired to become a mixed martial arts cage fighter to raise cash for his school. James tries so hard you'd think he would be funnier. There's nicer work from Salma Hayek as his love interest, the school

Norwegian hood: Nikolaj Coster-Waldau in Morten Tyldum's ingenious, breathless and sexy *Headhunters*.

nurse, and Henry Winkler, the beloved music teacher whose work is under threat. The movie's no world-beater but it knows its humble place and doesn't try too hard. DW

▶ Kevin James, Salma Hayek, Henry Winkler, Greg Germann, Charice, Baz Rutten, Gary Valentine, Reggie Lee.
▶ *Dir* Frank Coraci, *Pro* James and Todd Garner, *Screenplay* Kevin James, Allan Loeb and Rock Reuben, *Ph* Phil Meheux, *Pro Des* Perry Andelin Blake, *Ed* Scot Hill, *M* Rupert Gregson-Williams, *Cos* Hope Hanafin.

Columbia Pictures/Broken Road/Happy Madison/Hey Eddie/Sony Pictures Entertainment-Sony Pictures Releasing.
105 mins. USA. 2012. Rel: 9 Nov 2012. Cert. 12A.

Himizu ★½

Here is a disappointing film from Sion Sono, the director of *Love Exposure* and *Cold Fish*. Fifteen-year-old Sumida (Shota Sometani) and his schoolmate Keiko (Fumi Nikaido) live in tents after a devastating earthquake and struggle to survive. Sumida is now in charge of the family boat business and is followed blindly by Keiko, who has a crush on him. It's beautifully filmed in the harsh landscape of Japan's tsunami-hit areas but the arch and loud acting style becomes very irritating by the end. GS

▶ Shota Sometani, Fumi Nikaido, Megumi Kagurazaka, Asuka Kurosawa, Denden, Mitsuru Fukikoshi, Tetsu Watanabe.
▶ *Dir* Sion Sono, *Pro* Haruo Umekawa and Masashi Yamazaki, *Screenplay* Sono and Minoru Furuya, *Ph* Sôhei Tanikawa, *Art Dir* Takashi Matsuzuka, *Ed* Jun'ichi Itô, *M* Tomohide Harada.

Studio Three Co Ltd/Kodansha/GAGA-Third Window Films.
130 mins. Japan. 2011. Rel: 1 June 2012. Cert. 15.

Protection racket: Joy Bryant, Bradley Cooper and Ryan Hansen in Hit and Run.

Hit and Run ★★★

Dax Shepard writes, co-directs, co-produces and stars in this exciting action comedy thriller as Charlie Bronson, an ex-getaway driver who risks his place in the witness protection programme to help his girlfriend (Kristen Bell) get to LA. It turns into one long epic nail-biting car chase with laughs and jolts as both the FBI and his old associates give him a run for his money. Bradley Cooper is hilariously scary as one of the thugs and Tom Arnold is funny as the clueless marshal. With $2 million and some pals, it's a kind of expensive home movie, but a good one. DW

▶ Kristen Bell, Dax Shepard, Bradley Cooper, Beau Bridges, Ryan Hansen, Tom Arnold, Kristin Chenoweth, Michael Rosenbaum.
▶ *Dir* David Palmer and Dax Shepard, *Pro* Shepard, Andrew Panay, Kim Waltrip and Nate Tuck, *Screenplay* Shepard, *Ph* Bradley Stonesifer, *Pro Des* Emily Bloom, *Ed* Keith Kroket, *M* Robert Mervak and Julian Wass, *Cos* Brooke Dulien.

Exclusive Media/Panay Films/Kim and Jim Productions/ Primate Pictures-Momentum Pictures.
100 mins. USA. 2012. Rel: 12 Oct 2012. Cert. 15.

Hit So Hard ★★

What do The Bangles, The Go-Gos, The Runaways and The Velvet Underground have in common? They all had female drummers. Patty Schemel, percussionist for Courtney Love's band Hole, drug addict, alcoholic and lesbian, is probably a more colourful drummer than most. Even so, this subdued documentary, a compilation of home movies and talking heads, could only really appeal to the faithful. Punk has never felt so genial. JC-W

▶ Patty Schemel, Melissa Auf der Maur, Eric Erlandson, Courtney Love, Gina Schock, Kurt Cobain.
▶ *Dir* and *Ed* P David Ebersole, *Pro* Todd Hughes and Christina Soletti, *Screenplay* Ebersole and Hughes, *Ph* John Tanzer, Larra Anderson and Mark Putnam, *M* Roddy Bottum.

The Ebersole Hughes Company/Tight Ship Productions-Peccadillo Pictures.
103 mins. USA. 2011. Rel: 16 Nov 2012. No Cert.

The Hobbit: An Unexpected Journey ★½

Not since *The Phantom Menace* has such fevered expectation been met with such grave disappointment. Rendered unwatchable by 48fps visuals that deliver a disconcerting real-world look while simultaneously stripping the film of its magic, style and flow, this is the tiresomely padded first third of a slim kids' adventure that should never have been given the trilogy treatment. Lacking the grandeur, spirit and soul of director Peter Jackson's previous *Lord of the Rings* trilogy, it's immature, self-indulgent and poorly characterised, an unsightly and ennui-inducing patchwork of awkward errors in judgment. MJ

▶ Ian McKellen, Martin Freeman, Andy Serkis, Barry Humphries, Christopher Lee, Ken Stott, James Nesbitt, Ian Holm, Elijah Wood, Cate Blanchett, Hugo Weaving, Benedict Cumberbatch.
▶ *Dir* Peter Jackson, *Pro* Jackson, Zane Weiner, Fran Walsh and Carolynne Cunningham, *Screenplay* Jackson, Guillermo del Toro, Philippa Boyens and Fran Walsh, based on the book by JRR Tolkien, *Ph* Andrew Lesnie, *Pro Des* Dan Hennah, *Ed* Jabez Olssen, *M* Howard Shore, *Cos* Bob Buck, Ann Maskrey and Richard Taylor.

Metro Goldwyn Mayer Pictures/New Line Cinema/ WingNut Films-Warner Bros.
169 mins. USA/New Zealand 2012. Rel: 13 Dec 2012. Cert. 12A.

Hollywoo ★★½

Jeanne (Florence Foresti) is a French voiceover artist famous for dubbing American actress Jennifer Marshall (Nikki Deloach) in a popular television series. But when Jennifer announces she is giving up acting, Jeanne has no option but to travel to Hollywood and make her change her mind... This is a fun idea, and Foresti is a terrific comedienne, but the script feels forced and doesn't entirely ring true. GS

▶ Florence Foresti, Jamel Debbouze, Nikki Deloach, Jeff Roop, Muriel Robin, Sophie Mounicott, Alex Lutz.
▶ *Dir* Frederic Berthe and Pascal Serieis, *Pro* Jean-Baptiste Dupont and Cyril Colbeau-Justin, *Screenplay* Serieis, Foresti, Patrick Fouque and Xavier Maingon, *Ph* Ludovic Colbeau-Justin, *Pro Des* Franck Benezech, *M* Philippe Rombi, *Cos* Aurore Pierre and Jo Rosen.

LGM Cinéma/StudioCanal/TFI Films Production/Canal +/Backup Films/Coficup etc-StudioCanal .
107 mins. France. 2011. Rel: 20 Apr 2012. Cert. 15.

Holy Motors ★★★½

Everyone agrees that Leos Carax's extraordinary showcase for Denis Lavant is weird. He appears as a man in Paris who adopts and acts out many different roles in the course of a day. Its oddity invites either admiration or disdain according to taste, but its episodic nature means that it keeps moving on to new things so, although it's uneven, it's never boring. Technically it is very impressive and, at the very least, you will find it intriguing unless you are frustrated by the impossibility of deciding what is being said here. MS

▶ Denis Lavant, Edith Scob, Kylie Minogue, Michel Piccoli, Eva Mendes, Jeanne Disson, Leos Carax.
▶ *Dir* and *Screenplay* Leos Carax, *Pro* Martine

Marignac, *Ph* Caroline Champetier and Yves Cape, *Art Dir* Florian Sanson, *Ed* Nelly Quettier, *Cos* Anaïs Romand.

Pierre Grise Productions/Theo Films/Pandora Film/Arte France Cinéma etc-Artificial Eye.
116 mins. France/Germany. 2012. Rel: 28 Sep 2012. Cert. 18.

Hope Springs ★★★½

It's a shame that this film loses its footing late on, becoming coarser and over-determined to provide a feel-good ending. Until then, Vanessa Taylor's screenplay is admirably balanced between the comic and the serious as it portrays the increasingly sexless marriage of a couple long together. Meryl Streep and Tommy Lee Jones, unselfishly supported by Steve Carell as a therapist, are magnificent and much of the film is a joy. MS

▶ Meryl Streep, Tommy Lee Jones. Steve Carell, Jean Smart, Ben Rappaport, Elisabeth Shue.
▶ *Dir* David Frankel, *Pro* Todd Black and Guymon Casady, *Screenplay* Vanessa Taylor, *Ph* Florian Ballhaus, *Pro Des* Stuart Wurtzel, *Ed* Steven Weisberg, *M* Theodore Shapiro, *Cos* Ann Roth.

Columbia Pictures/Mandate Pictures/Metro-Goldwyn-Mayer etc-Momentum Pictures.
100 mins. USA. 2012. Rel: 14 Sep 2012. Cert. 12A.

Hotel Transylvania ★★★

Adam Sandler provides the voice of Dracula and Kevin James of Frankenstein for this lovingly crafted animated family comedy. It's set in the present day when Drac's home is now the Hotel Transylvania. He invites his monster pals to his daughter Mavis' 118th birthday party. Mavis (Selena Gomez) sees human boy Jonathan (Andy Samberg) in the forest, and there's a bit of an age gap – he's 21! Costly, charming and sweet natured, it's aimed mainly at kids, but it's quite fun for adults too. Sandler does a tasty job with the vocals. DW

Monster mash: Count Dracula (far right) and friends in Genddy Tartakovsky's *Hotel Transylvania*.

➤ With the voices of Adam Sandler, Andy Samberg, Selena Gomez, Kevin James, Fran Drescher, Steve Buscemi, Jon Lovitz.
➤ *Dir* Genndy Tartakovsky, *Pro* Michelle Murdocca, *Screenplay* Peter Baynham and Robert Smigel, based on a story by Tod Durham and Dan and Kevin Hageman, *Pro Des* Marcelo Vignali, *Ed* Catherine Apple, *M* Mark Mothersbaugh.

Columbia Pictures/Sony Pictures Animation-Sony Pictures Releasing.
91 mins. USA. 2012. Rel: 12 Oct 2012. Cert. U.

House at the End of the Street
★★★

A freshly divorced mother (Elisabeth Shue) and her teenage daughter (Jennifer Lawrence) move into a dream house, albeit next to a property with a dubious history. To say more would be to spoil the fun (?), but Mark Tonderai's thriller does veer from the standard to something a little more interesting in the second half. He's helped no end by Lawrence, who seems unable to make a false move. Consequently, the audience's sympathy is fully invested in her. But don't be fooled, this is still a generic piece, albeit a more gripping one than most. JC-W

➤ Jennifer Lawrence, Max Thieriot, Gil Bellows, Elisabeth Shue, Allie MacDonald.
➤ *Dir* Mark Tonderai, *Pro* Aaron Ryder, Peter Block and Ryan Kavanaugh, *Screenplay* David Loucka, from a story by Jonathan Mostow, *Ph* Miroslaw Baszak, *Pro Des* Lisa Soper, *Ed* Steve Mirkovich and Karen Porter, *M* Theo Green, *Cos* Jennifer Stroud.

Relativity Media/FilmNation Entertainment/A Bigger Boat/Zed Filmworks-Momentum Pictures.
100 mins. USA. 2012. Rel: 21 Sep 2012. Cert. 15.

The House I Live In ★★★★½

Although it could be pruned to advantage, this is an outstanding documentary. It's an admirably reasoned polemic against America's War on Drugs,

Dead man walking: A scene from Eugene Jarecki's eye-opening documentary The House I Live In.

a cause which has counted as a major factor in that country's politics since the 1970s. The ethnic, if not necessarily racist, aspects underlying laws which make matters worse instead of better are exposed, and there's even a judge on hand to express distaste for laws he has to administer. Over the end credits we discover that the title comes from a song by Paul Robeson. MS

➤ With Eugene Jarecki, Nannie Jeter, David Simon.
➤ *Dir* and *Written by* Eugene Jarecki, *Pro* Jarecki, Melinda Shopsin and others, *Ph* Sam Cullman and Derek Hallquist, *Pro Des* Joe Posner, *Ed* Paul Frost, *M* Robert Miller.

Charlotte Street Films/an Edgewood Way production/BBC Storyville etc-Dogwoof.
109 mins. USA/UK/Germany/Qatar/The Netherlands/Japan/Australia. 2012. Rel: 23 Nov 2012. Cert. 15.

House of Tolerance ★★★

Artistic rather than salacious, Bertrand Bonello's handsome film is about life in a high-class Parisian brothel at the very end of the 19th century. A girl deformed by a client with a knife provides just one of many plot threads, but nothing takes on enough weight (symbolic, social or otherwise) to justify the length, which is just over two hours. (Original title: *L'Apollonide: Souvenirs de la maison close*) MS

➤ Hafsia Herzi, Céline Sallette, Alice Barnole, Iliana Zabeth, Adèle Haenel, Jasmine Trinca.
➤ *Dir*, *Screenplay* and *M* Bertrand Bonello, *Pro* Kristina Larsen and Bonello, *Ph* Josée Deshaies, *Art Dir* Alain Guffroy, *Ed* Fabrice Rouaud, *Cos* Anaïs Romand.

Les Films du Lendemain/My New Picture/Arte France Cinéma etc-The Works.
126 mins. France. 2010. Rel: 27 Jan 2012. Cert. 18.

How I Spent My Summer Vacation ★★★½

Originally titled *Get the Gringo*, this went straight to DVD in the States, thanks largely to the toxic public image of its star, Mel Gibson. Reckless casting aside, director Adrian Grünberg's debut feature is actually a very spirited, exciting and darkly funny crime-themed actioner. Largely set in a tough Mexican prison that's more a lawless town, the movie features a pleasingly Martin Riggs-like performance from Gibson and is surprisingly good. (Original title: *Get the Gringo*) MJ

➤ Mel Gibson, Kevin Hernandez, Daniel Himénez Cacho, Dolores Heredia, Peter Stormare, Dean Norris.
➤ *Dir* Adrian Grünberg, *Pro* Gibson, Stacy Perskie and Bruce Davey, *Screenplay* Gibson, Grünberg and Perskie, *Ph* Benoît Debie, *Pro Des* Bernard Trujillo, *Ed* Steven Rosenblum, *M* Antonio Pinto, *Cos* Anna Terrazas.

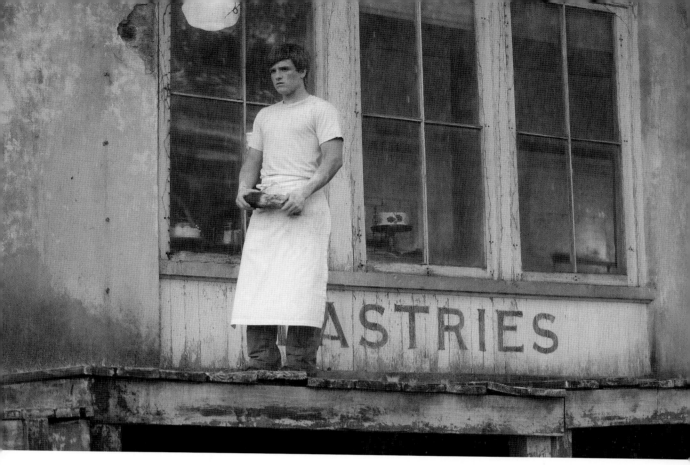

ASTRIES

Airborne Productions/Icon Productions-Icon Film
Distribution.
96 mins. USA. 2012. Rel: 11 May 2012. Cert. 15.

How to Re-establish a Vodka Empire ★★★★

Personal in the best sense, this engaging little
film by Daniel Edelstyn tells of his journey to the
Ukraine where his great grandfather had built up
a vodka factory, a centre of local employment.
He seeks to save the distillery from decay and
to support it by launching a new vodka label
in the UK. He additionally uncovers a touching
family history. This is a well-made piece, quirkily
individual and very endearing. MS

▶ Hilary Powell, Daniel Edelstyn, Conrad Asquith,
Anthony Styles, Esmé Edelstyn.
▶ Dir and Written by Daniel Edelstyn, Pro Edelstyn,
Hilary Powell and Christopher Hird, Pro Des Powell,
Ed John Mister, M Andrew Skeet.

Dartmouth Films/Optimistic Productions etc-Dartmouth
Films.
76 mins. UK. 2011. Rel: 16 Mar 2012. Cert. 12A.

Hungarian Rhapsody: Queen Live in Budapest '86 ★★★★

Queen fans will be in heaven with this fantastic
film featuring lovingly restored, digitally re-
mastered footage of their 1986 Budapest triumph.
It opens with a 25-minute documentary about
the year after Live Aid and their Wembley
Stadium gig, then the Budapest film really shows
them at their peak. Freddie Mercury comes over
as oddly shy and gauche in the interviews but
is stunningly confident in performance, the
consummate showman. The rest of the band are
interviewed too, giving articulate accounts of
themselves. DW

▶ With Freddie Mercury, Brian May, Roger Taylor,
John Deacon.
▶ Dir János Zsombolyai, Pro George Mihály,
Ph Elemér Ragályi, M Queen.

Sony Digital Cinema-Eagle Rock Entertainment.
118 mins. Hungary. 2012. Rel: 20 Sep 2012. No Cert.

The Hunger Games ★★★★

The premise is simple: teenagers in the future
are forced to kill each other in the name of
entertainment. And it's a theme that is becoming
worryingly popular. Still, if one can set aside the
story's inherent bloodlust, Gary Ross' adaptation
of Suzanne Collins' literary saga (translated
into 26 languages) is a skilfully managed and
gripping affair. Ross, who chooses his films with
infinite care (this is only his third feature after
Pleasantville and Seabiscuit), has had the good
sense to cast the excellent Jennifer Lawrence
as his young heroine, film the whole thing in
the picturesque Blue Ridge Mountains of North
Carolina and keep a tight rein on the nuanced
score. The rest, more or less, falls into place. JC-W

Food for thought:
Josh Hutcherson
in Gary Ross'
box-office smash,
The Hunger
Games.

Lie of the mind: Mads Mikkelsen attacks Daniel Engstrup in Thomas Vinterberg's *The Hunt*, for which Mikkelsen won the best actor award at Cannes.

▶ Jennifer Lawrence, Josh Hutcherson, Liam Hemsworth, Woody Harrelson, Elizabeth Banks, Donald Sutherland, Lenny Kravitz, Stanley Tucci, Wes Bentley, Toby Jones.
▶ *Dir* Gary Ross, *Pro* Nina Jacobson and Jon Kilik, *Screenplay* Ross, Suzanne Collins and Billy Ray, *Ph* Tom Stern, *Pro Des* Philip Messina, *Ed* Christopher S Capp, Stephen Mirrione and Juliette Welfling, *M* James Newton Howard, *Cos* Judianna Makovsky.

Lionsgate/Color Force-Lionsgate.
143 mins. USA. 2012. Rel: 23 Mar 2012. 12A.

Hunky Dory ★★★

In contrast to his earlier work, Marc Evans here offers us a feel-good piece with music. Set in Swansea during the hot summer of 1976, it's the tale of a spirited teacher (well-cast Minnie Driver) putting on with her pupils a rock musical version of Shakespeare's *The Tempest*. Various adolescent problems feature convincingly within the mix. The film is, however, over-long and naïve and it doesn't really take off as a musical – but its heart is emphatically in the right place. MS

▶ Minnie Driver, Aneurin Barnard, Danielle Branch, Haydn Gwynne, Bob Pugh, Owen Teale.
▶ *Dir* Marc Evans, *Pro* Jon Finn and Dan Lupovitz, *Screenplay* Laurence Coriat, *Ph* Charlotte Bruus Christensen, *Pro Des* Jacqueline Abrahams, *Ed* Mali Evans, *M* Joby Talbot, *Cos* Stewart Meacham.

The Film Agency for Wales & Wales Creative IP Fund/a

Big Pond/Big Bad Wolf production-E1 Films.
110 mins. UK. 2011. Rel: 2 Mar 2012. Cert. 15.

The Hunt ★★½

Mads Mikkelsen is excellent in this serious-minded Danish drama playing a teacher falsely accused of being a paedophile. Unfortunately as the story develops the screenplay (by Tobias Lindholm and director Thomas Vinterberg) builds up the hysteria against him in a way that fails to ring true. Admittedly I saw this movie before the Jimmy Savile story broke, but I found myself frequently questioning the likelihood of the events depicted. (Original title: *Jagten*) MS

▶ Mads Mikkelsen, Thomas Bo Larsen, Annika Wedderkopp, Lasse Fogelstrøm, Susse Wold.
▶ *Dir* Thomas Vinterberg, *Pro* Sisse Graum Jørgensen, Morten Kaufmann and others, *Screenplay* Vinterberg and Tobias Lindholm, *Ph* Charlotte Bruus Christensen, *Pro Des* Torben Stig Nielsen, *Ed* Anne Østerud and Janus Billeskov Jansen, *M* Nikolaj Egelund, *Cos* Stine Gudmundsen-Holmgreen.

Zentropa Entertainments/Film i Väst/Zentropa International Sweden etc-Arrow Films.
115 mins. Denmark/Sweden. 2012. Rel: 30 Nov 2012. Cert. 15.

The Hunter ★★★½

Willem Dafoe is exceedingly well cast in the titular role of this Australian drama about a man hired to hunt down the very rare Tasmanian tiger. He does so at the behest of a biotech company which can make use of DNA samples thus obtained. The unfamiliar location is an asset and the environmental issues are interesting, but the personal story that develops is less moving than it should be and the ending doesn't ring true. MS

▶ Willem Dafoe, Frances O'Connor, Sam Neill, Morgana Davies, Finn Woodlock.
▶ *Dir* Daniel Nettheim, *Pro* Vincent Sheehan, *Screenplay* Alice Addison, from the novel by Julia Leigh as adapted by Wain Fimeri and Nettheim, *Ph* Robert Humphreys, *Pro Des* Steven Jones-Evans, *Ed* Roland Gallois, *M* Matteo Zingales, Michael Lira and Andrew Lancaster, *Cos* Emily Seresin.

Magnolia Pictures/Screen Australia/Screen NSW/Screen Tasmania/Madman Entertainment etc-Artificial Eye. 102 mins. Australia. 2011. Rel: 6 July 2012. Cert. 15.

Hysteria ★★

In days of yore, or 1880 to be more precise, women suffering from insomnia, cramps or nerves – hysteria – were treated by certain practitioners of the medical profession with digital manipulation. This Victorian romp-com, a sort of *Carry On Coming*, takes a saucy seaside postcard approach to the subject, with the excellent Hugh Dancy cast in the Jim Dale part. Unfortunately, Mr Dancy is no comedian and most of the other actors try too hard. Still, it's better than *Rabbit Fever*. JC-W

▶ Hugh Dancy, Maggie Gyllenhaal, Jonathan Pryce, Felicity Jones, Rupert Everett, Ashley Jensen, Sheridan Smith, Gemma Jones, Anna Chancellor, David Ryall.
▶ *Dir* Tanya Wexler, *Pro* Tracey Becker, Judy Cairo and Sarah Curtis, *Screenplay* Stephen Dyer and Jonah Lisa Dyer, from a story by Howard Gensler, *Ph* Sean Bobbitt, *Pro Des* Sophie Becher, *Ed* Jon Gregory, *M* Gast Waltzing, *Cos* Nic Ede.

Informant Media/Forthcoming Films/Beachfront Films/ Canal +/Chimera Films/arte France Cinéma-Sony Pictures Releasing. 99 mins. UK/France/Germany/Luxembourg. 2011. Rel: 21 Sep 2012. Cert. 15.

I Against I ★★½

Kenny Doughty does well as a cocky youngish businessman who flees the scene of the murder of a city crime boss while mystery man Ingvar Eggert Sigurdsson watches. The victim's vengeful son (Mark Womack) rounds up the two suspects and forces them to try to kill each other. This visually stylish, nightmarish Brit gangster film achieves a haunting copy of the old film noir look. Though plot development is a bit clumsy and unsatisfying, the film is nevertheless intriguing and involving, achieving much on a tiny budget. It's co-written and co-directed by the son of Richard (*Jagged Edge*) Marquand. DW

▶ Kenny Doughty, Ingvar Eggert Sigurdsson, Mark Womack, Sónia Balacó, John Castle.
▶ *Dir* and *Screenplay* James Marquand, Mark Cripps and David Ellison, *Pro* Marquand, Matthew Whyte and Kristian Kozlowski, *Ph* Whyte, *Art Dir* Stuart May and Daniel Newton, *Ed* Anton Short, *M* Bernd Rest, *Cos* Raquel Azevedo and Anna Biggerstaff.

Stray Dog Films. 84 mins. UK. 2012. Rel: 12 Aug 2012. Cert. 15.

Spy of the tiger: Willem Dafoe in Daniel Nettheim's *The Hunter*.

Panic in Pangaea: Manny, Diego and friends take on the Gigantopithecus Captain Gutt (voiced by Peter Dinklage) in *Ice Age: Continental Drift*.

I Am Bruce Lee ★★½

"Water can flow or it can crash. Be like water." Though not inspired, this is a useful and interesting documentary about the great martial artist and beloved icon, packed with all the expected rare archive footage, vintage photographs and new interviews, most notably from his widow Linda, daughter Shannon (the film's producer) and fighter Daniel Inosanto, all set to an upbeat soundtrack. The story may be familiar but the film is clearly a well-edited labour of love, and most of the interviewees are either revealing or entertaining. Mickey Rourke's words of wisdom, for example, are especially amusing. DW

▶ With Shannon Lee, Daniele Bolelli, Paul Bowman, Richard Bustillo, Stephan Bonnar, Kobe Bryant, Daniel Inosanto, Mickey Rourke.
▶ *Dir* Pete McCormack, *Pro* Shannon Lee and Derik Murray, *Ph* Ian Kerr, *Ed* Tony Kent, *M* Schaun Tozer.
Network Entertainment-Freemantle Media Enterprises. 94 mins. Canada. 2011. Rel: 20 July 2012. Cert. 15.

I, Anna ★★★½

Switching the location from America to London, writer-director Barnaby Southcombe adapts Elsa Lewin's novel which combines a police investigation and a love story. The mood is that of film noir and Southcombe helpfully casts his mother, Charlotte Rampling, in the title role. There's a good supporting cast too but, while the film displays a flair for atmospheric visuals, the storytelling is less sure-footed and the finale too melodramatic. MS

▶ Charlotte Rampling, Gabriel Byrne, Eddie Marsan, Hayley Atwell, Jodhi May, Honor Blackman.
▶ *Dir* and *Screenplay* (based on the novel by Elsa Lewin) Barnaby Southcombe, *Pro* Felix Vossen, Christopher Simon and others, *Ph* Ben Smithard, *Pro Des* Tom Burton, *Ed* Peter Boyle, *M* K>i<D, *Cos* Pam Downe.

Global Screen/Exponential Media/Greenstreet Entertainment/Embargo Films etc.-Artificial Eye. 91 mins. UK/Germany/France. 2012. Rel: 7 Dec 2012. Cert. 15.

Ice Age 4: Continental Drift ★★★½

Be warned: *Ice Age 4* is not aimed at adults. Unlike the increasingly sophisticated, demographically two-ply cartoons of Pixar and their ilk, this is an old-fashioned, rollicking entertainment for the kids. While there are fleeting visual allusions to Aristotle, Atlantis and Mount Rushmore – which the exceptionally young will miss – for the most part this is a U-rated rollercoaster ride of anthropomorphic slapstick. It's an odd mix, an anything-goes medley of modern urban slang, Greek mythology, prehistoric cataclysm and pirate adventure – with a music video featuring Jennifer Lopez. But there are plenty of good lines, too, neatly balancing the constant rush of inventive pictorial gags. JC-W

▶ With the voices of Ray Romano, John Leguizamo, Denis Leary, Nicki Minaj, Drake, Jennifer Lopez, Queen Latifah, Seann William Scott, Keke Palmer, Peter Dinklage, Wanda Sykes, Nick Frost, Chris Wedge, Patrick Stewart, Simon Pegg.
▶ *Dir* Steve Martino and Mike Thurmeier, *Pro* John C Donkin and Lori Forte, *Screenplay* Michael Berg, Jason Fuchs and Mike Reiss, *Ph* Renato Falcão,

Art Dir Nash Dunnigan, *Ed* James Palumbo and David Ian Salter, *M* John Powell.

Blue Sky Studios-20th Century Fox.

92 mins. USA. 2012. Rel: 13 July 2012. Cert. U.

ID: A ★★★★

Set mainly in Copenhagen, this is a Danish thriller. Nevertheless, we meet the central character, a woman with memory loss, in France where men are looking for her and where the TV announces the local killing of a politician. There's a long flashback on the way to everything being explained and, if the material is hardly exceptional, this Hitchcockian movie, which incorporates links with the world of opera, is well played and stylishly directed. MS

▷ Tuva Novotny, Flemming Enevold, Carsten Bjørnlund, Arnaud Binard, Rogier Philipoom.
▷ *Dir* Christian E Christiansen, *Pro* Louise Vesth, *Screenplay* Tine Krull Petersen, based on Anne Chaplin Hansen's novel *På knivens æg*, *Ph* Ian Hansen, *Art Dir* Thomas Greve, *Ed* Bodil Kjærhauge, *M* Kristian Eidnes Anderson, *Cos* Rebecca Richmond.

Zentropa Entertainments10/Filmfyn/Holland Harbour/ Film i Väst etc-Artificial Eye.

104 mins. Denmark/The Netherlands/Sweden. 2011. Rel: 17 Feb 2012. Cert. 15.

If I Want to Whistle, I Whistle ★★★½

It's unlucky for this Romanian film, made in 2009, that it should reach us just after the superior *Breathing* [qv], which also concerns a teenager in a detention centre troubled by his relationship with his mother. Here it's George Pistereanu's Silviu fearing the effect of his mother's promiscuity on his younger brother. The work's stage origin is well hidden, but Silviu's reactions to a social worker (Ada Condeescu) are not always persuasive. The film is interesting but *Breathing* is far more sure-footed. (Original title: *Eu cand vreau sa fluier, fluier*) MS

▷ George Pistereanu, Ada Condeescu, Clara Voda, Mihai Constantin, Marian Bratu.
▷ *Dir* Florin Serban, *Pro* Catalin Mitulescu and Daniel Mitulescu, *Screenplay* Catalin Mitulescu and Serban, from a play by Andreea Valean, *Ph* Marius Panduru, *Pro Des* Ana Ioneci, *Ed* Catalin F Cristutiu and Sorin Baican, *Cos* Augustina Stanciu.

Strada Film/Film I Väst/The Chimney Pot etc-Artificial Eye.

94 mins. Romania/Sweden. 2009. Rel: 18 May 2012. Cert. 15.

If Not Us, Who? ★★★

Unlike other films referencing Germany's famed political terrorists the Baader-Meinhof group, this work by Andres Veiel is largely concerned with events before 1968. Indeed, even with Meinhof not appearing, its emphasis is less on Andreas Baader than on the roles played out by Bernward Vesper and Gudrun Esslin and it has been described as a radical love story. However, my own response is muted since I find these people notably unsympathetic, and the film's viewpoint strikes me as oddly indeterminate. It is well acted though. (Original title: *Wer wenn nicht wir*) MS

▷ August Diehl, Lena Lauzemis, Alexander Fehling, Susanne Lothar, Sebastian Blomberg.
▷ *Dir* and *Screenplay* Andres Veiel, *Pro* Thomas Kufus, *Ph* Judith Kaufmann, *Art Dir* Christian M Goldbeck, *Ed* Hansjörg Weissbrich, *M* Annette Focks, *Cos* Bettina Marx.

zero one film/SWR/Degeto/WDR/Deutschfilm/Senator Film Produktion etc.-Soda Pictures.

125 mins. Germany. 2011. Rel: 2 Mar 2012. Cert. 15.

Ill Manors ★★★★

Filmed in my own manor in East London, Ben (Plan B) Drew's directorial debut is an unflinching look at life on the streets where drugs, whores and gangsta culture are the norm. Several stories are interwoven in a seamless picture of a lost generation. Pimps, dealers and gang leaders rule the roost, forcing the innocent to commit abominable crimes, including murder, as initiation rites to an underground society that forms today's street life. It's a depressing picture but its almost documentary style lends it an all too credible realism. Drew's strong cast of new faces work wonders in their handling of the grosser side of life. MHD

▷ Riz Ahmed, Ed Skrein, Keith Coggins, Lee Allen, Nick Sagar, Ryan De La Cruz, Anouska Mond, Nathalie Press.
▷ *Dir* and *Screenplay* Ben Drew, *Pro* Atif Ghani, *Ph* Gary Shaw, *Pro Des* Greg Shaw and Fabrice Spelta, *Ed* David Freeman and Hugh Williams, Sotira Kyriakou and Farrah Drabu, *M* Plan B and Al Shux, *Cos* Violetta Kassapi.

Lest she forget: Tuva Novotny in Christian E Christiansen's *ID: A.*

BBC Films/Microwave/Film London/Gunslinger/
Aimimage Productions etc-Revolver Entertainment.
121 mins. UK. 2012. Rel: 6 June 2012. Cert. 18.

The Imposter ★★★★

This is a documentary film that isn't a
documentary, although it relates a true story
about a 14-year-old Texas boy who disappeared
in 1994 after playing basketball with his friends.
Three years later his mother has a phone call
from her son, who claims he has escaped from
the clutches of a child sex ring. Of course we
know that he is an imposter but the film goes
on to dramatise the events that happened
subsequently. It is an absorbing look at an odd
situation and makes use of the people involved in
the mystery, including the mother, her daughter
and the imposter himself. With its 'wrong man'
subject it could almost be a Hitchcock film – and
it's just as exciting as Hitch at his best. MHD

▶ With Frédéric Bourdin, Adam O'Brian, Anna
Ruben, Cathy Dresbach, Alan Teichman, Nancy
Fisher, Philip French.
▶ *Dir* Bart Layton, *Pro* Dimitri Doganis, *Ph* Erik
Alexander Wilson and Lynda Hall, *Ed* Andrew
Hulme, *M* Anne Nikitin.

A & E Indie Films/RAW/Film 4/Protagonists Pictures/
Randy Murray Productions-Revolver Entertainment.
99 mins. UK. 2012. Rel: 24 Aug 2012. Cert. 15.

The human drain:
Zofia Pieczynska
in Agnieszka
Holland's Oscar-
nominated
In Darkness.

In Darkness ★★★½

The ghost of Wajda's masterpiece *Kanal* (1956)
haunts Agnieszka Holland's take on real-life events
in the Polish town of Lvov in 1943. We are back in
the sewers where this time Jews trying desperately
to survive are in hiding. Holland is no less sincere
than Wajda, but with so many characters to
identify, so much darkness and such length (144
minutes to *Kanal*'s 97) this becomes something of
an endurance test for the audience. MS

▶ Robert Wieckiewicz, Benno Fürmann, Agnieszka
Grochowska, Maria Schrader, Herbert Knaupp.
▶ *Dir* Agnieszka Holland, *Pro* Steffen Reuter, Patrick
Knippel and others, *Screenplay* David F Shamoon,
from Robert Marshall's book *In the Sewers of Lvov*,
Ph Jolanta Dylewska, *Pro Des* Erwin Prib, *Ed* Michal
Czarnecki, *M* Antoni Komasa-Lazarkiewicz, *Cos*
Katarzyna Lewinska and Jagna Janicka.

Polish Film Institute/Studio Babelsberg/Cinegate
Germany/Filmissimo etc-Metrodome Distribution.
144 mins. Germany/Poland/USA/Italy/Canada. 2011.
Rel: 16 Mar 2012. Cert. 15.

In Search of Haydn ★★★★

Phil Grabsky's articulate documentary on the
great master of music follows his previous Mozart
and Beethoven 'searches'. Grabsky has clearly
discovered a winning formula in celebrating the

work of these wonderful composers and here again Juliet Stevenson provides the eloquent narration. Grabsky has the ability to capture on the screen both the historians' and the artists' immense enthusiasm for their subject and the result is illuminating and highly infectious. GS

▷ Documentary narrated by Juliet Stevenson, with readings by Henry Goodman and contributions by Roger Norrington, Emanuel Ax, Bayan Northcott, Ronald Brautigam, Frans Brüggen, Alison Balsom Marc-André Hamelin, the Endellion String Quartet etc.
▷ *Dir* and *Written by* Phil Grabsky.

PhilGrabskyFilms.com/Seventh Art Productions-Seventh Art Distribution.
102 mins. UK. 2012. Rel: 19 Jan 2012. Cert. U.

In the Dark Half ★½

A thriller set in the rural outskirts of Bristol, *In the Dark Half* lays on the atmosphere as densely as it can. The sound editing takes up most of the slack in this tale of grief and single parenthood, but the performances are not up to snuff. Having delivered two excellent turns in *Tamara Drewe* and *Hanna*, Jessica Barden has shown what a good actress she can be. But as a lonely 15-year-old haunted by the boy next door, she is unable to make us believe. In fact, everything about the film is unconvincing, right up to its inexplicable climax. JC-W

▷ Tony Curran, Lyndsey Marshal, Jessica Barden, Georgia Henshaw.
▷ *Dir* Alastair Siddons, *Pro* Margaret Matheson, *Screenplay* Lucy Catherine, *Ph* Neus Ollé, *Pro Des* Max Bellhouse, *Ed* Paul Carlin, *M* Dan Jones.

Cinema Six/Matador Pictures/Regent Capital-Verve Pictures.
111 mins. UK. 2012. Rel: 10 Aug 2012. Cert. 15.

In Your Hands ★★★

Belatedly released here, this French film's arrival may be down to the understandable appeal of its star, Kristin Scott Thomas. Once again she is excellent, and she's ably partnered by Pio Marmaï. He plays a man who kidnaps a surgeon, Anna (Scott Thomas), seeking revenge for what had happened to one of her patients. For some time the relationship between them is subtly and convincingly charted, but this psychological drama later loses conviction. By the end we are left with doubts and questions rather than a convincing resolution. (Original title: *Contre toi*) MS

▷ Kristin Scott Thomas, Pio Marmaï, Jean-Philippe Ecoffey, Marie Sohna-Condé.
▷ *Dir* and *Screenplay* Lola Doillon, *Pro* Saga Blanchard, *Ph* Mathieu Vadepied, *Art Dir* Stéphanie Guitard and Stanislas Reydellet, *Ed* Marie Da Costa, *M* Sandra Moubarak and others, *Cos* Mic Cheminal.

Origami Films/Ce qui me meut/Mars Films etc-Artificial Eye.
81 mins. France. 2010. Rel: 20 July 2012. Cert. 15.

Spectral bride Brenda Cooney haunts amateur ghost hunter Sara Paxton in Ti West's *The Innkeepers*.

Inbred ★★½

This is a true-Brit cheapo comedy horror as four teenage offenders and their two youth workers go to Yorkshire to spend the weekend at an old house near the remote village of Mortlake. The Yorkshire locals are weird and unfriendly, as they always are in Brit chillers, and the violence escalates. This modest but engaging effort is typically low budget (£1.25 million), but it's inventive, amusing and certainly bloody enough to satisfy fright fans. DW

▷ Jo Hartley, Seamus O'Neill, James Doherty, James Burrows, Neil Leiper, Dominic Brunt, Chris Waller.
▷ *Dir* Alex Chandon, *Pro* Margaret Milner, Michael Kraetzer and Yazid Benfeghoul, *Screenplay* Chandon and Paul Shrimpton, *Ph* Ollie Downey, *Pro Des* Melanie Light, *Ed* Oliver Griffin, *M* Dave Andrews, *Cos* Madeleine Millar.

New Flesh Films/Split Second Films-Anchor Bay Entertainment.
90 mins. Germany/UK. 2011. Rel: 21 Sep 2012. Cert. 18.

The Innkeepers ★★★

'A Ghost Story for the Minimum Wage' was one of the tag-lines, and the slow build-up in Ti West's film trades, not just on the part-comic camaraderie between two conspicuously unmotivated hotel clerks, but also the hopelessness of their dead-end situation. In truth, the build-up is just a bit *too* slow, though it's enlivened by a remarkable sound design (Graham Reznick) and some interesting side characters – Kelly McGillis as a sitcom star-turned-psychic and George Riddle's uniquely spooky old man. The setting is a real Connecticut hotel in which West stayed while making *The House of the Devil*. Though *The Innkeepers* is a disappointment after that film, West's retro approach remains bracingly offbeat and intelligent amid the puke-'em-up rank and file of 21st century horror. JR

▶ Sara Paxton, Pat Healy, Kelly McGillis, George Riddle, Lena Dunham, Alison Bartlett, Brenda Cooney.
▶ *Dir, Screenplay* and *Ed* Ti West, *Pro* West, Peter Phok, Derek Curl and Larry Fessenden, *Ph* Eliot Rockett, *Pro Des* Jade Healy, *M* Jeff Grace, *Cos* Elisabeth Vastola.

Dark Sky Films/Glass Eye Pix-Kaleidoscope Film Distribution.
101 mins. USA. 2011. Rel: 8 June 2012. Cert. 15.

Into the Abyss: A Tale of Death, A Tale of Life ★★★★½

Werner Herzog's feature-length documentary about the death penalty is a deeply humane film. It is set in Texas where, heard but not seen, Herzog carries out interviews. He speaks to those who work in jail, to those accused of murder (in particular to Michael James Perry not long before his death sentence was carried out) and to those connected with the victims. Life did not oblige by clarifying all the facts regarding the triple murder for which Perry died, but that's not central. It is Herzog's all-encompassing humanity that makes this film exceptional. MS

▶ With Michael James Perry, Rev. Richard Lopez, Werner Herzog, Fred Allen, Melyssa Burkett.
▶ *Dir* Werner Herzog, *Pro* Erik Nelson, *Ph* Peter Zeitlinger, *Ed* Joe Bini, *M* Mark degli Antoni.

Creative Differences/Skellig Rock/Spring Films/Werner Herzog Film etc-Revolver Entertainment.
107 mins. USA/UK/Germany. 2011. Rel: 30 Mar 2012. Cert. 12A.

On her mettle: Meryl Streep as Margaret Thatcher aka *The Iron Lady*.

Intruders ★½

Clive Owen takes the lead in this initially engaging and cerebral chiller, a tale of two children in different countries, each visited at night by a faceless goon who aims to possess them. It's a horror flick that eventually reveals itself to be psychological rather than supernatural, a switch that induces much grumbling and eye-rolling. Although it's quite stylish and thoughtfully put together, it's not terribly well written and leaves you with the feeling that you have just wasted 100 minutes. MJ

▶ Clive Owen, Carice van Houten, Ella Purnell, Pilar López de Ayala, Daniel Brühl, Mark Wingett, Lolita Chakrabarti, Kerry Fox.
▶ *Dir* Juan Carlos Fresnadillo, *Pro* Belén Atienza, Mercedes Gamero and Enrique López Lavigne, *Screenplay* Nicolás Casariego and Jaime Marques, *Ph* Enrique Chediak, *Pro Des* Alain Bainée, *Ed* Nacho Ruiz Capillas, *M* Roque Baños, *Cos* Tatiana Hernández.

Universal Pictures International/Canal +España/Antena 3 Films/Apaches Entertainment etc-Universal Pictures International.
100 mins. USA/UK/Spain. 2011. Rel: 27 Jan 2012. Cert. 15.

The Iron Lady ★★★½

Abi Morgan's screenplay for Phyllida Lloyd's *The Iron Lady* will obviously not be the last word we shall ever hear on Margaret Thatcher. Many actresses have 'done' her in the past and, if Meryl Streep's version is up there with the best of them, it's a pity she wasn't given a better script. This is biopic lite as it skims through scenes from a politician's life, seen in flashback while Margaret in her dotage talks with her imaginary late husband Denis. It's entertaining enough but hardly does the woman justice. Thatcher was a force to be reckoned with but this film does her down, wallowing in reminiscence and nostalgia. MHD

▶ Meryl Streep, Jim Broadbent, Susan Brown, Iain Glen, Alexandra Roach, Olivia Colman, Nicholas Farrell, John Sessions, Richard E Grant, Anthony Head, Roger Allam, Michael Pennington.
▶ *Dir* Phyllida Lloyd, *Pro* Damian Jones, *Screenplay* Abi Morgan, *Ph* Elliot Davis, *Pro Des* Simon Elliott, *Ed* Justine Wright, *M* Thomas Newman, *Cos* Consolata Boyle.

DJ Films/Pathé/Film 4/UK Film Council/The Weinstein Company/Yuk Films/Canal +/CineCinema/Goldcrest-Pathé International.
105 mins. UK/France. 2011. Rel: 6 Jan 2012. Cert. 12A.

Iron Sky ★★½

Years in the making and partly funded by fans enticed by online previews, *Iron Sky* is a unique Finnish-German-Australian co-production that delivers plenty of bang for the few bucks it cost.

A twisted tale of invading Nazis plotting on the dark side of the Moon, since things went tits-up bunker-wise, it's a cheeky cult comedy adventure with arresting visuals that belie its tiny budget. Though the movie itself is wildly uneven, you have to applaud the filmmakers' moxie. MJ

▶ Julia Dietze, Christopher Kirby, Gotz Otto, Peta Sergeant, Stephanie Paul, Udo Kier.
▶ *Dir* Timo Vuorensola, *Pro* Oliver Damian, Tero Kaukomaa and Samuli Torssonen, *Screenplay* Vuorensola and Michael Kalesniko, from a story by Johanna Sinisalo, based on an original concept by Jarmo Puskala, *Ph* Mika Orasmaa, *Pro Des* Ulrika von Vegesack, *Ed* Suresh Ayyar, *M* Laibach, *Cos* Jake Collier.

New Holland Pictures/Blind Spot Pictures Oy/27 Films Production etc-Revolver Entertainment.
93 mins. Finland/Germany/Australia. 2012. Rel: 23 May 2012. Cert. 15.

Irvine Welsh's Ecstasy ★★

Lloyd (Adam Sinclair) is living the high life on a continuous high – clubbing, women, and effortlessly smuggling drugs from Holland. But when he meets Heather (Kristin Kreuk) he begins to re-evaluate his priorities... Sinclair is a charismatic performer who gains sympathy from the start. But when the action turns into a series of violent acts, the film loses its grip. Rob Heydon's energetic direction lacks the cinematic flair of Danny Boyle's *Trainspotting*. GS

▶ Adam Sinclair, Kristin Kreuk, Billy Boyd, Carlo Rota, Natalie Brown, Stephen McHattie.
▶ *Dir* and *Pro* Rob Heydon, *Screenplay* Heydon and Ben Tucker, with Matt MacLennan and Paul McCafferty, based on *The Undefeated* by Irvine Welsh, *Ph* Brad Hruboska, *Pro Des* Dean A O'Dell, *Ed* Jeremiah Munce, *M* Craig McConnell, *Cos* Lisa D'Arcy.

Ecstasy Film Production Services/Silver Reel/We Are Enchanted Productions- Intandem Films.
99 mins. Canada/UK. 2011. Rel: 20 Apr 2012. Cert. 18.

The Island President ★★★★

Few of today's political figures are truly worthy of admiration, but an exception is Mohamed Nasheed, seen here as President of the Maldives. This film by Jon Shenk is at once a portrait of this man (who took on that role in 2008), an insight into life in those islands in recent decades and a comment on the urgency of tackling climate warming which endangers the Maldives. Sadly, after filming was completed the pressure from rival factions led to Nasheed's resignation in February 2012. See this film and you will recognise what a loss that was. MS

▶ With Mohamed Nasheed.
▶ *Dir* and *Ph* Jon Shenk, *Pro* Richard Berge and Bonni Cohen, *Ed* Pedro Kos.

Afterimage Public Media/Actual Films/Independent Television Service/Impact Partners etc-Dogwoof.
101 mins. USA/Germany. 2011. Rel: 30 Mar 2012. Cert. PG.

Jack and Jill ★

Adam Sandler picked a real dud here. He then co-wrote it and insisted on playing both title characters, identical siblings Jack and Jill. LA

Over the moon: A Nazi spaceship prepares for invasion in Timo Vuorensola's audacious *Iron Sky*.

advertising executive Jack hates both Thanksgiving and his visiting twin Jill, whose coarse habits always ruin the family holiday. The comedy of identity just has no point here, except that we know Sandler is doubling up. What is surprising is Al Pacino playing a version of himself, which involves getting the hots for Jill while being enticed into doing a commercial for a Dunkin Donuts drink called the Dunkicino – as if! Let's hope *Jack and Jill* goes down the hill to oblivion; I couldn't stomach *Jack and Jill 2* at any price. MHD

▶ Adam Sandler, Katie Holmes, Al Pacino, Eugenio Derbez, Dennis Dugan, Tim Meadows, Nick Swardson.
▶ *Dir* Dennis Dugan, *Pro* Adam Sandler, Todd Garner and Jack Giarraputo, *Screenplay* Sandler and Steve Koren, from a story by Ben Zook, *Ph* Dean Cundey, *Pro Des* Perry Andelin Blake, *Ed* Tom Costain, *M* Rupert Gregson-Williams and Waddy Wachtel, *Cos* Ellen Lutter.

Columbia Pictures/Broken Road/Happy Madison-Sony Pictures Releasing.
91 mins. USA. 2011. Rel: 3 Feb 2012. Cert. PG.

Jackpot ★★½

In some quarters this Norwegian thriller has been described as *Jo Nesbø's Jackpot* in the hope that it will duplicate the success of the Swedish films of Stig Larsson's Millennium Trilogy. But, unlike the able *Headhunters* [qv], this tale of killings consequent on a huge winning bet on a soccer match plays out as unimaginative black farce and is often silly. It needed the Coen brothers to make it work. (Original title: *Arme Riddere*) MS

▶ Kyrre Hellum, Mads Ousdal, Henrik Mestad, Arthur Berning, Lena Kristin Ellingsen.
▶ *Dir* and *Screenplay* (from a story by Jo Nesbø) Magnus Martens, *Pro* Martin Sundland and Are

Heidenstrøm, *Ph* Trond Høines, *Pro Des* Lina Nordqvist, *Ed* Jon Endre Mørk, *M* Magnus Beite, *Cos* Gabriella Ekman.

Fantefilm Fiksjon A/S/Film i Väst/Aschehoug etc-Metrodome Distribution.
86 mins. Norway/Denmark/Sweden. 2011. Rel: 10 Aug 2012. Cert. 15.

Jack Reacher ★★★

The hero of Lee Child's thrillers arrives on screen to investigate the guilt or innocence of a man arrested as the sniper who has killed five people. The film blends modern-day action with elements not far removed from the film noir world of private eyes, and the opening scenes are excellent. If the critical disdain for the film is understandable (albeit excessive), that's because Tom Cruise and Rosamund Pike are not well cast, and because the movie is much inferior to *The Usual Suspects* (1995), which, written by Christopher McQuarrie, set a standard he has not been able to match. MS

▶ Tom Cruise, Rosamund Pike, Richard Jenkins, Werner Herzog, Robert Duvall, David Oyelowo.
▶ *Dir* and *Screenplay* (from the novel *One Shot* by Lee Child) Christopher McQuarrie, *Pro* Tom Cruise, Don Granger and others, *Ph* Caleb Deschanel, *Pro Des* Jim Bissell, *Ed* Kevin Stitt, *M* Joe Kraemer, *Cos* Susan Matheson.

Paramount Pictures/Skydance Productions etc-Paramount.
130 mins. USA. 2012. Rel: 26 Dec 2012. Cert. 12A.

Jason Becker: Not Dead Yet ★★★★

How much you enjoy the music in this documentary featuring the singer-guitarist Jason Becker depends on how you respond to a style

Rain men: Tom Cruise punches above his weight as the humongous *Jack Reacher*. Jai Courtney (left) dares to confront him.

related to heavy metal and post-punk rock. But, if the on-screen acclaim for him as a genius is excessive, his extraordinary personal story is admirably told. As his career was taking off he became paralysed by a disease quickly expected to be fatal. That was in 1989 and his life since then has been heroic and uplifting. MS

▶ With Jason Becker, Steve Vai, Marty Friedman.
▶ *Dir* and *Pro* Jesse Vile, *Ph* Carl Burke, *Ed* Gideon Gold, *M* Michael Lee Firkins.
Opus Pocus Films-Dogwoof.
87 mins. USA. 2012. Rel: 16 Nov 2012. Cert. 15.

J. Edgar ★★★½

Previously the subject of Larry Cohen's interesting but uneven 1977 movie *The Private Files of J Edgar Hoover*, this new look at the infamous head of the FBI is no less variable. Director Clint Eastwood gets fine performances from Leonardo DiCaprio in the title role and from Judi Dench as Hoover's mother, but the old age make-up is distracting. In any case Dustin Lance Black's screenplay, which tells much of the story through flashbacks, makes for a shapeless piece and one which is less clear-cut and insightful than one might reasonably expect. MS

▶ Leonardo DiCaprio, Naomi Watts, Armie Hammer, Judi Dench, Josh Lucas.
▶ *Dir* and *M* Clint Eastwood, *Pro* Eastwood, Brian Grazer and Robert Loren, *Screenplay* Dustin Lance Black, *Ph* Tom Stern, *Pro Des* James J Murakami, *Ed* Joel Cox and Gary D Roach, *Cos* Deborah Hopper.
Warner Bros. Pictures/Imagine Entertainment/a Malpaso production-Warner Bros.
137 mins. USA. 2011. Rel: 20 Jan 2012. Cert. 15.

Jeff, Who Lives at Home ★★★

In *Cyrus* (2010) the 'Mumblecore' team of Jay and Mark Duplass were largely successful in adapting their indie style into something more mainstream. But, despite some helpful acting, this attempt to repeat the trick fails. That's down to their screenplay about two brothers with contrasted lifestyles. The aim is to be touching as well as humorous, but the gear changes are decidedly uneasy and the longer it goes on the sillier this initially engaging piece becomes. MS

▶ Jason Segal, Ed Helms, Judy Greer, Susan Sarandon, Rae Dawn Chong, Steve Zissis.
▶ *Dir* and *Screenplay* Jay and Mark Duplass, *Pro* Lianne Halfon, Russell Smith and Jason Reitman, *Ph* Jas Shelton, *Pro Des* Chris Spellman, *Ed* Jay Deuby, *M* Michael Andrews, *Cos* Meagan McLaughlin.
Paramount Vantage/Indian Paintbrush/a Right of Way production/Mr. Mudd-Paramount.
83 mins. USA. 2011. Rel: 11 May 2012. Cert. 15.

John Carter 3D ★★★★

A battle-weary Confederate captain (Taylor Kitsch) astral-projects into the middle of a

Thank you, Edgar Hoover: Leonardo DiCaprio plays the legendary director of the FBI in Clint Eastwood's *J. Edgar*.

Jungle fever: Michael Caine and Luis Guzmán in Brad Peyton's *Journey 2: The Mysterious Island.*

Martian civil war in this ingenious and irresistible adaptation of the enduring Edgar Rice Burroughs tale. Ineptly promoted, it died at the box-office. Regardless, *John Carter* has heart and enthusiasm, excitement and charm. The live-action feature debut of Pixar veteran Andrew Stanton, it's a dazzling fantasy epic with impossible walking cities, magnificent flying ships, believable alien species of every shape and size, and sweeping vistas reminiscent of vintage Hollywood historicals. MJ

❯ Taylor Kitsch, Lynn Collins, Samantha Morton, Mark Strong, Ciarán Hinds, Dominic West, James Purefoy, Willem Dafoe.
❯ *Dir* Andrew Stanton, *Pro* Jim Morris, Colin Wilson and Lindsey Collins, *Screenplay* Stanton, Mark Andrews and Michael Chabon, based on the story *A Princess of Mars* by Edgar Rice Burroughs, *Ph* Daniel Mindel, *Pro Des* Nathan Crowley, *Ed* Eric Zumbrunnen, *M* Michael Giacchino, *Cos* Mayes C Rubeo.
Disney-Buena Vista Distribution.
132 mins. USA. 2012. Rel: 9 Mar 2012. Cert. 12A.

Journey 2: The Mysterious Island ★★★

Seventeen-year-old Sean Anderson (Josh Hutcherson) is determined to discover a mysterious island after he receives a coded distress signal. Unable to stop him from going, Sean's new stepfather Hank (Dwayne Johnson) decides to join him. The early scenes when they're trying to break the code at breakneck speed are laughable, but once they reach the South Pacific island this develops into an exciting adventure with decent 3D effects. GS

❯ Dwayne Johnson, Michael Caine, Josh Hutcherson, Luis Guzmán, Vanessa Hudgens, Kristin Davis.
❯ *Dir* Brad Peyton, *Pro* Tripp Vinson, Charlotte Huggins and Beau Flynn, *Screenplay* Brian Gunn and Mark Gunn, from a story by them and Richard Outten, based on a novel by Jules Verne, *Ph* David Tattersall, *Pro Des* Bill Boes, *Ed* David Rennie, *M* Andrew Lockington, *Cos* Denise Wingate.
New Line Cinema/Contrafilm-Warner Bros.
94 mins. USA. 2012. Rel: 3 Feb 2012. Cert. PG.

The Joy of Six ★★★★

A compilation of six short films. Douglas Hart's unpredictable, well-acted *Long Distance Information* features Peter Mullan as a father on the phone to his son on Christmas Day. Will Jewell's stylish *Man in Fear* follows a paranoid young man (Luke Treadaway) desperate to escape from a certain calamity. Writer-director Matthew Holness stars in *A Gun for George*, a clever pastiche of 1970s cop movies. Romola Garai's assured directorial debut, *Scrubber*, features Amanda Hale as a single mother looking for a babysitter. Dan Sully's intriguing *The Ellington Kid* has the titular character finding refuge in a kebab shop after being stabbed. Judi Dench stars in Chris Foggin's entertaining *Friend Request Pending* as Mary, searching for a date on a social network. Well worth seeing. GS

❯ With Luke Treadaway, Judi Dench, Tim Healy, Peter Mullan, Amanda Hale, Tom Hiddleston, Philip Jackson, Matthew Holness, Hammid Animashaun, Durassie Kiangangu, Roger Ashton-Griffiths, Edward Halstead, Alan Tripney, Steven Robertson etc.
❯ *Dir* Douglas Hart, Romola Garai, Will Jewell,

Matthew Holness, Dan Sully, Chris Foggin, *Pro* Ohna Falby and Beth Montague, Daniel Nixon, Ally Gipps, Romola Garai and Shona Kerr, Rob Watson, Chris Croucher, *Screenplays* Douglas Hart, Will Jewell, Matthew Holness, Romola Garai, Dan Sully, Chris Croucher, *Ph* Stuart Bentley, Dominic Jones, David Rom, Kate Reid, Christopher Sabogal, Simon Tindall, *Pro Des* Louise Corcoran, Luis San Martin, Alison Butler, Caroline Collinge, Anna Rhodes, Chris Croucher, *Ed* Dan Robinson, David Wigram, Nick Fenton, Alastair Reid, Dan Sully, Chris & Christopher Ranson, *M* Gruff Rhys, Matthew Holness, Stuart Earl, Nic Nell, Michael Ferguson, *Cos* Emma Rees, Rob Nicholls, Hannah Wood.

Soda Pictures.
70 mins. UK. 2012. Rel: 9 Nov 2012. No Cert.

Joyful Noise ★½

The Divinity Church Choir in the small town of Pacashau, Georgia is determined to win the National Joyful Noise Competition but the rivalry between its new director Vi Rose Hill (Queen Latifah) and the old-fashioned traditionalist GG Sparrow (Dolly Parton) threatens to put a stop to their dream. To call this manipulative film predictable is a huge understatement; even the strong presence of its leading ladies can't rescue it. A lot of talent is wasted here. GS

▶ Queen Latifah, Dolly Parton, Keke Palmer, Jeremy Jordan, Courtney B Vance, Kris Kristofferson.
▶ *Dir* and *Screenplay* Todd Graff, *Pro* Joseph Farrell, Catherine Paura, Michael G Nathanson, Andrew

A Kosove and Broderick Johnson, *Ph* David Boyd, *Pro Des* Jeff Knipp, *Ed* Kathryn Himoff, *M* Mervyn Warren, *Cos* Tom Broecker.

Farrell Paura Productions/Gospel Truth Pictures/Alcon Entertainment/O N C Entertainment-Warner Bros Pictures.
118 mins. USA. 2012. Rel: 29 June 2012. Cert. PG.

Juan of the Dead ★★★

A cheeky take on the zomcom with a dash of social and political subtext, this sly Cuban effort sees 50-something slacker Juan (Alexis Díaz de Villegas) trying to cash in on the zombie apocalypse. A rude, irreverent satire with colourful characters and a bonkers screenplay, though neither scary nor even tense, it's a winning effort with some memorable moments and a great running joke about accidental harpooning. Held together by a grindhouse-style jazz score and a 'never say die' attitude, it's a flawed but foolishly fun low-budget bloodfest. (Original title: *Juan de los muertos*) MJ

▶ Alexis Díaz de Villegas, Jorge Molina, Andrea Duro, Andros Perugorria, Jazz Vilá.
▶ *Dir* and *Screenplay* Alejandro Brugués, *Pro* Gervesio Iglesias and Inti Herrera, *Ph* Carles Guzi, *Art Dir* Derubin Jácome, *Ed* Mercedes Cantero, *M* Julio de la Rosa, *Cos* Esther Vaquero.

La Zanfoña Producciones/Producciones de la 5ta Avenida-Metrodome Distribution.
92 mins. Spain/Cuba. 2011. Rel: 4 May 2012. Cert. 15.

Body Heap: Alexis Díaz de Villegas in Alejandro Brugués' *Juan of the Dead.*

Katy Perry: Part of Me 3D ★★★

A sunny, snappy concert movie with an access-all-areas backstage pass, this includes candid chats with Perry's friends and family, and also the girl herself, a seemingly genuine and likable sort who belts out her hits in a procession of wacky, colourful costumes. It also throws bones of positive affirmation to the freaks and geeks who love her. MJ

▶ Katy Perry, Adam Marcello, Casey Hopper, Patrick Matera, Max Hart, Joshua Moreau, Adele, Lady Gaga, Jessie J, Rihanna.
▶ *Dir* Dan Cutforth and Jane Lipsitz, *Pro* Perry, David Geffen, Brian Grazer, Bradford Cobb, Ron Howard, Martin Kirkup, Ted Kenney, Steven Jensen and Emer Patten, *Ph* Shanra Kehl, *Pro Des* Baz Halpin, *Ed* Scott Richter, Scott Evans and Brian Lazarte, *M* Deborah Lurie, *Cos* Johnny Wujek.

Insurge Pictures/MTV Films/Perry Productions/ Imagine Entertainment/AEG Live/EMI Music/Pulse Films/Splinter Films/Magical Elves Productions-Paramount Pictures International.
97 mins. USA. 2012. Rel: 5 July 2012. Cert. PG.

Keep the Lights On ★★★★

This is a gay film that tries its hardest to be realistic in its portrayal of the relationship between two men over a period of ten years. Danish Erik meets Paul in New York and what begins as a casual affair develops into something overwhelming. Paul is ostensibly straight and, no doubt on account of his confusion, gets hooked on drugs, a situation that starts to break up the relationship. The film is based loosely on a real-life situation experienced by director Ira Sachs, although the details are quite different. Unflinchingly good performances by Thure Lindhardt and Zachary Booth enhance an unexpectedly sharp look at gay relationships. MHD

▶ Thure Lindhardt, Zachary Booth, Marilyn Neimark, Julianne Nicholson, Souleymane Sy

Sex in the city: Thure Lindhardt and Zachary Booth in Ira Sachs' Keep the Lights On.

Savane, Paprika Steen, Sebastian La Cause.
▶ *Dir* Ira Sachs, *Pro* Sachs, Lucas Joaquin and Marie Therese Guirgis, *Screenplay* Sachs and Mauricio Zacharias, *Ph* Thimios Bakatakis, *Pro Des* Amy Williams, *Ed* Affonso Gonçalves, *M* Arthur Russell, *Cos* Elisabeth Vastola.

Alarum Pictures/Tiny Dancer Films/Parts and Labor-Peccadillo Pictures.
101 mins. USA. 2012. Rel: 2 Nov 2012. Cert. 18.

Keith Lemon The Film ★

Leigh Francis is the culprit here, starring as his alter ego Keith Lemon, who takes his 'securipole' invention to a convention in London. Meanwhile his girlfriend (Laura Aikman) finds she's in the family way. Soon no one wants the securipole and a million of the little blighters have arrived back home. There's just one thing for it. Lemon has to appear on David Hasselhoff's TV chat show. A ghastly train wreck of a comedy, with no wit, fun or laughs in sight. Deservedly, one of the internet 100 worst films of all time. DW

▶ Leigh Francis, Laura Aikman, Verne Troyer, Kelly Brook, Kevin Bishop, Fearne Cotton, David Hasselhoff, Holly Willoughby.
▶ *Dir* Paul Angunawela, *Pro* Mark Huffan and Aidan Elliott, *Screenplay* Angunawela and Leigh Francis, *Ph* Julian Court, *Pro Des* Jason Carlin and Tom McCullagh, *Ed* Peter Boyle, *M* Mark D Todd, *Cos* Hazel Webb-Crozier.

Generator Entertainment/Molinaire Studio-Lionsgate.
85 mins. UK. 2012. Rel: 24 Aug 2012. Cert. 15.

Keyhole ★★★

Love him or hate him, Guy Maddin is his own man. This film of his, mainly shot in black and white and set inside a house, fuses echoes of Greek tragedy (the central character is named Ulysses) with a tale of gangster types and ghosts. Early cinema styles are evoked here, but what Maddin wants to say through all the poetic symbolism and metaphor remains uncertain. If you dislike avant-garde cinema you will hate this but, as his skilful building of atmosphere confirms, Maddin is the real thing for those who can take it. MS

▶ Jason Patric, Isabella Rossellini, Udo Kier, Brooke Palsson, David Wontner, Louis Negin.
▶ *Dir* Guy Maddin, *Pro* Jody Shapiro and Jean du Toit, *Screenplay* George Toles and Maddin, *Ph* Ben Kasulke, *Pro Des* Ricardo Alms, *Ed* John Gurdebeke, *Cos* Heather Neale.

Entertainment One/Telefilm Canada/Manitoba Film & Music etc-Soda Pictures.
94 mins. Canada/USA. 2011. Rel: 14 Sep 2012. Cert. 12A.

Khodorkovsky ★★★½

Cyril Tuschi spent five years making this

documentary study of the Russian capitalist entrepreneur who became a thorn in the side of President Putin. Accused of fraud, embezzlement and tax evasion, Mikhail Khodorkovsky found himself in a Siberian gulag, but this film shows just how absurd the charges were. It's arguably over-long and some stylisation (such as the use of animation in recreated scenes) seems inappropriate, but the material is absorbing. MS

▶ With Mikhail Khodorkovsky, Pavel Khodorkovsky, Marina Khodorkovskaya, Cyril Tuschi.
▶ *Dir*, *Pro* and *Ph* Cyril Tuschi, *Ed* Salome Machaidze and Tuschi, *M* Arvo Pärt.

Rezo Films (Paris)/Fabfilm (Berlin)/a Lala Films production etc-Trinity Filmed Entertainment.
117 mins. Germany. 2011. Rel: 2 Mar 2012. Cert. 12A.

The Kid with a Bike ★★★★

Twelve-year-old Cyril was parked in a children's home for a month but his father never returned. The boy tries to contact him but to no avail. Accustomed to a lonely life, he does, however, solicit friendship from an older man, perhaps an alternative father figure, but keeps his distance from Samantha, a local hairdresser who wishes to adopt him. Meanwhile he rides his eponymous bicycle, if only to escape the adult world. Thomas Doret gives an incredible performance as the mischievous Cyril, reminding one of another free spirit 50-odd years ago, Antoine Doinel in *Les quatre cents coups*. The Dardenne brothers have a

winner in this one. (Original title: *Le Gamin au vélo*) MHD

▶ Thomas Doret, Cécile De France, Jérémie Renier, Egon Di Mateo, Fabrizio Rongione, Olivier Gourmet.
▶ *Dir* and *Screenplay* Jean-Pierre Dardenne and Luc Dardenne, *Pro* J-P & L Dardenne and Denis Freyd, *Ph* Alain Marcoen, *Pro Des* Igor Gabriel, *Ed* Marie-Hélène Dozo, *Cos* Maíra Ramedhan-Levi.

Les Films du Fleuve/France 2 Cinéma/ Belgacom/ Eurimages/Canal +/CinéCinéma/France Television/Wild Bunch etc-Artificial Eye.
87 mins. Belgium/Italy/France. 2011. Rel: 23 Mar 2012. Cert. 12A.

Killer Joe ★★★½

Having reached the grand old age of 72, William Friedkin, director of *The Exorcist*, has decided to show us that he can still shock. It's a compelling piece – if taken as a very black comedy – although the much-touted violence is not that realistic: there's a lot of blood, sound and fury but teeth and skin are spared. It's the controlled violence of the performances that is the thing, from the Baby Doll innocence of Juno Temple's Dottie to the almost comic defensiveness of Thomas Haden Church's hopelessly inept paterfamilias. However, it's Matthew McConaughey as Killer Joe who holds the suspense in place. JC-W

▶ Matthew McConaughey, Emile Hirsch, Juno Temple, Gina Gershon, Thomas Haden Church, Marc Macaulay.

No picnic: Thomas Doret and Cécile de France share a rare moment of harmony in Jean-Pierre Dardenne and Luc Dardenne's *The Kid with a Bike*, winner of the Grand Prix at Cannes.

Stir crazy:
A scene from
Marius Holst's
*The King of Devil's
Island*, based on
true events.

▶ *Dir* William Friedkin, *Pro* Nicolas Chartier and Scott Einbinder, *Screenplay* Tracy Letts, from his play, *Ph* Caleb Deschanel, *Pro Des* Franco-Giacomo Carbone, *Ed* Darrin Navarro, *M* Tyler Bates, *Cos* Peggy A. Schnitzer.

**Voltage Pictures/Picture Perfect/Worldview Entertainment/ANA Media- Entertainment One.
102 mins. USA. 2011. Rel: 29 June 2012. Cert. 18.**

Killing Them Softly ★★★★

Adapting a novel by George V Higgins, Andrew Dominik here comes up with something very unusual, a comment on modern American politics suggesting a parallel between that world and the world of mobsters. This aspect is almost over-emphasised, but it gives originality to a tale of minor crooks, out of their depth, whose actions lead to mayhem. The film is exceedingly violent, but the great cast is not to be faulted and Dominik's direction is masterly. MS

▶ Brad Pitt, Scoot McNairy, Ben Mendelsohn, Richard Jenkins, James Gandolfini, Ray Liotta.
▶ *Dir* and *Screenplay* (based on the novel *Cogan's Trade* by George V Higgins) Andrew Dominik, *Pro* Brad Pitt, Dede Gardner and others, *Ph* Greig Fraser, *Pro Des* and *Cos* Patricia Norris, *Ed* Brian A Kates, *M* Marc Streitenfeld.

**TWC/Inferno/a Plan B Entertainment production/a Chockstone Pictures production etc-Entertainment Film Distributors Ltd.
97 mins. USA. 2012. Rel: 21 Sep 2012. Cert. 18.**

The King of Devil's Island
★★★★★

Norway, 1915: the setting is Bastøy, a remote island prison for young offenders. When naval rating and murder suspect Erling (Benjamin Helstad) is sent there, he refuses to obey the draconian rules of prison director Håkon (Stellan Skarsgård), who, believing that he is obeying the will of God, ignores the abusive injustices wreaked by his staff. As Erling increasingly gains the respect of his fellow inmates, a rebellion ensues and the viciousness of overseer Braaten (Kristoffer Joner) knows no bounds. This is a bleak but brilliant portrait of the abuse of authority and punishment from director Marius Holst that cannot fail to evoke an emotional reaction. A really fine piece of film-making. (Original title: *Kongen av Bastøy*) MHD

▶ Stellan Skarsgård, Benjamin Helstad, Trond Nilssen Morten Løvstad, Kristoffer Joner, Daniel Bern.
▶ *Dir* Marius Holst, *Pro* Karin Julsrud, *Screenplay* Dennis Magnusson and Eric Schmid, from a story by Mette M Bølstad and Lars Saabye Christensen, *Ph* John Andreas Andersen, *Pro Des* Janusz Sosnowski, *Ed* Michal Leszczylowski, *M* Johan Söderqvist, *Cos* Katja Watkins.

**Opus Film/MACT Productions/St Paul Film/4 ½ Film-Arrow Films.
116 mins. Norway. 2010. Rel: 29 June 2012. Cert. 12A.**

The Knot ★

Alexandra (Talulah Riley) and Jeremy (Matthew McNulty) are getting married but their loathsome friends are determined to ruin their wedding day with their endless pranks. This vulgar gross-out comedy is a strong contender for the worst film of the year – and the less said about Noel Clarke's co-authored script and his smug performance the better. Avoid! GS

▶ Noel Clarke, Mena Suvari, Matthew McNulty, Talulah Riley, Jason Maza, Susannah Fielding, Davie Fairbanks, Geoff Carino, Liza Sadovy.
▶ *Dir* Jesse Lawrence, *Pro* Noel Clarke, Jason Maza, Roslyn Hill, Enrico Tessarin and Davie Fairbanks, *Screenplay* Clarke, Fairbanks and Geoff Carino, *Ph* Trevor Forrest, *Pro Des* Paul Burns, *Ed* Tom Hemmings, *M* Adam Lewis, *Cos* Andy Blake.

Unstoppable Entertainment/Beactive Entertainment/New Treatment-Universal Pictures.
92 mins. UK. 2012. Rel: 5 Oct 2012. Cert. 15.

Kosmos ★★★★½

This extraordinary Turkish film, an astonishing work of art, marks a huge step forward for Reha Erdem who here finds material ideally suited to his talents. Kosmos is the name adopted by an outsider who arrives at a border town where he seems capable of performing miracles. He may be a thief, but he also suggests a Christ figure or some kind of holy fool. However, the townsfolk turn against him. This is a weird, stylised film which, whether you find it pro-religion or the reverse, is often Bressonian in character. At times it may become too odd, but it's haunting to a degree. MS

▶ Sermet Yesil, Türkü Turan, Hakan Altuntas, Sabahat Doganyilmaz, Korel Kubilay.
▶ *Dir, Screenplay* and *Ed* Reha Erdem, *Pro* and *Art Dir* Ömer Atay, *Ph* Florent Herry, *Cos* Mehtap Tunay.

An Atlantik Film, Imaj, Kaboal Pictures, Hundek Isik co-production etc-Verve Pictures Ltd.
122 mins. Turkey/Bulgaria. 2009. Rel: 15 June 2012. Cert. 12A.

Last Flight to Abuja ★★★

Allegedly based on a real Nigerian air disaster from which there were no survivors, and premiered a week after a massive crash over Lagos took 150 passengers to their deaths, this film takes us back to those group jeopardy movies of the 1970s, so lovingly parodied in the *Airplane!* series. Obi Emelonye's blockbuster has been enormously successful in Nigeria, beating *The Dark Knight Rises* at the box-office, so could herald a new beginning for the burgeoning Nigerian film industry. PL

▶ Omotola Jalde-Ekeinde, Hakeem Kae-Kazim,

Jim Iyke, Anthony Monjaro, Uru Eke.
▶ *Dir* Obi Emelonye, *Pro* Emelonye and Charles Thompson, *Screenplay* Emelonye, Amaka Obi-Emelonye and Tunde Babalola, *Ph* James M. Costello, *Art Dir* Sango B'Song, *Ed* Ben Nugent, *M* Luke Corradine, *Cos* Precious Akomas.

Nollywood Film Factory.
81 mins. Nigeria/UK. 2012. Rel: 29 June 2012. Cert. 12A.

The Last Projectionist ★★★★★

The Electric in Birmingham is the oldest working cinema in Britain. It opened in 1909 and in its time has shown everything from silent movies to adult sex films. It fell into disrepair but the present owner, Thomas Lawes, who also directed this documentary, brought it back to working life in 2004. Here he interviews people associated with the cinema, including an old lady who remembers the Electric in 1917, and former cinema staff who bemoan the introduction of digital technology. The film also covers many of the other independent cinemas around the country, such as the splendid Rex, Berkhamsted and the Phoenix, East Finchley. MHD

▶ With John Brockington, Les Castree, Paul Curtin, Phil Fawke, Graham Lee and Thomas Lawes.
▶ *Dir, Pro, Ph, Ed* and *M* Thomas Lawes.

Electric Flix-E. C. Birmingham Ltd.
82 mins. UK. 2011. Rel: 22 June 2012. Cert. 12A.

Late September ★

There's a marionette that gives a first-class account of itself. And that's probably the only good thing one can say about this padded-out home movie. Eight people celebrate Ken's 65th birthday over the space of a weekend. Judging by the accents the location is England, although we are not even privy to an exterior shot of the house. This is the

Miraculous offender: Sermet Yesil in Reha Erdem's curious *Kosmos*.

sort of party in which very little happens, there's no food and a lot of banal (improvised) dialogue. One prays for a hint of Mike Leigh, but the plot – and acting – is not up to it. JC-W

▶ Anna Mottram, Richard Vanstone, Bob Goody.
▶ *Dir, Pro* and *Screenplay* Jon Sanders, *Ph* Jeff Baynes, *Ed* Nse Asuquo, *M* Douglas Finch.
Jon Sanders Films/Oxymoron Films-Late September. 87 mins. UK. 2012. Rel: 15 June 2012. Cert. 15.

Laurence Anyways ★★★

Talented young filmmaker Xavier Dolan is here too self-indulgent both as to length and in the use of self-conscious stylisation. That's a pity because Melvil Poupaud is outstanding as Laurence who disturbs his girlfriend in 1990s Montreal by revealing that he believes himself to be a woman trapped in a male body. This unsensational treatment of a trans-sexual's crisis plays so well at its best that it is infuriating to find it trapped within this film's grandiosity. MS

▶ Melvil Poupaud, Suzanne Clément, Nathalie Baye, Monia Chokri, Yves Jacques.
▶ *Dir, Screenplay* and *Ed* Xavier Dolan, *Pro* Lyse Lafontaine and Carole Mondello, *Ph* Yves Bélanger, *Art Dir* Colombe Raby, *M* Noia, *Cos* Dolan and François Barbeau.
Lyla Films/MK2/Arte France Cinéma etc-Network Releasing. 168 mins. Canada/France. 2012. Rel: 30 Nov 2012. Cert. 15.

Lawless ★★★★

Personally I don't care for the macho violence indulged in here, but John Hillcoat's film is directed with panache and features great performances. Mia Wasikowska is wonderful as ever and Guy Pearce's studiedly camp villain works well, but everybody is good. As a drama set in Prohibition America involving three brothers selling illegal liquor and refusing to be intimidated (or bribed) by the law, it's not exactly fresh-minted, but it's very good of its kind. MS

▶ Shia LaBeouf, Tom Hardy, Gary Oldman, Jessica Chastain, Mia Wasikowska, Guy Pearce.
▶ *Dir* John Hillcoat, *Pro* Douglas Wick, Lucy Fisher and others, *Screenplay* Nick Cave, from the book *The Wettest County in the World* by Matt Bondurant, *Ph* Benoît Delhomme, *Art Dir* Gershon Ginsburg, *Ed* Dylan Tichenor, *M* Cave and Warren Ellis, *Cos* Margot Wilson.
The Weinstein Company/Yuk Films/Benaroya Pictures/ Annapurna Pictures etc-Momentum Pictures. 116 mins. USA. 2011. Rel: 7 Sep 2012. Cert. 18.

Lawrence of Belgravia ★★★

Lawrence – here just Lawrence, but actually one Mr Hayward – was the guitarist and singer-songwriter responsible for the 1980s and '90s bands Felt and Denim; he also had a brief fling with something called Go Kart Mozart. Never overly successful, Lawrence kept at it and claimed he'd like to be the first pop pensioner, but then

Moonshine wars: Shia LaBeouf (running, right) in John Hillcoat's Lawless, formerly known as The Wettest County in the World.

the likes of Cliff and Elton must have already beaten him to it. For those who 'know' this documentary will have some fascination. Non-believers may be totally flummoxed. PL

▷ With Lawrence [Hayward].
▷ Dir, Pho and Ed Paul Kelly.
Heavenly Films-Heavenly Films.
86 mins. UK 2011. Rel: 2 May 2012. No Cert.

Lay the Favourite ★★★

One of my favourite actresses, Rebecca Hall, is astonishing here. The film itself, dealing with gamblers in Las Vegas, is nothing special (at times it's nearly *Bells Are Ringing* without the music), but Hall's comic performance as a girl caught up in this world as she seeks a better life is extraordinary. We knew she was wonderful, but who would have guessed that she could play a role like this, a seemingly dumb blonde of some intelligence who, supplying the film with its energy, reminds us of the heyday of Judy Holliday! MS

▷ Bruce Willis, Rebecca Hall, Catherine Zeta-Jones, Joshua Jackson, Joel Murray.
▷ Dir Stephen Frears, Pro Anthony Bregman, Paul Trijbits and others, Screenplay DV DeVicentis, from the book *Lay the Favorite: A Memoir of Gambling* by Beth Raymer, Ph Michael McDonough, Pro Des Dan Davis, Ed Mick Audsley, M James Seymour Brett, Cos Christopher Peterson.
A Likely Story-Emmett /Furla Films production/Wild Bunch/A Ruby Films production etc-E1 Films.
94 mins. USA/France/UK. 2012. Rel: 22 June 2012. Cert. 15.

Le Havre ★★★½

Working in France, Finland's Aki Kaurismäki comes up with a story about inhabitants of Le Havre helping illegal immigrants sought by the local police as they pass through. It's a love letter to the French cinema of yesteryear, but it's too stylised to work well as credible drama and less comic than I had expected. As for the image of hope at the end, it is far closer to schmaltz than one would expect from a filmmaker who admires Ozu! Nevertheless the acting is good and there is real warmth here. MS

▷ André Wilms, Kati Outinen, Jean-Pierre Darroussin, Evelyne Didi, Blondin Miguel, Jean-Pierre Léaud, Pierre Etaix, Laika.
▷ Dir and Screenplay Aki Kaurismäki, Pro Kaurismäki, Fabienne Vonier and Reinhard Brundig, Ph Timo Salminen, Art Dir Wouter Zoon, Ed Timo Linnasalo, Cos Fred Cambier.
Sputnik Oy/Pyramide Productions/Pandora Film/ARTE France Cinéma etc-Artificial Eye.
93 mins. Finland/France/Germany/Norway. 2011. Rel: 6 Apr 2012. Cert. PG.

Strange bedfellows: Pierre Étaix and Kati Outinen in Aki Kaurismäki's *Le Havre*.

Leave It on the Floor ★★½

This African-American musical takes place in downtown LA and follows the adventures of Brad (Ephraim Sykes), a homeless young man who finds refuge in the House of Eminence after his homophobic mother throws him out. In this exotic environment, ruled by the fiery diva Queen Latina (Miss Barbie-Q), Brad is welcomed with open arms by a group of dancers and artists. The energy of this colourful musical is admirable and almost makes you forget the clichéd dialogue and stereotypical characters. GS

▷ Ephraim Sykes, Andre Myers, Philip Evelyn, Miss Barbie-Q, Cameron Koa, James Alsop.
▷ Dir Sheldon Larry, Pro Larry, Glenn Gaylord and Gabriel Blanco, Screenplay Gaylord, Ph Tom Camarda, Pro Des Giao-Chau Ly, Ed Charles Bornstein, M Kimberly Burse, Cos Hunter Wells, Lee Frank Perez and Marsian.
Leave It On the Floor/Sheldon Larry Productions Inc-Peccadillo Pictures.
105 mins. Canada/USA. 2011. Rel: 3 Aug 2012. Cert. 15.

Let the Bullets Fly ★★

This superbly produced Chinese 'Western' boasts spectacular set-pieces but unfortunately its narrative lacks cohesion and clarity. The story takes place in 1920 and follows the adventures of Zhang (Wen Jiang), a notorious bandit who poses as the new mayor of Goose Town and inevitably comes into conflict with warlord Huang (Yun-Fat Chow). The designs are amazing and the actors seem to have a lot of fun in this over-the-top comedy. But, sadly, it fails to engage. (Original title: *Rang zidan fei*) GS

▷ Yun-Fat Chow, Kun Chen, Xiaogang Feng, Carina Lau, Wen Jiang, You Ge.
▷ Dir Wen Jiang, Pro Jiang, Albert Lee, Hai Cheng

Zhao, Homber Yin and Barbie Tung, *Screenplay* Jiang, Sujin Zhu, Xiao Wei, Ping Shu, Bukong Li and Junli Guo, *Ph* Fei Zhao, *Pro Des* Eddie Wong, Qing Hua Yu and Yi Guang Gao, *Ed* Wen Jiang and Wei Jie Cao, *M* Joe Hisaishi, *Cos* William Chang.

Emperor Motion Pictures/China Film Group/Beijing Bu Yi Le Hu Film Company-Kaleidoscope Film Distributors. 132 mins. China/Hong Kong. 2010. Rel: 17 Aug 2012. Cert. 15.

Liberal Arts ★★★½

Josh Radnor, writer and co-director as well as star, here aims to make a romcom to appeal to an intelligent audience. He plays a man in his thirties who is attracted to a student (the excellent Elizabeth Olsen) when returning to his old college for a teacher's retirement. Not everything works – it's much less sure-footed than, say, Todd Solondz at his best – but it's a sympathetic work containing another fine performance by Allison Janney. MS

▶ Josh Radnor, Elizabeth Olsen, Richard Jenkins, Allison Janney, Kate Burton, Zac Efron.
▶ *Dir* and *Screenplay* Josh Radnor, *Pro* Brice and Claude Dal Farra, Radnor and others, *Ph* Seamus Tierney, *Pro Des* Jade Healy, *Ed* Michael R Miller, *M* Ben Toth, *Cos* Deborah Newhall.

Strategic Motion Ventures/a BCDF Pictures production/ Tom Sawyer Entertainment-Picturehouse/Revolver Entertainment. 97 mins. USA. 2011. Rel: 5 Oct 2012. Cert. 12A.

Life Just Is ★½

Alex Barrett's grim film follows the lives of a group of friends. Their university days are over and now it's time to try to make sense of life and face the future. Meanwhile Jay (Jayne Wisener) begins dating an older man called Bobby (Paul Nicholls). The actors deliver committed performances, but the humourless script, which tries to imitate TV's *This Life*, is one-dimensional and lacks any sense of irony. GS

▶ Will de Meo, Paul Nicholls, Jack Gordon, Jayne Wisener, Nathaniel Martello-White, Fiona Ryan.
▶ *Dir* and *Screenplay* Alex Barrett, *Pro* Tom Stuart, *Ph* Yosuke Kato, *Pro Des* Niina Topp, *Ed* Murat Kebir, *Cos* Charmaine Parram.

Patchwork Productions/Asalva/Stanley Road Productions-Independent. 102 mins. UK. 2012. Rel: 7 Dec 2012. Cert. 15.

Life of Pi ★★★★½

Children may love the middle section of Ang Lee's wonderful if slightly over-long film: these are the scenes showing a teenage Indian boy who has survived a shipwreck adrift on the ocean in a small lifeboat accompanied by a Bengal tiger. But this is really a film for adults which questions what it is that draws people to believe in God. The animatronics are state of the art and for the first time 3D seems a crucial part of the experience. MS

▶ Suraj Sharma, Irrfan Khan, Rafe Spall, Tabu, Adil Hussain, Gérard Depardieu.
▶ *Dir* Ang Lee, *Pro* Gil Netter, Lee and David Womark, *Screenplay* David Magee, from the novel by Yann Martel, *Ph* Claudio Miranda, *Pro Des* David Gropman, *Ed* Tim Squyres, *M* Mychael Danna, *Cos* Arjun Bhasin.

Fox 2000 Pictures/a Haishang Films/Gil Netter production etc-20th Century Fox. 127 mins. USA/Taiwan/UK/Canada/Australia. 2012. Rel: 20 Dec 2012. Cert. PG.

Poetic licence: Josh Radnor and Elizabeth Olsen in Radnor's *Liberal Arts*.

Like Crazy ★★

We have here a delightful young cast: Anton Yelchin, Felicity Jones and Jennifer Lawrence. But that's the end of the good news. Debut director Drake Doremus is over-arty in his approach, but the great flaw in this tale, concerning a young couple (Yelchin and Jones) trying to sustain a relationship across the Atlantic Ocean, is that the two lovers blowing hot and cold are so unappealing. That's especially so in their appalling treatment of others and it's impossible to care about them. MS

▶ Anton Yelchin, Felicity Jones, Jennifer Lawrence, Charlie Bewley, Alex Kingston.
▶ *Dir* Drake Doremus, *Pro* Jonathan Schwartz and Andrea Sperling, *Screenplay* Doremus and Ben York Jones, *Ph* John Guleserian, *Pro Des* Katie Byron, *Ed* Jonathan Alberts, *M* Dustin O'Halloran, *Cos* Mari Chisholm.

Paramount Vantage/Indian Paintbrush/a Super Crispy Entertainment etc-Paramount.
90 mins. USA. 2011. Rel: 27 Jan 2012. Cert. 12A.

Lockout ★★

Although this outer space spin on John Carpenter's *Escape from New York* claims to be based on an original idea by co-writer Luc Besson, there's not a scrap of originality in this derivative rescue actioner with self-conscious old-school stylings. Solely notable for starring Guy Pearce, the movie certainly benefits from the actor's sardonic, world-weary charm as he battles to save the President's daughter (Maggie Grace) from a maximum security space prison. Sparkier repartee and more imaginative rough-and-tumble would have helped distinguish what amounts, in the end, to a mundane viewing experience. MJ

▶ Guy Pearce, Maggie Grace, Vincent Regan, Joseph Gilgun, Lenny James.
▶ *Dir* James Mather and Stephen Saint Leger, *Pro* Marc Libert and Leila Smith, *Screenplay* Mather, Saint Leger and Luc Besson, based on an idea by Besson, *Ph* James Mather, *Pro Des* Romek Delmata, *Ed* Camille Delamarre and Eamonn Power, *M* Alexandre Azaria, *Cos* Olivier Bériot.

Canal +/Cine +/Europa Corporation-Entertainment Film Distributors.
95 mins. France. 2012. Rel: 20 Apr 2012. Cert. 15.

LOL ★

Writer-director Lisa Azuelos recycles her 2008 French film (with Sophie Marceau) for this Chicago-set (but Detroit-filmed) remake, a formulaic teen comedy. Demi Moore plays Anne, who's shocked when she finds the secret diary of her internet-obsessed daughter Lola (Miley Cyrus). When Lola realises her boyfriend (George Finn) is a jerk, she takes up with her best friend (Douglas Booth), then heads for France with her class. The lame, cheesy script takes the long, dull route with nowhere to go, except the long-awaited reconciliation of mom and daughter. The Moore-Cyrus match doesn't light many sparks. DW

A raft of ideas: Suraj Sharma in Ang Lee's highly acclaimed *Life of Pi.*

▶ Miley Cyrus, Douglas Booth, Ashley Green,
George Finn, Demi Moore, Adam Sevani, Gina
Gershon, Marlo Thomas.
▶ *Dir* Lisa Azuelos, *Pro* Tish Cyrus, Esteban Martin,
Stacey Sher and Michael Shamberg, *Screenplay*
Azuelos and Kamir Aïnouz, based on the book *LOL
(Laugh Out Loud)* by Azuelos and Nans Delgado, *Ph*
Kieran McGuigan, *Pro Des* Happy Massee, *Ed* Myron I
Kerstein, *M* Rob Simonsen and pink, *Cos* Hope Hanafin.

**Lol Productions/Mandate Pictures/Double Feature
Films/PIC Agency-Lionsgate.
97 mins. USA. 2012. Rel: 1 June 2012. Cert. 12A.**

Lola Versus ★½

The world of 29-year-old Lola (Greta Gerwig)
simply crashes when her boyfriend Luke (Joel
Kinnaman) abandons her just three weeks before
their wedding. She begins dating but feels like
a fish out of water and seeks advice from her
best friend Alice (Zoe Lister Jones). Meanwhile
Lola's eccentric parents (Debra Winger and Bill
Pullman) never miss an opportunity to offer
their opinion. This is a charmless film with a
charisma-free performance from Gerwig and an
irritating one from Lister Jones. GS

▶ Greta Gerwig, Zoe Lister Jones, Hamish Linklater,
Joel Kinnaman, Debra Winger, Bill Pullman,
Cheyenne Jackson.
▶ *Dir* Daryl Wein, *Pro* Janice Williams, Jocelyn Hayes
and Michael London, *Screenplay* Wein and Zoe Lister
Jones, *Ph* Jakob Ihre, *Pro Des* Teresa Mastropierro, *Ed*
Suzy Elmiger and Susan Littenberg, *M* Phil Mossman,
Will Bates and Fall On Your Sword, *Cos* Jenny Gering.

**Groundswell Productions-20th Century Fox.
87 mins. USA. 2012. Rel: 20 July 2012. Cert. 15.**

London: The Modern Babylon
★★★½

There are great sequences in Julien Temple's film
in which sound and image seem inseparable.
Looking at London, that most cosmopolitan
of cities, over the last hundred years or so, the
film becomes an essay. It's often memorable
but sometimes too superficial and rather too
long. Film clips (unidentified) vie with songs in
bringing the city to life and, flawed though this
is, much here is immensely engaging, including
comments by a woman aged 106, still articulate
and able to share her memories vividly. MS

▶ With the voices of Michael Gambon, Imelda
Staunton, Bill Nighy.
▶ *Dir* and *Written by* Julien Temple, *Pro* Julien and
Amanda Temple and Stephen Malit, *Ph* Stephen
Organ, *Ed* Caroline Richards, *M* J C Carroll.

**BBC Films/BFI/a Nitrate Film production etc-BFI Films.
128 mins. UK. 2012. Rel: 3 Aug 2012. Cert. 15.**

Looper ★★★★

Although I am not drawn to science fiction I
enjoyed *Source Code* (2011) and this return to
form by writer-director Rian Johnson is similarly
entertaining. The narrative shifts back and forth
between 2044 and 2074 and concerns hired
'loopers', killers whose victims have been sent back
30 years through time in order to be eliminated

without leaving evidence. A story develops about a looper (Joseph Gordon-Levitt), expected to kill his older self (Bruce Willis), who eludes this fate; this leads into a search for a child who, if not stopped, will grow to be a dictator in 2074. It's intriguing, very well done and has a child actor, Pierce Gagnon, who is unforgettable. MS

➤ Bruce Willis, Joseph Gordon-Levitt, Emily Blunt, Paul Dano, Jeff Daniels, Pierce Gagnon.
➤ *Dir* and *Screenplay* Rian Johnson, *Pro* Ram Bergman and James D Stern, *Ph* Steve Yedlin, *Pro Des* Ed Verreaux, *Ed* Bob Ducsay, *M* Nathan Johnson with Son Lux and Chris Mears, *Cos* Sharen Davis, *Animation* Atomic Fiction.
Endgame Entertainment/DMG Entertainment/ FilmNation Entertainment etc-E1 Films.
118 mins. USA/China. 2012. Rel: 28 Sep 2012. Cert. 15.

Love ★★★★★

Funded by US rock band Angels & Airwaves, this began life as an avant-garde companion piece to their freely downloadable album *Love*. But then, under the guidance of writer-director-cinematographer William Eubank, it grew into an impressive science fiction essay about an astronaut stranded on a space station asking Big Questions about Life, the Universe and Everything. A floating dream of a movie with top-notch production values belying its minuscule budget. JC

➤ Gunner Wright, Corey Richardson, Bradley Horne, Roger E Fanter.
➤ *Dir, Ph, Pro Des* and *Screenplay* William Eubank, *Pro* Angels & Airwaves, Vertel Scott, Nate Kolbeck, Tom DeLonge, Mark Eaton and Dan Figur, *Ed* Brian

Berdan and Scott Chestnut, *M* Angels & Airwaves.
New Dog Media/Griffin Interplanetary Studios/Five VFX/Zoic Studios-High Fliers/Blue Dolphin.
84 mins. USA. 2011. Rel: 7 Sep 2012. Cert. 12.

Love Bite ★★½

Ed Speleers (*Eragon*, *Downton Abbey*) stars in this slightly posher, smarter, higher budget Brit comedy horror in which party-mad teens in a seaside town start to go missing. No wonder! A werewolf's on the loose. It's preying on virgins, so a lot of quick sex seems the best way out, especially with the arrival of sexy American Jessica Szohr on the party scene. Daft but entertaining, pacy and fun, it's rather well made, written and performed for this kind of thing. Speleers is a personable hero; Timothy Spall and Robert Pugh help as the adults. DW

➤ Ed Speleers, Jessica Szohr, Timothy Spall, Luke Pasqualino, Kierston Wareing, Robert Pugh, Robin Morrissey.
➤ *Dir* Andy De Emmony, *Pro* Paul Ritchie and Robert Bernstein, *Screenplay* Chris Cole and Ronan Blaney, *Ph* Tat Radcliffe, *Pro Des* Mike Gunn, *Ed* Matt Platt-Mills and Daniel Farrell, *M* Nick Green, *Cos* Anna Robbins.
West End Films/Ecosse Films/Spitfire Pictures/Scope Pictures-Entertainment Film Distribution.
91 mins. UK. 2012. Rel: 9 Nov 2012. Cert. 15.

Love Crime ★★★★

Made by the late Alain Corneau in 2010, this French drama begins as a study of the relationship, sexual or otherwise, between an ambitious business woman (Kristin Scott Thomas,

Office politics: Ludivine Sagnier and Kristin Scott Thomas in Alain Corneau's last feature, *Love Crime*.

splendid yet again) and the mousey but devoted and clever assistant (Ludivine Sagnier) with whom she plays games. Halfway through the film changes course, but if you then accept it as being in the style of Fritz Lang's *Beyond a Reasonable Doubt* (1956) it can be enjoyed as a very neatly turned example of this kind of thriller. (Original title: *Crime d'amour*) MS

▶ Ludivine Sagnier, Kristin Scott Thomas, Patrick Mille, Guillaume Marquet.
▶ *Dir* Alain Corneau, *Pro* Saïd Ben Saïd, *Screenplay* Corneau and Natalie Carter, *Ph* Yves Angelo, *Pro Des* Katia Wyszkop, *Ed* Thierry Derocles, *M* Pharoah Sanders, *Cos* Khadija Zeggaï.

UGC/an SBS Films production/France 2 Cinéma/Divali Films etc-Verve Pictures Ltd.
106 mins. France. 2010. Rel: 14 Dec 2012. Cert. 15.

Lovely Molly ★★½

When newlywed Molly (Gretchen Lodge) moves back to her long-abandoned family home her childhood nightmares begin to plague her once again after her husband goes on a business trip. Is it all in her mind or is there a supernatural force that threatens to possess her soul? Eduardo Sánchez creates enough suspense in the early stages of his claustrophobic film, benefiting from Lodge's committed performance, but as the story unfolds it loses its grip as well as any reality. GS

Memories of Molly: Gretchen Lodge in Eduardo Sánchez's Lovely Molly.

▶ Gretchen Lodge, Johnny Lewis, Alexandra Holden, Lauren Lakis, Ken Arnold.
▶ *Dir* Eduardo Sánchez, *Pro* Mark Ordesky, Gregg Hal, Robin Cowie and Jane Fleming, *Screenplay* Sánchez and Jaime Nash, from a story by Sánchez, *Ph* John W Rutland, *Pro Des* Andrew White, *Ed* Sánchez and Andrew Vona, *M* Tortoise, *Cos* Jamie Frazer.

Haxan Films/Amber Entertainment-Metrodome Distribution.
99 mins. USA. 2012. Rel: 29 June 2012. Cert. 15.

The Lucky One ★★

US Marine Logan Thibault first saw Beth's face in a photograph in the sand in Iraq. After finding the snapshot, he survived two ambushes and came to believe that Beth was a good luck totem, his destiny. So he walks from Colorado to Louisiana to find her… Taylor Schilling does the best she can with the sunny role of Beth and as her spirited grandmother there's Blythe Danner, who's always good value. Even so, for a film to tug at the heartstrings it does need a modicum of credibility. It's an adaptation of the novel by Nicholas Sparks, he who wrote *The Notebook* and *Dear John*, so you know what to expect. JC-W

▶ Zac Efron, Taylor Schilling, Blythe Danner, Jay R Ferguson, Adam LeFevre.
▶ *Dir* Scott Hicks, *Pro* Denise Di Novi and Kevin

Animal magic: Marty (voiced by Chris Rock) and Vitaly (Bryan Cranston) in Eric Darnell, Conrad Vernon and Tom McGrath's wondrous *Madagascar 3: Europe's Most Wanted.*

McCormick, *Screenplay* Will Fetters, *Ph* Alar Kivilo, *Pro Des* Barbara Ling, *Ed* Scott Gray, *M* Mark Isham, *Cos* Dayna Pink.

Village Roadshow/DiNovi Pictures/Langley Park Productions-Warner Bros.
100 mins. USA. 2012. Rel: 2 May 2012. Cert. 12A.

Madagascar 3: Europe's Most Wanted ★★★

This third entry in the hitherto irritating CG animated franchise about zoo animals escaping New York to live in Madagascar is a much more enjoyable movie than its predecessors, with our heroes joining a travelling circus and being tracked across Europe by a ruthlessly determined French policewoman. This is the first of the series that's actually worth seeing. JC

➤ With the voices of Ben Stiller, Chris Rock, David Schwimmer, Jada Pinkett Smith, Sacha Baron Cohen, Cedric the Entertainer, Frances McDormand, Jessica Chastain, Martin Short, Tom McGrath, Bryan Cranston.
➤ *Dir* Tom McGrath, Conrad Vernon and Eric Darnell, *Pro* Mark Swift and Mireille Soria, *Screenplay* Darnell and Noah Baumbach, *Pro Des* Kendal Cronkhite-Shaindlin, *Ed* Nick Fletcher, *M* Hans Zimmer.

DreamWorks Animation/Pacific Data Images-Paramount Pictures.
93 mins. USA. 2012. Rel: 19 Oct 2012. Cert. PG.

Madam Butterfly 3D ★★★★

Julian Napier's wonderful film version of Moshe Leiser and Patrice Caurier's Royal Opera production of Puccini's masterpiece tells the story of a Japanese geisha whose love for an American naval officer has tragic consequences. Liping Zhang is magnificent as the eponymous heroine and sings like an angel. It is a beautiful, deeply moving experience and the 3D is simply ravishing. A feast for the senses! GS

➤ James Valenti, Liping Zhang, Helene Schneiderman, Anthony Michaels-Moore, Robin Leggate, Jeremy White.
➤ *Dir* Julian Napier, *Pro* Phil Streather, *Pro Des* Christian Fenouillat, *Ed* Napier and Stroo Oloffson, *M* Giacomo Puccini, *Staging* Patrice Caurier and Moshe Leiser, *Conductor* Paul Wynne Griffiths, *Cos* Agostino Cavalca.

Royal Opera House/Real D-Royal Opera House Cinema Season.
170 mins. UK. 2012. Rel: 5 Mar 2012. Cert. PG.

Magic Mike ★★½

An unexpected choice of vehicle for Steven Soderbergh, this look at the world of male strippers initially finds the perfect tone. It's ideal for hen night parties as it sends up the men whose stage antics are sexy without being naughty enough to be pornographic. But then in order to find somewhere to go with the tale the film turns unconvincingly moralistic about the dangers of this lifestyle. It's technically very competent and well acted but a thorough mishmash. MS

➤ Channing Tatum, Alex Pettyfer, Matthew McConaughey, Cody Horn, Olivia Munn.
➤ *Dir* Steven Soderbergh, *Pro* Nick Wechsler, Gregory Jacobs, Channing Tatum and Reid Carolin, *Screenplay* Carolin, *Ph* Peter Andrews (ie, Soderbergh), *Pro Des* Howard Cummings, *Ed* Mary Ann Bernard (ie, Soderbergh), *Cos* Christopher Peterson.

Warner Bros. Pictures/Iron Horse etc-Lionsgate UK.
110 mins. USA. 2012. Rel: 11 July 2012. Cert. 15.

The Man Inside ★½

Clayton Murdoch (Ashley Thomas) is an idealistic young boxer haunted by violent childhood memories involving his brutal father (David Harewood), who is now serving a long prison sentence. But when violence again hits his family it's time for Clayton to face reality and exorcise his past demons. Dan Turner's muddled film lacks focus as he attempts to tackle far too many issues. Especially redundant is an unconvincing subplot involving the trainer's drug-addicted daughter (Michelle Ryan). GS

▸ Ashley Thomas, Michelle Ryan, David Harewood, Peter Mullan, Jason Maza, Theo Barklem-Biggs.
▸ *Dir* and *Screenplay* Dan Turner, *Pro* Dean Fisher, *Ph* Richard Swingle, *Pro Des* Mickaela Trodden, *Ed* Richard Alderson, *M* Laura Rossi, *Cos* Laura Jane Aitman.
Urban Way Productions/Northstar Ventures/Scanner-Rhodes Productions-Kaleidoscope Film Distributors.
99 mins. UK. 2012. Rel: 27 July 2012. Cert. 15.

Man on a Ledge ★★★

If *Fourteen Hours* (1951) dealt persuasively with a would-be suicide on a ledge, this thriller similarly set in New York incorporates a comparable situation but one that proves to be part of a plan for a heist, so the whole thing becomes significantly larger than life. This film's very good cast ought to be involved in something better than this, but the tone is at least consistent. The film delivers on its own terms, even if the goods are scarcely worth delivering. MS

▸ Sam Worthington, Elizabeth Banks, Jamie Bell, Anthony Mackie, Ed Burns, Kyra Sedgwick.
▸ *Dir* Asger Leth, *Pro* Lorenzo di Bonaventura and Mark Vahradian, *Screenplay* Pablo F Fenjves, *Ph* Paul Cameron, *Pro Des* Alec Hammond, *Ed* Kevin Stitt, *M* Henry Jackman, *Cos* Susan Lyall.
Summit Entertainment/a di Bonaventura Pictures production-E1 Films.
102 mins. USA. 2011. Rel: 3 Feb 2012. Cert. 12A.

The Man with the Iron Fists ★½

Director RZA wrote the story and co-wrote both screenplay and music; he also plays Blacksmith, the eponymous hero who joins forces with Jack Knife (Russell Crowe) in a battle against a brutal enemy in a rural Chinese village. This silly and often incomprehensible vanity project is a mixture of kung fu and western and is accompanied by a score with more than a nod to Ennio Morricone's iconic compositions. RZA makes a dull hero while Crowe's OTT performance seems to belong to a totally different film. GS

▸ Russell Crowe, Rick Yune, Lucy Liu, RZA, Byron Mann, Dave Bautista, Jamie Yung, Pam Grier.
▸ *Dir* RZA, *Pro* Eli Roth, Eric Newman, Thomas A Bliss and Mark Abraham, *Screenplay* RZA and Roth, from a story by RZA, *Ph* Chi Ying Chan, *Pro Des* Drew Boughton, *Ed* Joe D'Augustine, *M* RZA and Howard Drossin, *Cos* Thomas Chong.
Arcade Pictures/Iron Fists-Universal Pictures.
95 mins. USA/Hong Kong. 2012. Rel: 7 Dec 2012. Cert. 18.

The Man with the Jazz Guitar ★★★½

Ken Sykora began his career as a guitarist, having been a devotee of the great Django Reinhardt, and he was up there with the best. After

High crimes: Sam Worthington in Asger Leth's *Man on a Ledge.*

venturing into broadcasting he eventually gave it all up and went to live in Scotland to run a pub with his alcoholic wife Helen. What started as a great life and career ended in disappointment. A fascinating life, nonetheless, told here by Sykora's family, friends, associates and fellow musicians. PL

▶ With Ronnie Caiels, Julie Gleave, Jimmy Grant, Margaret Grant, Andy Park, Alison, Duncan and Dougal Sykora.
▶ *Dir, Ph* and *Ed* Marc Mason, *Pro* Mason and Linda Chirrey, *Music Superviser* Kirsten Lane.
Five Feet Films-Five Feet Films.
115 mins. UK. 2012. Rel: 15 May 2012. Cert. U.

A Man's Story ★★★★

Ozwald Boateng's work in fashion is of no great interest to me personally, but I was held by this documentary made with visual flair by Varon Bonicos: it's a revealing portrait of a fascinating man. Filmed over 12 years (what we see is largely chronological from 1998 onwards), it touches on failures in Boateng's personal and professional life as well as celebrating the essential triumph of a son of Ghanaian immigrants whose services to the clothing industry earned him an OBE. MS

▶ With Ozwald Boateng, Giorgio Armani, Don Cheadle, Michael Bay, Paul Bettany, Will Smith.
▶ *Dir* and *Ph* Varon Bonicos, *Pro* Rachel Robey and Alastair Clark, *Ed* Tom Hemmings, *M* Chad Hobson.
UK Film Council/Almega Projects/a b.b.f. & Wellington Films production etc-Trinity Filmed Entertainment.
98 mins. UK. 2010. Rel: 9 Mar 2012. Cert. 15.

Margin Call ★★★½

This moral drama set in the New York banking world at the time of the recent crisis is an ambitious debut for writer-director JC Chandor. But, while it convinces, it nevertheless leaves us as mere observers of a relatively predictable story rather than achieving any strong emotional involvement. There are, however, outstanding performances here, not least from Jeremy Irons and Stanley Tucci. MS

▶ Kevin Spacey, Paul Bettany, Jeremy Irons, Stanley Tucci, Zachary Quinto, Demi Moore.
▶ *Dir* and *Screenplay* JC Chandor, *Pro* Michael Benaroya, Zachary Quinto and others, *Ph* Frank G DeMarco, *Pro Des* John Paino, *Ed* Peter Beaudreau, *M* Nathan Larson, *Cos* Caroline Duncan.
Myriad Pictures/Benaroya Pictures/a Before the Door production etc-Stealth Media Group.
106 mins. USA. 2011. Rel: 13 Jan 2012. Cert. 15.

Marina Abramovic: The Artist is Present ★★★★½

"Playing with the edge of the knife is what makes her work so transcendent." So claimed an art critic about the incredible talent of Marina Abramovic – the world-renowned and fearless performance artist who shines in Matthew Akers and Jeff Dupre's must-see documentary. She proves her aphorism that "performance is all about a state of mind" following her three-month live act at the Museum of Modern Art, where thousands queued every day to stare at

Performance capture: A scene from Matthew Akers' and Jeff Dupre's documentary *Marina Abramovic: The Artist is Present.*

Cult favourite: Joaquin Phoenix in Paul Thomas Anderson's *The Master*.

this amazing woman's eyes. Truly inspirational and deeply moving. GS

▶ With Marina Abramovic, Ulay, Klaus Biesenbach, James Franco, Chrissie Iles, Arthur Danto, David Blaine.
▶ *Dir* Matthew Akers and Jeff Dupre, *Pro* Dupre and Maro Chermayeff, *Ph* Akers, *Ed* E. Donna Shepherd and Jim Hession, *M* Nathan Halpern.
Show of Force/Dakota Group/AVRO Television-Dogwoof. 106 mins. USA. 2012. Rel: 6 July 2012. Cert. 15.

Marley ★★★★

Kevin Macdonald's documentary on singer-songwriter Bob Marley is the first authorised film biography of this iconic figure. Marley was dubbed the King of Reggae and was a musical influence for many other artists and a spokesman on religion and philosophy. Born to a Jamaican mother and a white father, he became known not only for his music but also for promoting Black Power. Interviews with Marley's family, fellow musicians and friends, including his girlfriends (he had 11 children by seven women), are mixed with archive footage to build up an absorbing portrait of the man, his times and his short life. MHD

▶ With Bob Marley, Ziggy Marley, Rita Marley, Cedela Marley, Jimmy Cliff, Chris Blackwell, The Wailers.
▶ *Dir* Kevin Macdonald, *Pro* Charles Steel, *Ph* Mike Eley, Wally Pfister and Alwin H Kuchler, *Ed* Dan Glendenning, *Music Superviser* Liz Gallacher.
Cowboy Films/Tuff Going Pictures/Shangri-La Entertainment-Universal Pictures International. 144 mins. USA/UK. 2012. Rel: 20 Apr 2012. Cert. 15.

Martha Marcy May Marlene ★★★½

This film is worthy of note as the debut feature of writer-director Sean Durkin, but even more strikingly it introduces us to an immensely talented actress in Elizabeth Olsen. She plays a girl, variously known by all the names in the title, who, after fleeing a cult community to which she belonged for two years, worries her sister regarding her mental state. It's an unusual and intriguing film, but one seriously weakened by its abrupt and inconclusive ending. MS

▶ Elizabeth Olsen, John Hawkes, Hugh Dancy, Sarah Paulson, Brady Corbet.
▶ *Dir* and *Screenplay* Sean Durkin, *Pro* Josh Mond, Antonio Campos and others, *Ph* Jody Lee Lipes, *Pro Des* Chad Keith, *Ed* Zac Stuart-Pontier, *M* Saunder Jurriaans and Danny Bensi, *Cos* David Tabbert.
Fox Searchlight Pictures/a Borderline Films production/ This is That etc-20th Century Fox. 102 mins. USA. 2011. Rel: 3 Feb 2012. Cert. 15.

Marvel Avengers Assemble – see Avengers Assemble

The Master ★★½

The year's most divisive film (that means that everyone should judge it for themselves) finds me siding with the nay-sayers. Paul Thomas Anderson's movie looks great, but the story of a troubled ex-soldier (Joaquin Phoenix with an unhelpful accent)

falling under the spell of a religious guru (Philip Seymour Hoffman) is less engaging than it sounds. It's long, ambiguous as to what in it is real and what imagined, and unclear in its motivations. In a cameo role Laura Dern is riveting. MS

➤ Joaquin Phoenix, Philip Seymour Hoffman, Amy Adams, Laura Dern, Ambry Childers.
➤ *Dir* and *Screenplay* Paul Thomas Anderson, *Pro* Joanne Sellar, Anderson and others, *Ph* Mihai Malaimare Jr, *Pro Des* Jack Fisk and David Crank, *Ed* Leslie Jones and Peter McNulty, *M* Jonny Greenwood, *Cos* Mark Bridges.

The Weinstein Company/Ghoulardi Film Company/ Annapurna Pictures etc-Entertainment Film Distributors Ltd. 144 mins. USA. 2012. Rel: 2 Nov 2012. Cert. 15.

Matthew Bourne's Swan Lake ★★★★

Shot at Sadler's Wells in 2011, this enthralling film version of the all-male stage show of *Swan Lake* (first produced in 1995) records for posterity the sizzling performances of Richard Winsor as the Swan and Dominic North as the Prince. The makers don't really do much cinematically, just stick the cameras in there and focus hard on the dancing. But, with the 3D specs adding depth, that's all we need. The dancing is breathtaking, Winsor mesmerising, Bourne's reinterpretation vital and engrossing, the show raw and sexy. And, of course, Tchaikovsky's score works its magic. A glorious treat. DW

➤ Richard Winsor, Dominic North, Nina Goldman, Madelaine Brennan, Steve Kirkham, Joseph Vaughan.
➤ *Dir* Matthew Bourne and Ross MacGibbon, *Pro* Fiona Morris, *M* Tchaikovsky, *Conductor* David Lloyd-Jones.

Leopard Films-More2Screen. 120 mins. UK. 2012. Rel: 15 May 2012. Cert. PG.

Men in Black 3 ★★★★

Few popcorn movies in the summer of 2012 boasted as much wit, excitement, humour, charm, gore and ingenious special effects as this romp back in time. In order to save the life of his recently deceased partner Agent K (Tommy Lee Jones), Agent J (Will Smith) travels back to 1969 to apprehend the grotesque perpetrator of the crime... Like the previous outings, there's so much going on in the background here that one feels obliged to see the film again just to catch all the incidental visual gags. Incidentally, in spite of the film's PG certificate (what? *really*?), be warned, this 'fantasy' contains the most disgusting French kiss in cinema history. JC-W

➤ Will Smith, Tommy Lee Jones, Josh Brolin, Jemaine Clement, Michael Stuhlbarg, Emma Thompson, Alice Eve, Nicole Scherzinger, David Rasche, Bill Hader (as Andy Warhol).
➤ *Dir* Barry Sonnenfeld, *Pro* Walter F. Parkes and Laurie MacDonald, *Screenplay* Etan Cohen, *Ph* Bill Pope, *Pro Des* Bo Welch, *Ed* Don Zimmerman, *M* Danny Elfman, *Cos* Mary E Vogt.

Amblin Entertainment/Hemisphere Media Capital/Imagenation Abu Dhabi FZ/Media Magik Entertainment/Parkes/MacDonald Productions-Sony Pictures Releasing. 105 mins. USA. 2012. Rel: 25 May 2012. Cert. PG.

Mental ★★★★

When the free-spirited Shaz (Toni Colette) enters their lives, fragile housewife Shirley Moochmore (Rebecca Gibney) and her five daughters, who all believe that they suffer from some sort of mental illness, are encouraged to reassess their lives. This is PJ Hogan's best film since *Muriel's Wedding*, with a terrific opening sequence that pays tribute to *The Sound of Music*. He proves again how brilliant he is at creating fully fledged roles for women as well as embracing major issues with sensitivity and humour. GS

➤ Liev Schreiber, Toni Collette, Caroline Goodall, Anthony LaPaglia, Kerry Fox, Rebecca Gibney.
➤ *Dir* and *Screenplay* PJ Hogan, *Pro* Jerry & Janet Zucker and Jocelyn Moorhouse, *Ph* Donald McAlpine, *Pro Des* Graham 'Grace' Walker, *Ed* Jill Bilcock, *M* Michael Yezerski, *Cos* Tim Chappel.

Zucker Productions/Screen Australia/Story Bridge Films-Universal Pictures International. 116 mins. USA/Australia. 2012. Rel: 16 Nov 2012. Cert. 15.

Mercenaries ★½

The action takes place in Serbia following a military coup in which the President is assassinated. Soon after that a wanted war criminal kidnaps the American ambassador and his aide while ex-SAS officer Andy Marlow (Robert Fucilla) and his mercenaries are assigned to find them. The

Creature feature: An extra-terrestrial flunkey in Barry Sonnenfeld's weird and wonderful *Men in Black 3*.

premise is not bad but Paris Leonti's disappointing second film (following the impressive *Daylight Robbery*) lacks tension and suspense and feels like a vanity project for Fucilla. GS

▶ Robert Fucilla, Kirsty Mitchell, Rob-James Collier, Antony Byrne, Geoff Bell, Michael Nardone, Billy Zane.
▶ *Dir* and *Screenplay* Paris Leonti, *Pro* John Adams and Luc Chaudhary, *Ph* Roger Bonnici, *Pro Des* Paul Burns, *Ed* Anthony Willis, *M* Haim Frank Ilfman, *Cos* Alice Wolfbauer.
Angry Badger Pictures/International Artists Management-Kaleidoscope.
97 mins. UK. 2011. Rel: 27 Jan 2012. Cert. 15.

Michael ★★★

Echoing tragic realities, this Austrian film is a study of a paedophile, the titular character excellently played by Michael Fuith, who keeps an 11-year-old boy a prisoner in the cellar of his house. This is not exploitation cinema, and it's not a horror movie: instead it's a precision job in a style close to being minimalistic. Yet there are no real insights here, and I find it difficult to see this film as a worthwhile or useful achievement. MS

▶ Michael Fuith, David Rauchenberger, Christine Kain, Ursula Strauss, Viktor Tremmel.
▶ *Dir* and *Screenplay* Markus Schleinzer, *Pro* Nikolaus Geyrhalter, Markus Glaser and others, *Ph* Gerald Kerkletz, *Pro Des* Katrin Huber and Gerhard Dohr, *Ed* Wolfgang Widerhofer, *Cos* Hanya Barakat.
NGF/ORF Film/Fernseh-Abkommen etc-Artifical Eye.
96 mins. Austria. 2011. Rel: 2 Mar 2012. Cert. 18.

Midnight's Children ★★★

Director Deepa Mehta does well to avoid longueurs in this very long film adapted by Salman Rushdie from his 1980 novel. But, while it all flows, on screen parts of it play like soap opera as it tells a story spanning Indian history from the 1947 partition onwards. That aspect

Independence day: Shriya Saran and Satya Bhabha in Deepa Mehta's *Midnight's Children.*

hinges on the swap by a nurse of two babies from wealthy and poor backgrounds respectively, but the key elements are those in which magic realism is applied to highlight political and social comment. That's as per the book, but I confess to finding it an odd mix. MS

▶ Satya Bhabha, Seema Biswas, Shriya Saran, Shabana Azmi, Charles Dance, Siddharth, Salman Rushdie (narrator).
▶ *Dir* Deepa Mehta, *Pro* David Hamilton, *Screenplay* Salman Rushdie, from his novel, *Ph* Giles Nuttgens, *Pro Des* Dilip Mehta, *Ed* Colin Monie, *M* Nitin Sawhney, *Cos* Dolly Ahluwalia.
FilmNation Entertainment/Noble Nomad Pictures/ Number 9 Films etc-E1 Films.
146 mins. Canada/UK/USA. 2011. Rel: 26 Dec 2012. Cert. 12A.

Mirror Mirror ★★★★

Just as the plays of Shakespeare are incessantly re-imagined, so the fables of the Brothers Grimm never cease to entice filmmakers. This is a relatively straightforward dramatisation of *Snow White*, albeit told from the sarcy viewpoint of the vain and tyrannical stepmother (Julia Roberts camping it up deliciously – but not too much). The accent here is on humour and pictorial panache. Indeed, the visuals are so awesome that one almost forgets the film isn't animated. There's also some excellent puppetry – influenced by the Czech tradition – and even a Bollywood number during the closing credits, a nod to the background of its Punjabi director. JC-W

▶ Julia Roberts, Lily Collins, Armie Hammer, Nathan Lane, Sean Bean, Mare Winningham, Michael Lerner.
▶ *Dir* Tarsem Singh, *Pro* Ryan Kavanaugh, Bernie Goldmann, Brett Ratner and Kevin Misher, *Screenplay* Marc Klein and Jason Keller, *Ph* Brendan Galvin, *Pro Des* Tom Foden, *Ed* Robert Duffy and Nick Moore, *M* Alan Menken, *Cos* Eiko Ishioka.
Relativity Media/Yucaipa Films/Goldmann Pictures/Rat Entertainment/Misha Films-StudioCanal.
106 mins. USA. 2012. Rel: 2 April 2012. Cert. PG.

Mission to Lars ★★★★½

William and Kate Spicer's film is not only a brilliant documentary but also a heartfelt gift to their charismatic brother Tom, a man with learning disabilities. Tom's ambition is to meet his hero, Lars Ulrich of Metallica, and soon the siblings embark on a transatlantic adventure in order to fulfil their brother's dream. It is a very moving but also very funny film, a real-life *Rain Man* story. An uplifting and rewarding experience. GS

▶ With Lars Ulrich, Tom Spicer and the voices of Kate Spicer and William Spicer.

▶ *Dir* and *Pro* James Moore and William Spicer, *Ph* Moore, Spicer and Lee Alner, *Ed* Moore, Ben Luria, Tom Herington and Mags Arnold, *M* Mike Lindsay.

Spicer & Moore.
74 mins. UK/USA. 2012. Rel: 8 June 2012. No Cert.

Mitsuko Delivers ★★

This is a disappointing comedy from Yûya Ishii, the director of the quirky *Sawato Decides*. This time he tells the story of Mitsuko (Riisa Naka), a heavily pregnant woman who has no friends or money. Her parents believe she is still in California living the high life, whereas Mitsuko is in fact back in Tokyo searching for a purpose and the meaning of life. It's original and totally eccentric but lacks any reality, which prevents us from caring. (Original title: *Hara ga kore nande*) GS

▶ Riisa Naka, Aoi Nakamura, Ryo Ishibashi, Keiko Saito.
▶ *Dir* and *Screenplay* Yûya Ishii, *Pro* Hiroshi Kogure, Sachiko Sone and Yuichi Shibahara, *Ph* Yukihiro Okimura, *Ed* Naoichiro Sagara, *M* Takashi Watanabe, *Cos* Kyoko Baba.

Yahoo Japan/Smoke/Pony Canyon/Nippon Planning Center/Showgate/Smoke etc-Third Window Films.
109 mins. Japan. 2011. Rel: 11 May 2012. Cert. PG.

The Monk ★★★★

This 17th century drama from a famous novel set in a monastery may not fully satisfy, but it is very interesting and has been undervalued. As co-adaptor and director Dominik Moll has created a serious work rather than a full-blooded Gothic melodrama; the excellent Vincent Cassel in the title role was asked by Moll to tone down his acting. This treatment invites us to speculate on the work's attitude to religion and carries fascinating echoes of Goethe's *Faust*. An unusual and intriguing film. (Original title: *Le Moine*). MS

▶ Vincent Cassel, Déborah François, Joséphine Japy, Sergi López, Geraldine Chaplin.
▶ *Dir* Dominik Moll, *Pro* Michel Saint-Jean, *Screenplay* Moll and Anne-Louise Trividic, based on the novel by Matthew G Lewis, *Ph* Patrick Blossier, *Art Dir* Antxón Gómez, *Ed* François Gedigier and Sylvie Lager, *M* Alberto Iglesias, *Cos* Bina Daigeler.

Diaphana Films/Morena Films/France 3 Cinéma/Canal+ etc-Metrodome Distribution Ltd.
100 mins. France/Spain. 2011. Rel: 27 Apr 2012. Cert. 15.

Monsieur Lazhar ★★★½

Set in Montreal, this is a sensitive study concentrating not only on the titular figure, a teacher from Algeria, but on his attempts to help pupils after another teacher has killed herself in their classroom. It's an involving tale which hides its theatrical origin but, while some may welcome its comparatively upbeat ending, I felt that, given the subject matter, the film was less disturbing than it should have been. (Original title: *Bachir Lazhar*) MS

▶ Fellag, Sophie Nélisse, Émilien Néron, Brigitte Poupart, Danielle Proulx, Jules Philip.

Having a ball: Armie Hammer and Lily Collins (centre) in Tarsem Singh's witty and visually ravishing *Mirror Mirror*.

▶ *Dir* and *Screenplay* (based on the play *Bachir Lazhar* by Evelyne de la Chenelière) Philippe Falardeau, *Pro* Luc Déry and Kim McCraw, *Ph* Ronald Plante, *Pro Des* Emmanuel Fréchette, *Ed* Stéphane Lafleur, *M* Martin Léon, *Cos* Francesca Chamberland.

Les Films Christal/a micro_scope production etc-Soda Pictures.
95 mins. Canada. 2011. Rel: 4 May 2012. Cert. 15.

A Monster in Paris ★★★★

This delightful animation feature takes place in the 1920s. An experiment goes horribly wrong and Francoeur (Sean Lennon) is born, a monster of epic proportions but with a singing voice to die for. Maynott (Danny Huston), the ruthless police commissioner, is determined to catch him but the beautiful singer Lucille (Vanessa Paradis) is prepared to do anything in order to protect her new friend. The animation is stunning and the style quirky in this cross between *The Phantom of the Opera* and *The Fly*. (Original title: *Un Monstre à Paris*) GS

▶ With the voices of Bob Balaban, Adam Goldberg, Jay Harrington, Danny Huston, Sean Lennon, Vanessa Paradis, Catherine O'Hara (all for the English version).
▶ *Dir* Bibo Bergeron, *Pro* Luc Besson, *Screenplay* Bergeron and Stéphane Kazandjian, *Pro Des* François Moret, *Ed* Pascal Chevé and Nicolas Stretta, *M* Mathieu Chedid, *Animation Director* Fabrice Joubert.

Bibo Films/EuropaCorp/France 3 Cinéma/Canal+/ Walking the Dog/CinéCinéma etc-E1 Films.
90 mins. France. 2011. Rel: 27 Jan 2012. Cert. U.

Moonrise Kingdom ★★★★

New England, 1965… Two innocent 12-year-old outsiders, Sam (Jared Gilman) and Suzy (Kara Hayward), fall in love and decide to run away. Sam is an orphan and boy scout, Suzy loves science fiction and the songs of Françoise Hardy. Her parents (Frances McDormand and Bill Murray) are having marriage trouble. When the kids disappear, the adults over-react, calling in sheriff Bruce Willis and scout master Edward Norton, both in their own ways fairly inept. Wes Anderson's quirky take on American life and the chaste love between the two kids is quite charming and only occasionally too cute for its own good. The two young leads are exceptional while the starry cast of alleged grown-ups are perfect. Watch out for Tilda Swinton as a maniacal social worker. MHD

▶ Jared Gilman, Kara Hayward, Bruce Willis, Edward Norton, Bill Murray, Frances McDormand, Tilda Swinton, Jason Schwartzman, Bob Balaban, Harvey Keitel.
▶ *Dir* Wes Anderson, *Pro* Anderson, Scott Rudin, Jeremy Dawson and Steven Rales, *Screenplay* Anderson and Roman Coppola, *Ph* Robert D Yeoman, *Pro Des* Adam Stockhausen, *Ed* Andrew Weisblum, *M* Alexandre Desplat, *Cos* Kasia Walicka-Maimone.

Scott Rudin Productions/Moonrise/Indian Paintbrush/ American Empirical-Universal Pictures International.
94 mins. USA. 2012. Rel: 25 May 2012. Cert. 12A.

Mother and Child ★★★

There's a good cast here but, unexpectedly for a film with Alejandro Gonzalez Inárritu as an executive producer, the material is akin to women's pictures of the 1940s. If that's your bag, then this tale of mothers and children combining three narrative threads may appeal, but others (myself included) may well feel that players such as Naomi Watts and Annette Bening should be engaged in something better than soap opera. I myself would rather be watching Ingmar Bergman's *So Close to Life* but that's a matter of taste! MS

They'll always have Paris: Lucille and Francoeur in Bibo Bergeron's *A Monster in Paris*, loosely inspired by *The Phantom of the Opera*.

▶ Naomi Watts, Annette Bening. Kerry Washington, Jimmy Smits, Samuel L Jackson, Cherry Jones.
▶ *Dir* and *Screenplay* Rodrigo García, *Pro* Lisa Marie Falcone and Julie Lynn, *Ph* Xavier Pérez Grobet, *Pro Des* Christopher Tandon, *Ed* Steven Weisberg, *M* Edward Shearmur, *Cos* Susie DeSanto.

Sony Pictures Classics/Everest Entertainment/a Mockingbird Pictures production-Verve Pictures Ltd. 126 mins. USA. 2009. Rel: 6 Jan 2012. Cert. 15.

Mother's Milk ★★½

Set in Provence, this is a drama about a woman on her deathbed (the late Margaret Tyzack) threatening to disinherit her family and to leave her property there to an Irish con man. It sounds promising but, despite the cast's valiant efforts, it doesn't work at all. Drama and farce clash, the leading character is totally unsympathetic and this adaptation of Edward St Aubyn's novel swamps everybody with a very literary voice-over text, negating this as cinema. MS

▶ Jack Davenport, Annabel Mullion, Adrian Dunbar, Margaret Tyzack, Thomas Underhill, Diana Quick, Annette Badland, Flora Montgomery.
▶ *Dir* Gerry Fox, *Pro* Fox and Zara D'Abo, *Screenplay* Fox and Edward St Aubyn, from the latter's novel, *Ph* Steve Haskett, *Pro Des* Michel Rollant, *Ed* John Street, *M* David Ogilvy, *Cos* Leonie Hartard.

Guerilla Films/a Foxy Films production etc-Guerilla Films. 98 mins. UK. 2012. Rel: 9 Nov 2012. Cert. 15.

Mozart's Sister ★★★

René Féret gave us the excellent and too little-known *The Mystery of Alexina* (1985), and this historical drama, centred on Mozart's younger sister but also more widely concerned with the position of women in the second half of the 18th century, is not the family vanity project that the credits might lead you to suspect. All the same, despite being respectful and sincere, the piece lacks dramatic fire and seems tiresomely over-extended. One wishes that one could like it more. (Original title: *Nannerl, la soeur de Mozart*) MS

▶ Marie Féret, Marc Barbé, Delphine Chuillot, David Moreau, Clovis Fouin, Lisa Féret.
▶ *Dir* and *Screenplay* René Féret, *Pro* René and Fabienne Féret, *Ph* Benjamin Echazarreta, *Art Dir* Veronica Fruhbrodt, *Ed* Fabienne Féret, *M* Marie-Jeanne Séréro, *Cos* Dominique Louis.

Les Films Alyne etc.-Palisades Tartan. 120 mins. France. 2010. Rel: 13 Apr 2012. Cert. 12A.

The Muppets ★★★½

It's good to have the old gang back, even under their new bosses at Disney. Maybe they lost their way in some of their previous outings but here they're trying to re-open their old studio before evil oil man Chris Cooper gets his hands on it. Muppet fans Gary (Jason Segal, who also co-wrote), girlfriend Mary (Amy Adams) and Gary's

Elope trick: Kara Hayward and Jared Gilman in Wes Anderson's *Moonlight Kingdom*.

Muppet brother Walter round up Kermit, Fozzie, Miss Piggy, Gonzo, Animal, Statler and Waldorf, together with guests galore including Alan Arkin, Mickey Rooney, Emily Blunt, Whoopi Goldberg, Jack Black etc. More good news is that the Muppets will be back again in 2014! MHD

▶ Jason Segal, Amy Adams, Chris Cooper, Rashida Jones, Alan Arkin, Emily Blunt, Whoopi Goldberg, Neil Patrick Harris, Jack Black, Mickey Rooney and the voices of Steve Whitmire, Eric Jacobson, Dave Goelz, Bill Barretta, David Rudman, Matt Vogel.
▶ *Dir* James Bobin, *Pro* David Hoberman and Scott Lieberman, *Screenplay* Jason Segal and Nicholas Stoller, *Ph* Don Burgess, *Pro Des* Steve Saklad, *Ed* James Thomas, *M* Christophe Beck, *Cos* Rahel Afiley.
Walt Disney Pictures-Walt Disney Studios Motion Pictures. 103 mins. USA. 2011. Rel: 10 Feb 2012. Cert. U.

My Brother the Devil ★★★

Sally El Hosaini's first feature has been highly acclaimed and uses its Hackney locations well. Nevertheless the dangerous appeal to youngsters of being macho (and violent with it) was even more compellingly realised in Saul Dibb's *Bullet Boy* (2004). Here the second half sidetracks, not always convincingly, into issues dealing with sexuality. It's a promising debut, sincerely meant and well acted, but for all that I feel that it has been over-praised. MS

▶ Saïd Taghmaoui, James Floyd, Fady Elsayed, Aymen Hamdouchi, Elarica Gallacher.
▶ *Dir* and *Screenplay* Sally El Hosaini, *Pro* Gayle Griffiths, Julia Godzinskaya and Michael Sackler, *Ph* David Raedeker, *Pro Des* Stéphane Collonge, *Ed* Iain Kitching, *M* Stuart Earl, *Cos* Rob Nicholls.
A Wild Horses Film Company and Rooks Nest Entertainment production/Film Clinic etc-Verve Pictures. 112 mins. UK/Egypt/USA. 2012. Rel: 9 Nov 2012. Cert. 15.

Pride and prejudice: Fady Elsayed and James Floyd in Sally El Hosaini's remarkable film debut, *My Brother the Devil.*

The Myth of the American Sleepover ★★★★

David Robert Mitchell's debut feature is an unfashionably gentle portrait of adolescents in Detroit, Michigan. Limited to a period of 24 hours before a new school term starts, it shows the students partying while their parents are away. The slightly older Scott (Brett Jacobsen), still obsessed with a pair of twin sisters, provides one plot thread, but it's largely a film of sympathetic everyday detail convincingly conveyed by unknown players rather than an attempt at strong drama. MS

▶ Claire Soma, Brett Jacobsen, Marlon Morton, Amanda Bauer, Nikita Ramsey, Jade Ramsey.
▶ *Dir* and *Screenplay* David Robert Mitchell, *Pro* Adele Romanski, *Ph* James Laxton, *Pro Des* Jeanine A. Nicholas, *Ed* Julio C Perez IV, *M* Kyle Newmaster.
Roman Spring Pictures/Screen Actors Guild/IFP-Independent Distribution. 96 mins. USA. 2010. Rel: 31 Aug 2012. Cert. 15.

Nativity 2: Danger in the Manger ★★★

The adventures of the well-meaning but inept infants classroom assistant Mr Poppy (Marc Wootton) continue, with idealistic new teacher David Tennant arriving at the school and getting sucked into taking the kids on an unauthorised school trip to enter the national school choir 'Song for Christmas' competition. It all goes horribly wrong. Like its predecessor, this is surprisingly funny. JC

▶ David Tennant, Marc Wootton, Jason Watkins, Pam Ferris, Jessica Hynes, Shannon Maguire, Ian McNeice, Joanna Page.
▶ *Dir* and *Screenplay* Debbie Isitt, *Pro* Nick Jones, *Ph* Sean Van Hales, *Pro Des* Chris Roope, *Ed* Nicky Ager, *M* Isitt and Nicky Ager, *Cos* Stephanie Collie.
Premier Picture/Media Pro Six/Moviehouse Entertainment/Mirrorball Films-Entertainment One. 105 mins. UK. 2012. Rel: 23 Nov 2012. Cert. U.

Neil Young Journeys ★★½

Jonathan Demme's documentary is a clear labour of love as his cameras follow 65-year-old music legend Neil Young's return to his Toronto birth place (where he performs in the city's iconic Massey Hall), as well as his road trip in a 1956 Ford Crown Victoria to revisit his old haunts in Ontario. Demme makes the most of two nights' concert footage, which includes performances of new material from Young's album *Le Noise* and the vintage stuff that fans hope for like 'Ohio' and 'I Believe in You'. A nostalgia fest for older folk – appealing, attractive and soulful. DW

▶ With Neil Young in performance.

Spring awakening: Jelle Florizoone and Thomas Coumans in Bavo Defurne's *North Sea Texas.*

▸ *Dir* Jonathan Demme, *Pro* Demme and Elliot Rabinowitz, *Ph* Declan Quinn, *Ed* Glenn Allen, *M* Neil Young.

Shakey Pictures/Clinica Estetico-Sony Pictures Classics. 87 mins. USA. 2011. Rel: 14 Dec 2012. Cert. PG.

A Night in the Woods ★½

Horror films composed of fabricated camcorder footage have become so commonplace that one would have thought the genre was ripe for parody. However, this three-actor cheapie behaves as if it were a true original, as if nobody had seen or heard of *The Blair Witch Project*. An annoying American with a camcorder (Scoot McNairy), his girlfriend (Anna Skellern) and her 'cousin' (Andrew Hawley) go on a camping trip on Dartmoor. What follows is mainly artless, self-indulgent padding; the rest is unconvincing, derivative and very, very tedious. JC-W

▸ Scoot McNairy, Anna Skellern, Andrew Hawley.
▸ *Dir* and *Screenplay* Richard Parry, *Pro* Allan Niblo, Nick Love and James Richardson, *Ph* Elliot Ebel, *Ed* Christine Pancott.

Vertigo Films-Vertigo Films. 82 mins. UK. 2011. Rel: 7 Sep 2012. Cert. 15.

The Nine Muses ★★★★

John Akomfrah's experimental film cleverly mixes poetry, music and striking imagery in retelling the history of the migrant's life in post-war Britain through the lens of Homer's epic *The Odyssey*. It is also devised and scripted from the writings of Beckett, Shakespeare and Sophocles amongst others, mixing archival material with specially filmed scenes in the United States and the UK. It is a rich, imaginative and deeply moving film. GS

▸ *Dir* and *Screenplay* John Akomfrah, *Pro* David Lawson and Nina Gopaul, *Ph* Dewald Aukema, *Ed* Mikka Leskinen and Ben Hunt, *M* Trevor Mathison.

Smoking Dogs Films-New Wave Films. 90 mins. Ghana/UK. 2010. Rel: 20 Jan 2012. No Cert.

North Sea Texas ★★★★★

Pim is an odd soul who from childhood has always kept objects that have meant something to him in a secret box. As an adolescent he falls for Gino, the boy next door. Their relationship is only a means for Gino to let off sexual steam, but for Pim it is something more. When Gino moves on to girls, Pim starts flirting with Zoltan, his mother's lodger. As usual for teenagers, life is not predictable, although Pim knows who he is and what he wants. Set in the 1970s, this is a very affecting, subtly moving film. An excellent performance by Jelle Florizoone as Pim is matched by fine playing from the rest of the cast in a truly honest portrayal of adolescence by Belgian director Bavo Defurne. (Original title: *Noordzee, Texas*) MHD

▸ Jelle Florizoone, Mathias Vergels, Thomas Coumans, Ben Van den Heuvel, Eva van der Gucht, Katelijne Damen, Nathan Naenen, Nina Marie Kortekaas.
▸ *Dir* Bavo Defurne, *Pro* Yves Verbraeken and Luc Roggen, *Screenplay* Defurne, Yves Verbraeken and

Andre Sollie, based on his novel *Nooit gaat dit over*, *Ph* Anton Mertens, *Pro Des* Kurt Rigolle, *Ed* Els Voorspoels, *M* Adriano Cominotto, *Cos* Nathalie Lermytte.

Indeed Films/Mollywood/Eén etc-Peccadillo Pictures. 94 mins. Belgium. 2011. Rel: 6 Apr 2012. Cert. 15.

Nostalgia for the Light ★★★½

Patricio Guzmán's essay film set in the Atacama Desert contains images which should ideally be seen on the big screen since they represent a visual coup de cinéma on the level of Kubrick's *2001*. But this film tries to link the concept of astronomers studying the heavens through telescopes in that region with the continuing search for any bones or remnants there confirming the fate of those who disappeared in Pinochet's Chile. The attempt to bring these two elements together seems forced and heavy-handed, but in isolation there are utterly stunning moments here. MS

❯ With Patricio Guzmán, Gaspar Galaz, George Preston.
❯ *Dir* and *Written by* Patricio Guzmán, *Pro* Renate Sachse, *Ph* Katell Djian, *Ed* Guzmán and Emmanuelle Joly, *M* Miguel Miranda and José Miguel Tobar.

Atacama Productions S.A.R.L./Blinker Filmproduktion GmBH etc- New Wave Films 94 mins. France/Germany/Chile/USA. 2010. Rel: 13 July 2012. Cert. 12A.

Now is Good ★★½

Adapted from the Jenny Downham novel *Before I Die*, *Now is Good* aims for a tender and understated approach, a tone mirrored in the performance of Dakota Fanning as Tessa Scott, a 17-year-old English girl dying in Brighton. As she has leukaemia, one wants to forgive her everything, but she's self-righteous and not a very engaging protagonist. As Tessa draws up a bucket list of things she wants to achieve before she dies, one prays that her more seditious and impudent aspirations may be echoed in her behaviour. Sadly, they aren't. JC-W

❯ Dakota Fanning, Jeremy Irvine, Paddy Considine, Olivia Williams, Kaya Scodelario, Julian Wadham, Joe Cole, Kate Dickie.
❯ *Dir* and *Screenplay* Ol Parker, from Jenny Downham's novel *Before I Die*, *Pro* Graham Broadbent and Peter Czernin, *Ph* Erik Wilson, *Pro Des* Amanda McArthur, *Ed* Peter Lambert, *M* Dustin O'Halloran, *Cos* Suzie Harman.

Goldcrest/BBC Films/Blueprint Pictures/Lipsync Prods/ UK Film Council-Warner Bros. 103 mins. UK. 2012. Rel: 19 Sep 2012. Cert. 12A.

Nuremburg: Its Lesson for Today ★★★★

Stuart Schulberg's 1948 documentary receives its first ever UK release in this restored version narrated by Liev Schreiber. It's a powerful document of the 1945-46 trial of 22 of the top Nazi leaders, including Hermann Goering, but it's the background material of the Nazis' own films and records (which international prosecutors used to build their cases) that make this film an unforgettable experience. GS

❯ Narrated by Liev Schreiber.
❯ *Dir* and *Written by* Stuart Schulberg, from documentary material recovered by Sandra Schulberg and Josh Waletzky, *Pro* Stuart Schulberg and Pare Lorentz, *Ed* Joseph Zigman, *M* Hans Otto Borgmann.

Schulberg Productions/Metropolis Productions- Schulberg Productions. 78 mins. USA. 1948. Rel: 15 June 2012. Cert. 12A.

Dying in Brighton: Kaya Scodelario and Dakota Fanning in Ol Parker's *Now is Good.*

Offender ★★★

Offender purports to be a hard-hitting drama focusing on the fallout of the London riots of 2011. And if you believe the publicity, it plays out as a modern-day version of *Scum*, Alan Clarke's seminal 1979 portrait of teenage violence. Yeah, right. It's actually a conventional prison drama that fails to deliver any of the authenticity of the recent slew of such dramas. Having said that, it's a surprisingly compelling cocktail of the old ultra-violence, helped no end by a markedly scary performance by Joe Cole as a weedy convict bent on revenge. JC-W

▶ Joe Cole, English Frank, Kimberley Nixon, G Frsh, Shaun Dooley, Ruth Gemmell, Vas Blackwood.
▶ *Dir* Ron Scalpello, *Pro* Paul Van Carter and Nick Taussig, *Screenplay* Van Carter, *Ph* Richard Mott, *Pro Des* Marie Lanna, *Ed* Johnny Rayner, *M* Chad Hobson, *Cos* Matthew Price.

Gunslinger-Revolver Entertainment.
101 mins. UK. 2012. Rel: 8 Aug 2012. Cert. 15.

Oliver Sherman ★★★½

Garret Dillahunt stars as veteran Sherman Oliver, who turns up at the home of the soldier who saved his life in the war. That man now has a happy life with a wife, two kids and a job – but when Sherman enters their house, and their lives, he emerges as increasingly troubled. An involving, brooding tale, Ryan Redford's first full-length film works well as a character study, actors' showcase and comment on war. Redford manages plenty of tension; Dillahunt does crazy perfectly. DW

▶ Garret Dillahunt, Donal Logue, Molly Parker, Kaelan Meunier, Duane Murray, Marla J. Hayes, Fiona Highet.
▶ *Dir* and *Screenplay* Ryan Redford, from Rachel Ingalls' short story *Veterans*, *Pro* Eric Jordan and Paul Stephens, *Ph* Antonio Calvache, *Pro Des* Oleg M. Savytski, *Ed* Matthew Hannam, *Sound Mixer* Bissa Scekic, *Cos* Lea Carlson.

The Film Works-Cinefile World.
82 mins. Canada. 2010. Rel: 20 Apr 2012. Cert. 15.

On the Road ★★★½

This adaptation of Jack Kerouac's classic book comes from Walter Salles who gave us *The Motorcycle Diaries* (2004). This semi-autobiographical work about rebel drop-outs in America foreshadows the hippie movement, being set mainly between 1947 and 1949. To my eyes at least, the characters are very unappealing (especially in their treatment of women), but admirers of the book may be impressed. What is great beyond dispute is the look of the film (photographed by Eric Gautier) and the superb evocation of the period. MS

▶ Garrett Hedlund, Sam Riley, Kristen Stewart, Amy Adams, Tom Sturridge, Alice Braga, Kirsten Dunst, Viggo Mortensen, Steve Buscemi.

Echoes of war: Kaelan Meunier and Garret Dillahunt in Ryan Redford's Oliver Sherman.

Night without end: Cansu Demirci in Nuri Bilge Ceylan's acclaimed *Once Upon a Time in Anatolia*.

▷ *Dir* Walter Salles, *Pro* Nathanael Karmitz, Charles Gillibert and others, *Screenplay* José Rivera, from the novel by Jack Kerouac, *Ph* Eric Gautier, *Pro Des* Carlos Conti, *Ed* François Gedigier, *M* Gustavo Santaolalla, *Cos* Danny Glicker.

MK2/American Zoetrope/a Jerry Leider Company production etc-Lionsgate UK.
124 mins. France/UK/Brazil/USA/Canada. 2012.
Rel: 12 Oct 2012. Cert. 15.

On the Sly ★★★

This French-Belgian co-production released in an English language version looks at life through the eyes of a six-year-old girl. The voice-over by this disaffected child makes for a divertingly comic start but later becomes rather tiresome. Indeed, even at 77 minutes the work feels too extended. Also unhelpful is our uncertainty as to whether the girl's escape from her parents should be taken as realistic drama or as fantasy. Nevertheless the film is original and the director's daughter in the central role avoids being too cute. (Original title: *À pas de loup*) MS

▷ Wynona Ringer, Olivier Ringer, Macha Ringer, Ursula Noyer, Pierre Leroux.
▷ *Dir*, *Ph* and *Ed* Olivier Ringer, *Pro* Yves Ringer and Antoine Simkine, *Screenplay* Olivier and Yves Ringer, *M* Bruno Alexiu.

Ring Prod & Les Films d'Antoine-Showcomotion Films.
77 mins. Belgium/France. 2011. Rel: 1 June 2012. Cert. U.

Once Upon a Time in Anatolia ★★★★★

This is a true work of art, but a demanding one since the film is long and slow. Although it begins with the authorities investigating a killing, this is not a police procedural. Instead with Chekhovian subtlety it studies the way in which we treat one another and raises complex moral questions. Talk may be crucial, but Ceylan's film is stunningly well photographed. Although it depicts events in Turkey, what it has to say has universal validity. It could be argued that, whereas Kieslowski made works based on each of the Ten Commandments, this piece takes as its text the biblical saying "Let he who is without sin cast the first stone." (Original title: *Bir zamanlar Anadolu'da*) MS

▷ Muhammet Uzuner, Yilmaz Erdogan, Taner Birsel, Ahmet Mümtaz Taylan, Firat Tanis, Ercan Kesal.
▷ *Dir* Nuri Bilge Ceylan, *Pro* Zeynep Özbatur Atakan, *Screenplay* Ercan Kesal, Ebru Ceylan and Nuri Bilge Ceylan, from a story by the latter and Bora Göksingöl, *Ph* Gökhan Tiryaki, *Art Dir* Dilek Yapkuöz Ayaztuna, *Ed* Göksingöl, *Cos* Meral Efe, Nildag Batur and Özlem Batur.

A Zeyno Film, Production2006 d.o.o. Sarajevo, 1000 Volt Post production etc-New Wave Films.
158 mins. Turkey/Bosnia and Herzegovina. 2011. Rel: 16 Mar 2012. Cert. 15.

One for the Money ★★★

Katherine Heigl delights as a newly divorced, jobless lingerie clerk called Stephanie Plum who gets a job with her cousin's bail bond business. Her first task is to track down a cop (Jason O'Mara), a murder suspect who by chance is one of her ex's. She finds him, he gets away, she finds him again, he says he's innocent, she tries to help him, that kind of thing. This fairly big-budget ($40 million) mix of comedy, action and thriller lit no fireworks at the box-office and is no earth-mover, but it is quite a lot of easygoing, enjoyable, escapist fun. John Leguizamo, Debra Monk and Debbie Reynolds are assets. DW

❥ Katherine Heigl, Jason O'Mara, Daniel Sunjata, John Leguizamo, Debra Monk, Debbie Reynolds.
❥ *Dir* Julie Anne Robinson, *Pro* Sidney Kimmel, Tom Rosenberg, Gary Lucchesi and Wendy Finerman, *Screenplay* Stacy Sherman, Liz Brixius and Karen Ray, from the novel by Janet Evanovich, *Ph* James Whitaker, *Pro Des* Franco-Giacomo Carbone, *Ed* Lisa Zeno Churgin, *M* Deborah Lurie, *Cos* Michael Dennison.
Lakeshore Entertainment/Sidney Kimmel Entertainment-Entertainment Film Distributors. 91 mins. USA. 2012. Rel: 24 Feb 2012. Cert. 12A.

The Oranges ★★½

What a promising cast (see below) and what a disappointing film! The movie features two neighbouring families living in West Orange, New Jersey. Central to it is the father of one family (Hugh Laurie) who begins an adulterous liaison with the daughter of the other (Leighton Meester). The couple are so self-centred as to be downright unappealing and, in contrast to, say, *Win Win* (2011) or *Please Give* (2009), there are no characters to make it touching as well as comic. Throw in a heavy-handed excess of Christmas songs and it's an all-round letdown. MS

❥ Hugh Laurie, Catherine Keener, Oliver Platt, Allison Janney, Alia Shawkat, Leighton Meester.
❥ *Dir* Julian Farino, *Pro* Anthony Bregman, Leslie Urdang and Dean Vanech, *Screenplay* Jay Reiss and Ian Helfer, *Ph* Steven Fierberg, *Pro Des* Dan Davis, *Ed* Jeffrey M Werner and Carole Kravetz Aykanian, *M* Klaus Badelt and Andrew Raiher, *Cos* David Robinson.
ATO Pictures/an Olympus Pictures production/a Likely Story production etc-Paramount. 90 mins. USA. 2012. Rel: 7 Dec 2012. Cert. 15.

Outside Bet ★½

When the feel-good factor is laid on with a nudge, a wink and a blast of 1980s music, it can make one feel quite nauseous. And beware films that feature a raft of lovable eccentrics with lightly sketched back stories: it's hard to identify with or know or care about anybody. This film, traipsing in the shadow of *Made in Dagenham*, is set in 1985 and is spotted with colourful East London types revolting against the unions and attempting to keep their heads above water. The story is inspired by true events but that doesn't make it any less predictable. JC-W

❥ Bob Hoskins, Phil Davis, Jenny Agutter, Calum MacNab, Adam Deacon, Kate Magowan, Rita Tushingham, Emily Atack, Vincent Regan, Perry Benson, Dudley Sutton, Jason Maza, Linda Robson, Sacha Bennett, Richard Blackwood.
❥ *Dir* Sacha Bennett, *Pro* Carolyn Bennett, Tony Humphreys and Terry Stone, *Screenplay* Bennett and Nigel Smith, *Ph* Nic Lawson, *Pro Des* Matthew Button, *Ed* Kate Evans, *M* Greg Hatwell, *Cos* Hayley Nebauer.
Gateway Films/Talent Films-The Works UK. 101 mins. UK. 2012. Rel: 27 April 2012. Cert. 12A.

The Pact ★★★

Spooky goings on are the order of the day in this efficient haunted houser from first-time feature maker Nicholas McCarthy. Troubled by the disappearance of her estranged sister after their unloved mother's passing, Annie (Caity Lotz) is pestered by an increasingly hands-on spook with something on its mind… With a moderately mysterious plot, a couple of decent jumps, an ominous, shadowy atmosphere and a neatly surprising third act development, *The Pact* is a perfectly acceptable chiller. MJ

❥ Caity Lotz, Casper Van Dien, Agnes Bruckner, Haley Hudson, Kathleen Rose Perkins, Samuel Ball, Mark Steger.
❥ *Dir* and *Screenplay* Nicholas McCarthy, *Pro* Ross M. Dinerstein, *Ph* Bridger Nielson, *Pro Des* Walter

Ghosts of childhood past: Caity Lotz in Nicholas McCarthy's horror opus *The Pact*.

Seeing dead people: Norman Babcock (far right) and friends in Sam Fell and Chris Butler's *ParaNorman*.

Barnett, *Ed* Adriaan van Zyl, *M* Ronen Landa, *Cos* Azalia Snail.

Preferred Content-Entertainment One.
89 mins. USA. 2012. Rel: 8 June 2012. Cert. 15.

Paranormal Activity 4 ★★★½

This new story takes place five years after the disappearance of Kate and Hunter, focusing on teenage Alex (Kathryn Newton), whose family welcome new-to-the-neighbourhood Robbie (Brady Allen) when his mother falls ill. New characters and new surveillance technology are introduced to this successful franchise, which curiously gets better every time; in this case, it's much scarier than the original. GS

▶ Kathryn Newton, Matt Shively, Aidan Lovecamp, Brady Allen, Stephen Dunham, Alexondra Lee, Katie Featherston.
▶ *Dir* Henry Joost and Ariel Schulman, *Pro* Oren Peli, *Screenplay* Christopher Landon, based on a story by Chad Feehan, inspired by Peli's film *Paranormal Activity*, *Ph* Doug Emmett, *Pro Des* Jennifer Spence, *Ed* Gregory Plotkin, *Cos* Leah Butler.

Paramount Pictures/Solana Films/Room 101 Inc/
Blumhouse-Paramount Pictures.
88 mins. USA. 2012. Rel: 17 Oct 2012. Cert. 15.

ParaNorman ★★★

The Oregon-based Laika studio believes in the hand-tooled approach. The company's first full-length feature, *Coraline*, was hypnotic, darkly comic and delightfully macabre. It was also exquisitely crafted in stop-motion animation. Laika's second full-length film, *ParaNorman* (great title), draws on the same attention to detail. Here we have curses, zombies and witches, which are the bread-and-butter of children's literature but, in spite of some ample doses of comedy, the accumulation of horror may prove too intense for younger viewers. Once the charm and throwaway visual gags have worn off, the film lapses into all-too-familiar zombie fare. JC-W

▶ With the voices of Kodi Smit-McPhee, Tucker Albrizzi, Anna Kendrick, Casey Affleck, Christopher Mintz-Plasse, Leslie Mann, Jeff Garlin, Elaine Stritch, Bernard Hill, Jodelle Ferland, John Goodman.
▶ *Dir* Sam Fell and Chris Butler, *Pro* Travis Knight and Arianne Sutner, *Screenplay* Butler, *Ph* Tristan Oliver, *Pro Des* Nelson Lowry, *Ed* Christopher Murrie, *M* Jon Brion.

Laika Entertainment-Universal.
92 mins. USA. 2012. Rel: 14 Sep 2012. Cert. PG.

Parental Guidance ★★½

Artie and Diane Becker (Billy Crystal and Bette Midler) agree to babysit for their daughter's (Marisa Tomei) three children while she's away on holiday with her eccentric husband (Tom Everett Scott). But the grandparents' old methods and tough rules are not welcome. Crystal and Midler have fun together but need a better script than this. Some of the set-pieces fall into the gross-out category and aren't that funny, but overall this is not as bad as it sounds. GS

‣ Billy Crystal, Bette Midler, Marisa Tomei, Tom Everett Scott, Bailee Madison, Joshua Rush, Kyle Harrison Breitkopf.
‣ *Dir* Andy Flickman, *Pro* Billy Crystal, Peter Chernin and Samantha Sprecher, *Screenplay* Lisa Addario and Joe Syracuse, *Ph* Dean Semler, *Pro Des* David J Bomba, *Ed* Kent Beyda, *M* Marc Shaiman, *Cos* Genevieve Tyrrell.

Chernin Entertainment/Walden Media-20th Century Fox. 105 mins. USA. 2012. Rel: 28 Dec 2012. Cert. U.

Patience (After Sebald) ★★★★

This intelligent documentary takes the form of a meditation centred on the writer WG Sebald and in particular on his book *The Rings of Saturn*. Shot mainly in black and white in East Anglia, it follows the walk which provided the framework for that book while also incorporating interviews with academics and other writers and admirers of Sebald. The film has an integrity reminiscent of the best work in that famous TV series *Monitor*. MS

‣ With Adam Phillips, Marina Warner, Andrew Motion, Katie Mitchell, Chris Petit.
‣ *Dir* and *Ph* Grant Gee, *Pro* Sarah Caddy, Gareth Evans and Di Robson, *Ed* Gee and Jerry Chater, *M* The Caretaker.

UK Film Council/An Artevents production/The Re-Enchantment/Screen South etc-Soda Pictures. 86 mins. UK. 2011. Rel: 27 Jan 2012. Cert. 12A.

Payback Season ★

Jerome Davies (Adam Deacon) is a Premiership superstar who's even Better Than Beckham, although he's just 5'5" and as skinny as a spliff. He's got the threads, the ride, the bitches and the fans – but we don't exactly see the moves. In fact, he spends much of the film knocking back such vast quantities of alcohol that he makes George Best look like a lightweight. Be that as it may, this is a morality tale that suggests that once you've capitalised on your dreams, you'd better leave your less savoury childhood friends behind... The standard of acting is astonishing! JC-W

‣ Adam Deacon, Nichola Burley, David Ajala, Anna Popplewell, Leo Gregory, Geoff Hurst, Bronson Webb.
‣ *Dir* Danny Donnelly, *Pro* Donnelly, John Adams and Justin King, *Screenplay* Donnelly and Jenny Fitzpatrick, *Ph* James Martin, *Pro Des* Paul Burns and Ana Viana, *Ed* Oliver Parker, *Cos* Alex Watherston.

Pure Film Prods/Angry Badger Pictures-Revolver Entertainment. 91 mins. UK. 2012. Rel: 9 March 2012. Cert. 15.

The Penguin King 3D ★★★

Given the temperatures, the nature of the terrain and the heavy equipment needed for 3D shooting, it was a brave venture to go to the South Sandwich Islands to make this film about a year in the life of a King Penguin. However, films of this kind are far from new (the 3D adds little), the film's approach seems over-dramatised and, considering that the voice-over is by Sir David Attenborough, the commentary is surprisingly banal. MS

‣ With David Attenborough (narrator).
‣ *Dir* Anthony Geffen and Sias Wilson, *Pro* Geffen, *Written by* David Attenborough, *Ph* Simon Niblett, *Ed* Rob Hall, *M* James Edward Barker.

An Atlantic Productions film/Sky 3D/Galileo Digital Entertainment-Kaleidoscope Entertainment. 78 mins. UK. 2012. Rel: 24 Oct 2012. Cert. U.

People Like Us ★★★

Writer turned director Alex Kurtzman here creates what seems like a personal project. It's the story of a man who, reluctantly attending his father's funeral, makes the discovery that the dead man, unknown to him, had had a second family. There's novelty in this material, but sadly the second half is misjudged (the central character behaves in ways that are presumably more alienating than intended) and sentimentality eventually takes over. MS

‣ Chris Pine, Elizabeth Banks, Olivia Wilde, Michelle Pfeiffer, Mark Duplass, Philip Baker Hall.
‣ *Dir* Alex Kurtzman, *Pro* Roberto Orci, Bobby Cohen and Clayton Townsend, *Screenplay* Kurtzman, Orci and Jody Lambert, *Ph* Salvatore Totino, *Pro Des* Ida Random, *Ed* Robert Leighton, *M* AR Rahman, *Cos* Mary Zophres.

DreamWorks Pictures/Reliance Entertainment/a K/O Paper Products production-Buena Vista. 114 mins. USA. 2012. Rel: 9 Nov 2012. Cert. 12A.

Sovereign Spheniscidae: The stars of *The Penguin King*.

Personal Best ★½

Personal Best follows the four-year preparatory arc of a quartet of British sprinters training for the London Olympics. In the tradition of such documentaries as *Spellbound* and *Sounds Like Teen Spirit*, Sam Blair's film focuses on its protagonists as they gear up for the competition, but it's far too light on back story. Consequently, the sprinters fail to shine as personalities and we don't really get to know them or even root for them. *Chariots of Fire* this ain't. JC-W

▶ James Ellington, Jeanette Kwakye, Richard Alleyne, Omardo Anson.
▶ *Dir* and *Ed* Sam Blair, *Pro* Jessica Levick, *Ph* Jean-Louis Schuller, *M* Lukid and Gunnar Oskarsson.
Magnified Pictures-Verve Pictures.
89 mins. UK. 2012. Rel: 25 May 2012. Cert. 12A.

The Perks of Being a Wallflower ★★★½

The vaults of Hollywood are littered with tales of the classroom outcast. This one is adapted from a 1999 novel by Stephen Chbosky and, interestingly, is directed by Chbosky himself. It's perhaps predictably quirky but is also quite sweet and touching, while gearing up the viewer for some major revelation. However, there are a surprising number of untied loose ends – a reason, perhaps, to read the novel – but overall the film casts a wistful glow with an original, slow-burning radiance. JC-W

▶ Logan Lerman, Emma Watson, Ezra Miller, Mae Whitman, Paul Rudd, Dylan McDermott, Nina Dobrev, Melanie Lynskey, Johnny Simmons, Joan Cusack.
▶ *Dir* and *Screenplay* Stephen Chbosky, *Pro* Russell Smith, Lianne Halfon and John Malkovich, *Ph* Andrew Dunn, *Pro Des* Inbal Weinberg, *Ed* Yana Gorskaya and Mary Jo Markey, *M* Michael Brook, *Cos* David C Robinson.
Summit Entertainment/Mr. Mudd-Entertainment One.
102 mins. USA. 2012. Rel: 3 Oct 2012. Cert. 12A.

Family values: Maxime Godart and Valérie Lemercier in Laurent Tirard's *Petit Nicolas*.

Le petit Nicolas ★★★½

Derived from illustrated children's tales popular in France, this film, aimed at adults as well as children, deals with the adventures of young Nicolas (Maxime Godart). When he jumps to the conclusion that his mother is pregnant, he is jealous enough of the unborn child to plan the kidnapping of the baby. Responses to comedy vary greatly and you will find this either agreeable yet lacking the imagination to take off fully (my own view) or the kind of simple pleasure which is a delight. MS

▶ Maxime Godart, Sandrine Kiberlain, Valérie Lemercier, Kad Merad, Virgile Tirard, Michel Duchaussoy.
▶ *Dir* Laurent Tirard, *Pro* Olivier Delbosc and Marc Missonnier, *Screenplay* Tirard, Grégoire Vigneron and Alain Chabat, from the work of René Goscinny and Jean-Jacques Sempé, *Ph* Denis Rouden, *Art Dir* Françoise Dupertuis, *Ed* Valérie Deseine, *M* Klaus Bedelt, *Cos* Pierre-Jean Larroque.
Fidélité/IMAV/Wild Bunch/M6 Films/Scope Pictures etc-Soda Pictures.
91 mins. France/Belgium. 2009. Rel: 24 Aug 2012. Cert. PG.

Piggy ★½

This deeply violent film tells the story of Joe (Martin Compston), an easy-going London lad whose life is shattered when his beloved brother is brutally murdered. He is unable to cope until he meets Piggy (Paul Anderson), one of his brother's old friends. Kieron Hawkes' flashy direction is let down by his underdeveloped script, which relies more on endless violent acts rather than fully developed characters. GS

▶ Martin Compston, Paul Anderson, Neil Maskell, Josh Herdman, Ed Skrein.
▶ *Dir* and *Screenplay* Kieron Hawkes, *Pro* Danny Potts and Leo Perlman, *Ph* James Friend, *Pro Des* Paul Burns, *Ed* Benjamin Turner, *M* Bill Ryder-Jones, *Cos* Jessie Fell and Holly Austin.
DP Films/Fulwell 73-Metrodome Distribution.
106 mins. UK. 2012. Rel: 4 May 2012. Cert. 18.

Ping Pong ★★★★★

This film's tag-line 'Never too old for gold' would have been a better title since those not much interested in the game of ping pong will, if they understandably ignore the film, miss out on a documentary which offers the best and most optimistic portrait of old age that I can recall seeing in any film. It follows eight contestants who participated in 2009 in the Table Tennis Championships for the over-eighties in Inner Mongolia. It's not the sport that counts here but the people and they are wonderful. *Ping Pong* will delight those who see it. MS

▶ With Les D'Arcy, Terry Donlon, Ursula Bihl, Dorothy DeLow, Lisa Modlich, Sun Lao.
▶ *Dir* Hugh Hartford, *Pro* Anson Hartford, *Ph* Hugh and Anson Hartford, *Ed* John Mister, *M* Orlando Roberton.

Banyak Films/BRITDOC/Channel 4/a Hartford Brothers film etc-Brit Doc Films.
76 mins. UK. 2012. Rel: 6 July 2012. Cert. PG.

Piranha 3DD ★★

A film so wildly, gorily, crazily over-the-top mental, it makes the 2010 original seem like a posh period drama. *Piranha 3DD* sees the toothsome troublemakers of the title setting their sights on a newly opened waterpark. A manically mindless collision of blood, breasts and crass comedy horror, it's both a giddy guilty pleasure and blundering, exploitative trash. A sea of boobs awaits, the largest being David Hasselhoff, who plays himself so badly in this he's like a car crash in a swimsuit. MJ

▶ Danielle Panabaker, David Koechner, Chris Zylka, Gary Busey, Christopher Lloyd, David Hasselhoff, Matt Bush, Katrina Bowden.
▶ *Dir* John Gulager, *Pro* Mark Canton, Marc Toberoff and Joel Soisson, *Screenplay* Soisson, Marcus Dunstan and Patrick Melton, based on characters created by Pete Goldfinger and Josh Stolberg, *Ph* Alexandre Lehmann, *Pro Des* Ermano Di Febo-Orsini, *Ed* Kirk Morri, Devin C. Lussier and Martin Bernfeld, *M* Elia Cmiral, *Cos* Carol Cutshall.

Dimension Films/Mark Canton/IPW/Neo Art & Logic-Entertainment Film Distributors.
83 mins. USA. 2012. Rel: 11 May 2012. Cert. 18.

The Pirates! In an Adventure with Scientists ★★★★½

This season's fun fare from Aardman Animation is a roistering tale of the high seas that knocks Disney's live-action pirate series into a tricorn. Hugh Grant is the voice of the Pirate Captain who wants to win the Pirate of the Year contest. Trouble is he has a rather dozy crew. The scientists they meet on their travels include Charles Darwin, who tells them that if they take the Pirate Captain's parrot (it's actually a dodo) back to England, they will be hailed as heroes for finding an extinct bird. It's all great stuff with Aardman's usual sly sense of humour and regulation punning. There's a terrific chase sequence to outdo all chases and nearly every British actor alive has a voice part. (US title: *The Pirates! Band of Misfits*) MHD

▶ With the voices of Hugh Grant, Martin Freeman, Imelda Staunton, David Tennant, Jeremy Piven, Salma Hayek, Lenny Henry, Brian Blessed, Russell Tovey, Brendan Gleeson, Ashley Jensen.
▶ *Dir* Peter Lord and Jeff Newitt, *Pro* Lord, Julie Lockhart and David Sproxton, *Screenplay* Gideon Defoe, based on his own book, *Ph* Frank Passingham, *Pro Des* Norman Garwood, *Ed* Justin Krish, *M* Theodore Shapiro.

Aardman Animations/Sony Pictures Animation-Sony Pictures Releasing.
88 mins. UK/USA. 2012. Rel: 28 Mar 2012. Cert. U.

Pitch Perfect ★★★

Beca (Anna Kendrick) is the new girl at Barden University and soon joins The Bellas, an all-girl

A hard man from Aardman: The Pirate Captain (voiced by Hugh Grant, of all people) in *The Pirates! In An Adventure With Scientists!*

a capella group. The Bellas are determined to challenge their male rivals and win this year's campus singing competition to make up for their disaster of the previous year. Kendrick and Skylar Astin, as the leader of the male group, work well together but it's Rebel Wilson as fat Amy who steals the show. An enjoyable comedy but unfortunately it runs out of steam towards the end. GS

▶ Anna Kendrick, Skylar Astin, Rebel Wilson, Anna Camp, Brittany Snow, Ester Dean, Alexis Knapp, Hana Mae Lee, Ben Platt.
▶ *Dir* Jason Moore, *Pro* Max Handelman, Paul Brooks and Elizabeth Banks, *Screenplay* Kay Cannon, based on the book by Mickey Rapkin, *Ph* Julio Macat, *Pro Des* Barry Robison, *Ed* Zach Chemberlene, *M* Christophe Beck and Mark Kilian, *Cos* Salvador Pérez Jr.

Brownstone Productions/Relativity Media/Gold Circle Films-Universal Pictures.
112 mins. USA. 2012. Rel: 21 Dec 2012. Cert. 12A.

Planet of Snail ★★★★

Seung-jun Yi's remarkable documentary tells the story of Yeong-chan, a young man who has been deaf and blind since childhood, and his loving wife Soon-Ho, also physically handicapped. It is an incredible story of their daily struggle to survive but mostly one of great love and dependence. But it's the little things in life, like tapping on each other's fingers or fixing the bedroom light, that show the strength of their relationship in this unique and absorbing film. GS

▶ With Yeong-chan Jo, Soon-ho Kim.
▶ *Dir* and *Ph* Seung-jun Yi, *Pro* Min Chul Kim and Gary Byung-seok Kam, *Ed* Seung-jun Yi and Simon El Habre, *M* Seong-ki Min.

NHK/Imamura Ken-ichi-Dogwoof.
88 mins. Finland/Japan/South Korea. 2011. Rel: 22 June 2012. No Cert.

Destiny's child: Karin Viard with a victim of child abuse in Maïwenn's daring and compelling *Polisse*.

The Players ★★½

A series of short films about infidelity directed by a host of French filmmakers including *The Artist* director Michel Hazanavicius. It's a fascinating mixture of vulgarity and hilarity as the talented duo of Jean Dujardin and Gilles Lellouche pose in a series of womanising roles, but with a touch of homoeroticism as well. Some segments work better than others, especially the central sequence where all the characters get together for a sex therapy group led by the puzzled Sandrine Kiberlain. A mixed bag. (Original title: *Les Infidèles*) GS

▶ Jean Dujardin, Gilles Lellouche, Pierre Benoist, Sandrine Kiberlain, Violette Blanckaert, Aina Clotet, Etienne Durot.
▶ *Dir* Emmanuelle Bercot, Fred Cavayé, Alexandre Courtès, Jean Dujardin, Michel Hazanavicius, Jan Kounen, Eric Lartigau, Gilles Lellouche, *Pro* Jean & Marc Dujardin, Guillaume Lacroix and Eric Hannezo, *Screenplay* Dujardin, Lellouche, Nicolas Bedos, Stéphane Joly, Philippe Caverivière, *Ph* Guillaume Schiffman, *Pro Des* Maamar Ech-Cheikh, *Ed* Anny Danché and Julien Leloup, *M* Pino D'Angiò and Evgueni Galperine, *Cos* Carine Sarfati.

JD Prod/Black Dynamite Films/Mars Films/Canal +/Ciné +/Wild Bunch-Alliance Films.
109 mins. France. 2012. Rel: 6 July 2012. Cert. 18.

Polisse ★★★★★

You think you've seen everything in the cinema and then you see a child giving birth. But then *Polisse* is a policier with a difference: it's a film about the Child Protection Unit of Paris. Tackling the taboo subject of child abuse from the perspective of the police, the children, the parents and the perpetrators, *Polisse* is a film that couldn't have been made in Hollywood. But it's not only a ferociously daring portrait of an escalating problem, it's human as well, and even funny. And, naturellement, it is constantly shocking. This is what cinema should be: compelling, believable drama that gives its audience something to think about long after the smell of popcorn has evaporated. JC-W

▶ Karin Viard, Joeystarr, Marina Foïs, Nicolas Duvauchelle, Maïwenn, Karole Rocher, Emmanuelle Bercot, Frédéric Pierrot, Sandrine Kiberlain, Anthony Delon.
▶ *Dir* Maïwenn, *Pro* Alain Attal, *Screenplay* Maïwenn and Emmanuelle Bercot, *Ph* Pierre Aïm, *Pro Des* Nicolas de Boiscuillé, *Ed* Laure Gardette, *M* Stephen Warbeck, *Cos* Marité Coutard.

Les Productions du Trésor/arte France Cinéma/Mars Distribution/ Canal+/CinéCinéma/Arte France/Wild Bunch-Artificial Eye.
127 mins. France. 2011. Rel: 15 June 2012. Cert. 15.

The Pool ★★★½

Belatedly released here (it was made in 2007), this is a story about street kids in Goa. It traces the envious interest of one of them in a property owner and his daughter whose house has a magnificent pool. Based on a short story, it needed the craft of a Satyajit Ray to make the simplicity of the piece telling and to sustain feature length satisfactorily. Chris Smith's work falls short of that, but it's sympathetic and certainly well meant. MS

▶ Venkatesh Chavan, Ayesha Mohan, Nana Patekar, Jhangir Badshah. Malcolm Faria.
▶ *Dir* and *Ph* Chris Smith, *Pro* Kate Noble, *Screenplay* Smith and Randy Russell, from a short story by Russell, *Ed* Barry Polterman, *M* Noisola, Didier Leplae and Joe Wong.

Bluemark-Blue Dolphin Films.
94 mins. USA. 2007. Rel: 16 Nov 2012. Cert. 12A.

Position Among the Stars ★★★★★

This portrait of an Indonesian family is the final part of a trilogy but it readily stands alone. It touches on three generations and moves from village life to Jakarta and back again. Strictly speaking this is a documentary which in the manner of Flaherty may include re-enactments. However, what matters is that the depth of human concern and sensitivity echoes the work of India's Satyajit Ray, while in addition it also possesses a sense of poetry which is all its own. This is not a well-known film, but it is amongst the year's best. (Original title: *Stand van de Sterren*) MS

▶ With members of the Sjamsuddin family.
▶ *Dir* and *Ph* Leonard Retel Helmrich, *Pro* Hetty Naaijkens-Retel Helmrich, *Written by* Naaijkens-Retel Helmrich and Helmrich, *Ed* Jasper Naaijkens, *M* Danang Faturahman and Fahmy Al-Attas.

Scarabeefilms/HUMAN Broadcasting etc-Dogwoof.
109 mins. The Netherlands/USA. 2010. Rel: 17 Feb 2012. No Cert.

The Possession ★★½

Playing a recently divorced couple, Jeffrey Dean Morgan and Kyra Sedgwick add acting chops to this smooth Canadian-made horror thriller. Their girls Hannah and Em (Madison Davenport, Natasha Calis) share time with them. Morgan drives to a yard sale where Calis buys an ancient box and becomes obsessed. When an old professor (Jay Brazeau) says it's a dybbuk box containing a demon, Morgan goes to New York and gets the rabbi's son (Matisyahu) to agree to an exorcism. With its over-familiar theme and stately

Slum citizens: Rumidjah and her son Bakti in their Jakarta ghetto, in Leonard Retel Helmrich's documentary *Position Among the Stars.*

pacing, the film's a bit tame, but it still delivers enough mayhem and scares to be effective. The well-honed screenplay, atmospheric camerawork and classy direction make it a polished ride. DW

▸ Jeffrey Dean Morgan, Kyra Sedgwick, Natasha Calis, Madison Davenport, Matisyahu, Jay Brazeau.
▸ *Dir* Ole Bornedal, *Pro* Sam Raimi, Robert G Tapert and JR Young, *Screenplay* Juliet Snowden and Stiles White, based on Leslie Gornstein's article *Jinx in a Box*, *Ph* Dan Laustsen, *Pro Des* Rachel O'Toole, *Ed* Eric L Beason and Anders Villadsen, *M* Anton Sanko, *Cos* Carla Hetland.

North Box Productions/Ghost House Pictures-Lionsgate. 92 mins. USA/Canada. 2012. Rel: 31 Aug 2012. Cert. 15

Premium Rush ★★★★

David Koepp's film does what it says on the tin, and does it well. An energetic action movie, it features a New York bicycle messenger (the ever reliable Joseph Gordon-Levitt) who finds himself in danger from a crooked cop (Michael Shannon) when he refuses to yield up a mysterious envelope that he is due to deliver. Excellently edited and with two well-placed pauses for breath, this is a chase movie that plays out in what is almost real time. MS

▸ Joseph Gordon-Levitt, Michael Shannon, Dania Ramirez, Jamie Chung, Wolé Parks.
▸ *Dir* David Koepp, *Pro* Gavin Polone, *Screenplay* Koepp and John Kamps, *Ph* Mitchell Amundsen, *Pro Des* Thérèse DePrez, *Ed* Jill Savitt and Derek Ambrosi, *M* David Sardy, *Cos* Luca Mosca.

Columbia Pictures/a Pariah production-Sony Pictures Releasing. 91 mins. USA. 2012. Rel: 14 Sep 2012. Cert. 12A.

The Prey ★★★★

Franck Adrien (Albert Dupontel) is an escaped prisoner who begins a race against time in order to track down Maurel (Stéphane Debac), a former cellmate who frames him for a series of murders. But first Franck needs to outsmart the police and also save his family... Eric Valette's tight thriller is superbly shot in the best Hitchcock tradition, with some very exciting set-pieces, and boasts a raw and highly physical performance from Dupontel. See it before the inevitable Hollywood remake. (Original title: *La Proie*) GS

▸ Albert Dupontel, Alice Taglioni, Stéphane Debac, Natacha Régnier, Sergi López, Serge Hazanavicius, Lucien Jean-Baptiste.
▸ *Dir* Eric Valette, *Pro* Luc Bossi, *Screenplay* Bossi and Laurent Turner, *Ph* Vincent Mathias, *Pro Des* Bertrand Seitz, *Ed* Christophe Pinel, *M* Noko, *Cos* Fabienne Katany.

Brio Films/StudioCanal/Canal +/CinéCinéma/Cinémage 5 etc-StudioCanal. 102 mins. France. 2011. Rel: 13 July 2012. Cert. 15.

Private Peaceful ★★★

Michael Morpurgo, author of *War Horse*, is an executive producer for this adaptation of another novel of his focusing on the First World War. The cost of that war is illustrated by the fate of two brothers of the Peaceful family. The material prompts thoughts of both Losey's *King and Country* (1964) and Kubrick's *Paths of Glory* (1957). Inevitably this is very simplistic by comparison, but young viewers won't have those films in mind and it's certainly sincere. MS

▸ George Mackay, Jack O'Connell, Alexandra Roach, Frances de la Tour, Richard Griffiths, John Lynch, Maxine Peake, Anna Carteret, James Laurenson.
▸ *Dir* Pat O'Connor, *Pro* Guy de Beaujeu and Simon Reade, *Screenplay* Reade, from Michael Morpurgo's novel, *Ph* Jerzy Zielinski, *Pro Des* Adrian Smith, *Ed* Humphrey Dixon, *M* Rachel Portman, *Cos* Anushia Nieradzik.

Eagle Media/Fluidity Films/Poonamallee Productions etc-Eagle Rock Group. 102 mins. UK. 2012. Rel: 12 Oct 2012. Cert. 12A.

Project X ★★★

Seventeen-year-old Thomas (Thomas Mann) and his equally nerdy high school friends decide to throw a party on his birthday while his parents are away. To their surprise thousands turn up. The set-up is routine and the inevitable handheld camera gets in the way when one of the friends decides to capture this momentous occasion for posterity. But once the way over-the-top party gets going it is surprisingly funny, due mainly to the razor-sharp editing. GS

▸ Thomas Mann, Oliver Cooper, Jonathan Daniel Brown, Dax Flame, Kirby Bliss Blanton, Alexis Knapp.

Speed is of the essence: Joseph Gordon-Levitt and Dania Ramirez in David Koepp's *Premium Rush*.

▶ *Dir* Nima Nourizadeh, *Pro* Todd Phillips, *Screenplay* Matt Drake and Michael Bacall, from a story by Bacall, *Ph* Ken Seng, *Pro Des* Bill Brzeski, *Ed* Jeff Groth, *Cos* Alison McCosh.

Green Hat Films/Silver Pictures-Warner Bros. 88 mins. USA. 2012. Rel: 2 Mar 2012. Cert. 18.

Prometheus ★★★★½

The excitement of Ridley Scott's original *Alien* was the whole new world he created within the parameters of science fiction. For the first time he brought both a credibility and human form to a genre previously defined by bright lights and tinfoil. To Scott's credit, he now takes the franchise he created in 1979 and steers it back to its creditable beginnings – far, far from the excesses of the later films. Consequently, the jaw-dropping set-pieces retain all the power of the first film in the series. And you'll never look at a caesarean in the same light again. JC-W

▶ Noomi Rapace, Michael Fassbender, Guy Pearce, Idris Elba, Logan Marshall-Green, Charlize Theron, Sean Harris, Rafe Spall, Kate Dickie, Emun Elliott, Benedict Wong, Patrick Wilson.
▶ *Dir* Ridley Scott, *Pro* Scott, David Giler and Walter Hill, *Screenplay* Jon Spaihts and Damon Lindelof, *Ph* Dariusz Wolski, *Pro Des* Arthur Max, *Ed* Pietro Scalia, *M* Marc Streitenfeld and Harry Gregson-Williams, *Cos* Janty Yates.

Twentieth Century Fox/Dune Entertainment/Scott Free/ Brandywine-20th Century Fox. 123 mins. USA. 2012. Rel: 1 June 2012. Cert. 15.

The Prophet ★★★★

Gary Tarn's lyrical documentary takes Kahlil Gibran's 1923 cult novel and turns it into a unique cinematic experience. Tarn travels to Serbia, Lebanon, New York, Milan and London and photographs people, situations and places that reflect Gibran's text. It's a rich tapestry of culture, love and death and is perfectly complemented by Thandie Newton's eloquent narration, which adds class and style to this mesmerising and hypnotic experience. GS

▶ Narrated by Thandie Newton.
▶ *Dir, Pro, Pho, Ed, M* Gary Tarn.

Land Media Productions-ICO/City Screen. 75 mins. UK/Italy/Lebanon/USA/Serbia & Montenegro. 2011. Rel: 21 Sep 2012. No Cert.

Pusher ★★★★

This remake of Nicolas Winding Refn's 1996 Danish film relocated to London finds him on board as an executive producer and, briefly, as an actor on screen. That's apt because this tighter version of a drug dealer's desperate attempt to escape to a new life is very well done. Richard Coyle's anti-hero is admirably judged, and there's a great villain, the equal of Gert Froebe's Goldfinger, in Zlatko Buric's reprise of his original role. MS

▶ Richard Coyle, Bronson Webb, Agyness Deyn, Mem Ferda, Paul Kaye, Zlatko Buric, Neil Maskell.
▶ *Dir* Luis Prieto, *Pro* Rupert Preston, Christopher

Future fresh: Noomi Rapace in Ridley Scott's powerful, thrilling and jaw-dropping Prometheus.

Simon and Felix Vossen, *Screenplay* Matthew Read, based on the original screenplay by Nicolas Winding Refn and Jens Dahl, *Ph* Simon Dennis, *Pro Des* Sarah Webster, *Ed* Kim Gaster, *M* Orbital, *Cos* Alexandra Mann.

A Vertigo Films & Embargo Films production/ Exponential Media-Vertigo Films.
89 mins. UK. 2012. Rel: 12 Oct 2012. Cert. 18.

The Queen of Versailles ★★★★

Lauren Greenfield's intriguing documentary looks at the lives of the billionaire David Siegel and his much younger third wife, Jackie. Initially we see them when Siegel's business success with property (timeshare apartments a special feature) enables him to commission the building of the largest house in America, modelled on Versailles. Then comes the financial crash. To some extent a comment on the American dream, the film rewardingly leaves it to the audience to forge their own attitudes to this extraordinary couple. MS

⯈ With David Siegel, Jacqueline Siegel, Richard Siegel.
⯈ *Dir* Lauren Greenfield, *Pro* Greenfield and Danielle Renfrew Behrens, *Ph* Tom Hurwitz, *Ed* Victor Livingston, *M* Jeff Beal.
Evergreen Pictures/BBC Storyville/Impact Partners/ Candescent Films etc-Dogwoof.
101 mins. Sweden/Norway/Switzerland/Finland. 2012. Rel: 7 Sep 2012. Cert. PG.

Radioman ★★★★

Mary Kerr's excellent documentary follows Radioman around New York: he is a unique, well-known personality, an experienced supporting artist considered a friend by many film actors, including Meryl Streep and Tom Hanks. He may look like a homeless man, bearing an uncanny resemblance to Robin Williams in *The Fisher King*, but he's also an essential feature of any New York film location and knows where every film is being shot even before the actors receive their call sheets. An exceptional film about an inimitable personality. GS

⯈ With Josh Brolin, George Clooney, Craig Castaldo, Matt Damon, Johnny Depp, Tom Hanks, Jude Law, Eva Mendes, Helen Mirren, Meryl Streep, Tilda Swinton, Sting and Radioman.
⯈ *Dir* and *Ph* Mary Kerr, *Pro* Paul Fischer, *Ed* Gary Forrester, *M* Julia Newmann and Cody Westheimer.
Ten Cent Adventures-Ten Cent Adventures.
75 mins. UK. 2012. Rel: 12 Oct 2012. Cert. 15.

The Raid ★★★★★

No need to ask why a Welshman directed a superb action movie in Indonesia. Just know that Gareth Huw Evans has made the best action film of the year. A SWAT team has to break into a Jakarta tower block from where drugs baron Tama operates. How can they get past his machete-wielding guards? What follows is a bombardment by the cops who hack their way in, literally cutting a swathe from the ground floor up to the 15th and Mr Big's HQ. As they go at it with knives, blades, machetes and anything else that comes to hand, including fisticuffs, it's like taking part in a computer game over which you have no control. The totally committed cast are brilliant, the running time is 101 minutes, the body count about double that. (Original title: *Serbuan maut*) MHD

⯈ Iko Iwais, Ananda George, Ray Sahetapy, Tegar Setryar, Doni Alamsyah, Yahan Ruhian, Pierre Gruno, Joe Taslim, Verdi Solaiman.
⯈ *Dir, Screenplay* and *Ed* Gareth Huw Evans, *Pro* Ario Sagantoro, *Ph* Mat Flannery and Dimas Imam Subhono, *Art Dir* Moti D Setyanto, *M* Fajar Yuskemal, Aria Prayogi, Mike Shinoda and Joseph Trapanese, *Costume Superviser* Upay Mariani.
Merantau Films/Celluloid Nightmares/XYZ Films-Momentum Films.
101 mins. Indonesia/USA. 2011. Rel: 18 May 2012. Cert. 18.

Rampart ★★

The title of this police drama refers to the headquarters of the LAPD and a corrupt officer (Woody Harrelson) is at the film's centre. He strikes me as a wholly repulsive character and that applies no less when one takes his personal life into account. A different screenplay might render him a pitiable, tragic figure but, as told, I found his story wholly antipathetic. Some lovers of tough dramas may disagree. MS

⯈ Woody Harrelson, Ned Beatty, Ben Foster, Anne Heche, Ice Cube, Sigourney Weaver, Robin Wright, Steve Buscemi, Francis Capra.
⯈ *Dir* Oren Moverman, *Pro* Lawrence Inglee, Ben

Special extra: Craig Castaldo, the colourful subject of Mary Kerr's documentary, *Radioman*.

Foster and others, *Screenplay* James Ellroy and Moverman, *Ph* Bobby Bukowski, *Pro Des* David Wasco, *Ed* Jay Rabinowitz, *M* Dickon Hinchcliffe, *Cos* Catherine George.

Lightstream Pictures/a Waypoint Entertainment production/The Third Mind Pictures-StudioCanal Limited. 108 mins. USA. 2011. Rel: 24 Feb 2012. Cert. 15.

The Raven ★½

John Cusack plays Edgar Allan Poe during the unaccounted-for last days of his life. Blending fact and fiction, James McTeigue's film conjures up a story in which the penniless and drunken poet is further tormented by the grisly executions of a serial killer emulating scenes from Poe's own stories. Not an original idea, of course (cf *Copycat*, ABC TV's *Castle*, etc), and one performed with a surprisingly straight face (Poe-faced, one might say). Yet, even when the film borders on torture porn in spirit, it's actually more Hammer horror without the ham. But an arched eyebrow might have paid dividends. JC-W

❥ John Cusack, Luke Evans, Alice Eve, Kevin R McNally, Brendan Gleeson, Sam Hazeldine, Pam Ferris.
❥ *Dir* James McTeigue, *Pro* Marc D Evans, Trevor Macy and Aaron Ryder, *Screenplay* Ben Livingston and Hannah Shakespeare, *Ph* Danny Ruhlmann,

Pro Des Roger Ford, *Ed* Niven Howie, *M* Lucas Vidal, *Cos* Carlo Poggioli.

Intrepid Pictures/FilmNation Entertainment/Galavis Film/Pioneer Pictures/Relativity Media-Universal. 110 mins. USA/Hungary/Spain. 2012. Rel: 9 March 2012. Cert. 15.

Ray Harryhausen: Special Effects Titan ★★★★

Although many famous directors pay tribute here, Ray Harryhausen himself is the wholly engaging star personality in this admirable documentary looking back at his career. At times the other contributors are allowed to repeat themselves, but this is a delightful reminder of Harryhausen's work, recalling such pleasures as *The 7th Voyage of Sinbad* and *Jason and the Argonauts* and celebrating a time when one man rather than a team was crucial in that kind of movie. MS

❥ With Ray Harryhausen, Tim Burton, James Cameron, Terry Gilliam, Steven Spielberg.
❥ *Dir*, *Written by* and *Ed* Gilles Penso, *Pro* and *M* Alexandre Poncet.

Frenetic Arts/The Ray & Diana Harryhausen Foundation-Arrow Films. 97 mins. France/UK/USA. 2012. Rel: 9 Nov 2012. Cert. PG.

Puppet master Ray Harryhausen, the subject of Gilles Penso's *Ray Harryhausen: Special Effects Titan.*

The bridal bug: Newlyweds Diego Martin and Leticia Dolera in Paco Plaza's *[REC]³ Génesis*.

[Rec]3 Génesis ★★★

The third in the supernatural horror series moves away from the claustrophobic environment of the Barcelona apartment building of *[Rec]* 1 and 2 to the wedding of Kordo and Clara, the happiest day of their lives until their uncle arrives with a huge bandage on his arm. The production values and set-pieces are more impressive this time around and the story has more fun elements than before. The eerie atmosphere of the original has been lost, but thankfully the handheld camera filming style is also abandoned halfway through. GS

▶ Leticio Dolero, Diego Martin, Javier Botet, Ismael Martínez, Àlex Monner, Mireia Ros, Carla Nieto.
▶ *Dir* Paco Plaza, *Pro* Julio Fernández, *Screenplay* Plaza, David Gallart and Luiso Berdejo, *Ph* Pablo Rosso, *Pro Des* Gemma Fauria, *Ed* David Gallart, *M* Mikel Salas, *Cos* Olga Rodal.

Canal + España/Filmax/Ono/Rec Genesis AEI/Televisió de Catalunya (TV3)/Televisión Espanola (TVE) etc-Entertainment One.
80 mins. Spain. 2012. Rel: 31 Aug 2012. Cert. 18.

Red Dog ★★

I applaud any dog lover who embraced the 2009 film *My Dog Tulip*, but this Australian hit, a legendary tale of a real-life kelpie of the 1970s, could not be more sentimental and contrived. It tries ineptly to switch from comedy to tragedy and yet to come up with a happy ending.

Nevertheless, there will be those who find pathos where I found bathos. The location shooting is admirable. MS

▶ Josh Lucas, Rachael Taylor, Rohan Nichol, Luke Ford, John Batchelor, Koko.
▶ *Dir* Kriv Stenders, *Pro* Nelson Woss and Julie Ryan, *Screenplay* Daniel Taplitz, from the book by Louis de Bernières, *Ph* Geoffrey Hall, *Pro Des* Ian Gracie, *Ed* Jill Bilcock, *M* Cezary Skubiszewski, *Cos* Mariot Kerr.

Screen Australia/Endymion Films/Essential Entertainment/a Woss Group production-G2 Pictures.
92 mins. Australia/USA. 2010. Rel: 24 Feb 2012. Cert. PG.

Red Light Revolution ★½

Shunzi (Zhao Jun) has reached rock bottom: he loses his job and subsequently his wife leaves him for another man. He is desperate to make ends meet so he agrees to secretly open a sex shop in a conservative neighbourhood. But his supplier is a gangster who threatens Shunzi for his weekly payments. Director Sam Voutas' unfunny comedy claims to be 'China's first sex shop comedy', but sadly the script lacks subtlety and the performers are encouraged to overact. GS

▶ Zhao Jun, Vivid Wang, Xidu Jiang, Masanobu Otsuka, Tes Liu, Bing Bo.
▶ *Dir, Screenplay* and *Ed* Sam Voutas, *Pro* Melanie Ansley, *Ph* Yifan Wang, *Art Dir* Yuan Feng, *Cos* Wei Xiaoyan.

Scopofile-Terracotta Distribution.
91 mins. China. 2010. Rel: 20 Jan 2012. Cert. 18.

Red Lights ★★

The 2010 film *Buried* was a tour de force for its director Rodrigo Cortés. Sadly he can do nothing here to hide the fact that the story being told is pure hokum. This is emphasised by a music score which underlines every would-be terrifying moment. The cast for this tale of a possibly bogus blind psychic is surprisingly distinguished, but the film isn't good enough to be taken seriously and too daft to be fun. It's sunk by its script – which this time is Cortés' own. MS

➤ Cillian Murphy, Sigourney Weaver, Robert De Niro, Toby Jones, Elizabeth Olsen, Joely Richardson, Craig Roberts.
➤ *Dir*, *Screenplay* and *Ed* Rodrigo Cortés, *Pro* Adrian Guerra and Cortés, *Ph* Xavi Giménez, *Pro Des* Antón Laguna, *M* Victor Reyes, *Cos* Patricia Monné.
Parlay Films/a Nostromo Pictures production/Cindy Cowan Entertainment etc-Momentum Pictures.
113 mins. Spain/USA. 2012. Rel: 15 June 2012. Cert. 15.

Red Tails ★★½

This is inspired by World War II's first African-American fighter squadron and boasts superb aerial photography. The powerful story about this valiant group of pilots, who overcame racial discrimination in order to become one of the most distinguished squadrons in the war, needs to be told but is let down by a one-dimensional script and Anthony Hemingway's unimaginative direction. Producer George Lucas' impressive production values are simply not enough to fulfil the story's potential. GS

➤ Cuba Gooding Jr, Nate Parker, David Oyelowo, Bryan Cranston, Tristan Wilds, Rupert Penry-Jones, Ne-Yo, Daniela Ruah.
➤ *Dir* Anthony Hemingway, *Pro* Charles Floyd Johnson and Rick McCallum, *Screenplay* John Ridley and Aaron McGruder, from a story by Ridley based on John B Holway's book *Red Tails, Black Wings: The Men of America's Black Air Force*, *Ph* John Aronson, *Pro Des* Michael Carlin and Nicholas Palmer, *Ed* Ben Burt and Michael O'Halloran, *M* Terence Blanchard, *Cos* Alison Mitchell.
Twentieth Century Fox/Lucasfilm Group/Partnership Pictures-Momentum Pictures.
125 mins. USA. 2012. Rel: 6 June 2012. Cert. 12A.

Requiem for a Killer ★★★★

Lucrece (Mélanie Laurent) is a highly skilled assassin assigned to one last job during the Festival d'Ermeux in the Swiss Alps. But first she has to pose as a soprano before killing one of her fellow performers, the British baritone Alexander Child (Christopher Stills). Laurent delivers another luminous performance as the classy assassin caught in the middle of double-cross and deceit in this stylish thriller. (Original title: *Requiem pour une tueuse*) GS

➤ Mélanie Laurent, Clovis Cornillac, Xavier Gallais, Christopher Stills.
➤ *Dir* and *Screenplay* Jérôme Le Gris *Pro* Alain Terzian, *Ph* Antoine Monod, *Pro Des* Maamar Ech-Cheihk, *Ed* Claire Fieschi, *M* Jiri Heger, Anne-Sophie Versnaeyen and Regis Vogëlène, *Cos* Catherine Rigaud.
Alter Films/StudioCanal/France 2 Cinéma/France Télévision/Canal+/ CinéCinéma etc-StudioCanal.
91 mins. France. 2011. Rel: 15 June 2012. Cert. 12A.

Resident Evil: Retribution ★

There have now been five *Resident Evil* movies. With each one much the same as the last, it's a

Musical chairs: Clovis Cornillac and Tchéky Karyo in Jérôme Le Gris' *Requiem for a Killer*.

Death's a bitch: Milla Jovovich (left) aims for completion in Paul WS Anderson's *Resident Evil: Retribution*.

stubbornly unremarkable franchise that delivers in-one-eye-and-out-the-other SF-horror action that's neither clever nor scary nor exciting. Milla Jovovich battles through a convoluted, po-faced and personality-free videogame plot, wasting monstrous mutants and gun-toting zombies on her way to yet another open ending. Strictly for heavily sedated fans of the franchise who, contrary to all natural laws, enjoyed the previous offerings. MJ

► Milla Jovovich, Sienna Guillory, Michelle Rodriguez, Aryana Engineer, Colin Salmon.
► *Dir* and *Screenplay* Paul WS Anderson, *Pro* Anderson, Don Carmody, Jeremy Bolt and Samuel Hadida, *Ph* Glen MacPherson, *Pro Des* Kevin Phipps, *Ed* Niven Howie, *M* tomandandy, *Cos* Wendy Partridge.

Constantin Film International/Davis Films/Impact Pictures-Sony Pictures Releasing.
96 mins. Germany/Canada/USA. 2012. Rel: 28 Sep 2012. Cert. 15.

Return ★★★½

When Kelli, a woman soldier, returns home from Afghanistan to Ohio, we recognise that her experiences of war have traumatised her more than she is prepared to admit. Her marriage suffers accordingly. Director Liza Johnson captures superbly the feel of American provincial life, but as the story develops the issues raised are not always investigated with the clarity and detail one would like. However, lead actress Linda Cardellini is excellent and Michael Shannon offers unselfish support. MS

► Linda Cardellini, Michael Shannon, John Slattery, Talia Balsam, Paul Sparks.
► *Dir* and *Screenplay* Liza Johnson, *Pro* Noah Harlan, Ben Howe and Johnson, *Ph* Anne Etheridge, *Pro Des* Inbal Weinberg, *Ed* Paul Zucker and Affonso Goncalves, *M* T Griffin, *Cos* Erica Munro.

Fork Films/a 2.1 Films/True Enough production/Meredith Vieira Productions etc-Network Releasing.
98 mins. USA. 2011. Rel: 6 Apr 2012. Cert. 15.

Revenge of the Electric Car
★★★½

A follow-up to the earlier documentary *Who Killed the Electric Car?* (2006), this is a more positive update tracing the industry's changed attitude to the electric car that it once excoriated. This time it's a less compelling tale, but ably told nevertheless. It contains the most intriguing of credits regarding a star whose endorsement of the car appears in this film: 'Danny DeVito photographed by Haskell Wexler'. MS

► With Carlos Ghosn, Elon Musk, Bob Lutz, Danny DeVito. Narrated by Tim Robbins.
► *Dir* Chris Paine, *Pro* Jessie Deeter and PG Morgan, *Written by* Morgan and Paine, *Ph* Thaddeus Wadleigh, *Ed* Chris A Peterson, *M* David Robbins.

Westmidwest Productions-Dogwoof.
90 mins. USA. 2011. Rel: 20 July 2012. Cert. PG.

The Reverend ★★½

Stuart Brennan does well as the young Reverend gentleman in question, bloodily bitten by a vampire on the very first day of his new job (bad luck that!) when he welcomes a mystery girl into his chapel at night. Now he has a mission from God – to clean up his lawless village. Script, effects and budget seem a bit skimpy, but the striking visuals, high gore quota and practised villainy of Tamer Hassan (plus Rutger Hauer and Doug Bradley in cameos) give this graphic-novel-based horror a boost. DW

► Stuart Brennan, Tamer Hassan, Rutger Hauer, Doug Bradley, Giovanni Lombardo Radice, Emily Booth, Shane Richie.
► *Dir* and *Screenplay* Neil Jones, *Pro* Jones and Brennan, *Ph* Alessio Valori, *Pro Des* Felix Coles, *M* Alan Deacon, *Cos* Gemma Bedeau.

Burn Hand Film Productions/Templeheart Fims-Metrodome Distribution.
98 mins. UK. 2011. Rel: 3 Aug 2012. Cert. 18.

The Rise and Fall of a White Collar Hooligan ★½

The hooligan in question is Mike Jacobs (Nick Nevern), an unemployed man who after a chance meeting with old friend Eddie Hill (Simon Phillips) begins to work for him as a courier. Unsurprisingly he soon finds himself locked up in a French prison with no one to care about his fate. Though slick and fast, this is also hollow thanks to its uninteresting characters. Nevern does his best in an unexplored and over-familiar script while Phillips delivers yet another smug performance. GS

► Nick Nevern, Simon Phillips, Rita Ramnani, Peter Barrett, Rebecca Ferdinando.
► *Dir* and *Screenplay* Paul Tanter, from a story by

Raheel Riaz, *Pro* Tanter, Alain Wildberger, Jonathan Sothcott and Patricia Rybarczyk, *Ph* Haider Zafar, *Pro Des* Felix Coles, *Ed* Richard Colton and Andi Sloss, *Cos* Alice Woodward.

Press On Features/Silver Town Films/Templeheart Films/ Chata Pictures-Momentum Pictures.
81 mins. UK. 2012. Rel: 7 May 2012. Cert. 18.

Rise of the Guardians ★★½

An adaptation of William Joyce's series of books *The Guardians of Childhood*, this sounds like a folkloric version of *Avengers Assemble*. With the Bogeyman attempting a comeback, Father Christmas, the Easter Bunny, the Tooth Fairy, the Sandman, Jack Frost and the Man in the Moon join forces to stop him in his tracks. Visually the film is astonishing but the charm is forced and the wit woefully lacking. And it's a shame that so much violence seems to save the day. JC-W

▶ With the voices of Chris Pine, Alec Baldwin, Jude Law, Isla Fisher, Hugh Jackman, Dakota Goyo.
▶ *Dir* Peter Ramsey, *Pro* Christina Steinberg and Nancy Bernstein, *Screenplay* David Lindsay-Abaire, based on William Joyce's series of books *The Guardians of Childhood*, *Visual Consultant* Roger Deakins, *Pro Des* Patrick Hanenberger, *Ed* Joyce Arrastia, *M* Alexandre Desplat.

DreamWorks Animation-Paramount Pictures.
97 mins. USA. 2012. Rel: 30 Nov 2012. Cert. PG.

Rock of Ages ★★

This has got to stop. The trend for filching songs from the jukebox and adding Polyfilla plots must be giving Cole Porter and Irving Berlin cause to spin. Here, the Broadway 'musical' *Rock of Ages* is given the cinematic treatment courtesy of Adam Shankman, director of *Hairspray* – the film of the musical of the film, that is. And the cheese is three Camemberts high. Thank Axl Rose, then, for the music, supplied by the likes of Guns N' Roses, Def Leppard, Foreigner, and their mates. Otherwise this might have been a rather rusty nail in the coffin of the rock 'n' roll musical. JC-W

▶ Julianne Hough, Diego Boneta, Russell Brand, Paul Giamatti, Catherine Zeta-Jones, Mary J Blige, Alec Baldwin, Tom Cruise, Malin Akerman, Bryan Cranston, Will Forte.
▶ *Dir* Adam Shankman, *Pro* Shankman, Jennifer Gibgot, Tobey Maguire, Matthew Weaver, Scott Prisand, Carl Levin and Garrett Grant, *Screenplay* Justin Theroux, Chris D'Arienzo and Allan Loeb, *Ph* Bojan Bazelli, *Pro Des* Jon Hutman, *Ed* Emma E Hickox, *M* Adam Anders and Peer Åström, *Cos* Rita Ryack, *Choreography* Mia Michaels.

New Line Cinema/Corner Store Entertainment/ Material Pictures/Offspring Entertainment/Maguire Entertainment-Warner Bros.
123 mins. USA. 2012. Rel: 13 June 2012. Cert. 12A.

The Rolling Stones: Crossfire Hurricane ★★★½

Films about The Rolling Stones just keep on coming. From Jean-Luc Godard's *Sympathy for the Devil* (1968) to Martin Scorsese's *Shine a Light* (2008), the great and the good seem to be transfixed by the boys from London. This film chronicles the early years with archive footage commented on by The Stones themselves. It's an elegant tribute, but never ingratiatingly so,

Guardians congregate: Santa Claus (centre) gives Jack Frost (right) a talking to in *Rise of the Guardians*.

and includes never-before-seen footage from some of the older documentaries. And because the musicians contribute their words off-camera, their revelations seem all the more revealing and un-selfconscious. CB

▶ Mick Jagger, Charlie Watts, Keith Richards, Ron Wood, Bill Wyman, Mick Taylor, Brian Jones (archive).
▶ *Dir* and *Written by* Brett Morgan, *Pro* Jagger and Victoria Pearman, *Ed* Stuart Levy and Conor O'Neill.
Milkwood Films/Tremolo Productions-Eagle Rock Entertainment.
111 mins. UK/USA. 2012. Rel: 18 Oct 2012. Cert. 15.

Room 237 ★★

If you are obsessed by Stanley Kubrick's film *The Shining*, you might conceivably be fascinated by this documentary in which five unseen commentators expound their theories as to its hidden meanings. Edited together with little sense of structure, these notions range from it being a comment on the Holocaust or on the genocide of the American Indians to Kubrick's confession that he faked the footage of the moon landing. At this length, and with no insight into the individuals with these bizarre notions, one is left wishing that it had been relegated to a much shorter version as a DVD extra. MS

▶ With Bill Blakemore, Geoffrey Cocks, Juli Kearns, John Fell Ryan, Jay Weidner.
▶ *Dir* Rodney Ascher, *Pro* Tim Kirk, *M* William Hutson and Jonathan Snipes.
Highland Park Classics-Metrodome Distribution Ltd.
102 mins. USA. 2012. Rel: 26 Oct 2012. Cert. 15.

A Royal Affair ★★★★

Denmark-Norway in the 18th century... English Princess Caroline Mathilde is to marry the appalling and almost certifiable King Christian VII. After giving birth to a royal heir, Caroline begins a loving relationship with the King's German physician, Doctor Struensee. The doctor tries to convince the mad King that his country should become more progressive and enlightened. It works for a time but the rigid courtiers realise what is happening and eventually the love affair is brought to an end. Nikolaj Arcel's film is beautifully made, with stunning performances by Alicia Vikander as Caroline, Mads Mikkelsen as Struensee and Mikkel Boe Følsgaard as the King. A fascinating but little-known true story brought to brimming life. (Original title: *En kongelig affaere*) MHD

▶ Alicia Vikander, Mads Mikkelsen, Mikkel Boe Følsgaard, Trine Dyrholm, David Dencik, Harriet Walter.
▶ *Dir* Nikolaj Arcel, *Pro* Meta Luise Foldager, Sisse Graum Jørgensen and Louise Vesth, *Screenplay* Arcel and Rasmuss Heisterberg, from Bodil Steensen-Leth's novel *Prinsesse af blodet*, *Ph* Rasmus Videbæk, *Pro Des* Niels Sejer, *Ed* Kasper Leick and Mikel E. G. Nielsen, *M* Cyrille Aufort and Gabriel Yared, *Cos* Manon Rasmussen.
Zentropa Entertainments/Sirena Film/DR TV/Trollhätten Film AB/Film i Vast/
Sveriges Television-Metrodome Distribution.
137 mins. Denmark/Sweden/Czech Republic. 2012. Rel: 15 June 2012. Cert. 15.

Ruby Sparks ★★★½

Zoe Kazan, who wrote it and who delights us in the leading role, is the key figure in this uneven but ambitious piece. Paul Dano, also ideally cast, is a novelist with writer's block whose dream girl, Ruby, literally comes to life. The comedy that develops avoids cloying whimsy and then turns serious about the possessive side of relationships, eventually becoming as dark as *Secretary* (2002). But when it backtracks into comedy again for a happy ending, it misfires. Yet it's original and worth seeing despite its faults. MS

▶ Zoe Kazan, Paul Dano, Antonio Banderas, Annette Bening, Steve Coogan, Elliott Gould.
▶ *Dir* Jonathan Dayton and Valerie Faris, *Pro* Albert Berger and Ron Yerxa, *Screenplay* Zoe Kazan, *Ph* Matthew Libatique, *Pro Des* Judy Becker, *Ed* Pamela Martin, *M* Nick Urata, *Cos* Nancy Steiner.
Fox Searchlight Pictures/a Bona Fide production/Dune Entertainment-20th Century Fox.
102 mins. USA. 2012. Rel: 12 Oct 2012. Cert. 12A.

Rust and Bone ★★★

This French film from Jacques Audiard stars the splendid Marion Cotillard and instantly became famous for using the latest techniques to show the actress legless after her character

Character development: Zoe Kazan and Paul Dano in Jonathan Dayton and Valerie Faris' *Ruby Sparks*.

suffers an accident at the pool where she works with whales. One is expecting to see a story about this woman and her adjustment to life aided by a new acquaintance (able newcomer Matthias Schoenaerts). Instead it's the man who becomes the chief focus in the second half, which also disappoints by leading to a flagrantly melodramatic climax. Belatedly I learnt that the film is based on two short stories and that helps to explain why it seems wrong. (Original title: *De Rouille et d'os*) MS

‣ Marion Cotillard, Matthias Schoenaerts, Armand Verdure, Bouli Lanners, Céline Sallette.
‣ *Dir* Jacques Audiard, *Pro* Pascal Caucheteux, Martine Cassinelli and Audiard, *Screenplay* Thomas Bidegain and Audiard, from *De Rouille et d'os* by Craig Davidson, *Ph* Stéphane Fontaine, *Art Dir* Michel Barthélémy, *Ed* Juliette Welfling, *M* Alexandre Desplat, *Cos* Virginie Montel.

Why Not Productions/Page 114/France 2 Cinéma/Les Films du Fleuve etc-StudioCanal Ltd.
123 mins. France/Belgium. 2012. Rel: 2 Nov 2012. Cert. 15.

Safe ★★★½

Computers have a habit of leaving traces of code behind. Not so the human brain. In this case, the brain of an 11-year-old Chinese girl proves extremely useful to the Triad of New York, the Russian Mafia and the noble boys in blue of the NYPD – not to mention the city's mayor… Whatever one thinks of Jason Statham, one can't deny that he makes movies that deliver. As the erstwhile cop in *Safe* he tears New York apart by the hinges. In short, *Safe* is vicious, ruthless and proficient B-movie escapism that keeps the pulse racing on overdrive. JC-W

‣ Jason Statham, Robert John Burke, Chris Sarandon, Catherine Chan, James Hong, Anson Mount.
‣ *Dir* and *Screenplay* Boaz Yakin, *Pro* Lawrence Bender and Dana Brunetti, *Ph* Stefan Czapsky, *Pro Des* Joseph Nemec III, *Ed* Frederic Thoraval, *M* Mark Mothersbaugh, *Cos* Ann Roth.

IM Global/Automatik Entertainment/Lawrence Bender Prods/Trigger Street Prods/87Eleven-Momentum Pictures.
94 mins. USA. 2012. Rel: 4 May 2012. Cert. 15.

Safe House ★★

There's no safety and not a lot of houses in this non-stop, testosterone-centric star vehicle. Denzel Washington plays a man wanted by the CIA and no end of shadowy bad guys, and Ryan Reynolds is the cop who ends up employed as his babysitter. Denzel proves to be a decidedly slippery customer – even as half of Cape Town pursues our mismatched heroes through the rooms, streets and shanty towns of South Africa. Much of it is incomprehensible but what isn't is mind-numbingly familiar and formulaic. JC-W

‣ Denzel Washington, Ryan Reynolds, Vera Farmiga, Brendan Gleeson, Sam Shepard, Rubén Blades, Robert Patrick, Liam Cunningham.

Sea change: Marion Cotillard in Jacques Audiard's *Rust and Bone*, winner of four César awards.

Fish out of water: Amr Waked and Ewan McGregor in Lasse Hallström's *Salmon Fishing in the Yemen*.

▶ *Dir* Daniel Espinosa, *Pro* Scott Stuber, *Screenplay* David Guggenheim, *Ph* Oliver Wood, *Pro Des* Brigitte Broch, *Ed* Rick Pearson, *M* Ramin Djawadi, *Cos* Susan Matheson.

Universal Pictures/Relativity Media/Bluegrass Films-Universal.
114 mins. USA. 2012. Rel: 24 February 2012. Cert. 15.

Safety Not Guaranteed ★★★½

There may be echoes here of the classic *Mr Deeds Goes to Town*, but there's also obvious originality in this story of a magazine intern (female) involved in getting a story out of the fact that an eccentric advertiser (male) is looking for a companion for a trip back through time to 2001. The film has an engaging, youthful freshness but, having earlier adroitly added serious touches to the humour within it, it fails to find an ending that satisfies on both levels. MS

▶ Aubrey Plaza, Mark Duplass, Jake Johnson, Karan Soni, Jenica Bergere, Kristen Bell.
▶ *Dir* Colin Trevorrow, *Pro* Marc Turtletraub, Trevorrow, Derek Connolly and others, *Screenplay* Connolly, *Ph* Benjamin Kasulke, *Pro Des* Ben Blankenship, *Ed* Franklin Peterson and Joe Landauer, *M* Ryan Miller, *Cos* Rebecca Luke.

Filmdistrict/a Big Beach and Duplass Brothers production-Vertigo Films.
86 mins. USA. 2012. Rel: 26 Dec 2012. Cert. 15.

Saints and Soldiers 2: Airborne Creed ★★★

This modest but well-crafted adventure takes place on 15 August 1944 and tells the story of a few survivors of the Parachute Regimental Combat Team. Three isolated paratroopers land in the south of France, their mission to protect and support the Allied Troops. It works because director Ryan Little takes his time in introducing his characters with some effective use of flashback sequences. It's hardly a groundbreaking war film but it delivers. GS

▶ Corbin Allred, David Nibley, Jason Wade, Lincoln Hoppe, Nichelle Aiden.
▶ *Dir* and *Ph* Ryan Little, *Pro* Little and Adam Abel, *Screenplay* Lamont Gray and Lincoln Hoppe, *Pro Des* Debbie Farrer, *Ed* Burke Lewis and Rhett Lewis, *M* J Bateman.

Go Films-KOAN.
94 mins. USA. 2012. Rel: 24 Sep 2012. Cert. 15.

Salmon Fishing in the Yemen ★★★★

Thanks to the considerable skills of Ewan McGregor and Emily Blunt this film carries off admirably a switch halfway through from comedy to romantic drama. The humour involves mocking bureaucracy over a sheikh's unlikely scheme to promote salmon fishing in his own country and its tone is decidedly Ealingesque. As for the drama, it's engaging without becoming heavy-handed. For once Kristin Scott Thomas takes on a comic role in support, and the whole film is an admirable example of a movie offering good popular entertainment. MS

➤ Ewan McGregor, Emily Blunt, Kristin Scott Thomas, Amr Waked, Rachael Sterling.
➤ *Dir* Lasse Hallström, *Pro* Paul Webster, *Screenplay* Simon Beaufoy, from the novel by Paul Torday, *Ph* Terry Stacey, *Pro Des* Michael Carlin, *Ed* Lisa Gunning, *M* Dario Marianelli, *Cos* Julian Day.

BBC Films/Lionsgate UK/UK Film Council/a Kudos Pictures production etc-Lionsgate UK.
107 mins. UK/France. 2011. Rel: 20 Apr 2012. Cert. 12A.

Salute ★★★★

Filmmaker Matt Norman here provides an apt tribute to his uncle, the Australian athlete Peter Norman, who paid the penalty after supporting black colleagues who gave the Black Power salute in the 1968 Olympics. More about racism than sprinting, this engaging documentary honours a good man who died in 2006 but not before seeing a rough cut of this film. MS

➤ With Peter Norman, Tommie Smith, John Carlos.
➤ *Dir* and *Written by* Matt Norman, *Pro* Norman and David Redman, *Ph* Martin Smith, *Ed* Jane Moran and John Leonard, *M* David Hirschfelder.

Film Finance Corporation Australia/Instinct Entertainment etc-Verve Pictures Ltd.
92 mins. Australia. 2008. Rel: 13 July 2012. Cert. PG.

Samsara ★★★

If looks were all *Samsara*, shot in Panavision Super 70 over five years, would be a knockout. It's Ron Fricke's follow-up to 1992's *Baraka* and almost a re-run of that movie, which was itself built on what he had learnt from working on films like *Koyaanisqatsi* (1982). A wordless meditation on the cycle of birth, death and rebirth uniting man and nature, it needs more

shape and clarification (locations go unnamed for example). Without that, the images are what count and the message gets left behind. MS

➤ With Olivier de Sagazan, Kikumaru.
➤ *Dir* and *Ph* Ron Fricke, *Pro* Mark Magidson, *Concept/Treatment written by* and *Ed* Fricke and Magidson, *M* Michael Stearns, Lisa Gerrard and Marcello De Francisci.

Oscilloscope Laboratories/Magidson Films Inc-Arrow Films.
102 mins. USA. 2011. Rel: 31 Aug 2012. Cert. 12A.

The Sapphires ★★★½

Wayne Blair's engaging debut taken from a stage play (although you wouldn't guess it) is a musical based on fact featuring women members of an Aborigine family who sang for the American troops in Vietnam. Chris O'Dowd shines as their manager, and so do co-stars Deborah Mailman and Jessica Mauboy. As a soul musical it's great stuff, but it falls into cliché (for which you will probably forgive it) when it tries to manipulate the emotions. MS

➤ Chris O'Dowd, Deborah Mailman, Jessica Mauboy, Shari Sebbens, Miranda Tapsell, Tory Kittles.
➤ *Dir* Wayne Blair, *Pro* Rosemary Blight and Kyle du Fresne, *Screenplay* Keith Thompson and Tony Briggs, from the latter's stage play, *Ph* Warwick Thornton, *Pro Des* Melinda Doring, *Ed* Dany Cooper, *M* Cezary Skubiszewski, *Cos* Tess Schofield.

Screen Australia/a Goldpost Pictures production/Screen NSW etc-E1 Films.
103 mins. Australia. 2012. Rel: 7 Nov 2012. Cert. PG.

Savages ★★

At one point in Oliver Stone's violent drug cartel thriller, Blake Lively's Ophelia cites *Butch Cassidy and the Sundance Kid*, she being the girl coupled with two hunky criminal boyfriends. But whereas the earlier film was an exquisitely crafted adventure with lashings of charm and humour – and with two charismatic leads – *Savages* is a brutal, formulaic and extremely unpleasant

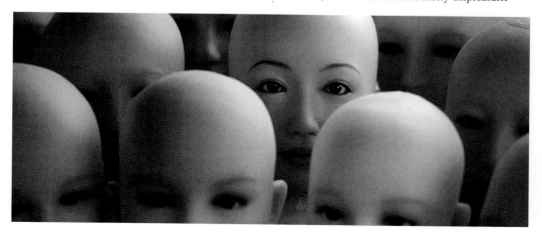

A world of faces: A shot from Ron Fricke's *Samsara*, filmed across 25 countries over a period of five years.

trudge over familiar territory. Only Benicio Del Toro's powerful turn as a daunting and sadistic gangster (who kills out of habit) saves the film from being an artistic wasteland. JC-W

▶ Taylor Kitsch, Blake Lively, Aaron Johnson, John Travolta, Benicio Del Toro, Salma Hayek, Demián Bichir, Emile Hirsch.
▶ *Dir* Oliver Stone, *Pro* Moritz Borman and Eric Copeloff, *Screenplay* Stone, Shane Salerno and Don Winslow, *Ph* Dan Mindel, *Pro Des* Tomás Voth, *Ed* Joe Hutshing, Stuart Levy and Alex Marquez, *M* Adam Peters, *Cos* Cindy Evans.
Ixtian/Onda Entertainment/Relativity Media-Universal. 129 mins. USA. 2012. Rel: 21 Sep 2012. Cert. 15.

Searching for Sugar Man ★★★½

This is a documentary investigating what happened to the singer-songwriter Sixto Rodriguez, who made recordings in the late 1960s that inspired comparisons with Bob Dylan. That was before he disappeared and was believed dead. His recordings were a failure in America commercially, but he was later acclaimed in South Africa where he inspired those involved in the anti-Apartheid movement. For those who don't know, it's best not to reveal what the filmmakers discovered. Despite some weaknesses, their film is intriguing. MS

▶ With Steve 'Sugar' Segerman, Craig Bartholomew, Sixto Rodriguez.
▶ *Dir*, *Written by* and *Ed* Malik Bendjelloul, *Pro* Simon Chinn and Bendjelloul, *Ph* Camilla Skagerström.
A Red Box Films & Passion Pictures production/Canfield Pictures/The Documentary Company-StudioCanal Limited. 86 mins. UK. 2012. Rel: 26 July 2012. Cert. 12A.

Seeking a Friend for the End of the World ★★

The end of the world is an odd subject for a romantic comedy. But then Lorene Scafaria's directorial debut strains for originality at every

Artistic wasteland: Benicio Del Toro (left) adds heft to Oliver Stone's formulaic and unpleasant *Savages*. Aaron Taylor-Johnson listens up.

turn. Steve Carell plays a morose insurance broker, Dodge Petersen, whose wife leaves him three weeks before Earth is due to collide with an asteroid called Matilda. A pragmatic soul, Dodge returns to work while Los Angeles descends into violence and anarchy. However, after befriending his neighbour Penny (Keira Knightley), Dodge finds himself on a road trip where anything can happen... For a dystopian romcom, the sugar is surprisingly thick. JC-W

▶ Steve Carell, Keira Knightley, Adam Brody, Derek Luke, William Petersen, Melanie Lynskey, Rob Corddry, Patton Oswalt, Martin Sheen, Nancy Carell, Melinda Dillon.
▶ *Dir* and *Screenplay* Lorene Scafaria, *Pro* Steve Golin, Joy Gorman, Mark Roybal and Steven M. Rales, *Ph* Tim Orr, *Pro Des* Chris L Spellman, *Ed* Zene Baker, *M* Jonathan Sadoff and Rob Simonsen, *Cos* Kristin M Burke.
Anonymous Content/Indian Paintbrush/Mandate Pictures-StudioCanal. 101 mins. USA. 2012. Rel: 13 July 2012. Cert. 15.

Seven Psychopaths ★★★½

Colin Farrell plays Marty, a screenwriter with writer's block who has been dumped by girlfriend Abbie Cornish. He stays with his mate Billy (Sam Rockwell) who, together with Hans (Christopher Walken), kidnaps dogs for a living. More trouble looms when they nick the favourite shihtzu belonging to mad criminal Charlie (Woody Harrelson)... Martin McDonagh follows his success with *In Bruges* with a film that has charm, great dialogue and delirious performances. But the plot is on shaky ground. Billy wants to help Marty with his screenplay for a film called *Seven Psychopaths*; the impression given is that they are making it up as they go along. Worth it, anyway. MHD

▶ Sam Rockwell, Colin Farrell, Abbie Cornish, Christopher Walken, Harry Dean Stanton, Woody Harrelson, Tom Waits.
▶ *Dir* and *Screenplay* Martin McDonagh, *Pro* McDonagh, Graham Broadbent and Peter Czernin, *Ph* Ben Davis, *Pro Des* David Wasco, *Ed* Lisa Gunning, *M* Carter Burwell, *Cos* Karen Patch.
Blueprint Pictures/Film 4/British Film Institute-Momentum Pictures. 110 mins. UK. 2012. Rel: 5 Dec 2012. Cert. 15.

Shadow Dancer ★★★½

That very fine actress Andrea Riseborough is still searching for a film as good as what she brings to it. Although her performance here impresses, this tale of an Irish girl with two brothers in the IRA rather falls between two stools. Much of it plays like a thriller, but it's really a personal tragedy about somebody forced to report to the British and to deceive her family in the process.

It's that story that loses out to the conventional excitements of the action genre, but the film remains interesting. MS

▶ Andrea Riseborough, Clive Owen, Aidan Gillen, Domhnall Gleeson, Brid Brennan, Gillian Anderson.
▶ *Dir* James Marsh, *Pro* Chris Coen, Andrew Lowe and Ed Guiney, *Screenplay* Tom Bradby, from his novel, *Ph* Rob Hardy *Pro Des* Jon Henson, *Ed* Jinx Godfrey, *M* Dickon Hinchliffe, *Cos* Lorna Marie Mugan.
BFI/BBC Films/a Unanimous Entertainment/Element Pictures/Wild Bunch production etc-Paramount. 102 mins. UK/Ireland/France. 2012. Rel: 24 Aug 2012. Cert. 15.

Shady Lady ★★★½

It may sound like a Marlene Dietrich remake, but this is actually the name of a B-24 'Liberator' aircraft that, in 1943, embarked on a bombing mission from Darwin, Australia to Borneo. At the time this was the world's longest bombing expedition and the 'Shady Lady' encountered some pretty serious setbacks, from tropical thunderstorms to Japanese fighter planes. It's a fascinating tale, a mix of drama, documentary and cuticle-chewing stuff, a remarkable feather in the cap for Sussex-based film company Fact Not Fiction Films. CB

▶ Narrated by Michael Dorn, with Ross Neuenfeldt, Gregory Kanter, Jim Alexander, Robert H Wainwright, Sean Morton.

▶ *Dir, Pro* and *Ed* Tristan Loraine, *Screenplay* Loraine and Viv Young, *Ph* Nathalie Grace, *Pro Des* Chloë Potter, *M* Moritz Schmittat, *Cos* Alexandra, Genevieve and Karen Rawlins.
Fact Not Fiction Films-DFT Enterprises. 87 mins. UK. 2012. Rel: 9 Nov 2012. No Cert.

Shame ★★★★

Less a story than a character study, this second feature from Steve McQueen (the artist whose debut feature was *Hunger* in 2008) is set in America and is a portrait of a sex addict. The man in question, admirably played by Michael Fassbender, is not a glamourised figure but someone who is a prisoner of his obsession. Carey Mulligan is equally impressive as his sister, whose own troubled existence is stunningly conveyed when she sings 'New York, New York' in downbeat mode. Within its chosen limitations, this serious film works well. MS

▶ Michael Fassbender, Carey Mulligan, James Badge Dale, Nicole Beharie.
▶ *Dir* Steve McQueen, *Pro* Iain Canning and Emile Sherman, *Screenplay* McQueen and Abi Morgan, *Ph* Sean Bobbitt, *Pro Des* Judy Becker, *Ed* Joe Walker, *M* Harry Escott, *Cos* David Robinson.
Film4/UK Film Council/Alliance Films/a See-Saw Films production etc-Momentum Pictures. 101 mins. UK/Canada. 2011. Rel: 13 Jan 2012. Cert. 18.

Hare apparent: Tom Waits in Martin McDonagh's *Seven Psychopaths.*

She Monkeys ★★★½

This provocative drama by Sweden's Lisa Aschan shows sexual relationships as power games, and it's compelling but also disturbing. What we see is a believable but unsympathetic portrait of a lesbian couple against a background of competitive horsemanship. Is this just an individual story or Aschan's view of life generally? Either way there's no sense of pity and this technically assured film feels cold. (Original title: *Apflickorna*) MS

▶ Mathilda Paradeiser, Linda Molin, Isabella Lindquist, Adam Lundgren, Sigmund Hovind.
▶ *Dir* Lisa Aschan, *Pro* Helene Lindholm, *Screenplay* Aschan and Josefine Adolfsson, *Ph* Linda Wassberg, *Pro Des* and *Cos* Kia Nordqvist, *Ed* Kristofer Nordin, *M* Sami Sänpäkkilä.

Atmo Production AB/FIlm i Väst/Swedish Television etc-Peccadillo Pictures.
83 mins. Sweden/Denmark. 2011. Rel: 18 May 2012. Cert. 12A.

Shut Up and Play the Hits ★★★★

On 2 April 2011 the lead singer of LCD Soundsystem, James Murphy, gave one last performance at Madison Square Garden before an early retirement. This fascinating documentary allows Murphy to share his thoughts about his controversial decision through a series of honest interviews before as well as after the show. Most importantly there are highlights of his mesmerising performance, playing to thousands of admirers who are elated but also hugely disappointed to see their hero for one last time. GS

▶ James Murphy, Stephen Colbert, Chuck Closterman, Reggie Watts, Arcade Fire, Win Butler, Soulwax and LCD Soundsystem.
▶ *Dir* Will Lovelace and Dylan Southern, *Pro* Thomas Benski, Lucas Ochoa and James Murphy, *Ph* Reed Morano and Spike Jonze, *Art Dir* John Fergason, *Ed* Mark Burnett.

Oscilloscope Laboratories/Killer Films-Pulse Films.
108 mins. UK. 2012. Rel: 7 Sep 2012. Cert. 15.

Sightseers ★★★½

After *Kill List* Ben Wheatley offers another view of serial killing but with a comic approach rather than a violently dramatic one; it's a sort of latterday *Kind Hearts and Coronets*. Tina flouts her controlling mother's wishes and goes caravanning with her new boyfriend Chris. To avoid their holiday being spoiled, when they meet up with somebody they don't like, Chris does them in. They're a kind of vigilante twosome on the prowl for disposable bores, the sort of creatures that inhabit the films of Mike Leigh. It may be black but it's also very funny and due acknowledgment should be paid to the leading actors, Alice Lowe and Steve Oram, who also wrote the hilarious screenplay. MHD

▶ Alice Lowe, Steve Oram, Eileen Davies, Richard Glover, Monica Dolan, Jonathan Aris.
▶ *Dir* Ben Wheatley, *Pro* Andrew Starke, Nira Park

Country carnage: Alice Lowe and Steve Oram in their self-penned *Sightseers*.

and Claire Jones, *Screenplay* Steve Oram, Alice Lowe and Amy Jump, *Ph* Laurie Rose, *Pro Des* Jane Levick, *Ed* Wheatley, Jump and Robin Hill, *M* Jim Williams, *Cos* Rosa Dias.

StudioCanal/Film4/British Film Institute/Rook Films/Big Talk Pictures-StudioCanal.

88 mins. UK. 2012. Rel: 30 Nov 2012. Cert. 15.

Silent Hill: Revelation 3D ★

This sequel, based on the survival horror video game, is as lame as the original if not worse. On the eve of her 18th birthday, and after her father's (Sean Bean) disappearance, Heather Mason (Adelaide Clemens) learns that her identity is false; still plagued by childhood nightmares, she enters an alternate dimension. This is a dull, not very scary horror film and feels as if they made it up as they went along. GS

➤ Sean Bean, Malcolm McDowell, Martin Donovan, Carrie-Anne Moss, Radha Mitchell, Adelaide Clemens, Kit Harington.
➤ *Dir* and *Screenplay* Michael J Bassett, *Pro* Don Carmody and Samuel Hadida, *Ph* Maxime Alexandre, *Pro Des* Alicia Keywan, *Ed* Michele Conroy, *M* Jeff Danna and Akira Yamaoka, *Cos* Wendy Partridge.

Anibrain Digital Technologies/Silent Hill 2 DCP/Davis-Films/Konami-Open Road Films.

94 mins. France/Canada/USA. 2012. Rel: 31 Oct 2012. Cert. 15.

Silent House ★★½

This is a remake of a Uruguayan thriller (see Jonathan Rigby's review in last year's annual), based on a true story that happened in a small village in the late 1940s. Elizabeth Olsen confirms her rising star status following *Martha Marcy May Marlene* and this time she plays a young woman trapped inside her family's lakeside retreat. Like Hitchcock's *Rope* this intriguing thriller was shot in one continuous, real-time take, which is

impressive. It is dark and atmospheric but doesn't succeed in being scary. GS

➤ Elizabeth Olsen, Adam Trese, Eric Sheffer Stevens, Julia Taylor Ross.
➤ *Dir* Chris Kentis and Laura Lau, *Pro* Lau and Agnès Mentre, *Screenplay* Lau, based on the screenplay *La casa muda* by Oscar Estevez, *Ph* Igor Martinovic, *Pro Des* Roshelle Berliner, *Ed* Andrew Pang, *M* Nathan Larson and Jason Domnarski, *Cos* Lynn Falconer.

Elle Driver/Tazora Films-StudioCanal.

86 mins. USA/France. 2011. Rel: 4 May 2012. Cert. 15.

Silent Souls ★★★

Although Aleksei Fedorchenko's film carries echoes of Tarkovsky (albeit on a much briefer scale since it lasts only 78 minutes), I can't subscribe to the view of those who regard it as arthouse heaven. It's a road movie in which a husband and his employer take a trip to dispose of the wife's body in accordance with ancient rites. At times both poetic and erotic, the film's approach is minimalistic but its ultimate purpose is decidedly obscure. (Original title: *Ovsyanki*) MS

➤ Igor Sergeyev, Yuriy Tsurilo, Yuliya Aug, Viktor Sukhorukov, Ivan Tushin.
➤ *Dir* Aleksei Fedorchenko, *Pro* Igor Mishin and Mary Nazari, *Screenplay* Denis Osokin, from the novel *Buntings* by Aist Sergeyev, *Ph* Mikhail Krichman, *Art Dir* Andrey Ponckratov and Aleksei Potapov, *Ed* Sergei Ivanov and Anna Virgun, *M* Andrei Karasyov, *Cos* Anna Barthuly and Lidiya Archakova.

Igor Mishin-Artificial Eye.

78 mins. Russia/USA. 2010. Rel: 22 June 2012. Cert. 15.

Silver Linings Playbook ★★★★

A troubled young widow (Jennifer Lawrence) agrees to help when a violent, possibly bipolar, man (Bradley Cooper) is released from a mental hospital into home care. He asks her to deliver

Sex and death: Larisa Domaskina and Olga Dobrina in Aleksei Fedorchenko's Silent Souls.

Snuff already: Clare Foley with Nicholas King as Mr Boogie in Scott Derrickson's *Sinister*.

a letter to his wife, whom he wants to regain despite being under a restraining order not to approach her. Notwithstanding the dark implications, this is at heart a romcom, and more and more overtly so as it leads towards a finale involving a dance competition. That makes it an odd piece, but writer-director David O Russell handles it with great assurance. Cooper is fine, the supporting cast (Robert De Niro included) are admirable and Jennifer Lawrence, identifying wholly with her role, is astoundingly real. MS

▶ Bradley Cooper, Jennifer Lawrence, Robert De Niro, Jacki Weaver, Chris Tucker, Anupam Kher, John Oritz, Shea Whigham, Julia Stiles.
▶ *Dir* and *Screenplay* (from the novel by Matthew Quick) David O Russell, *Pro* Donna Gigliotti, Bruce Cohen and Jonathan Gordon, *Ph* Masanobu Takayanagi, *Pro Des* Judy Becker, *Ed* Jay Cassidy, *M* Danny Elfman, *Cos* Mark Bridges.
The Weinstein Company/Pennsylvania Film Office etc-Entertainment.
122 mins. USA. 2012. Rel: 23 Nov 2012. Cert. 15.

A Simple Life ★★★

The Hong Kong director Ann Hui resurfaces with this somewhat minimalistic piece based on real-life events. It concerns a film producer and his concern for the family retainer (Deanie Ip) forced by a stroke to live in a nursing home. It's unsentimental, but the characters remain largely undeveloped and there's a lack of real dramatic momentum. But it's an award winner and, if I merely respect it, others much admire it. (Original title: *Tao jie*) MS

▶ Andy Lau, Deanie Ip, Wang Fuli, Anthony Wong, Qin Hailu, Eman Lam, Hui Bik Kee.
▶ *Dir* Ann Hui, *Pro* Roger Lee, Chan Pui-wah and Hui, *Screenplay* Susan Chan and Lee, *Ph* Yu Lik-wai,

Pro Des Albert Poon, *Ed* Kwong Chi-leung, *M* Law Wing-fai, *Cos* Boey Wong.
Bona Entertainment Co./Focus Films/Sil-Metropole Organization-Arrow Films.
118 mins. Hong Kong. 2011. Rel: 3 Aug 2012. Cert. PG.

Sing Your Song ★★★★

Now an octogenarian, Harry Belafonte appears here to give us his life story. The film – informative and engaging – allows him to tell it his way and some matters are bypassed. Nevertheless, the portrait that emerges is both social and personal and Belafonte's continuing concern with and involvement in social issues is admirable. Some film clips are in the wrong ratio, but the final section of the movie is particularly strong and this is an enjoyable watch. MS

▶ With Harry Belafonte.
▶ *Dir* Susanne Rostock, *Pro* Michael Cohl, Gina Belafonte and others, *Ed* Rostock and Jason L Pollard, *M* Hahn Rowe.
Belafonte Enterprises/S2BN Entertainment/Julius R Nasso Productions-Verve Pictures.
104 mins. USA. 2011. Rel: 8 June 2012. Cert. 12A.

Sinister ★★★★

The classic horror scenarios always need tarting up for each new generation, and in *Sinister* the 'bad place' motif (a very popular one in 2012, from *The Pact* to *The Woman in Black*) gets as expert a make-over as could be wished for. Ethan Hawke is excellent as a twitchy 'true crime' author, desperate for another hit, who moves with his (unknowing) family to a murder scene. Direction, photography, editing, music; all conspire to wring maximum apprehension – indeed, dread – from the house's multiplying dark spaces. Similar to but more focused than the same producer's *Insidious*, *Sinister* benefits from scraps of ageing Super 8 home movies (eg, 'Lawn Work 86') that are authentically bowel-loosening. Only a crass jump scare at the *very* last moment lets the side down. JR

▶ Ethan Hawke, Juliet Rylance, Michael Hall D'Addario, Clare Foley, Rob Riley, Fred Dalton Thompson, Vincent D'Onofrio (uncredited).
▶ *Dir* Scott Derrickson, *Pro* Jason Blum and Brian Kavanaugh-Jones, *Screenplay* Derrickson and C Robert Cargill, *Ph* Christopher Norr, *Pro Des* David Brisbin, *Ed* Frédéric Thoraval, *M* Christopher Young, *Cos* Abby O'Sullivan.
Alliance Films/Possessed Pictures/Automatik/Blumhouse Productions/IM Global-Momentum Pictures.
110 mins. USA. 2012. Rel: 5 Oct 2012. Cert. 15.

Sister ★★★½

Despite some incidental symbolism, Ursula Meier's successor to *Home* (2008) is a naturalistic piece set in Switzerland and featuring a boy who lives at the foot of a mountain. This enables him to ascend it to steal from visitors at a ski resort, in order, it would seem, to support himself and his older sister. Kacey Mottet Klein is terrific as the boy, the setting has some novelty value and the story grips, but ultimately it lacks the resolution which would round it off satisfactorily. (Original title: *L'Enfant d'en haut*) MS

➤ Léa Seydoux, Kacey Mottet Klein, Martin Compston, Gillian Anderson, Jean-François Stévenin.
➤ *Dir* Ursula Meier, *Pro* Denis Freyd and Ruth Waldburger, *Screenplay* Antoine Jaccoud and Meier with Gilles Taurand, *Ph* Agnès Godard, *Art Dir* Ivan Niclass, *Ed* Nelly Quettier, *M* John Parish, *Cos* Anna Van Brée.

Archipel 35/Vega Film/RTS Radio Télévision Suisse/Bande à part Films etc-Soda Pictures.
97 mins. France/Switzerland. 2012. Rel: 26 Oct 2012. Cert. 15.

The Sitter ★

A foul-mouthed, grossly overweight slacker (Jonah Hill) is guilted into babysitting. However, the three children in his charge are even more obnoxious than he is. Over an evening of far-fetched misadventure, the four learn a few life lessons about exploitative women, being homosexual and blowing stuff up. Loosely inspired by Chris Columbus' *Adventures in Babysitting* (1987), this vehicle for the questionable charms of Jonah Hill is actually meant to be funny (it's billed as a comedy). Whatever its intentions, it doesn't have much respect for humanity. Even sadder is that the director's first film, *George Washington*, was declared a masterpiece. JC-W

➤ Jonah Hill, Max Records, Ari Graynor, JB Smoove, Sam Rockwell, DW Moffett, Jessica Hecht, Bruce Altman.
➤ *Dir* David Gordon Green, *Pro* Michael De Luca, *Screenplay* Brian Gatewood and Alessandro Tanaka, *Ph* Tim Orr, *Pro Des* Richard A. Wright, *Ed* Craig Alpert, *M* David Wingo and Jeff McIlwain, *Cos* Leah Katznelson.

Twentieth Century Fox/Michael De Luca Prods/Rough House Pictures-20th Century Fox.
81 mins. USA. 2011. Rel: 20 January 2012. Cert. 15.

Skyfall ★★★★½

Director Sam Mendes' screenwriters have re-invented 007 for the cinematic character's 50th anniversary. Gone are the excessive gadgets as Bond comes home to enjoy a romp around the British Isles. Some vital info has been purloined by regulation nasty Silva (Javier Bardem on brilliant, creepy form), who plans to use it against the British Establishment. After a taxing time on a Turkish train, James (Daniel Craig) recovers in order to track down Silva and take in the Scottish Highlands, like his ur-hero Richard Hannay in *The Thirty-Nine Steps*. M (Judi Dench) is along for

Inspecting gadgets: Ben Whishaw and Daniel Craig in Sam Mendes' box-office breaking *Skyfall*.

Legend has it: Chris Hemsworth and Kristen Stewart in Rupert Sanders' *Snow White and the Huntsman*.

the ride and it's the first time she's been a proper Bond girl. It's all so refreshingly different, but brings the franchise back to its roots and it turns out to be one of the best-ever 007 outings. MHD

▶ Daniel Craig, Javier Bardem, Judi Dench, Ralph Fiennes, Naomie Harris, Albert Finney, Bérénice Lim Mahlohe, Ben Whishaw, Rory Kinnear, Ola Rapace, Helen McCrory.
▶ *Dir* Sam Mendes, *Pro* Barbara Broccoli and Michael G Wilson, *Screenplay* John Logan, Robert Wade and Neal Purvis, based on characters created by Ian Fleming, *Ph* Roger Deakins, *Pro Des* Dennis Gassner, *Ed* Stuart Baird, *M* Thomas Newman, *Cos* Jany Temime.

Eon Productions/Danjaq-Sony Pictures International. 143 mins. UK/USA. 2012. Rel: 26 Oct 2012. Cert. 12A.

Smashed ★★★★

For Kate and Charlie every evening is a party, often leading to the morning after the night before. But Kate, an elementary school teacher, is turning up to class with a hangover, and worse… The cinema is crowded with bravura dramas about alcoholism – *The Lost Weekend, Days of Wine and Roses, My Name is Joe* – and *Smashed*, as petite and unassuming as it is, should rank among them. Its narrative simplicity is actually part of its strength; it refuses to be distracted. It also knows of what it speaks and former

scream queen Mary Elizabeth Winstead nails her character with chilling accuracy. JC-W

▶ Mary Elizabeth Winstead, Aaron Paul, Octavia Spencer, Nick Offerman, Megan Mullally, Mary Kay Place, Richmond Arquette.
▶ *Dir* James Ponsoldt, *Pro* Jennifer Cochis, Jonathan Schwartz and Andrea Sperling, *Screenplay* Ponsoldt and Susan Burke, *Ph* Tobias Datum, *Pro Des* Linda Sena, *Ed* Suzanne Spangler, *M* Eric D Johnson and Andy Cabic, *Cos* Diaz.

Super Crispy Entertainment-Sony Pictures Releasing. 81 mins. USA. 2012. Rel: 14 Dec 2012. Cert. 15.

Snow White and the Huntsman ★★★½

It may be regarded as a misfortune that Snow White popped up earlier in the year in the camp, joyous and pictorially ravishing *Mirror Mirror*. However, this is a visual banquet in its own right, and an entirely different take on the Grimms' fairy tale – and a very impressive one at that. The English commercials director Rupert Sanders is obviously a talent to watch and exhibits the same remarkable eye for a picturesque flourish as Ridley Scott. In fact, the film is brimming with stupendous set-pieces and, although the story may be familiar, the setting and palette bring a surreal freshness to the legend. JC-W

Kristen Stewart, Charlize Theron, Chris Hemsworth, Sam Claflin, Ian McShane, Bob Hoskins, Ray Winstone, Sam Spruell, Nick Frost, Eddie Marsan, Toby Jones, Brian Gleeson, Vincent Regan, Lily Cole, Rachael Stirling, Anastasia Hille.
Dir Rupert Sanders, *Pro* Sam Mercer, Palak Patel and Joe Roth, *Screenplay* Evan Daugherty, John Lee Hancock and Hossein Amini, *Ph* Greig Fraser, *Pro Des* Dominic Watkins, *Ed* Conrad Buff IV and Neil Smith, *M* James Newton Howard, *Cos* Colleen Atwood.

Roth Films/Universal-Universal.
127 mins. USA. 2012. Rel: 30 May 2012. Cert. 12A.

The Snows of Kilimanjaro ★★★★

Not a Hemingway adaptation but another Marseille drama from Robert Guédiguian. It may not be his very best, but it's a well-acted and engaging story. Central to it are a couple, once ardent working class socialists who, suffering a robbery by a needy youth, confront the issue of middle age making them more bourgeois in their outlook. This reminds us of the affinities between Guédiguian and Ken Loach and, if you like the latter but don't know Guédiguian's work, you should certainly try this. (Original title: *Les Neiges du Kilimandjaro*) MS

Ariane Ascaride, Jean-Pierre Darrousin, Gérard Máylan, Grégoire Leprince-Ringuet.
Dir Robert Guédiguian, *Screenplay* Jean-Louis Milesi and Guédiguian, *Ph* Pierre Milon, *Art Dir* Michel Vandestien, *Ed* Bernard Sasia, *Cos* Juliette Chanaud.

Agat Films et Cie/France 3 Cinéma/Canal+/CinéCinéma etc-Cinefile.
107 mins. France. 2011. Rel: 14 Sep 2012. Cert. 15.

So Undercover ★★

Likable performer Miley Cyrus struggles on gamely with her acting career. Unfortunately she's not done many favours here by her iffy casting as a tough, street-smart Dallas private eye hired by FBI agent Jeremy Piven to have a make-over and go undercover in a posh New Orleans college sorority. There's a problem with ledgers and identities – gosh! This tame *Miss Congeniality / Kindergarten Cop* mash-up doesn't produce many surprises or thrills, but it's harmless, brain-in-neutral entertainment for undemanding teenage girls. DW

Miley Cyrus, Jeremy Piven, Mike O'Malley, Joshua Bowman, Lauren McKnight, Kelly Osbourne, Megan Park.
Dir Tom Vaughan, *Pro* Tish Cyrus, Steven Pearl, Alan Loeb, Guy East, and Nigel Sinclair, *Screenplay* Loeb and Pearl, *Ph* Denis Lenoir, *Pro Des* Daniel B Clancy, *Ed* Michael Berenbaum and Wendy Greene Bricmont, *M* Steven Trask and Bryce Jacobs, *Cos* Wendy Chuck.

Hope Town Entertainment/Crystal City Entertainment/Scarlet Fire Entertainment etc-Exclusive Media Group.
94 mins. USA. 2012. Rel: 7 Dec 2012. Cert. 12A.

Some Guy who Kills People ★★★

Kevin Corrigan plays the depressed, lonely and crazy Ken Boyd, some guy who kills the people he thinks have caused all his miseries – those who put him in the mental hospital from which he's recently been released to start a new life in a diner. Another cheapo black comedy horror-thriller, this one stands out by being cleverly written and confidently realised, as well as particularly lusty and vicious. Barry Bostwick plays the local sheriff, who's having a thing with Ken's sarcastic, chain-smoking mom, Karen Black, and starts to suspect Ken. Both vintage actors are a treat. DW

Kevin Corrigan, Barry Bostwick, Karen Black, Leo Fitzpatrick, Ariel Gade, Eric Price, Lucy Davis.
Dir Jack Perez, *Pro* Ryan Levin, Michael Wormser and Micah Goldman, *Screenplay* Levin, *Ph* Shawn Maurer, *Pro Des* Zach Bangma, *Ed* Chris Conlee, *M* David Kitchens and Ben Zarai, *Cos* Vania Ouzounova.

Level Ten Films/Litn Up Films/Battle of Ireland Films-Koch Media Entertainment.
97 mins. USA. 2011. Rel: 5 Oct 2012. Cert. 15.

Something from Nothing: The Art of Rap ★★★

Ice-T's entertaining but over-long documentary celebrates the world of rap by interviewing artists who reveal the roots and history of the art. They include Afrika Bambaataa, Ice Cube, Snoop Dogg and Yasiin Bey, formerly known as Mos Def, plus the white artist Eminem. This is an illuminating and enjoyable film on the creative process behind rap music, despite the fact that only a couple of female performers are featured in this very male art form. GS

Ice Cube, Chuck D, Snoop Dogg, Doctor Dre, Eminem, Ice-T, MC Lyte, Q-Tip, Puerto Rico, Kanye West, WC, Xzibit, Afrika Bambaataa, Yasiin Bey etc.

Silly slaughter: Kevin Corrigan as *Some Guy who Kills People*.

> *Dir* Ice-T and Andy Baybutt, *Pro* Paul Toogood, *Ph* Baybutt and Jeremy Hewson, *Ed* Kieran Smyth, *M* Adam F.

Jollygood Films/Westmount Films/Final Level Entertainment-Kaleidoscope Film Distribution. 106 mins. UK/USA. 2012. Rel: 19 July 2012. Cert. 15.

The Soul of Flies ★★★

This first feature from Spain's Jonathan Cenzual Burley is all of a piece. However, how much you like it may well be a matter of personal taste for this is a surreal road movie blending humour and philosophy. It's the tale of a philandering father who hopes that his funeral will bring together the two contrasted half-brothers who are his sons. Episodic, odd, different, and yet perhaps too slight to register strongly, the movie exists in its own world. (Original title: *El alma de las moscas*) MS

> Andrea Calabrese, Javier Sáez, Felix Cenzual, Louis Cenzual, Francisca Lucas, Diana Pintado.
> *Dir*, *Screenplay*, *Ph* and *Ed* Jonathan Cenzual Burley, *Pro* Burley and Luis Cenzual, *M* Tim Walters and Andrea Calabrese.

El Mailan Films-El Mailan. 78 mins. Spain. 2009/11. Rel: 13 July 2012. Cert. 15.

Sound of My Voice ★★★★

Co-writer Brit Marling is nice and creepy as an icily aloof cult leader who claims to have travelled back from the future to help her true believers in this excellent mystery drama. Hoax or reality? Christopher Denham and Nicole Vicius feel just right as a journalist and his girlfriend, documentary filmmakers who infiltrate the cult to expose the truth. Eerie, tense and engrossing, even quite chilling at times, this surprisingly polished film maintains its hauntingly enigmatic air of mystery till the very end. We eagerly await writer-director Zal Batmanglij's next two episodes. DW

> Christopher Denham, Nicole Vicius, Brit Marling, Davenia McFadden, Richard Wharton, James Urbaniak, Matthew Carey, Constance Wu.
> *Dir* Zal Batmanglij, *Pro* Brit Marling, Hans C Ritter and Shelley Surpin, *Screenplay* Batmanglij and Marling, *Ph* Rachel Morrison, *Pro Des* Scott Enge, *Ed* Tamara Meem, *M* Batmanglij, *Cos* Sarah de Sa Rego.

Skyscraper Films-Fox Searchlight Pictures. 85 mins. USA. 2011. Rel: 3 Aug 2012. Cert. 15.

The Source ★★★½

Colourful but socially engaged, this is a tale of village life somewhere in North Africa which borrows from *Lysistrata* when the women, campaigning to be better treated, deny sex to their men. Unfortunately its last section is weak (too many plot threads to be tied up in a film which in any case is too long). Nevertheless there is a lot here that is engaging and sympathetic, not least the presence of Biyouna, who is memorable as a widow who is a source of wisdom. (Original title: *La Source des femmes*) MS

> Leïla Bekhti, Hafsia Herzi, Biyouna, Saleh Bakri, Hiam Abbass, Mohamed Majd, Karim Leklou.
> *Dir* Radu Mihaileanu, *Pro* Denis Carot, Marie Masmonteil and Mihaileanu, *Screenplay* Mihaileanu and Alan-Michel Blanc with Catherine Ramnberg, *Ph* Glynn Speeckaert, *Art Dir* Cristian Niculesco, *Ed* Ludo Troch, *M* Armand Amar, *Cos* Viorica Petrovici.

An Elzevir Films and Oï Oï Oï Productions production/ Europacorp etc-Picturehouse Entertainment. 125 mins. France/Belgium/Italy/Morocco. 2011. Rel: 18 May 2012. Cert. 15.

Sparkle ★★★

Anyone remember the 1976 original with Irene Cara as Sparkle? This snazzy remake of the 1960s-set musical drama puts a fresh, glossy coat of paint on the old, old story about three sisters who form a singing group, become a sensation and start to fall apart as fame strikes. The over-earnest, cliché-ridden story sometimes sucks but the songs ('One Wing', 'His Eyes Are on the Sparrow') and the performances easily carry the movie. Making her debut, singer Jordin Sparks puts the sparks into her star part as Sparkle and Whitney Houston (in her last role) is outstanding as Mom. But the knockout turn comes from Carmen Ejogo as Sparkle's older, sexy sister. Derek Luke and Mike Epps score for the boys. DW

> Jordin Sparks, Whitney Houston, Carmen Ejogo, Derek Luke, Mike Epps, Tika Sumpter, Cee-Lo Green, Curtis Armstrong.
> *Dir* Salim Akil, *Pro* Salim Akil, Mara Brock Akil, Debra Martin Chase, Curtis Wallace and TD Jakes,

In the name of water: Leila Bekhti in Radu Mihaileanu's The Source, loosely inspired by Aristophanes' Lysistrata.

Screenplay Mara Brock Akil, from a story by Joel Schumacher and Howard Rosenman, *Ph* Anastas Michos, *Pro Des* Gary Frutkoff, *Ed* Terilyn A Shropshire, *M* Salaam Remi, *Cos* Ruth E Carter.

Akil Production Company/Sony Pictures Entertainment/ Stage 6 Filmsetc-Sony Pictures Releasing. 116 mins. USA. 2012. Rel: 5 Oct 2012. Cert. 12A.

The Squad ★★★½

This film combines two genres, the war film and the horror movie. A group of soldiers descend on a remote mountain outpost in search of a lost squadron. As one of the team enters the base, another soldier tries to stop him but is killed by a landmine. The base is deserted and surrounded by an impenetrable fog. When the squad settles in, they find a strange woman locked up and, on releasing her, she flees. Thinking her a witch, the squad face the unknown horrors about to beset them. Tension is kept throughout most of the film until a less effective ending. (Original title: *El páramo*) PL

▷ Juan David Restrepo, Juan Pablo Barragán, Alejandro Aguilar, Mauricio Navas.
▷ *Dir* Jaime Osorio Marquez, *Pro* Federico Durán, *Screenplay* Marquez, Diego Vivanco and Tania Cardenas from a story by Marquez, *Ph* Alejandro Moreno, *Pro Dir* Oscar Navarro, *Ed* Felipe Guerrero and Sebastián Hernández, *M* Ruy Folguera.

Alta Films/Rhayuela Films/Sudestada Cine etc-Momentum Pictures. 100 mins. Colombia. 2011. Rel: 15 June 2012. Cert. 15.

St George's Day ★★★

This is a first-rate Brit crime thriller that delivers both brutal action and exciting thrills on an epic scale, taking off to Amsterdam and Berlin for a diamond heist. Frank Harper and Craig Fairbrass shine as notorious London criminals who are in complete charge of their game – until, that is, a shipment of cocaine belonging to the Russian Mafia goes missing. Clever Mr Harper shows his virtuosity, co-writing and directing as well as starring as the scarily monstrous anti-hero Mickey Mannock, and he manages strong work in all three departments. There's also a bit of a dream cast in support, with Charles Dance and Luke Treadaway outstanding. DW

▷ Frank Harper, Craig Fairbrass, Charles Dance, Dexter Fletcher, Vincent Regan, Sean Pertwee, Keeley Hazell, Luke Treadaway, Nick Moran, Jamie Foreman, Clemency Burton-Hill.
▷ *Dir* Frank Harper, *Pro* Lars Sylvest, Steve Harvey, Nick Hamson and Warren Derosa, *Screenplay* Harper and Urs Buehler, *Ph* Mike Southon, *Pro Des* Monica Black, *Ed* Nick McCahearty, *M* Tim Atack, *Cos* Jacky Levy.

Elstree Studio Productions-Metrodome Distribution. 109 mins. UK. 2012. Rel: 7 Sep 2012. Cert. 18.

Starbuck ★★★★

This is a French language movie from Canada about a former sperm donor who, under his pseudonym 'Starbuck', finds himself the subject

Sister act: Tika Sumpter, Carmen Ejogo and Jordin Sparks in Salim Akil's *Sparkle*.

of a class action lawsuit by 142 children to whom he is technically the father. To make life even more interesting, he's just got his girlfriend pregnant too. Taboo material is sensitively handled with no small degree of charm and it is intermittently hilarious. JC

▶ Patrick Huard, Julie LeBreton, Antoine Bertrand, Dominique Philie, Marc Bélanger, Igor Ovadis.
▶ *Dir* Ken Scott, *Pro* André Rouleau and Jasmyth Lemoine, *Screenplay* Scott and Martin Petit, *Ph* Pierre Gill, *Art Dir* Danielle Labrie, *Ed* Yvann Thibaudeau, *M* David Lafleche, *Cos* Sharon Scott.
Caramel Film-Signature Entertainment.
109 mins. Canada. 2011. Rel: 23 Nov 2012. Cert. 15.

Star Wars Episode 1: The Phantom Menace 3D ★

The 3D presentation of the *Star Wars* movies was announced as a major event, but many fans must have been disappointed that the first re-release was the unloved Episode I, *The Phantom Menace*, and not the original *Star Wars* from 1977. Box-office receipts for *The Phantom Menace* in 3D were presumably weak, as plans to re-release Episodes II-VI in 3D have been abandoned. Disney's new ownership of the franchise promises more genuine innovation in 2015.

▶ Liam Neeson, Ewan McGregor, Natalie Portman, Jake Lloyd, Ian McDiarmid, Oliver Ford Davies, Hugh Quarshie, Kenny Baker, Frank Oz, Terence Stamp.
▶ *Dir and Screenplay* George Lucas, *Pro* Rick McCallum, *Ph* David Tattersall, *Pro Des* Gavin Bocquet, *Ed* Ben Burtt and Paul Martin Smith, *M* John Williams, *Cos* Trisha Biggar.
Lucasfilm-Twentieth Century Fox.
136 mins. USA. 1999. Re-release 3D version: 9 Feb 2012. Cert. U.

Is it better to give...? Patrick Huard as the sperm donor in Starbuck.

Step Up 4: Miami Heat ★★½

Another year, another *Step Up*, but now there's no relation to Channing Tatum's 2006 original. Kathryn McCormick stars as Emily, daughter of rich entrepreneur/developer Peter Gallagher, the Mr Pretty Evil who plans to pull down the Miami neighbourhood where the nice young folks just wanna have fun dancing in the streets or wherever no one's expecting them. McCormick dances and acts fairly well and has some star presence and appeal, while Gallagher has fun as the lip-smacking near-villain of the piece. But it's Ryan Guzman's show. The model and mixed martial arts fighter looks like an angel and dances like a dream. (Original title: *Step Up Revolution*) DW

▶ Kathryn McCormick, Peter Gallagher, Ryan Guzman, Misha Gabriel, Michael Langebeck, Stephen 'Twitch' Boss.
▶ *Dir* Scott Speer, *Pro* Jennifer Gibgot, Garrett Grant, Erik Feig, Patrick Wachsberger and Adam Shankman, *Screenplay* Amanda Brody, based on characters created by Duane Adler, *Ph* Karsten 'Crash' Gopinath, *Pro Des* Carlos Menéndez, *Ed* Matt Friedman and Avi Youabian, *M* Aaron Zigman, *Cos* Rebecca Hoffherr.
Offspring Entertainment/Summit Entertainment-Universal Pictures International.
99 mins. USA. 2012. Rel: 10 Aug 2012. Cert. PG.

Stitches ★★½

Comedian Ross Noble is very funny on TV and, although not really an actor, proves a skilled star presence as a clown who comes back from the dead to avenge himself on the now-teenage birthday party kids who accidentally killed him. Weird and grisly stuff, there's a much better film trying to squeeze itself out of here, but this non-PC comedy take on teen slasher movies is not too bad anyway. There's enough gore and bad taste laughs to fill the 85 minutes and, if only the script had been wittier, this could have had us in stitches. DW

▶ Ross Noble, Tommy Knight, Shane Murray Corcoran, Gemma Leah-Devereux,
▶ *Dir* Conor McMahon, *Pro* Ruth Treacy, Brendan McCarthy, John McDonnell and Julianne Forde, *Screenplay* McMahon and David O'Brien, *Ph* Patrick Jordan, *Pro Des* Ferdia Murphy, *Ed* Chris Gill, *M* Paul McDonnell, *Cos* Allison Byrne.
Fantastic Films/Irish Film Board/Tailored Films/MPI Media Group-Signature Entertainment.
85 mins. Ireland. 2012. Rel: 26 Oct 2012. Cert. 18.

Storage 24 ★★★

Charlie (Noel Clarke) and Shelley (Antonia Campbell Hughes) are in Storage 24 with their friends, dividing their possessions after a recent break-up, but their petty arguments are soon

interrupted when a military cargo plane crashes into London. They get trapped underground while a mysterious entity is hunting them. This SF-horror is inspired by 1950s B-movies and, thankfully, Johannes Roberts' tight direction relies more on character than on spectacular special effects, which seems to work well. GS

▶ Noel Clarke, Colin O'Donoghue, Antonia Campbell-Hughes, Laura Haddock.
▶ *Dir* Johannes Roberts, *Pro* Noel Clarke and Manu Kumaran, *Screenplay* Clarke, Marc Small and Dave Fairbanks, *Ph* Tim Sidell, *Pro Des* Malin Lindholm, *Ed* Martin Brinkler, *M* Christian Henson, *Cos* Andy Blake and Miss Molly.
Unstoppable Entertainment/Medient Entertainment/ BigYellow Films-Universal Pictures.
87 mins. UK. 2011. Rel: 29 June 2012. Cert. 15.

Strawberry Fields ★★

Kent, a relatively unfamiliar location, is the setting here, but it is, alas, wasted on a tiresome drama about two troubled sisters, one of whom is cruelly demanding toward her sibling. Both of the sisters share with the other figures in the story a total inability to make the audience care about them. Even the sudden dramatic climax lacks weight. For a more interesting film from a woman director making her feature debut try instead DR Hood's *Wreckers* (2010). MS

▶ Anna Madeley, Christine Bottomley, Emun Elliott, Jonathan Bonnici, Florence Bell.
▶ *Dir* Frances Lea, *Pro* Liam Beatty and Lucie Wenigerová, *Screenplay* Judith Johnson and Lea, *Ph*

Dave Miller, *Pro Des* John Bramble, *Ed* Cinzia Balderassi, *M* Bryony Afferson and James Stone, *Cos* Emma Moore.
Film London/a Spring Pictures production/a Microwave Film/BBC Films etc-Soda Pictures.
87 mins. UK. 2011. Rel: 6 July 2012. Cert. 15.

StreetDance 2 3D ★½

Streetdancer Ash (Falk Hentschel) and his new friend Eddie (George Sampson) travel around Europe searching for dancers to join their group for a forthcoming dance competition. There's no reality in this premise as these two rather penniless dancers jet-set around Europe – who is financing this enterprise? And then they reach Paris where Ash falls for the beautiful salsa dancer Eva (Sofia Boutella). Boutella adds class to this lazy sequel but her uncle is played by Tom Conti as if he just walked off the set of *'Allo 'Allo*. GS

▶ Sofia Boutella, Falk Hentschel, George Sampson, Tom Conti, Stephanie Nguyen
▶ *Dir* Max Giwa and Dania Pasquini, *Pro* Allan Niblo and James Richardson, *Screenplay* Jane English, *Ph* Sam McCurdy, *Pro Des* Richard Bullock, *Ed* Tim Murrell, *M* Lloyd Perrin (original score) plus tracks by various artists, *Cos* Andrew Cox.
BBC Films/Vertigo Films/BFI/Square One Entertainment/ Film 1/Eagle Pictures/
Deutsche Filmförderfonds-Vertigo Films.
85 mins. UK/Germany. 2012. Rel: 30 Mar 2012. Cert. PG.

Strippers vs Werewolves ★

A stripper kills a hairy, violent punter (Martin Kemp) who turns out to have been a member of

The uninvited guest: Laura Haddock, Antonia Campbell-Hughes, Ned Dennehy and Noel Clarke in *Storage 24*.

a vicious gang of werewolves. Led by Jack Ferris (Billy Murray), the werewolves scour London for the culprit, finally arriving at the strip club for the big showdown with the strippers. With such a brilliant title, the mix of blood, bullets and boobs should be irresistible, but this horror comedy fumbles it. The cast is fine, it's the script that's the problem. It doesn't really know what to do with the action or how to give anyone any memorable, let alone really funny, lines. DW

▶ Martin Compston, Sarah Douglas, Simon Phillips, Billy Murray, Alan Ford, Martin Kemp, Lysette Anthony, Steven Berkoff, Robert Englund.
▶ *Dir* Jonathan Glendening, *Pro* Simon Phillips, Billy Murray, Jonathan Sothcott, Patricia Rybarczyk, Ciaran Mullaney and Gareth Mullaney, *Screenplay* Phillip Barron and Pat Higgins, *Ph* David Meadows, *Pro Des* Felix Coles, *Ed* Richard Colton, *M* Neil Chaney, *Cos* Millie Sloan.

Black and Blue Films-Kaleidoscope Film Distribution.
93 mins. UK. 2012. Rel: 27 Apr 2012. Cert. 15.

Swandown ★★★

Andrew (*Gallivant*) Kotting's BFI-supported documentary is another oddball pleasure from him. It follows the filmmaker's trip with some pals from Hastings to Hackney in a swan-shaped pedalo called Edith. Pondering on the idyllic landscapes they pass and on the state of the nation, Kotting and writer Iain Sinclair remain amusing, sympathetic and provocative presences. And their eccentric act is bolstered successfully by quirky chats with locals and screen-hogging appearances by actor Dudley Sutton, comedian

Stewart Lee and graphic novelist Alan Moore. DW

▶ Andrew Kotting, Iain Sinclair, Stewart Lee, Alan Moore, Marcia Farquhar, Mark Lythgoe, Dudley Sutton.
▶ *Dir* Andrew Kotting, *Pro* Lisa Marie Russo, *Screenplay* Kotting and Iain Sinclair, *Ph* Nick Gordon Smith, *Ed* Cliff West, *M* Jem Finer.

British Film Institute/Swandown Productions/Fly Film Company-Cornerhouse Artist Film.
98 mins. UK. 2012. Rel: 20 July 2012. Cert. 12.

The Sweeney ★★

On paper, Ray Winstone would appear to be the perfect actor to resurrect John Thaw's Jack Regan from the 1975-1978 TV series. But much of the charm of the programme was the banter between Regan and fellow Flying Squad detective George Carter (Dennis Waterman). In addition, there was even a modicum of plausibility in amongst the car chases and tough guy antics. In the update, Regan has been turned into a foul-mouthed monster who beats up suspects and humps the boss' wife. And Ben Drew as Carter is a drawback as he has zero presence – and zero chemistry with Winstone. JC-W

▶ Ray Winstone, Ben Drew, Hayley Atwell, Steven Mackintosh, Paul Anderson, Alan Ford, Damian Lewis, Allan Corduner.
▶ *Dir* and *Screenplay* Nick Love, *Pro* Allan Niblo, Rupert Preston, James Richardson, Christopher Simon and Felix Vossen, *Ph* Simon Dennis, *Pro Des* Morgan Kennedy, *Ed* James Herbert, *M* Lorne Balfe, *Cos* Andrew Cox.

Vertigo Films/Embargo Films-E1 Films.
112 mins. UK. 2012. Rel: 12 September 2012. Cert. 15.

Switch ★★★½

Sophie (Karine Vanasse) jumps at the chance to exchange her apartment in Montreal for a luxurious one in Paris when she hears about holiday house-swapping SWITCH.com. But her dream holiday turns into a nightmare when a body is found in her bedroom and she is accused of murder. Detective Forgeat (Eric Cantona) disbelieves her story but when she escapes he begins to question her motives. This is a suspenseful thriller in the best Hitchcock tradition with a thrilling chase sequence through the streets of Paris, but sadly it loses its grip towards the end. GS

▷ Karine Vanasse, Eric Cantona, Mehdi Nebbou, Aurélien Recoing, Karina Testa, Maxim Roy.
▷ *Dir* Frédéric Schoendoerffer, *Pro* Schoendoerffer, Jean-Christophe Grangé and Éric Névé, *Screenplay* Schoendoerffer and Grangé, *Ph* Vincent Gallot, *Pro Des* Jean-Marc Kerdelhue, *Ed* Elsa Fernández and Dominique Mazzoleni, *M* Bruno Coulais, *Cos* Claire Lacaze and Marie-Laure Lasson.

Carcharodon/L & G/Pathé/France 2 Cinéma/France Télévision/Jouor/ CinéCinéma/Canal+ etc-Pathé International.
104 mins. France. 2011. Rel: 30 Mar 2012. Cert. 15.

Tabu ★★★★½

This wholly individual work by Portugal's Miguel Gomes is challenging but rewarding. Presented in two parts following a stylised prologue, it is in essence the story of a love that survived the parting of the lovers. What might have emerged as melodrama gains transcendental power through the form adopted. The first part, set in contemporary Portugal, invites us to ponder the motivations of the characters before switching to a silent second half, set in Africa years earlier, to reveal the history behind what we have seen thus far. In a fine cast Teresa Madruga is outstanding. MS

▷ Teresa Madruga, Laura Soveral, Ana Moreira, Carloto Cotta, Henrique Espírito Santo.
▷ *Dir* Miguel Gomes, *Pro* Luís Urbano and Sandro Anguilar, *Screenplay* Gomes and Mariana Ricardo, *Ph* Rui Poças, *Art Dir* Bruno Duarte, *Ed* Telmo Churro and Gomes, *Cos* Silvia Grabowski.

O Som e a Fúria/Komplizen Film/Gullane/Shellac Sud etc-New Wave Films.
118 mins. Portugal/Germany/France. 2012. Rel: 7 Sep 2012. Cert. 15.

Take This Waltz ★

What a disappointment! Michelle Williams is a fine actress and Sarah Polley turned director adroitly with *Away from Her* (2006). Here, however, they bring us a modishly frank triangle drama in which Williams' tiresome wife has to choose between her husband (Seth Rogen playing it for character) and a younger man (Luke Kirby). The triangle in the recent *Mademoiselle Chambon* made one care, but here we just want Williams to choose so that the film can end. It manages to be both pretentious and banal. MS

▷ Michelle Williams, Seth Rogen, Luke Kirby, Sarah Silverman, Jennifer Podemski.
▷ *Dir* and *Screenplay* Sarah Polley, *Pro* Susan Cavan and Polley, *Ph* Luc Montpellier, *Pro Des* Matthew Davies, *Ed* Christopher Donaldson, *M* Jonathan Goldsmith, *Cos* Lea Carlson.

Joe's Daughter & Mongrel Media/TF1 Droits Audiovisuels/Telefilm Canada etc-StudioCanal Limited.
116 mins. Canada/France. 2011. Rel: 17 Aug 2012. Cert. 15.

Taken 2 ★★★★

In *Taken*, retired CIA agent Bryan Mills (Liam Neeson) killed the Albanian pimp who kidnapped his daughter Kim (Maggie Grace) for sex slavery. Now the pimp's father is back to wreak revenge. He has Mills and his wife Lenore (Famke Janssen) abducted in Istanbul. Luckily Mills has enough gadgets about his person to contact Kim and get her out of harm's way. She manages to get a gun to him and so begins an all-out effort by Mills to reach his daughter and then rescue his wife. As in *Taken* there are enough great action set-pieces, car chases, explosions and the like to keep the audience hooked throughout. It may be ludicrous but it is good fun. Neeson proves he still has it as an action hero and there is room for a *Taken 3*. Bring it on, say I. MHD

▷ Liam Neeson, Maggie Grace, Famke Janssen, Rade Šerbedžija, Leland Orser, Jon Gries, DB Sweeney, Kevork Malikian.
▷ *Dir* Olivier Megaton, *Pro* Luc Besson, *Screenplay* Besson and Robert Mark Kamen, *Ph* Romain Lacourbas, *Pro Des* Sébastien Inizan, *Ed* Camille Delamarre and Vincent Tabaillon,

Point taken: Karine Vanasse takes command in Frédéric Schoendoerffer's *Switch*.

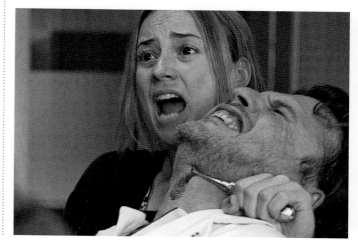

M Nathaniel Méchaly, *Cos* Olivier Beriot.
EuropaCorp/Grive Productions/Cine +/Canal +/M6 Films-20th Century Fox.
92 mins. France. 2012. Rel: 4 Oct 2012. Cert. 12A.

Tales of the Night 3D ★★★★★

That great animator Michel Ocelot here offers a portmanteau movie as six distinct tales are introduced when artists meet in an old cinema. Ranging from Africa to the Caribbean in their settings, these are fantastical tales with the underlying wisdom that you expect from Ocelot. Save for adding 3D here he ignores fashion and he makes films for adults and for children equally. If a film that collects anecdotes together suggests a slight work, that's more than compensated for by the rich and varied visual stylings. It's an immensely satisfying film. (Original title: *Les Contes de la nuit*) MS

▶ With the voices of Marine Griset, Julien Beramis, Christophe Rossignon, Michel Ocelot.
▶ *Dir*, *Screenplay* and *Art Dir* Michel Ocelot, *Pro* Christophe Rossignon and Philip Boëffard, *Ed* Patrick Ducruet, *M* Christian Maire, *Visual Effects* Mac Giff Ligne.
Nord-Ouest Films/Studio O/StudioCanal etc-Soda Pictures.
84 mins. France. 2011. Rel: 25 May 2012. Cert. PG.

Tatsumi ★★★½

This highly unusual work is an animated feature which, illustrating the life of Yoshihiro Tatsumi, also incorporates adaptations of no less than five of his manga stories. The first and best of these, *Hell*, is linked to the dropping of the atomic bomb on Hiroshima, and there are dark and disturbing elements in the others too. The original drawings are arguably more appealing than the animations and the various tales are

uneven in quality, but this is an intriguing film nevertheless. MS

▶ With the voices of Tetsuya Bessho, Yoshihiro Tatsumi, Motoko Gollent, Hiroaki Osada.
▶ *Dir* Eric Khoo, *Pro* Tan Fong Cheng, Esaf Andreas Sinaulan, Khoo and others, *Screenplay* based on *A Drifting Life* and the short stories of Yoshihiro Tatsumi, *Art Dir* Widhi Saputro, *Ed* and *Creative Animation Dir* Phil Mitchell, *M* Christopher Khoo and Christine Sham.
Zhao Wei Films/Infinite Frameworks etc-Soda Pictures.
96 mins. Singapore/Japan. 2011. Rel: 13 Jan 2012. Cert. 15.

Ted ★★★½

When a man commits to a woman for life he must expect to make a few compromises. John Bennett (Mark Wahlberg) is 35 years old and has been dating Lori (Mila Kunis) for four years – but he still talks to his teddy bear. More problematic, his teddy bear talks back… The template of Seth MacFarlane's first film as writer-director is pretty standard-issue, except for the teddy bear thing. But because MacFarlane plays his romcom absolutely straight, it's all the more uproarious. It's also edgy stuff, albeit wrapped up in a cosy American love story that too often beggars belief. Still, it's very, very funny – even funnier than *The Beaver*. JC-W

▶ Mark Wahlberg, Mila Kunis, Seth MacFarlane (voice of Ted), Giovanni Ribisi, Joel McHale, Patrick Warburton, Matt Walsh, Patrick Stewart (narrator), Sam Jones, Nora Jones, Ryan Reynolds, Tom Skerritt.
▶ *Dir* Seth MacFarlane, *Pro* MacFarlane, Scott Stuber, John Jacobs and Jason Clark, *Screenplay* MacFarlane, Alec Sulkin and Wellesley Wild, *Ph* Michael Barrett, *Pro Des* Stephen J Lineweaver, *Ed* Jeff Freeman, *M* Walter Murphy, *Cos* Debra McGuire.
Universal/Media Rights Capital/Fuzzy Door Prods/ Bluegrass Films/Smart Entertainment-Universal.
106 mins. USA. 2012. Rel: 1 Aug 2012. Cert. 15.

A drifting life: A scene from Eric Khoo's *Tatsumi*, adapted from the short stories of the manga artist Yoshihiro Tatsumi.

Tempest ★★½

After Helen Mirren's lady Prospero in 2011, Shakespeare's masterwork gets another new spin. It happens in a shoestring drama-doc about a group of South London teens meeting twice a week for ten months to rehearse the re-imagined play near the Oval cricket ground. It ends of course with their show. Connecting Shakespeare's themes to a riot-afflicted Britain of 2011 seems strained, but it is imaginatively developed with a good heart. Though it could be better edited, the film stays involving, relevant and truthful. Zephryn Taitte gets the plum role as Prospero. DW

▶ Mitchell Bonsra, Kieran Edwards, Paris Campbell, Zephryn Taitte, Roy A Weise, Nathan Wharton.
▶ *Dir* and *Pro* Rob Curry and Anthony Fletcher, *Screenplay* William Shakespeare, *Ph* Richard Mitchell *Ed* Francesco Caradonna and Mark Townsend, *M* Roi Erez.

Fifth Column Films-Fifth Column Films.
90 mins. UK. 2012. Rel: 2 Nov 2012. Cert. 12A.

That's My Boy ★

Adam Sandler won the Razzie award as Worst Actor for this struggling, abrasive comedy, in which he (slackly) plays Donny, who turns up uninvited for the wedding of Todd, the boy he fathered in his teens and brought up single-handedly. Todd moved out when he was 18 and they have understandably not seen each other in quite a while, but Donny needs to reconnect. Charmless though Sandler is here, Andy Samberg (actually only 12 years younger than Sandler) is worse as Todd. Far too long, too witless and too smutty, the film finds the laughs are few and far between. It only recovered half its $70million cost at the US box-office. DW

▶ Adam Sandler, Andy Samberg, Leighton Meester, Susan Sarandon, Vanilla Ice, James Caan, Milo Ventimiglia.
▶ *Dir* Sean Anders, *Pro* Adam Sandler, Heather Parry, Jack Giarraputo and Alan Covert, *Screenplay* David Caspe, *Ph* Brandon Trost, *Pro Des* Aaron Osborne, *Ed* Tom Costain, *M* Rupert Gregson-Williams, *Cos* Ellen Lutter.

Columbia Pictures/Happy Madison Productions/
Relativity Media-Sony Pictures Releasing.
116 mins. USA. 2012. Rel: 7 Sep 2012. Cert. 15.

Think Like a Man ★★★½

This comedy is similar in structure to the recent *What to Expect When You're Expecting* but much funnier and with a talented ensemble of actors. The book *Act Like a Lady, Think Like a Man* becomes a bible to a group of women who are keen to 'get their man'. But when the men get hold of the book things get complicated... It's slick and classy but looks more like a glossy commercial than a slice of life. GS

▶ Michael Ealy, Regina Hall, Jerry Ferrara, Meagan Good, Kevin Hart, Terrence Jenkins, Taraji P Henson, Gabriele Union, Romany Malco.
▶ *Dir* Tim Story, *Pro* William Packer, *Screenplay* Keith

Boys aloud: Jerry Ferarra, Michael Ealy, Kevin Hart, Terrence Jenkins, Gary Owen and Romany Malco in Tim Story's *Think Like a Man.*

Displaced distinction: Sean Penn in one of the best performances of his career, in Paolo Sorrentino's *This Must Be the Place*.

Merryman and David A Newman, based on Steve Harvey's book *Act Like a Lady, Think Like a Man*, *Ph* Larry Blanford, *Pro Des* Chris Cornwell, *Ed* Peter S Elliot, *M* Christopher Lennertz, *Cos* Salvador Pérez Jr.

Screen Gems/Rainforest Films-Sony Pictures Releasing. 122 mins. USA. 2012. Rel: 22 June 2012. Cert. 12A.

This is Not a Film ★★★★

This unique document is an act of defiance by the Iranian filmmaker Jafar Panahi, who had been banned from filming by the authorities. In his flat we see him reading from a script they had refused to accept while awaiting news of his appeal against a prison sentence. Other social issues surface when he talks to a student struggling to get by in Tehran while this 'effort' (that is the word used in the end credits) witnesses his own claustrophobic isolation. It's a work of specialised interest by its very nature, but one stands back and salutes a brave man. MS

▶ With Jafar Panahi, Mojtaba Mirtahmasb, Hassan.
▶ *Dir* Jafar Panahi, *Ph* Mojtaba Mirtahmasb.

An effort by Jafar Panahi and Mojtaba Mirtahmasb-Palisades Tartan Ltd. 75 mins. Iran. 2011. Rel: 30 Mar 2012. Cert. U.

This Means War ★★½

When CIA agents FDR and Tuck (Chris Pine and Tom Hardy) fall for Lauren Scott (Reece Witherspoon), a senior product evaluator, it's time to forget about their friendship and get the knives out. This is loud and fast but the plot never rings true. The attractive cast bounce off

each other nicely while director McG keeps the action flowing, but they're all in desperate need of a better script. GS

▶ Reese Witherspoon, Chris Pine, Tom Hardy, Til Schweiger, Chelsea Handler, Rosemary Harris, Angela Bassett.
▶ *Dir* McG (Joseph McGinty Nichol), *Pro* Will Smith, Simon Kinberg, James Lassiter and Robert Simonds, *Screenplay* Timothy Dowling and Simon Kinberg, from a story by Dowling and Marcus Gautesen, *Ph* Russell Carpenter, *Pro Des* Martin Laing, *Ed* Nicolas De Toth, *M* Christophe Beck, *Cos* Sophie de Rakoff.

Overbrook Entertainments/Robert Simonds Company-Twentieth Century Fox. 97 mins. USA. 2012. Rel: 2 Mar 2012. Cert. 12A.

This Must Be the Place ★★★★

Italy's Paolo Sorrentino, he of *Il Divo* (2008), turns to an English language work set mainly in America. There a son (Sean Penn), a retired pop singer with a gender-bending image, hunts down the Nazi who humiliated his father in the camps. This underrated film, which finds Penn on top form, is less than perfect, but the climactic scene in which the two come face to face brilliantly confronts the audience with the issue of what is right when it comes to the question of former war criminals. MS

▶ Sean Penn, Judd Hirsch, Eve Hewson, Harry Dean Stanton, Frances McDormand, David Byrne, Kerry Condon, Joyce Van Patten, Shea Whigham, Heinz Lieven.
▶ *Dir* Paolo Sorrentino, *Pro* Nicola Giuliano, Andrea Occhipinti and others, *Screenplay* Sorrentino and Umberto Contarello, from Sorrentino's story, *Ph* Luca Bigazzi, *Pro Des* Stefania Cella, *Ed* Cristiano Travaglioli, *M* David Byrne, *Cos* Karen Patch.

An Indigo Film, Lucky Red, Medusa Film production/France 2 Cinéma etc-Trinity Filmed Entertainment. 112 mins. Italy/France/Ireland. 2011. Rel: 6 Apr 2012. Cert. 15.

A Thousand Kisses Deep ★

Mia (Jodie Whittaker), a young woman plagued by memories of her former lover Ludwig (Dougray Scott), must face up to her past in order to prevent a future tragedy. Whittaker is effective but is let down by Scott's rather indifferent and one-dimensional performance. The premise isn't bad but not very exciting, especially under Dana Lustig's unimaginative direction. File this under pretentious. GS

▶ Dougray Scott, Emilia Fox, David Warner, Jodie Whittaker, Allan Corduner, Charlotte Lucas, Jonathan Slinger.
▶ *Dir* Dana Lustig, *Pro* Ofir Kedar, *Screenplay* Alex Kustanovich and Vadim Moldovan, *Ph* George

Richmond, *Pro Des* Alison Riva, *Ed* Humphrey Dixon, *M* Mike Moran, Sandy McLelland and Ross Cullum, *Cos* Allison Wyldeck.

Tomori Films-Kaleidoscope Film Distribution.
84 mins. UK/USA. 2011. Rel: 15 June 2012. Cert. 15.

The Three Stooges ★★★

In a nutshell, the boys are dumb, dumber and dumbest. They break stuff, fall over a lot, get chased by angry guards through hospitals, zoos and the like. Wisely dividing an almost plotless excuse for slapstick comedy violence into three linked shorts, the Farrellys crack out gags at an alarming rate. At the centre of the chaos is a trio of flawless Stooge impersonations, though Larry David is particularly hilarious as a grouchy, Stooge-hating nun. Broad as a bean, winningly daft and packed with eye-watering yet consequence-free cartoon violence. MJ

‣ Sean Hayes, Chris Diamantopoulos, Will Sasso, Jane Lynch, Sofia Vergara, Jennifer Hudson, Larry David, Craig Bierko.
‣ *Dir* Bobby Farrelly and Peter Farrelly, *Pro* Farrelly Brothers, Bradley Thomas and Charles B Wessler, *Screenplay* Farrelly Brothers and Mike Cerrone, based on the Three Stooges short films, *Ph* Mathew F Leonetti, *Pro Des* Arlan Jay Vetter, *Ed* Sam Seig, *M* John Debney, *Cos* Cindy Carr.

Twentieth Century Fox/Dune Entertainment/
Conundrum Entertainment/C3 Entertainment Inc/
Wessler Entertainment-20th Century Fox.
92 mins. USA. 2012. Rel: 22 Aug 2012. Cert. PG.

Tim and Eric's Billion Dollar Movie ★

Tim Heidecker and Eric Wareheim get a billion dollars to make a movie. Things go pear-shaped. They'll be killed if they don't recoup the money, so they try to revamp a shopping mall. Tim and Eric's TV show was a hoot, but their movie effort as writers-directors-stars is strained. The story is clunky and not essentially funny, The occasional laughs just don't flow, most gags coming over as stale, predictable and contrived. It is lucky, then, that old reliables Robert Loggia, Will Ferrell, Will Forte, John C Reilly and Jeff Goldblum do actually raise some chuckles and that Tim and Eric stay likable. DW

‣ Tim Heidecker, Eric Wareheim, Jeff Goldblum, Robert Loggia, Will Ferrell, Will Forte, John C Reilly, Bob Ross, William Atherton. Narrated by Michael Gross.
‣ *Dir* Tim Heidecker and Eric Wareheim, *Pro* Heidecker, Wareheim, Ferrell, Todd Wagner, Jon Mugar, Chris Henchy, Dave Kneebone etc, *Screenplay* Heidecker, Wareheim, Jon Mugar, Doug Lussenhop and Jonathan Krisel, *Ph* Rachel Morrison, *Pro Des* Rosie Sanders, *Ed* Lussenhop and Daniel

Haworth, *M* Davin Wood, *Cos* Diana Contreras-Gonzalez.

2929 Productions/Gary Sanchez Productions/Funny or
Die/Abso Lutely Productions etc-Magnolia Pictures.
93 mins. USA. 2012. Rel: 24 Aug 2012. Cert. 18.

Tinkerbell and the Secret of the Wings 3D ★★★½

This is the fourth in Disney's adventures of the little fairy from *Peter Pan*, although what JM Barrie would make of them doesn't bear thinking about. Here our little gossamer-winged heroine goes into the Winter Woods where she meets Periwinkle, who turns out to be her sister. However, the Winter Woods Lord and the Queen of Pixie Hollow are against their meeting. Then, when the cold weather comes, the winter and the fair weather fairy friends have to fight together to save their wonderful world. Well-voiced by a familiar cast, this is pleasant, undemanding animation for little girls. (Original title: *Secret of the Wings*) PL

‣ Voices of Timothy Dalton, Anjelica Huston, Lucy Hale, Megan Hilty, Jesse McCartney, Mae Whitman, Lucy Liu.
‣ *Dir* Peggy Holmes and Bobs Gannaway, *Pro* John Lasseter and Makul Wigert, *Screenplay* Gannaway, Holmes, Ryan Rowe and Tom Rogers, *Art Dir* Barry Atkinson, *M* Joel McNeely.

Walt Disney Pictures/Disney Toon Studios-Walt Disney
Studios Motion Pictures.
75 mins. USA. 2012. Rel: 14 Dec 2012. Cert. U.

Tiny Furniture ★★★★

Recent college graduate Aura (played by writer-director Lena Dunham) returns home to New York after obtaining a degree in film theory from a university in the mid-west. Her mother Siri (Laurie Simmons) is a successful photographer while her younger sister Nadine (Grace Dunham) is about to graduate from high school. Aura has no idea what to do with her life but dreams of making movies... Dunham's script shines with originality; it's witty, perceptive and laugh-out-loud funny. GS

All she needs now is a very small apartment: Lena Dunham in Tiny Furniture.

▶ Lena Dunham, Laurie Simmons, Grace Dunham, David Call, Jemima Kirke, Amy Seimetz, Merritt Wever, Alex Karpovsky.
▶ *Dir* and *Screenplay* Lena Dunham, *Pro* Alicia Van Couvering and Kyle Martin, *Ph* Jody Lee Lipes, *Art Dir* Jade Healy, *Ed* Lance Edmands, *M* Teddy Blanks.

Tiny Ponies-Independent Distribution.
98 mins. USA. 2010. Rel: 30 Mar 2012. Cert. 15.

Titanic 3D ★★★★★

James Cameron's iconic film is even better second time around and looks absolutely dazzling in 3D. Re-released as part of the Titanic centenary, this tragic story of the doomed voyage needs no introduction. Leonardo DiCaprio and Kate Winslet are terrific as the young lovers caught up in devastating events and, under Cameron's immaculate direction, not a single shot is wasted. GS

▶ Leonardo DiCaprio, Kate Winslet, Billy Zane, Kathy Bates, Frances Fisher, Gloria Stuart, Bill Paxton, David Warner, Victor Garber.
▶ *Dir* and *Screenplay* James Cameron, *Pro* Cameron and Jon Landau, *Ph* Russell Carpenter, *Pro Des* Peter Lamont, *Ed* Cameron, Conrad Buff and Richard A Harris, *M* James Horner, *Cos* Deborah L Scott.

Twentieth Century Fox/Paramount Pictures/Lightstorm Entertainment-20th Century Fox.
194 mins. USA. 1997. Re-Release 6 Apr 2012. Cert. 12.

To Rome with Love ★★★

Woody Allen continues his travels with this comic portmanteau film intertwining five stories made in Italy. Compared to *Midnight in Paris*, this is light, slipshod stuff (one illogical thread echoes Allen's superior *Celebrity* of 1998). What makes it watchable is the acting: Allen himself is back on screen, but the real scene-stealers are his leading ladies: Penélope Cruz, Judy Davis, Ellen Page and not least the (to me) unknown Alessandra Mastronardi. MS

Woody Allen's Italian odyssey: Alessandro Tiberi and Penélope Cruz in *To Rome with Love*.

▶ Woody Allen, Penélope Cruz, Judy Davis, Alec Baldwin, Roberto Benigni, Ellen Page, Jesse Eisenberg, Alessandra Mastronardi, Greta Gerwig, Antonio Albanese, Alison Pill, Ornella Muti.
▶ *Dir* and *Screenplay* Woody Allen, *Pro* Letty Aronson, Stephen Tenenbaum and others, *Ph* Darius Khondji, *Pro Des* Anne Seibel, *Ed* Alisa Lepselter, *Cos* Sonia Grande.

Sony Pictures Classics/a Medusa Film & Gravier production/a Perdido production-Sony Pictures Releasing.
112mins. USA. 2012. Rel: 14 Sep 2012. Cert. 12A.

Top Cat The Movie ★★½

Top Cat and his gang – Benny the Ball, Fancy Fancy, Choo Choo, Spook and Brains – are back at war with the police, especially now that the evil megalomaniac Strickland is in charge. With the help of a robot police force and surveillance cameras, Strickland demands blind obedience from everyone, but TC and friends have other plans. The popular Hanna-Barbera cartoon gets the cinematic 3D treatment in this enjoyable but hollow adventure, with vibrant colours and retro designs matching the 1960s original. GS

▶ With the voices of Jason Harris, Bil Lobley, Ben Diskin, Matthew Piazzi, Melissa Disney, Chris Edgerly.
▶ *Dir* Alberto Mar, *Pro* Fernando de Fuentes and Jose C Garcia de Letona, *Screenplay* Tim McKeon and Kevin Seccia, *Art Dir* Mario Pons Morales, *Ed* Andrés Fernández, *M* Leoncio Lara, *Animation Director* José Alejandro Garcia Muñoz.

Anima Estudios/Illusion Studios-Vertigo Films.
90 mins. Mexico/Argentina/UK. 2011. Rel: 1 June 2012. Cert. U.

The Topp Twins: Untouchable Girls ★★★½

The Topp twins are utterly unique! They are New Zealand's wonderful yodelling lesbian twin sisters whose popular performances combine country singing with eccentric sketches, including The Two Kens, Camp Mother and Camp Leader, and The Bowling Ladies. This loving documentary celebrates their life and career with archive footage and home movies, including interviews with colleagues and their parents. It's an honest film about natural born talents who are real survivors – not only in a cut-throat business but also in beating breast cancer. GS

▶ With Jools Topp, Jean Topp, Lynda Topp, Helen Clark, Paul Horan, Peter Topp, Bruce Topp, Billy Bragg.
▶ *Dir* Leanne Pooley, *Pro* Arani Cuthbert, *Ph* Leon Narbey and Wayne Vinten, *Ed* Tim Woodhouse, *M* Jules & Lynda Topp and David Long.

Diva Productions/New Zealand Film Commission/New Zealand On Air/Sweeney Valley-November Films.
84 mins. New Zealand. 2009. Rel: 15 Feb 2012. Cert. PG.

Folk-singing folk from New Zealand in *The Topp Twins: Untouchable Girls*.

Tortoise in Love ★★★

Led by Guy Browning, this film was, as a credit puts it, "made by almost the entire village of Kingston Bagprize." As such, it should not be judged by the criteria usually applied to commercial movies. It's a very basic comedy set in the village with a shy hero falling for a Polish au pair and becoming caught up in complications surrounding the annual fête. It's always simplistic and sometimes feeble, but you have to admire the spirit and enterprise behind it. MS

▶ Tom Mitchelson, Alice Zawadzki, Tom Yates, Toby Longworth, Ingrid Evans.
▶ *Dir* and *Screenplay* Guy Browning, *Pro* Steffan Aquarone, *Ph* Balazs Bolygo, *Pro Des* Jan Carlisle, *Ed* David Stephenson, *M* Geoff Cottrell.

KBS Films/an Immense production-Immense Productions. 84 mins. UK. 2011. Rel: 13 July 2012. Cert. 12A.

Total Recall ★★★★

Set in the latter part of the 21st century, this riveting remake exudes a gritty reality – and the sets are to die for. London has become a futuristic metropolis and is now the centre of the all-powerful United Federation of Britain. It is here that Colin Farrell's factory worker discovers that he is not who he thinks he is – due to a 'memory implant'… Unlike the Schwarzenegger original – which was a comic-strip extravaganza set on Mars – this is a relentless, earthbound rollercoaster ride, a seemingly far-fetched but technically logical mind-trip. JC-W

▶ Colin Farrell, Kate Beckinsale, Jessica Biel, Bryan Cranston, Bill Nighy, Bokeem Woodbine, John Cho.
▶ *Dir* Ken Wiseman, *Pro* Neal H Moritz and Toby Jaffe, *Screenplay* Kurt Wimmer and Mark Bomback, *Ph* Paul Cameron, *Pro Des* Patrick Tatopoulos, *Ed* Christian Wagner, *M* Harry Gregson-Williams, *Cos* Sanja Milkovic Hays.

Total Recall/Original Film/Rekall Prods-Sony. 118 mins. USA/Canada. 2012. Rel: 29 Aug 2012. Cert. 12A.

Tower Block ★★★

After one of the residents of a decayed 1950s London tower block is beaten to death, the others lock themselves in, waiting for the council to re-house them. Months afterwards, a sniper starts picking them off and it's up to those left to battle for survival. There are plenty of jolts and tension throughout this exciting, high-impact thriller, with strong work on the score and camera. Sheridan Smith and Jack O'Connell stand out in the fine ensemble cast who bring to life some 'real' characters you care about. DW

▶ Sheridan Smith, Russell Tovey, Jack O'Connell, Ralph Brown, Julie Graham, Christopher Fulford.
▶ *Dir* James Nunn and Ronnie Thompson, *Pro* Thompson, Mark Lane and James Harris, *Screenplay*

D'Urberville twist: Riz Ahmed and Freida Pinto in *Trishna*, Michael Winterbottom's modern take on the Thomas Hardy classic.

James Moran, *Ph* Ben Moulden, *Pro Des* Kajsa Soderlund, *Ed* Kate Coggins, *M* Owen Morris, *Cos* Matthew Price.

Creativity Media/Tea Shop and Film Company-Lionsgate. 90 mins. UK. 2012. Rel: 21 Sep 2012. Cert. 15.

Town of Runners ★★★★

Filmed over three years in Ethiopia, Jerry Rothwell's documentary offers an appealing look at small-town life there, with particular emphasis on teenagers and on those from Bekoji who are keen to take up running. It could be better shaped and more succinct, but the people come across well and, even if it is not particularly cinematic, this is essentially a nice little film. MS

❧ With Sentayehu Esthu, Hawii Megersa, Alemi Tsegaye, Biruk.
❧ *Dir* and *Ph* Jerry Rothwell, *Pro* Dan Demissie and Al Morrow, *Ed* Alan Mackay, *M* Vincent Watts.

Met Film/an ITVS International co-production/Klikk/ Britdoc/Channel 4 etc-Dogwoof. 89 mins. UK/USA/Hong Kong. 2011. Rel: 20 Apr 2012. Cert. PG.

Transit ★★★★

The Sidwells' family holiday turns into a nightmare when a group of violent robbers hide a bag of money in the camping gear on top of their Land Rover… just before it approaches a road blockade. Antonio Negret's taut and superbly directed thriller puts the beautiful but hostile Louisiana landscape and its swamps to great effect. Jim Caviezel delivers a strong performance as the determined father prepared to do anything in order to protect his family. GS

❧ Jim Caviezel, Diora Baird, James Frain, Sterling Knight, Ryan Donowho, Elisabeth Röhm, Jake Cherry, Harold Perrineau.

❧ *Dir* Antonio Negret, *Pro* Moshe Diamant and Courtney Solomon, *Screenplay* Michael Gilvary, *Ph* Yaron Levy, *Pro Des* Nate Jones, *Ed* William Yeh, *M* Chris Westlake, *Cos* Kim Martinez.

After Dark Films/Signature Entertainment/Curtis Productions/Bettis Productions Ltd/Dark Castle Entertainment-G2 Pictures. 88 mins. USA. 2012. Rel: 20 Apr 2012. Cert. 15.

Trishna ★★★★★

Michael Winterbottom is at his best here. He gives us a contemporary variation on Thomas Hardy's *Tess of the d'Urbervilles* which, set in India, says a great deal about life in that country while gaining extra power through its echoes of the novel. Tess becomes Trishna and, more controversially, Hardy's two contrasted central male figures are represented by one man and the dual sides of his nature. For me this works and, as the powerful tragic climax confirms, Freida Pinto has never been better than she is here. The colour photography is superb. MS

❧ Freida Pinto, Riz Ahmed, Roshan Seth, Meeta Vasisht, Harish Khanna, Leela Madhauram.
❧ *Dir* and *Screenplay* (based on the novel *Tess of the d'Urbervilles* by Thomas Hardy) Michael Winterbottom, *Pro* Melissa Parmenter and Winterbottom, *Ph* Marcel Zyskind, *Pro Des* David Bryan, *Ed* Mags Arnold, *M* Shigeru Umebayashi and Amit Trivedi, *Cos* Niharika Khan.

Head Gear Films/UK Film Council/a Revolution Films production/Bob Film Sweden etc-Artificial Eye. 113 mins. UK/Sweden/India. 2011. Rel: 9 Mar 2012. Cert. 15.

Trouble with the Curve ★★★★

Clint Eastwood here yields the direction to his colleague Robert Lorenz but takes the lead role, so *Gran Torino* (2009) did not, as expected, contain his last performance. Randy Brown's story is both about baseball (Eastwood plays an ageing scout who still has a true instinct) and about a troubled father-daughter relationship (Eastwood and Amy Adams). It's a commercial mainstream movie set up to deliver a happy ending, but of its kind it's good. Both stars do well, and Eastwood limits the sentimentality by making his role suitably prickly. MS

❧ Clint Eastwood, Amy Adams, Justin Timberlake, John Goodman, Matthew Lillard.
❧ *Dir* Robert Lorenz, *Pro* Clint Eastwood, Lorenz and Michele Weisler, *Screenplay* Randy Brown, *Ph* Tom Stern, *Pro Des* James J Murakami, *Ed* Gary D Roach and Joel Cox, *M* Marco Beltrami, *Cos* Deborah Hopper.

Warner Bros Pictures/a Malpaso production etc-Warner Bros. 111 mins. USA. 2012. Rel: 30 Nov 2012. Cert. 12A.

Truth or Dare ★★★

There's a party, then it's spin the bottle, truth or dare, but one boy gets bullied. Months after, two carloads of kids head to his house for a birthday party. He isn't in, so they have to trek off to the keeper's cabin, where his brother (David Oakes) awaits… Yet another British horror thriller about a group of teens in a lonely cabin with a psycho killer out there, but this one is a decent surprise, quite entertaining throughout and with a few plot twists up its sleeve. The acting from a little-known cast is expert, especially Jennie Jacques, Liam Boyle as her boyfriend and Florence Hall as her friend. DW

▶ Liam Boyle, Jack Gordon, Florence Hall, Nicky Henson, Jennie Jacques, Tom Kane, Jason Maza.
▶ *Dir* Robert Heath, *Pro* Richard Johns and Rupert Jermyn, *Screenplay* Matthew McGuchan, *Ph* James Friend, *Pro Des* John Bramble, *Ed* Oliver Parker, *M* Richard Pryn, *Cos* Raquel Azevedo.

Corona Pictures-Showbox Media Group.
95 mins. UK. 2012. Rel: 6 Aug 2012. Cert. 15.

The Turin Horse ★★★★

The Hungarian avant-garde filmmaker Béla Tarr regards this film as his last. It's a long, demanding watch, but heartfelt. A father and daughter rely on a failing horse as they live off the land in a remote area. Fred Kelemen's black and white photography is magnificent, and in covering six days in their lives Tarr turns the personal story into a lament for a society which, largely rejecting religion, has found no holy values to replace it. Certainly of specialist appeal, this is a deeply pessimistic work which could be better shaped, but it's unquestionably a great work of art. (Original title: *A Torinói ló*) MS

▶ Erika Bók, János Derzsi, Mihály Kormos, Ricsi and the voice of Mihály Raday.
▶ *Dir* Béla Tarr with Ágnes Hranitzky, *Pro* Gábor Téni, Marie-Pierre Macia and others, *Screenplay* László Krasznahorkai and Tarr, *Ph* Fred Kelemen, *Art Dir* Sándor Kállay, *Ed* Hranitzky, *M* Mihály Víg, *Cos* János Breckl.

T.T.Filmmuhely/MPM Film/Vega Film/zero fiction film/Werc Werk Works-Artificial Eye.
155 mins. Hungary/France/Switzerland/Germany. 2011. Rel: 1 June 2012. Cert. 15.

Twenty 8K ★★★½

Journalist Parminder Nagra tries to clear her brother of the killing of a teenage boy outside a nightclub in this rousing, gritty Brit detective thriller, imaginatively directed in a realistic-looking London. Shot against the background of the 2011 riots, it manages to not only be an exciting thriller but also has a truthful relevance. Above all *Shameless* creator Paul Abbott has a good tale to tell, and directors David Kew and Neil Thompson make an excellent, fast-paced job of filming it. Nagra is an excellent, unusual heroine and Stephen Dillane adds effortless authority as the police inspector. DW

▶ Kay Scodelario, Parminder Nagra, Stephen Dillane, Kierston Wareing, Jonas Armstrong, Michael Socha, Nichola Burley, Melanie Hill.
▶ *Dir* David Kew and Neil Thompson, *Pro* Thompson and Martin Carr, *Screenplay* Paul Abbott and Jimmy Dowdall, *Ph* Mike Beresford-Jones, *Pro Des* Chris Richmond, *Ed* Kew, *M* Ruth Barrett, *Cos* Lisa Mitton.

Formosa Films/Abbott Vision-Showbox Media Group.
106 mins. UK. 2012. Rel: 10 Sep 2012. Cert. 15.

Horse opera: Erika Bók in Béla Tarr and Ágnes Hranitzky's *The Turin Horse*, winner of the Jury Grand Prix at Berlin.

Twilight Saga: Breaking Dawn Part 2 ★

This anaemic supernatural drama draws the curtain on an ill-conceived pentalogy beset by weakness at every turn. Slowly crawling towards a cop-out climax, the movie sees Edward and newborn vamp Bella gathering their far-flung relations for a final showdown with the villainous Volturi. Shallow and shoddily scripted, lazily plotted and blandly played with uninspired direction and soppy musical accompaniments, it's as disappointing as the worst of what came before. MJ

▷ Kristen Stewart, Robert Pattinson, Taylor Lautner, Dakota Fanning, Michael Sheen, Mackenzie Foy, Maggie Grace.
▷ *Dir* Bill Condon, *Pro* Stephenie Meyer, Wyck Godfrey and Karen Rosenfelt, *Screenplay* Melissa Rosenberg, from the novel *Breaking Dawn* by Meyer, *Ph* Guillermo Navarro, *Pro Des* Richard Sherman, *Ed* Virginia Katz and Ian Slater, *M* Carter Burwell, *Cos* Michael Wilkinson.

Summit Entertainment/Templehill Entertainment/ Sunswept Entertainment-Summit Entertainment. 115 mins. USA. 2012. Rel: 16 Nov 2012. Cert. 12A

Two Years at Sea ★★

Rightly shown at the London Film Festival in the 'Experimenta' section, Ben Rivers' film is based on what I regard as a misapprehension: he assumes that time spent with a loner, Jake Williams, living remotely in Scotland will convey to the viewer what it means to *be* this man. It doesn't because he rarely speaks. We can't get inside his mind and no background is supplied. Nor do I find beauty in the precisely composed black and white images since they are blotchy from being blown up from 16mm. MS

▷ With Jake Williams.
▷ *Dir*, *Pro*, *Ph* and *Ed* Ben Rivers.

Commissioned by FLAMIN Productions through Film

London Artists' Moving Image Network with funding from Arts Council England-Soda Pictures.
88 mins. UK. 2011. Rel: 4 May 2012. Cert. U.

UFO ★★

Try to remain calm, everybody, an alien army is menacing a Derby housing estate! Five friends wake to find the power gone, there's a UFO in the sky and they have to battle to survive. Pierce Brosnan's lookalike son Sean plays the shirtless, hot-headed hero and Jean-Claude Van Damme's daughter Bianca Bree co-stars as his new girlfriend, while Van Damme himself turns up to save mankind as a recluse with great survival skills. The highlight is the imaginatively staged attack on the supermarket, but otherwise director Dominic Burns just doesn't have enough money or tricks up his sleeve to overcome the weak story and rough dialogue. Nice try, though. DW

▷ Bianca Bree, Sean Brosnan, Simon Phillips, Jazz Lintott, Maya Grant, Jean-Claude Van Damme.
▷ *Dir* and *Screenplay* Dominic Burns, *Pro* Burns, Tim Major, Alain Wildberger, Andy Thompson and Simon Phillips, *Ph* Luke Bryant, *Pro Des* Felix Coles, *Ed* Richard Colton, *M* Si Begg, *Cos* Zoe Howerska.

Hawthorn Productions-Revolver Entertainment. 101 mins. UK. 2012. Rel: 14 Dec 2012. Cert. 15.

Undefeated ★★★½

How satisfying that the 2012 Oscar for Best Documentary went to this stylish and winning sports documentary. Even for non-sports fans, it's rousing and inspiring to follow over an entire season this David vs Goliath tale of the Memphis Manassas Tigers football club as the inner-city kids turn their troubled fortunes around and become winners thanks to a great, determined coach in Bill Courtney. The film won its own battle against the odds: the Sundance Festival rejected it but it was screened in Austin, bought for distribution and went on to gold. DW

▷ With the Memphis Manassas Tigers football team and their coach Bill Courtney.
▷ *Dir*, *Ph* and *Ed* Daniel Lindsay and TJ Martin, *Pro* Lindsay, Glen Zipper, Rich Middlemas, Seth Gordon and Ed Cunningham, *M* Michael Brook, Miles Nielsen and Daniel McMahon.

Five Smooth Stones Productions/Zipper Bros Films/ Level 22 Productions/Spitfire Pictures-Dogwoof. 113 mins. USA. 2011. Rel: 3 Aug 2012. Cert. 12A.

Underworld Awakening (3D) ★½

This is the fourth in the anaemic series about vampire warriors. Selene (Kate Beckinsale) escapes imprisonment but must fight the humans when they discover the existence of the Vampire

American football goes under the arc lights in the Academy Award winning documentary Undefeated.

and Lycan clans. The original was less than average in the first place and by now the feeble plot is almost incomprehensible. The 3D effects enhance the action sequences and Beckinsale knows how to kick ass, but she's in desperate need of a better script. GS

▶ Kate Beckinsale Sandrine Holt, Stephen Rea, Michael Ealy, Theo James, India Eisley, Charles Dance.
▶ *Dir* Måns Mårlind and Björn Stein, *Pro* Len Wiseman, Tom Rosenberg and Gary Luchesi, *Screenplay* Wiseman, John Hlavin, Allison Burnet and J Michael Straczynski, from a story by Wiseman and Hlavin, based on characters by Wiseman, Danny McBride and Kevin Grevioux, *Ph* Scot Kevan, *Pro Des* Claude Paré, *Ed* Jeff McEvoy, *M* Paul Haslinger, *Cos* Monique Prudhomme.

Screen Gems/Saturn Films/Sketch Films/Lakeshore Entertainment/UW4 Productions-Entertainment Film Distributors.
88 mins. USA. 2012. Rel: 20 Jan 2012. Cert. 18.

Untouchable ★★★★

Although based on fact, this is a feel-good movie and specifically French in character. It reassures by showing how an Algerian from the banlieues of Paris and a rich quadriplegic became best friends despite coming from opposite extremes of society. The opening scene mistakenly believes that dangerous driving is comically endearing, but thereafter it never puts a foot wrong. François Cluzet is excellent but it is Omar Sy as the Algerian who, perfectly cast, carries off the film with his César-winning performance: he's a

delight. (Original title: *Intouchables*) MS

▶ François Cluzet, Omar Sy, Anne Le Ny, Audrey Fleurot, Clothilde Mollet, Cyril Mendy.
▶ *Dir* and *Screenplay* Eric Toledano and Olivier Nakache, *Pro* Nicolas Duval Adassovsky, Yann Zenou and Laurent Zeitoun, *Ph* Mathieu Vadepied, *Pro Des* François Emmanuelli, *Ed* Dorian Rigal-Ansous, *M* Ludovico Einaudi, *Cos* Isabelle Pannetier.

Quad/Gaumont/TF1 Films Production/Ten Films/ Chaocorp etc-Entertainment Film Distributors Ltd.
112 mins. France. 2011. Rel: 21 Sep 2012. Cert. 15.

Up There ★★★

The smile-challenged Burn Gorman is spot on as the depressed late hero Martin. He just wants to be elevated 'up there' but is currently in limbo, having to welcome recently dead folks into the afterlife. When a new arrival disappears, he has to team up with the chatty Rash (Aymen Hamdouchi) to go to a deadend Scots seaside town to find the lost soul. There they meet a lot of quirky locals, including the suicidal Liz (Kate O'Flynn). There's plenty of fun to be had in this appealingly different Brit comedy, with warm performances, plus funny writing and expert direction by Zam Salim. DW

▶ Burn Gorman, Jo Hartley, Kate O'Flynn, Aymen Hamdouchi, Kulvinder Ghir, Farren Morgan, Alexander Morton, Chris Waitt, Warren Brown.
▶ *Dir* and *Screenplay* Zam Salim, *Pro* Annalise Davis, *Ph* Ole Bratt Birkeland, *Pro Des* Mike McLoughlin, *Ed* Richard Graham, *M* Christian Henson, *Cos* Anna Robbins.

The prosperous paraplegic: François Cluzet (in wheelchair) is given a new lease of life by Omar Sy, in Olivier Nakache and Éric Toledano's *Untouchable*.

UK Film Council/BBC Films/Creative Scotland/Eyeline Entertainment-Wilder Films.
80 mins. UK. 2012. Rel: 16 Nov 2012. Cert. 15.

A Useful Life ★★★

Shot in black and white and telling a story centred on a struggle to prevent a cinema in Montevideo from closing, this sounds like an ideal film for all who loved *Cinema Paradiso*. But, while it is heartfelt, this is a minimalist work and its portrayal of the cinema programmer, including his hesitant wooing of a teacher, is less engaging than one would hope. There are moments of effective quiet humour, but somehow warmth is lacking and the conclusion fails to resonate. (Original title: *La vida útil*) MS

▶ Jorge Jellinek, Manuel Martínez Carril, Paola Venditto, Gonzalo Delgado.
▶ *Dir* Federico Veiroj, *Pro* Laura Gutman and Juan José López, *Screenplay* Arauco Hernández Holz, Inés Bortagaray, Gonzalo Delgado and Veiroj, *Ph* Holz, *Art Dir* and *Cos* Emilia Carlevaro, *Ed* Holz and Veiroj.

Cinekdoque/Mediapro/Versátil Cinema etc-Dogwoof.
63 mins. Uruguay/Spain/The Netherlands. 2010.
Rel: 13 Jan 2012. Cert. U.

Victim ★★

Tyson (Ashley Chin) is a young man desperate to make a clean break from his gang, especially when he meets Tia (Ashley Madekwe), but his childhood friends and fellow criminals Mannie (Jason Maza) and Jason (Michael Maris) want to do one last job... Alex Pillai directs confidently and draws realistic performances from his actors, but he needs a more cinematic script in order to lift this above routine television drama. GS

▶ Ashley Chin, Ashley Madekwe, Jason Maza, Anna Nightingale, Michael Maris, David Harewood.
▶ *Dir* Alex Pillai, *Pro* Danny Donnelly and Jason Maza, *Screenplay* Adrian Scott, Michael Maris, Ashley Chin and Michael Kyei, *Ph* Peter Butler, *Pro Des* Lucy Gahagan, *Ed* Iain Mitchell, *M* Howard Rees, *Cos* Charlie Jones.

Pure Film Productions/Think Big Productions-Kaleidoscope Film Distributors.
86 mins. UK. 2011. Rel: 22 June 2012. Cert. 15.

The Vow ★★★★

Paige (Rachel McAdams) and Leo (Channing Tatum) are blissfully married in Chicago, but after a car accident Paige wakes up from a coma with her recent memory erased. She doesn't recognise Leo but remembers her estranged parents (Jessica Lange and Sam Neill), who take advantage of the situation. This is a beautiful love story, inspired by true events, which under Michael Sucsy's careful direction never sinks into sentimentality. Tatum and McAdams share a lovely chemistry, but the icing on the cake is Lange's controlled and vanity-free performance. GS

▶ Rachel McAdams, Channing Tatum, Sam Neill, Scott Speedman, Wendy Crewson, Jessica Lange.
▶ *Dir* Michael Sucsy, *Pro* Roger Birnbaum, Jonathan Glickman, Paul Taublieb and Gary Barber, *Screenplay* Jason Katims, Marc Silverstein and Abby Kohn, from a story by Stuart Sender, *Ph* Rogier Stoffers, *Pro Des* Kalina Ivanov, *Ed* Nancy Richardson and Melissa Kent, *M* Rachel Portman and Michael Brook, *Cos* Alex Kavanagh.

Screen Gems/Spyglass Entertainment-Sony Pictures Releasing.
104 mins. USA/France/Australia/UK/Germany. 2012.
Rel: 10 Feb 2012. Cert. 12A.

Memories may be beautiful... but not for Rachel McAdams and Channing Tatum in the unsentimental *The Vow*.

W.E. ★★

Against a backdrop of the Wallis Simpson-Duke
of Windsor affair that knocked the British
monarchy for six, Madonna places another story
of battered wife Wally Winthrop, who's besotted
by the Duke and Duchess. At a Sotheby's sale of
Simpson's artefacts she meets Evgeni, working as
a security guard, and they fall in love – hence the
title: Wallis and Edward and Wally and Evgeni –
geddit? The trouble is, one story cancels out the
other and neither comes out of it too well. Andrea
Riseborough as Wallis and James D'Arcy as Edward
look their parts, but Abbie Cornish as Wally and
Oscar Isaac as Evgeni appear mere fabrications. The
decor and couture throughout are gorgeous. MHD

❯ Abbie Cornish, Andrea Riseborough, James D'Arcy,
Oscar Isaac, Richard Coyle, James Fox, Judy Parfitt.
❯ *Dir* Madonna, *Pro* Madonna and Kris Thykier,
Screenplay Madonna and Alex Keshishian, *Ph* Hagen
Bogdanski, *Pro Des* Martin Childs, *Ed* Danny B Tull,
M Abel Korzeniowski, *Cos* Arianne Phillips.
Semtex Films-Optimum Releasing.
119 mins. UK. 2011. Rel: 20 Jan 2012. Cert. 15.

Wagner's Dream ★★★½

This is a documentary on the preparation
and staging between 2008 and 2012 of a new
production of Richard Wagner's Ring cycle at the
Metropolitan Opera House in New York. Director
Robert Lepage is never less than controversial and
his massive, 16-hour, four-opera staging seems to
have tested not only the skills of the production
team but also the patience of the opera house
staff and its audience. Depending on your point
of view, Susan Froemke's film is a valuable record
of either an innovative masterwork or a complete
folly. The jury is out on whether Wagner would
have approved. PL

❯ With Robert Lepage, James Levine, Fabio Luisi,
Jay Hunter Morris, Deborah Voigt, Peter Gelb etc
❯ *Dir* Susan Froemke, *Pro* Froemke and Douglas
Graves, *Ph* Don Lenzer, *Ed* Bob Eisenhardt.
Susan Froemke Productions-Susan Froemke Productions.
115 mins. USA. 2012. Rel: 20 June 2012. Cert. U.

Wanderlust ★★★

Unable to afford New York any more, George and
Linda decide to move on and work for George's
brother Rick. En route they happen across a
commune of hippies and get waylaid. When life
at Rick's place doesn't work out they return to the
commune, but then things get complicated and
the pressures on their love life become too much
to handle. Can the marriage survive the upheaval
or will they go their separate ways? In tone this
comedy has a dated feel to it, with all the usual
stereotypical ideas about hippies and free love. Paul
Rudd and Jennifer Aniston do their best to raise the
level above the mundane, but it is hard going. MHD

❯ Paul Rudd, Jennifer Aniston, Justin Theroux, Alan
Alda, Malin Akerman, Kathryn Hahn, Lauren Ambrose.
❯ *Dir* David Wain, *Pro* Wain, Judd Apatow, Paul
Rudd and Ken Marino, *Screenplay* Wain and Marino,
Ph Michael Bonvillain, *Pro Des* Aaron Osborne, *Ed*

Stage struck:
A scene from
Susan Froemke's
Wagner's Dream,
a documentary
on the mounting
of the 'Ring' cycle
at the Met.

Black Beauty Goes to War: Benedict Cumberbatch in Steven Spielberg's *War Horse.*

David Moritz and Robert Nassau, *M* Caig Wedren, *Cos* Debra McGuire.

Universal Pictures/Relativity Media/A Hot Dog-Universal Pictures International.
98 mins. USA. 2012. Rel: 2 Mar 2012. Cert. 15.

War Horse ★★★★½

The National Theatre's ongoing success with Michael Morpurgo's story using life-size puppet horses is theatrical history. Steven Spielberg couldn't have filmed it as presented on stage but has opted instead for a kind of fantastic realism that works perfectly in the cinema. Horses were needed for the trenches in World War I and young Albert (the excellent Jeremy Irvine) has to train his favourite steed, Joey, before seeing him sent to the front. Albert enlists, determined that eventually they will be together again. Despite all odds the film works thanks to Lee Hall and Richard Curtis' screenplay, steering clear of sentimentality but going for true emotion. It looks stunning in Janusz Kaminski's fine cinematography and has many moving performances from Spielberg's cast. MHD

▸ Jeremy Irvine, Emily Watson, David Thewlis, Peter Mullan, Niels Arestrup, Tom Hiddleston, Benedict Cumberbatch, Eddie Marsan.
▸ *Dir* Steven Spielberg, *Pro* Spielberg and Kathleen Kennedy, *Screenplay* Lee Hall and Richard Curtis, based on the novel by Michael Morpurgo and the stage play by Nick Stafford, *Ph* Janusz Kaminski, *Pro*

Des Rick Carter, *Ed* Michael Kahn, *M* John Williams, *Cos* Joanna Johnston.

DreamWorks Pictures/Amblin Entertainment/Kennedy-Marshall Company/Reliance Entertainment-Buena Vista International.
146 mins. USA. 2011. Rel: 13 Jan 2012. Cert. 12A.

The Watch ★½

The tale of a disparate quartet of suburban types whose fledgling neighbourhood watch is sorely tested when aliens invade their leafy corner of the world, this stars highly-strung imp Ben Stiller, shouty dough-boy Vince Vaughn, former funny fatty Jonah Hill and bizarre London talent Richard Ayoade. A glossy, by-the-numbers tale of men behaving badly, this seems like the sort of movie that was a lot of fun to make. Sadly the cast and crew's good time comes at the expense of ours, as viewers are saddled with a lamentable flurry of lame jokes and thin characters. MJ

▸ Ben Stiller, Vince Vaughn, Jonah Hill, Richard Ayoade, Rosemarie DeWitt.
▸ *Dir* Akiva Schaffer, *Pro* Shawn Levy and Tom McNulty, *Screenplay* Evan Goldberg, Seth Rogen and Jared Stern, *Ph* Barry Peterson, *Pro Des* Doug J Meerdink, *Ed* Dean Zimmerman, *M* Christophe Beck, *Cos* Wendy Chuck.
Twentieth Century Fox/Ingenious Film Partners/21 Laps Entertainment/Dune Entertainment-20th Century Fox.
102 mins. USA. 2012. Rel: 27 Aug 2012. Cert. 15.

We Are Poets ★★★★

This feel-good documentary follows six teenage poets from Leeds Young Authors after they're chosen to represent Britain at the prestigious Poetry Slams competition in Washington DC. It's an honest portrayal of this talented group's determination to fulfil their dream and find a way of expressing themselves. An assured work from first-time directors Alex Ramseyer-Bache and Daniel Lucchesi, it's both inspirational and deeply engaging. GS

‣ With the Leeds Young Authors Poetry Team: Saju Ahmed, Maryam Alam, Joseph Buckley, Kadish Morris, Rheima 'Mimz' Ibrahim, Azalia Anisko.
‣ *Dir* Daniel Lucchesi and Alex Ramseyer-Bache, *Pro* Lucchesi, Ramseyer-Bache and Martin John Harris, *M* Samuel Sim, The Pattern Theory, Tom Stewart and Bob Bradley.

Alex Ramseyer-Bache and Daniel Lucchesi production in association with Leeds Young Authors, The Northern Film School, Leeds etc-Dogwoof.
84 mins. UK/USA. 20112. Rel: 28 June 2012. No Cert.

We Bought a Zoo ★★★

Benjamin Mee acquired a country property with a zoo attached which he then re-established. That was in England, but this film builds it up into a feel-good tale set in America and then milks it for all it's worth. It's well acted by all, but in trying to please everyone (young children, teenagers, adults) it ends up with a mix that will satisfy nobody all of the time, and that's so even if they accept its contrivances. MS

‣ Matt Damon, Scarlett Johansson, Thomas Haden Church, Colin Ford, Elle Fanning.
‣ *Dir* Cameron Crowe, *Pro* Julie Yorn, Crowe and Rick Yorn, *Screenplay* Aline Brosh McKenna and Crowe, based on the book by Benjamin Mee, *Ph* Rodrigo Prieto, *Pro Des* Clay Griffith, *Ed* Mark Livolsi, *M* Jónsi, *Cos* Deborah L Scott.

Twentieth Century Fox/an LBI Entertainment/Vinyl Films production etc-20th Century Fox.
124 mins. USA. 2011. Rel: 16 Mar 2012. Cert. PG.

The Wedding Video ★★

Take the tried and tested format of 'let's make a video' and blend it with the thoroughly exhausted wedding romcom and you get what you deserve. As the obnoxious Raif (Rufus Hound, a sort of English Seth Rogen) implausibly records the six weeks, three days leading up to his brother's wedding, we are subjected to a series of extended skits. Having said that, there is a terrific turn from Lucy Punch as the posh bride (although, as Miriam Margolyes points out, you can varnish an infected toenail...) and good support from Michelle Gomez and Harriet Walter. JC-W

‣ Rufus Hound, Lucy Punch, Robert Webb, Harriet Walter, Miriam Margolyes, Michelle Gomez.
‣ *Dir* Nigel Cole, *Pro* James Gay-Rees, *Screenplay* Tim Firth, *Ph* Simon Tindall, *Pro Des* Kristian Milsted, *Ed* Laura Morrod, *M* Matt Berry, *Cos* Ian Fulcher.

Squirrel Films/Timeless Films-Entertainment Film Distributors.
93 mins. UK. 2012. Rel: 17 August 2012. Cert. 15.

Welcome Aboard ★★★½

A haunting little tale about a depressed man in his sixties and the runaway teenage girl he gives a lift to becomes a delightful experience in the expert hands of veteran Jean Becker (80 in 2013). Ideally cast, Patrick Chesnais and Jeanne Lambert give perfectly honed performances as the couple in question. The feelgood script might be a shade manipulative but it knows exactly what it is doing and when to do it, and Becker times the charming story (based on Eric Holder's novel) as if with a vintage stopwatch. (Original title: *Bienvenue parmi nous*) DW

‣ Patrick Chesnais, Jeanne Lambert, Miou-Miou, Jacques Weber, Xavier Gallais, Raphaëline Goupilleau.
‣ *Dir* Jean Becker, *Pro* Louis Becker, *Screenplay* Becker, François d'Épenoux and Marie-Sabine Roger, from the novel by Eric Holder, *Ph* Arthur Cloquet, *Pro Des* Thérèse Ripaud, *Ed* Jacques Witta and Franck Nakache, *Cos* Annie Perier Bertaux.

StudioCanal/K J B Production/ICE 3/France 3 Cinéma/Canal +/Ciné +/France Télévision etc-StudioCanal.
92 mins. France. 2012. Rel: 26 Oct 2012. Cert. 15.

West of Memphis ★★★★½

This ambitious documentary tells the story of the 'West Memphis 3', teenagers found guilty of a supposed Satanic ritual involving the killing and mutilation of three eight-year-old boys in 1994. It took 18 years to get them out of prison and this superbly structured film covers the whole complex story of an injustice. It's investigative journalism

Old man and teenage girl on the lam: Patrick Chesnais and Jeanne Lambert in Jean Becker's delightful *Welcome Aboard*.

Blind Justice: Henry Rollins and Amy Berg in Berg's documentary *West of Memphis.*

at its best, a strong indictment of the Arkansas courts and an invitation to consider the evidence pointing to another culprit. Arguably it's a shade too long at 147 minutes and an intermission might have been helpful. Even so, it's riveting. MS

❯ With Damien Echols, Lorri Davis, Jessie Misskelley, Jason Baldwin, Peter Jackson.
❯ *Dir* Amy Berg, *Pro* Berg, Fran Walsh, Peter Jackson, Damien Echols and Lorri Davis, *Written by* Berg and Billy McMillin, *Ph* Maryse Alberti and Ronan Killeen, *Pro Des* Linda Sena, *Ed* McMillin, *M* Nick Cave and Warren Ellis, *Cos* Diaz Jacobs.

A Wingnut Films production/Disarming Films-Sony Pictures Releasing.
147 mins. USA/New Zealand. 2012. Rel: 21 Dec 2012. Cert. 15.

What to Expect When You're Expecting ★★½

Think *Pregnant, Actually* and you get the general drift of this ensemble romcom. But when the likes of Cameron Diaz, Jennifer Lopez and Brooklyn Decker are rolling up to Mothercare (or its American equivalent), there aren't going to be many stretch marks of reality. Even so, the movie stirs up as many variations of Hollywood pregnancy as will sit comfortably within two hours, without any hope of the viewer getting to care for a single character. The humour is the thing, with flatulent mothers-to-be, accident-prone toddlers and sensitive nipples. Just don't go expecting any amniotic fluid. JC-W

❯ Cameron Diaz, Jennifer Lopez, Elizabeth Banks, Chase Crawford, Brooklyn Decker, Ben Falcone, Anna Kendrick, Matthew Morrison, Dennis Quaid, Chris Rock, Rodrigo Santoro.
❯ *Dir* Kirk Jones, *Pro* Mike Medavoy, Arnold Messer and David Thwaites, *Screenplay* Shauna Cross and Heather Hach, *Ph* Xavier Grobet, *Pro Des* Andrew Laws, *Ed* Michael Berenbaum, *M* Mark Mothersbaugh, *Cos* Karen Patch.

Lionsgate/Alcon Entertainment/Phoenix Pictures-Lionsgate.
109 mins. USA. 2012. Rel: 25 May 2012. Cert. 12A.

When Santa Fell to Earth ★

The title should give you a clue. It sounds like one of those ghastly B-movies of the 1950s. It's actually based on the relatively respected children's novel by Cornelia Funke, but it's a gruesome translation. An uncharacteristically youthful (and clean-shaven) Vater Christmas is chased out of Christmastown by the money-grabbing Goblynch and is forced to enlist the help of two children to save that special day on 25 December. Some awful CGI, disjointed action and the American dubbing really doesn't help. CB

❯ Alexander Scheer, Noah Joël Kraus, Mercedes Jadea Diaz, Jessica Schwarz, Fritz Karl.
❯ *Dir* Oliver Dieckmann, *Pro* Uschi Reich and Bernd Krause, *Screenplay* Reich, Robin Getrost and Benjamin Biehn, based on the novel by Cornelia

Funke, *Ph* Alexander Fischerkoessen, *Pro Des* Maximilian Lange, *Ed* Christian Nauheimer, *M* Nick Reiser and Péter Wolf, *Cos* Andrea Spanier.

Bavaria Film/Wega Film/Kiddinx Filmproduktion/ Zweites Deutsches Fernsehen-Sola Media.
107 mins. Germany. 2011. Rel: 7 Dec 2012. Cert. U.

When the Lights Went Out ★★

A family's dream council home turns into a nightmare as Kate Ashfield's Jenny, Steven Waddington's Len and their daughter Sally (Tasha Connor) battle things that go bump in the dark. Writer-director Pat Holden's film is based on real-life events that happened to his own family, which adds credibility to a far-fetched tale about poltergeists attacking a household in Yorkshire just as the 1974 power cuts hit. The acting is solid, the 1970s mood is well caught, and so is the eerie air of mounting hysteria, but it's a bit tame and on one-note as a horror movie. DW

▶ Kate Ashfield, Tasha Connor, Steven Waddington, Craig Parkinson, Jo Hartley, Nicky Bell, Alan Brent, Martin Compston, Peter Egan.
▶ *Dir* and *Screenplay* Pat Holden, *Pro* Bill Bungay and Deepak Nayar, *Ph* Jonathan Harvey, *Pro Des* Jane Levick, *Ed* Robert Hall and Gary Scullion, *M* Marc Canham, *Cos* Sarah Blenkinsop.

Kintop Pictures-Revolver Entertainment.
86 mins. UK. 2012. Rel: 14 Sep 2012. Cert. 15.

Where Do We Go Now? ★

Apart from a neat ending, this film from Nadine Labaki, who gave us *Caramel* (2007), is abysmal. Its theme of a woman leading the way to reconcile hostile men of different beliefs may be admirable, but as told here the story switches from mood to mood – it's now farce, now drama, now grim reality and now fairy tale. This creates a work which can never cohere and which is therefore an insult to the intelligence. (Original title: *Et maintenant on va où?*) MS

▶ Claude Baz Moussawbaa, Layla Hakim, Nadine Labaki, Yvonne Maalouf, Julien Farhat.
▶ *Dir* Nadine Labaki, *Pro* Anne-Dominique Toussaint, *Screenplay* Labaki, Jihad Hojeily and others, *Ph* Christophe Offenstein, *Pro Des* Cynthia Zahar, *Ed* Véronique Lange, *M* Khaled Mouzanar, *Cos* Caroline Labaki.

Les Films des Tournelles/Pathé/Chaocorp/France 2 Cinéma etc.-Revolver Entertainment.
102 mins. France/Lebanon/Egypt/Italy. 2011. Rel: 22 June 2012. Cert. 12A.

Wild Bill ★★★★½

Dexter Fletcher makes a remarkable debut as director on *Wild Bill*, which he co-wrote with Danny King. Bill (Charlie Creed-Miles) comes out of prison determined to go straight. Returning to the East London family home, he finds Dean and Jimmy, his two underage sons, living on their own, their mother having fled to Spain with her new boyfriend. Local drug dealers are trying to get Bill's sons working for them so, in order to save his family from a life of crime, Bill has to decide what sort of father he needs to be. Brilliant performances all round, especially from Creed-Miles as Bill and Will Poulter and Sammy Williams as the sons, coupled with a razor-sharp screenplay and Dexter's sure-footed direction make this a real boost to independent British films. MHD

▶ Charlie Creed-Miles, Will Poulter, Sammy Williams, Charlotte Spencer, Liz White, Leo Gregory, Neil Maskell, Jason Flemyng, Jaime Winstone, Olivia Williams, Andy Serkis.
▶ *Dir* Dexter Fletcher, *Pro* Tim Cole and Sam Tromans, *Screenplay* Fletcher and Danny King, *Ph* George Richmond, *Pro Des* Murray McKeown, *Ed* Stuart Gazzard, *M* Christian Henson, *Cos* Matt Price.

20ten Media-The Works.
98 mins. UK. 2011. Rel: 23 Mar 2012. Cert. 15.

The Woman in Black ★★★★

Scary but not too scary, this adroit adaptation of Susan Hill's novel, which also became a successful stage play, is an ideal post-Harry Potter vehicle for Daniel Radcliffe. As a young lawyer who is also a widower, he becomes involved with events in a dead client's house which is haunted. The thrills that follow may not be subtle, but the film knows how to hold its audience and proves that Radcliffe, with an able supporting cast, can carry a movie single-handedly. MS

▶ Daniel Radcliffe, Ciarán Hinds, Janet McTeer, Liz White, Roger Allam.
▶ *Dir* James Watkins, *Pro* Richard Jackson, Simon Oakes and Brian Oliver, *Screenplay* Jane Goldman,

Soul destroying: The ghosts of victims past, in James Watkins' chilling *The Woman in Black*.

Maids in Paris: Carmen Maura, Sandrine Kiberlain, Natalia Verbeke, Lola Dueñas and Berta Ojea in *The Women on the 6th Floor*.

from the novel by Susan Hill, *Ph* Tim Maurice-Jones, *Pro Des* Kave Quinn, *Ed* Jon Harris, *M* Marco Beltrami, *Cos* Keith Madden.

Alliance Films/Hammer/UK Film Council/a Talisman production etc-Momentum Pictures.
95 mins. USA/UK/Canada/Sweden. 2011. Rel: 10 Feb 2012. Cert. 12A.

The Woman in the Fifth ★★

To have Kristin Scott Thomas in a film by Pawel Pawlikowski (praised for *Last Resort* and *Summer of Love*) sounds exciting. Unfortunately what we have on screen is perplexingly elusive. Ethan Hawke plays an American novelist visiting Paris, where he encounters a somewhat underused Scott Thomas as the widow of a Hungarian writer. The mysteries that develop prove impenetrable: after the screening a colleague was heard to say "That was cryptic." Just so, and not in an appealing way. MS

▶ Ethan Hawke, Kristin Scott Thomas, Joanna Kulig, Samir Guesmi, Delphine Chuillot.
▶ *Dir* and *Screenplay* (based on the novel by Douglas Kennedy) Pawel Pawlikowski, *Pro* Caroline Benjo and Carole Scotta, *Ph* Ryszard Lenczewski, *Pro Des* Benoit Barouh, *Ed* David Charap, *M* Max de Wardener, *Cos* Julian Day and Shaida Day.

Haut et Court/Film4/UK Film Council/SPI International Poland/The Bureau etc-Artificial Eye.
84 mins. France/UK/Poland. 2011. Rel: 17 Feb 2012. Cert. 15.

The Women on the 6th Floor ★★★½

Like *Salmon Fishing in the Yemen* [qv], this film from France starts as comedy but segues into romantic drama. Fabrice Luchini is the man who rebels against his snobbish wife (Sandrine Kiberlain) to empathise with the immigrant working class women living above him on the sixth floor. The tonal switch is less than perfect, but this is enjoyable, with a great cast extending from famous names to the less familiar Natalia Verbeke, who steals the show. (Original title: *Les Femmes du 6ème étage*). MS

▶ Fabrice Luchini, Sandrine Kiberlain, Natalia Verbeke, Carmen Maura, Lola Dueñas.
▶ *Dir* Philippe Le Guay, *Pro* Philippe Rousselet, *Screenplay* Le Guay and Jérôme Tonnerre, *Ph* Jean-Claude Larrieu, *Art Dir* Pierre-François Limbosch, *Ed* Monica Coleman, *M* Jorge Arriagada, *Cos* Christian Gasc.

A Vendome Production/France 2 Cinéma//SND/Canal+ etc-Cinefile World.
106 mins. France. 2010. Rel: 6 July 2012. Cert. 12A.

Woody Allen: A Documentary ★★★★

The reticent gag-writer and stand-up who became a prolific actor-writer-director is depicted as an obsessive figure who never stops working. He has written 70 films and directed nearly 50, making a feature film virtually every year since the 1970s. Robert B Weide (who directed the TV series *Curb Your Enthusiasm* with Larry David, the new Woody) here takes a worthy trawl through Allen's career, using new material and archive footage of Allen's collaborators and fans. If it avoids going into detail about Allen's private life, it is still an absorbing look at one of cinema's great auteurs. Made for HBO, the TV version runs over three hours; the DVD release has many fascinating extras. MHD

▶ Woody Allen, Letty Aronson, Marshall Brickman, Larry David, John Cusack, Penélope Cruz, Josh Brolin, Dick Cavett, Diane Keaton, Julie Kavner etc.
▶ *Dir, Pro* and *Written by* Robert B Weide, *Ph* Buddy Squires, Bill Sheehy, Nancy Schreiber, Anthony Savini and Neve Cunningham, *Ed* Weide and Karoliina Tuovinen, *M* Paul Cantelon.

Whyaduck Productions/Insurgent Media/Rat Entertainment/Mike's Movies/Thirteen's American Masters-Soda Pictures.
113 mins. USA. 2012. Rel: 8 June 2012. Cert. 15.

Wrath of the Titans 3D ★★

The action of this sequel takes place ten years after the defeat of the monstrous Kraken. Perseus (Sam Worthington), the demi-god son of Zeus (Liam Neeson), has returned to his fishing but is called back on duty when his father is imprisoned by Hades (Ralph Fiennes). The set-up of this spectacular adventure looks absolutely splendid on the giant IMAX screen, but the repetitive and almost identical action sequences lose their impact long before the final credits. GS

▶ Sam Worthington, Rosamund Pike, Bill Nighy, Édgar Ramirez, Toby Kebbell, Danny Huston, Ralph Fiennes, Liam Neeson.
▶ *Dir* Jonathan Liebesman, *Pro* Basil Iwanyk and Polly Cohen Johnsen, *Screenplay* Dan Mazeau and David Leslie Johnson, from a story by Mazeau, Johnson and Greg Berlanti, *Ph* Ben Davis, *Pro Des* Charles Wood, *Ed* Martin Walsh, *M* Javier Navarrete, *Cos* Jany Temime.

Warner Bros Pictures/Legendary Pictures/Cott Productions/Thunder Road etc- Warner Bros.
99 mins. USA. 2012. Rel: 30 Mar 2012. Cert. 12A.

X: Night of Vengeance ★

This Australian thriller follows the story of high-class call girl Holly Rowe (Viva Bianca), who one night pairs up with young and homeless Shay Ryan (Hannah Mangan Lawrence) for a date with a rich client. But the night goes disastrously wrong when they witness his murder and have to run for their lives. The premise sounds better than the final result – it is gratuitous, slow and dull. (Original title: *X*) GS

▶ Viva Bianca, Hanna Mangan Lawrence, Peter Docker, Stephen Phillips.
▶ *Dir* Jon Hewitt, *Pro* Lizzette Atkins, *Screenplay* Hewitt and Belinda McClory, *Ph* Mark Pugh, *Pro Des* Michelle Southeran, *Ed* Cindy Clarkson, *M* David Franzke and Byron Joel Scullin, *Cos* Vanessa Loh.

Circe Films/Rough Beast-Celluloid Nightmares.
90 mins. Australia. 2011. Rel: 20 Jan 2012. Cert. 18.

Yossi ★★★★

This sequel to 2002's *Yossi and Jagger* can stand alone. Set in Tel Aviv, it's a quiet, thoughtful film about a gay doctor, secretive about his sexuality and still haunted by the loss of his lover ten years earlier. A chance meeting with a younger gay soldier underlines how the past decade has changed attitudes to homosexuality. The affirmative ending may seem contrived, but Eytan Fox's film has you rooting for it all the same. (Original title: *Ha-sippur shel Yossi*) MS

▶ Ohad Knoller, Oz Zehavi, Orly Silbersatz, Ola Schur Selektar, Lior Ashkenazi, Meir Golan.
▶ *Dir* Eytan Fox, *Pro* Ayelet Kait, Fox and others, *Screenplay* Itay Segal, *Ph* Guy Raz, *Art Dir* Mor Barak, *Ed* Yosef Grunfeld, *M* Keren Ann, *Cos* Mira Karmely and Chen Carmi.

United King Films/Lama Films etc-Peccadillo Pictures.
81 mins. Israel. 2012. Rel: 30 Nov 2012. Cert. 15.

No peace for a demi-god: Sam Worthington back on duty as Perseus in *Wrath of the Titans 3D*.

Young Adult ★★★★

Mavis Cody (Charlize Theron) is a writer of romantic fiction for adolescent girls, yet her own love life leaves much to be desired. Experiencing writer's block, she has her latest books cancelled. Learning that her former boyfriend Buddy (Patrick Wilson) is happily married with a new baby in tow, she freaks out and determines to settle a score and get him back. En route she encounters some old acquaintances but has difficulty in re-writing her own life story so that it has a happy ending. With a stunning and quite hilarious performance by Theron, both she and the film go into overdrive in this impressive playing-out of a life falling apart. MHD

‣ Charlize Theron, Patton Oswalt, Patrick Wilson, Elizabeth Reaser, Jill Eikenberry, Mary Beth Hurt.
‣ *Dir* Jason Reitman, *Pro* Reitman, Diablo Cody, Lianne Halfon, Mason Novick etc, *Screenplay* Diablo Cody, *Ph* Eric Steelberg, *Pro Des* Kevin Thompson, *Ed* Dana E Glauberman, *M* Rolfe Kent, *Cos* David Robinson.

Paramount Pictures/Denver and Delilah Productions/Right of Way Films/Mandate Pictures etc-Paramount Pictures. 94 mins. USA. 2011. Rel: 3 Feb 2012. Cert. 15.

Your Sister's Sister ★★★½

Lynn Shelton, who made the promising *Humpday* (2009), opts here for bigger names, retaining Mark Duplass but adding Emily Blunt – and, as originally planned, Rachel Weisz, whose role eventually went to the excellent Rosemarie De Witt instead. As well as featuring a troubled yet essentially loving relationship between sisters, Shelton's film retains her individual voice in its comic yet sympathetic take on messed-up sexual relationships. However, the full-scale happy ending does not convince. MS

‣ Emily Blunt, Rosemarie DeWitt, Mark Duplass, Mike Birbiglia.
‣ *Dir* and *Screenplay* Lynn Shelton, *Pro* Steven Schardt, *Ph* Benjamin Kasulke, *Pro Des* John Lavin, *Ed* Nat Sanders, *M* Vinny Smith.

Ada Films-StudioCanal Limited. 90 mins. USA. 2011. Rel: 29 June 2012. Cert. 15.

You've Been Trumped ★★★★

Anthony Baxter's documentary grippingly records what members of the Menie Estate in Aberdeenshire had to put up with when the American billionaire Donald Trump was authorised by the Scottish parliament to go ahead with a controversial development, imposing two golf courses, a posh hotel and time-share apartments on a site noted as a wildlife habitat. The filmmaking can occasionally be questioned, but that hardly matters for by the close there will be few viewers who do not feel anger at the behaviour of Trump and of the authorities. MS

‣ With Michael Forbes, Anthony Baxter.
‣ *Dir* and *Ph* Anthony Baxter, *Pro* Richard Phinney, *Written by* Phinney and Baxter, *Ed* William Rice, *M* Jonny Pilcher.

Montrose Pictures/a Bell Rock production-Montrose Films. 101 mins. UK. 2011. Rel: 6 July 2012. Cert. PG.

You Will Be My Son ★★★½

This is a drama about inheritance. It concerns the wealthy owner of a French vineyard who comes to see the son of a colleague as better suited than his own son to take over. The novel setting is an asset and, if slightly staid in its approach, Gilles Legrand's film holds the interest. The debit side is a climax which needs to be better prepared

Pillow talk: Emily Blunt and Rosemarie DeWitt in Lynn Shelton's *Your Sister's Sister.*

for if it is not to feel over-melodramatic in this context. (Original title: *Tu seras mon fils*) MS

▶ Niels Arestrup, Lorànt Deutsch, Patrick Chesnais, Anne Marivin, Nicolas Bridet.
▶ *Dir* Gilles Legrand, *Pro* Frédéric Brillion and Legrand, *Screenplay* Legrand and Delphine De Vigan, *Ph* Yves Angelo, *Art Dir* Aline Bonetto, *Ed* Andréa Sedlackova, *M* Armand Amar, *Cos* Tess Hammami, Hélène Vaduva and others.

Epithète Films/Orange Cinéma Séries/Soficas Banque Postale Image 4 etc-Swipe Films.
101 mins. France. 2011. Rel: 7 Dec 2012. Cert. PG.

Yuma ★★★½

Jakub Gierszal is magnetic as the early 20-something Zyga in the riveting tale of a Polish anti-hero who's dragged into the gangster life in the chaos after the fall of communism. Though the film is not consistently brilliant, Piotr Malaruk often dazzles as both co-writer and director, delivering an edgy, entertaining *Goodfellas*-style crime thriller while seriously tackling the theme of the moral collapse at the time of the birth of capitalism in Poland. DW

▶ Jakub Gierszal, Krzysztof Skonieczny, Jakub Kamienski, Tomasz Kot, Katarzyna Figura, Karolina Chapko
▶ *Dir* Piotr Mularuk, *Pro* Mularuk, Magdalena Napieracz and Pavel Bercik, *Screenplay* Mularuk and

Wojciech Gajewicz, *Ph* Tomasz Dobroewolski and Jacek Podgorski, *Pro Des* Aneta Suskiewicz, *Ed* Agnieszka Glinska, *M* Jan P Muchow, *Cos* Magdalena Rutkiewicz and Emilia Skalska.

Yeti Films/Evolution Films-Giant Film.
113 mins. Poland/Czech Republic. 2012. Rel: 31 Aug 2012. Cert. 15.

Zaytoun ★★★

Like the much superior *Free Men* [qv], this is an honourable film that asserts common humanity in a situation where strife reigns. Here it is Beirut in 1982 where the lives of a downed Israeli airman and a Palestinian boy from a refugee camp intertwine as hostility between them yields to affection. It starts with brutal realism and that ill prepares us for a contrived story that would work better if offered as a fable. Yet its heart is emphatically in the right place, as one would expect of the director of *Lemon Tree* (2008). MS

▶ Stephen Dorff, Abdallah El Akal, Alice Taglioni, Loai Noufi, Tarik Copti, Joni Arbid.
▶ *Dir* Eran Riklis, *Pro* Gareth Ellis-Unwin and Fred Ritzenberg, *Screenplay* Nader Rizq, *Ph* Dan Lausten, *Pro Des* Yoel Herzberg, *Ed* Herve Schneid, *M* Cyril Morin, *Cos* Hamada Atallah.

A Zaytoun Productions, Pathé, Erin Riklis Productions & United King Films co-production etc-Artificial Eye.
110 mins. UK/France/Israel/USA. 2012. Rel: 26 Dec 2012. Cert. 15.

Last refuge: Abdallah El Akal and Stephen Dorff in Eran Riklis' *Zaytoun.*

Awards and Festivals

85th American Academy of Motion Picture Arts and Sciences Awards ('The Oscars') and Nominations for 2012
24 February 2013

▶ **Best Film:** *Argo.* Nominations: *Amour; Beasts of the Southern Wild; Django Unchained; Les Misérables; Life of Pi; Lincoln; Silver Linings Playbook; Zero Dark Thirty.*

▶ **Best Director:** Ang Lee, for *Life of Pi.* Nominations: Michael Haneke, for *Amour;* David O Russell, for *Silver Linings Playbook;* Steven Spielberg, for *Lincoln;* Behn Zeitlin, for *Beasts of the Southern Wild.*

▶ **Best Actor:** Daniel Day-Lewis, for *Lincoln.* Nominations: Bradley Cooper, for *Silver Linings Playbook;* Hugh Jackman, for *Les Misérables;* Joaquin Phoenix, for *The Master;* Denzel Washington, for *Flight.*

▶ **Best Actress:** Jennifer Lawrence, for *Silver Linings Playbook.* Nominations: Jessica Chastain, for *Zero Dark Thirty;* Emmanuelle Riva, for *Amour;* Quvenzhané Wallis, for *Beasts of the Southern Wild;* Naomi Watts, for *The Impossible.*

▶ **Best Supporting Actor:** Christoph Waltz, for *Django Unchained.* Nominations: Alan Arkin, for *Argo;* Robert De Niro, for *Silver Linings Playbook;* Tommy Lee Jones, for *Lincoln;* Philip Seymour Hoffman, for *The Master.*

▶ **Best Supporting Actress:** Anne Hathaway, for *Les Misérables.* Nominations: Amy Adams, for *The Master;* Sally Field, for *Lincoln;* Helen Hunt, for *The Sessions;* Jacki Weaver, for *Silver Linings Playbook.*

▶ **Best Original Screenplay:** Quentin Tarantino, for *Django Unchained.* Nominations: Michael Haneke, for *Amour;* John Gatins, for *Flight;* Wes Anderson and Roman Coppola, for *Moonrise Kingdom;* Mark Boal, for *Zero Dark Thirty.*

▶ **Best Screenplay Adaptation:** Chris Terrio, for *Argo.* Nominations: Lucy Alibar and Benh Zeitlin, for *Beasts of the Southern Wild;* David Magee, for *Life of Pi;* Tony Kushner, for *Lincoln;* David O Russell, for *Silver Linings Playbook.*

▶ **Best Cinematography:** Claudio Miranda, for *Life of Pi.* Nominations: Seamus McGarvey, for *Anna Karenina;* Robert Richardson, for *Django Unchained;* Janusz Kaminski, for *Lincoln;* Roger Deakins, for *Skyfall.*

▶ **Best Editing:** William Goldenberg, for *Argo.* Nominations: Tim Squyres, for *Life of Pi;* Michael Kahn, for *Lincoln;* Jay Cassidy and Crispin Struthers, for *Silver Linings Playbook;* Dylan Tichenor and William Goldenberg, for *Zero Dark Thirty.*

▶ **Best Original Score:** Mychael Danna, for *Life of Pi.* Nominations: Dario Marianelli, for *Anna Karenina;* Alexandre Desplat, for *Argo;* John Williams, for *Lincoln;* Thomas Newman, for *Skyfall.*

▶ **Best Original Song:** 'Skyfall' from *Skyfall,* by Adele and Paul Epworth. Nominations: 'Before My Time' from *Chasing Ice,* by J Ralph; 'Pi's Lullaby' from *Life of Pi,* by Mychael Danna (music) and Bombay Jayashri (lyrics); 'Suddenly' from *Les Misérables,* by Claude-Michel Schönberg (music) and Herbert Kretzmer and Alain Boublil (lyrics); 'Everybody Needs A Best Friend' from *Ted,* by Walter Murphy (music) and Seth MacFarlane (lyrics).

▶ **Best Art Direction:** Rick Carter and Jim Erickson, for *Lincoln.* Nominations: Sarah Greenwood and Katie Spencer, for *Anna Karenina;* Dan Hennah, Ra Vincent and Simon Bright, for *The Hobbit: An Unexpected Journey;* Eve Stewart and Anna Lynch-Robinson, for *Les Misérables;* David Gropman and Anna Pinnock, for *Life of Pi.*

▶ **Best Costume Design:** Jacqueline Durran, for *Anna Karenina.* Nominations: Paco Delgado, for *Les Misérables;* Joanna Johnston, for *Lincoln;* Eiko Ishioka, for *Mirror Mirror;* Colleen Atwood, for *Snow White and the Huntsman.*

▶ **Best Sound Editing:** Per Hallberg and Karen Baker Landers, for *Skyfall.* Nominations: Erik Aadahl and Ethan Van der Ryn, for *Argo;* Wylie Stateman, for *Django Unchained;* Eugene Gearty and Philip Stockton, for *Life of Pi;* Paul NJ Ottosson, for *Zero Dark Thirty.*

▶ **Best Sound Mixing:** Andy Nelson, Mark Paterson and Simon Hayes, for *Les Misérables.* Nominations: John Reitz, Gregg Rudloff and Jose Antonio Garcia, *Argo;* Ron Bartlett, DM Hemphill and Drew Kunin, for *Life of Pi;* Andy Nelson, Gary Rydstrom and Ronald Judkins, for *Lincoln;* Scott Millan, Greg P Russell and Stuart Wilson, for *Skyfall.*

Above: Quvenzhané Wallis in *Beasts of the Southern Wild.*
Opposite: Joaquin Phoenix in *The Master.*

▶ **Best Makeup and Hairstyling**: Lisa Westcott and Julie Dartnell, *Les Misérables*. Nominations: Howard Berger, Peter Montagna and Martin Samuel, for *Hitchcock*; Peter Swords King, Rick Findlater and Tami Lane, for *The Hobbit: An Unexpected Journey*.

▶ **Best Visual Effects**: Bill Westenhofer, Guillaume Rocheron, Erik-Jan De Boer and Donald R. Elliott, for *Life of Pi*. Nominations: Joe Letteri, Eric Saindon, David Clayton and R Christopher White, for *The Hobbit: An Unexpected Journey*; Janek Sirrs, Jeff White, Guy Williams and Dan Sudick, for *Marvel's The Avengers*; Richard Stammers, Trevor Wood, Charley Henley and Martin Hill, for *Prometheus*; Cedric Nicolas-Troyan, Philip Brennan, Neil Corbould and Michael Dawson, for *Snow White and the Huntsman*.

▶ **Best Animated Short Film**: *Paperman*. Nominations: *Adam and Dog*; *Fresh Guacamole*; *Head over Heels*; *Maggie Simpson in 'The Longest Daycare'*.

▶ **Best Animated Feature**: *Brave*. Nominations: *Frankenweenie*; *ParaNorman*; *The Pirates! Band of Misfits* (aka *The Pirates! In an Adventure with Scientists!*); *Wreck-It Ralph*.

▶ **Best Documentary Feature**: *Searching for Sugar Man*. Nominations: *5 Broken Cameras*; *The Gatekeepers*; *How to Survive a Plague*; *The Invisible War*.

▶ **Best Documentary Short**: *Inocente*. Nominations:

Sixto Rodriguez in *Searching for Sugar Man*.

Kings Point; *Mondays at Racine*; *Open Heart*; *Redemption*.

▶ **Best Foreign-Language Film**: *Amour* (Austria). Nominations: *Kon-Tiki* (Norway); *No* (Chile); *A Royal Affair* (Denmark); *War Witch* (Canada).

▶ **Jean Hersholt Humanitarian Award**: Jeffrey Katzenberg.

The 63rd Berlin International Film Festival
7-17 February 2013

▶ **Golden Bear for Best Film**: *Child's Pose* (Romania), by Călin Peter Netzer.

▶ **Silver Bear, Jury Grand Prix**: *An Episode in the Life of an Iron Picker* (Bosnia and Herzegovina), by Danis Tanović.

▶ **Silver Bear, Best Director**: David Gordon Green, for *Prince Avalanche* (USA).

▶ **Silver Bear, Best Actress**: Paulina García, for *Gloria* (Chile).

▶ **Silver Bear, Best Actor**: Nazif Mujić, for *An Episode in the Life of an Iron Picker*.

▶ **Silver Bear for Outstanding Artistic Achievement**: Aziz Zhambakiyev, for *Harmony Lessons* (Kazakhstan/Germany).

▶ **Best Screenplay**: Jafar Panahi, for *Closed Curtain* (Iran).

▶ **Alfred Bauer Prize for a work of particular innovation**: *Vic and Flo Saw a Bear* by Denis Côté.

▶ **Special Mentions**: *Promised Land* (USA) by Gus Van Sant and *Layla Fourie* (Germany/South Africa/France/The Netherlands) by Pia Marais.

▶ **Golden Bear for Best Short Film**: *The Runaway*, by Jean-Bernard Marlin.

▶ **Jury**: *Wong Kar-wai* (president), *Susanne Bier, Andreas Dresen, Ellen Kuras, Shirin Neshat, Tim Robbins* and *Athina Rachel Tsangari*.

The 2012 British Academy of Film and Television Arts Awards ('Baftas')
10 February 2013

▶ **Best Film**: *Argo*.
▶ **Outstanding British Film**: *Skyfall*.
▶ **Best Director**: Ben Affleck, for *Argo*.
▶ **Best Actor**: Daniel Day-Lewis, for *Lincoln*.
▶ **Best Actress**: Emmanuelle Riva, for *Amour*.
▶ **Best Supporting Actor**: Christoph Waltz, for *Django Unchained*.
▶ **Best Supporting Actress**: Anne Hathaway, for *Les Misérables*.
▶ **Best Original Screenplay**: Quentin Tarantino, for *Django Unchained*.
▶ **Best Adapted Screenplay**: David O Russell, for *Silver Linings Playbook*.
▶ **Best Cinematography**: Claudio Miranda, for *Life of Pi*.
▶ **Best Production Design**: Eve Stewart and Anna Lynch-Robinson, for *Les Misérables*.
▶ **Best Editing**: William Goldenberg, for *Argo*.
▶ **Best Music**: Thomas Newman, for *Skyfall*.

▸▸ **Best Costumes**: Jacqueline Durran, for *Anna Karenina*.

▸▸ **Best Sound**: Simon Hayes, Andy Nelson, Mark Paterson, Jonathan Allen, Lee Walpole and John Warhurst, for *Les Misérables*.

▸▸ **Best Special Visual Effects**: Bill Westenhofer, Guillaume Rocheron, Erik-Jan De Boer and Donald R Elliott, for *Life of Pi*.

▸▸ **Best Make-Up/Hair**: Lisa Westcott, for *Les Misérables*.

▸▸ **Best Non-English Language Film**: *Amour* (Austria).

▸▸ **Best Documentary**: *Searching For Sugar Man*.

▸▸ **Best Short Film**: *Swimmer*.

▸▸ **Best Animated Film**: *Brave*.

▸▸ **Best Short Animated Film**: *The Making of Longbird*.

▸▸ **Best Outstanding Debut by a British Writer, Director or Producer**: Bart Layton and Dimitri Doganis, for *The Imposter*.

▸▸ **The Orange Rising Star Award**: Juno Temple.

▸▸ **Bafta Fellowship**: Sir Alan Parker.

▸▸ **Outstanding British Contribution to Cinema**: Tessa Ross (Controlller of Film and Drama at Channel 4).

The 65th Cannes Film Festival Awards
16-27 May 2012

▸▸ **Palme d'Or (Golden Palm)**: *Amour* (Austria), by Michael Haneke.

▸▸ **Grand Prix du Jury**: *Reality* (Italy), by Matteo Garrone.

▸▸ **Jury Prize**: *The Angels' Share* (UK), by Ken Loach.

▸▸ **Camera d'Or** (first-time filmmaker): Benh Zeitlin, for *Beasts of the Southern Wild* (USA).

▸▸ **Best Actor**: Mads Mikkelsen, for *The Hunt* (Denmark).

▸▸ **Best Actress**: Cosmina Stratan and Cristina Flutur, for *Beyond the Hills* (Romania).

▸▸ **Best Director**: Carlos Reygadas for *Post Tenebras Lux* (Mexico).

▸▸ **Best Screenplay**: Cristian Mungiu, for *Beyond the Hills* (Romania).

▸▸ **Un Certain Regard Prize**: *Después de Lucía* (*After Lucía*) (Mexico), by Michel Franco.

▸▸ **Special Jury Prize**: *Le grand soir* (France/Belgium), by Benoît Delépine and Gustave de Kervern.

▸▸ **Best Actress**: Émilie Dequenne, for *Loving Without Reason* (aka *Our Children*) (Belgium/France), and Suzanne Clément, for *Laurence Anyways* (Canada).

▸▸ **Palme d'Or – Short Film**: *Silent* (Turkey), by L Rezan Yesilbas.

❯ **Jury**: *Nanni Moretti (president), Hiam Abbass, Andrea Arnold, Emmanuelle Devos, Jean Paul Gaultier, Diane Kruger, Ewan McGregor, Alexander Payne* and *Raoul Peck*.

The 70th Hollywood Foreign Press Association ('Golden Globes') Awards
13 January 2013

▸▸ **Best Motion Picture – Drama**: *Argo*.

▸▸ **Best Motion Picture – Musical or Comedy**: *Les Misérables*.

Toby Jones in *Berberian Sound Studio*.

▸▸ **Best Director**: Ben Affleck, for *Argo*.

▸▸ **Best Actor – Drama**: Daniel Day-Lewis, for *Lincoln*.

▸▸ **Best Actress – Drama**: Jessica Chastain, for *Zero Dark Thirty*.

▸▸ **Best Actor – Musical or Comedy**: Hugh Jackman, for *Les Misérables*.

▸▸ **Best Actress – Musical or Comedy**: Jennifer Lawrence, for *Silver Linings Playbook*.

▸▸ **Best Supporting Actor**: Christoph Waltz, for *Django Unchained*.

▸▸ **Best Supporting Actress**: Anne Hathaway, for *Les Misérables*.

▸▸ **Best Foreign Language Film**: *Amour* (Austria).

▸▸ **Best Animated Feature Film**: *Brave*.

▸▸ **Best Screenplay**: Quentin Tarantino, for *Django Unchained*.

▸▸ **Best Original Score**: Mychael Danna, for *Life of Pi*.

▸▸ **Best Original Song**: 'Skyfall', music and lyrics by Adele and Paul Epworth, from *Skyfall*.

The 33rd London Film Critics' Circle Awards 2012
20 January 2013

▸▸ **Film of the Year**: *Amour*.

▸▸ **British Film of the Year**: *Berberian Sound Studio*.

▸▸ **Foreign Language Film of the Year**: *Rust and Bone* (France/Belgium).

▸▸ **Documentary of the Year**: *The Imposter*.

Ben Goodman and Ben Affleck in *Argo*.

▶▶ **Director of the Year**: Ang Lee, for *Life of Pi*.

▶▶ **Breakthrough British Film-Makers**: Alice Lowe and Steve Oram, for *Sightseers*.

▶▶ **Technical Achievement**: Bill Westenhofer, visual effects, for *Life of Pi*.

▶▶ **Actor of the Year**: Joaquin Phoenix, for *The Master*.

▶▶ **Actress of the Year**: Emmanuelle Riva, for *Amour*.

▶▶ **British Actor of the Year**: Toby Jones, for *Berberian Sound Studio*.

▶▶ **British Actress of the Year**: Andrea Riseborough, for *Shadow Dancer*.

▶▶ **Supporting Actor of the Year**: Philip Seymour Hoffman, for *The Master*.

▶▶ **Supporting Actress of the Year**: Anne Hathaway, for *Les Misérables*.

▶▶ **Screenwriter of the Year**: Michael Haneke, for *Amour*.

▶▶ **Young British Performer of the Year**: Tom Holland, for *The Impossible*.

▶▶ **Dilys Powell Award for Excellence in Film**: Helena Bonham Carter.

69th Venice International Film Festival
29 August-8 September 2012

▶▶ **Golden Lion for Best Film**: *Pieta*, by Kim Ki-duk (South Korea).

▶▶ **Silver Lion for Best Director**: Paul Thomas Anderson, for *The Master* (USA).

▶▶ **Special Jury Prize**: *Paradies: Glaube*, by Ulrich Seidl (Austria/Germany/France).

▶▶ **Coppa Volpi for Best Actor**: Joaquin Phoenix and Philip Seymour Hoffman, for *The Master*.

▶▶ **Coppa Volpi for Best Actress**: Hadas Yaron, for *Lemale et Ha'chalal* (Israel).

▶▶ **Marcello Mastroianni Award for Best New Young Actor or Actress**: Fabrizio Falco, for *Bella Addormentata* (Italy), by Marco Bellocchio, and *È Stato Il Figlio* (Italy), by Daniele Ciprí.

▶▶ **Best Screenplay:** Olivier Assayas, for *APRES MAI* (France).

▶▶ **Best Technical Contribution (Cinematography)**: Daniele Ciprì, for *È Stato Il Figlio*.

▶▶ **Lion of the Future – 'Luigi De Laurentiis' Venice Award for a Debut Film**: *Küf* (*Mold*), by Ali Aydin (Turkey/Germany).

▶▶ **Golden Lion for Lifetime Achievement**: Francesco Rosi.

▶▶ **Jaeger-LeCoultre Glory to the Filmmaker Award**: Spike Lee.

▶▶ **Persol Award**: Michael Cimino.

▶▶ **L'Oréal Paris Award for Cinema**: Giulia Bevilacqua.

◆▶ **The Orizzonti section of the festival highlights the newest trends in world cinema:**

▶▶ **Orizzonti Award** (full-length films): *San Zi Mei*, by Wang Bing (France/Hong Kong).

▶▶ **Special Orizzonti Jury Prize** (full-length films): *Tango Libre*, by Frédéric Fonteyne (France/Belgium/Luxembourg).

▶▶ **Orizzonti You Tube Award for Best Short Film:** *Cho-De*, by Yoo Min-young (South Korea).

▶▶ **European Film Award** (**2012-EFA**): *Titloi Telous*, by Yorgos Zois (Greece).

◆▶ **Jury:** *Michael Mann* (president), *Marina Abramovic, Laetitia Casta, Peter Ho-Sun Chan, Ari Folman, Matteo Garrone, Ursula Meier, Samantha Morton* and *Pablo Trapero*.

Their Name is Bond, James Bond

Mansel Stimpson compares Skyfall *with its predecessors and concludes that 007 is a changed man.*

When Harry Saltzman and Albert R Broccoli produced *Dr No* in 1962 no one could have foreseen that 50 years on the adventures of James Bond would still be filling cinemas on a regular basis.

Back then, Ian Fleming's secret agent may have had the potential to become a franchise, but that had also been true of figures such as Charlie Chan, The Saint and Tarzan. Successful as they had been, none of those characters was to spawn a series of movies lasting half a century. (Admittedly Tarzan had appeared in silent films, but as a series one thinks of the period from 1932 to 1968, from Johnny Weissmuller to Mike Henry.) The fact that *Skyfall*'s huge success puts Bond well in front of all the competition and finds him on peak form is cause for celebration.

Looking back to the first Bond movies, I recall the extent to which I saw *Dr No*, *From Russia with Love* and *Goldfinger* as films which were a reflection of their times. It was *Goldfinger*, made in 1964, which was my favourite, and in large part that was due to the wit of the screenplay by Richard Maibaum and the distinguished former film critic Paul Dehn.

The decade which saw the start of this franchise is frequently referred to as the Swinging Sixties, but how widespread the new lifestyle was is something of an open question, even though it undoubtedly gained momentum as the decade went on. In 1962, however, with such related phenomena as The Beatles only just starting to make their mark, changes associated with the 1960s had not yet taken hold. Despite that, the fantasies of the man and woman in the street had moved on.

Back in the post-war heyday of cinemagoing it had been Herbert Wilcox who, directing his wife Anna Neagle in a series of films, had provided the dream fantasy that the British public wished to feast on. The epitome of this was his 1948 picture *Spring in Park Lane*, a romantic comedy in which, as so often, Neagle starred with Michael Wilding. In an age of austerity it invited audiences to

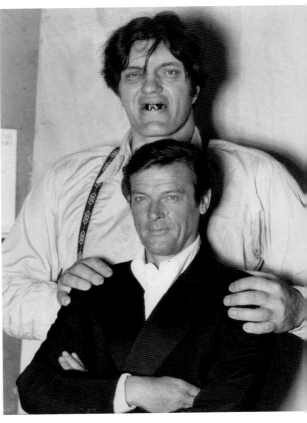

Above: Lois Maxwell, Akiko Wakabayashi, Sean Connery, Karin Dor and Mie Hama on the spectacular set of *You Only Live Twice* (1967).

Above right: James Bond III Roger Moore with his *Moonraker* co-star Richard Kiel in 1979.

enjoy the escapism of a story set among the well-heeled of Mayfair. British cinema would soon turn away from that to cater to a different kind of dream. This it did not by featuring a different lifestyle from that of their audiences but by providing memories of British pluck and courage, reminding viewers of the days when Britain was great. The 1950s was the decade when our cinema looked back again and again to the days of the Second World War.

The arrival of James Bond on screen was in marked contrast to this, and yet it reverted to

the Wilcox concept of providing the public with contemporary material that fed into a dream. While austerity may have become a thing of the past, those living in this country were still for the most part leading dull, circumscribed lives. *Spring in Park Lane* may have appealed to women more than it did to men, but now the early 007 films gave the men a hero with whom they wished to identify. It was not just that he lived an exciting, exotic life with plenty of action all around the world, but furthermore that he was unfettered. Bond was a man who, officially authorised, had a licence to kill and, what is more, he found himself in situations where he encountered glamorous women. Bedding them was accepted as part of his regular routine, a routine that in every way contrasted with the lives of most in the audience.

What this meant was that James Bond was a fantasy figure. His quips, like his actions, could be outrageous but were always beguiling, not least to the men who dreamt of being him. As the years went by and Sean Connery yielded the role to a series of successors, most notably Roger Moore and Pierce Brosnan, the tone changed. If at one time the now virtually forgotten Matt Helm series starring Dean Martin had been a jokier version of Bond, Bond himself became for a time a hero whose actions were increasingly tongue-in-cheek and over the top. The serious business of espionage was left to Michael Caine's Harry Palmer, followed by the yet darker tones

Right: The Dame who died: Diana Rigg and George Lazenby in *On Her Majesty's Secret Service* (1969).

Previous page: Honor Blackman and Sean Connery step out in Guy Hamilton's 1964 classic *Goldfinger*.

of John Le Carré's stories. But by the time Daniel Craig came on board with *Casino Royale* in 2006 the broader jokes had been left behind, even if the action remained far more exaggerated than anything to be found in the world of George Smiley.

This is the point at which I want to move forward to define what *Skyfall* tells us about where James Bond stands today. This latest Bond film inevitably retains the big action scenes and hasn't denied Bond the right to make quips. Nevertheless, in a move that echoes recent trends displayed in the Bourne and Batman franchises, to some extent darker material has been allowed in. It's all relative, of course, but the very opening of *Skyfall* features a splendidly judged pursuit sequence which leads to M (Judi Dench) giving an order to shoot, in the hope of hitting the man pursued by 007 and with whom he is now fighting. But the shot, far from having the desired effect, results in Bond himself appearing to plunge to his death. Inevitably very few viewers will be deceived by appearances – after all, killing off Bond would be even more unlikely than Sherlock Holmes being allowed to die at the Reichenbach Falls. Even so, the sequence does underline the ruthlessness required when giving risky orders in situations of this kind. More importantly, the recuperating Bond who emerges from this prologue is not the man he was.

Because James Bond had always been a fantasy figure able to escape from certain death in film after film, it is all the more striking that this near-death experience results in a Bond who is a shadow of his former self and no longer confident. But the world around Bond is transformed too. For many years our hero existed in settings which bore little relationship to actuality, but in *Skyfall* that is no longer the case. As scripted by Neil Purvis, Robert Wade and John Logan, this is a film that engages with reality – and with contemporary reality at that. We have London as a major setting here, and the attack on the Intelligence HQ reminds us of terrorists and the tragedy of 7/7.

It was once the case in Bond films that gadgets were there for the fun that they provided, but now they are bigger and better and the role they play can be devastating. Thanks to computers

and a whole range of modern technology they can be key to launching an attack from a safe distance or to publicising worldwide the names of agents in a calculated leak. Indeed, when the film shows us scenes of an enquiry into how a list of such names was obtained, we are reminded of real-life investigations into security lapses. In short, *Skyfall* brings us face to face with a world that we know and recognise.

Although I have always found the theory far-fetched, it has been suggested more than once that the celebrated Ealing comedy *The Ladykillers*, made in 1955, was intended in part as social comment. According to that theory, the old lady, Mrs Wilberforce, represented reactionary Tory Britain while the gang were to be seen as the Labour party trying in

Before the fall: Daniel Craig during the opening sequence of *Skyfall*.

London pride: Daniel Craig surveys his realm in *Skyfall*.

Above: Javier Bardem touches a nerve with Daniel Craig, in *Skyfall*.

Above right: The return of a 53-year-old Sean Connery in *Never Say Never Again* (1983).

vain to take over. I find it far easier to believe that in *Skyfall* James Bond stands for Britain today. The emphasis is on how he is getting older, losing his skills and finding himself a relic no longer suited to the present age. When the screenplay was being written, the Olympic games of 2012 still lay ahead and the film seems to express all the doubts of that period prior to the games: uncertainty as to how Britain was seen by the rest of the world and as to whether or not Britain stood for anything very much at all.

One cannot be certain that these points were in the minds of the writers, but it is possible, and the film certainly plays that way. But what is even more remarkable is that *Skyfall* seems to foresee the reassertion of pride in this country which came about when the Olympics proved to be a triumph. The Olympics were in August and *Skyfall* didn't appear until late October; the screenplay was obviously finalised well ahead of that change in public feeling, yet it all seems to be present in *Skyfall*, which, in summing up Britain in 2012, encompasses both the before and the after.

For all his self-doubts in this film, Bond does win through in spite of everything. The credit designs seen at the close reassert this and the statement that James Bond will return expresses all the new-found confidence of post-Olympic Britain as 2012 drew to a close. Far from being outmoded and uncertain that he still has a role to play, James Bond takes pleasure in the idea of continuing his work in the service of Britain, and the mood of Britain when the film premiered made this not just the usual advertising gimmick for another Bond movie but something that felt meaningful and resonated with the audience.

If one sees *Skyfall* in this light, it adds to the interest of a film which was a deserved success

for director Sam Mendes and for its actors, who were all on top form. (Javier Bardem's villain is one of the best in the whole series.) Indeed, many have declared this 23rd film in the franchise to be the best Bond ever. Whether it is or not may be a matter of taste. It could be argued that, taken as a whole, *Goldfinger* is a film with a more consistent tone – since, if *Skyfall* is felt to contain darker elements and allegorical content on the lines I have suggested, that doesn't always fit easily with the more outlandish action scenes without which Bond would not be Bond.

That leaves us with the question of who represents the ideal Bond on screen. For many years Sean Connery was clearly the favourite, although some have spoken out for others; indeed in recent times even George Lazenby's star has risen in this context if you follow some voices. After *Skyfall* however it suddenly became a more open contest. While many still supported Connery, there were others, hardly less in number, who were heard to declare that with his performance in *Skyfall* it was Daniel Craig who now took the honours. What needs to be asserted, I believe, is that you can't say that Craig is *better* than Connery, or vice versa. That's because *Skyfall* sees Craig giving us an in-depth James Bond who is dealing with his own doubts and uncertainties and thus presenting him, despite his engagement in the usual heroics, as a real person. In contrast Connery was, and remains, the ideal personification of 007 as the iconic figure of your dreams.

Thus, we now have two James Bonds, not one, and in consequence both Craig and Connery are the best. Which one you prefer is simply down to which James Bond most appeals to you.

It's all an act, really

Something that has become a regular feature of the film industry is actors turning to directing. **James Cameron-Wilson** *considers some recent moves from in front of the camera to behind it.*

Ben Affleck (right) discusses an angle of motivation with Alan Arkin on the set of *Argo*.

The Academy of Motion Picture Arts and Sciences just loves actors. In fact, they love actors so much that they prefer them to filmmakers. At least, real filmmakers.

So when the likes of Kevin Costner, Mel Gibson and Robert Redford slip behind the camera to shout "Action," they often beat their more experienced peers and pick up an Oscar for Best Director. In 1996, when Gibson stepped up to the podium to receive his gong for directing *Braveheart*, he beat out fellow nominee Tim Robbins for *his* work on *Dead Man Walking*. And this was the year that Ang Lee's *Sense and Sensibility* was short-listed for Best Film. Yet Ang Lee wasn't even nominated as director.

Of course, the Academy has since made up for this oversight by bestowing two golden statuettes on Lee, while denying the films themselves – *Brokeback Mountain* and *Life of Pi* – the top award. It's a strange business.

In their eagerness to reward actors for changing their stripes, the Academy has honoured Woody Allen, Warren Beatty, Richard Attenborough, Clint Eastwood (twice) and the aforementioned Costner, Gibson and Redford with best directing Oscars. There are, of course, grey areas. Richard Attenborough virtually gave up his career as an actor to take on directing full time, and Ron Howard (who won a best directing Oscar for *A Beautiful Mind*) did so completely.

Which brings us to Ben Affleck.

Already the recipient of an Academy Award for Best Screenplay for *Good Will Hunting* (shared with his long-time friend Matt Damon), Affleck took up the directorial reins in 2006 to make *Gone Baby Gone*. A powerful, emotionally and politically complex kidnapping thriller starring his younger brother Casey, the film was a huge critical success. Affleck followed this with *The Town* (2010), another thriller set in and around Boston, which, if anything, received even greater acclaim. This time Affleck also took the central role and saw his co-star Jeremy Renner pick up an Academy Award nomination for Best Supporting Actor. There were no two ways about it: Ben Affleck was an extremely accomplished filmmaker.

With his third film as director, *Argo* (2012), he spread his net further to incorporate locations in

Above: Dustin Hoffman on location for *Quartet* with his cinematographer John de Borman (in glasses).

Above right: Woody Allen at work on *Midnight in Paris*.

Los Angeles and Istanbul (doubling for Tehran) and took on a true story. Again, he stepped into the starring part and surrounded himself with outstanding actors; Alan Arkin nabbed an Oscar nomination for his role as a dyspeptic movie mogul. Of course, Affleck, being an actor himself, has a knack for coaxing good performances from his cast. Indeed, Amy Ryan, in *Gone Baby Gone*, also received an Oscar nomination under Affleck's guidance. And that's a pretty good track record for a director.

Members of the Academy like to vote for a face, rather than just a name. This may explain the Oscar that Affleck and Damon received for *Good Will Hunting*, the statuette Emma Thompson picked up for her adaptation of *Sense and Sensibility* and Billy Bob Thornton's gong for *Sling Blade*. One could even stretch the theory to include Woody Allen's Oscars for *Annie Hall* and *Midnight in Paris*. So why didn't the Academy acknowledge Affleck for his directing chores on *Argo* – particularly as they gave the film their greatest accolade of all? Did *Argo* really direct itself?

Of course, most people – including journalists – seem to regard Oscar as a monster with just one head, or at most a boardroom of electing officials. What one has to take into consideration is that 'Oscar' is made up of 6014 individuals with their own political and aesthetic agendas. Or, for those voting for the Best Director prize, 371 individuals. These things are complicated. So, 5643 more people voted for the Best Film award than for Best Director. And taking those statistics on board, the majority must have more sway than the 371 filmmakers who opted to crown Ang Lee.

But there's another point. *Argo* was good because it had a great premise (inspired by fact), a terrific screenplay (by the Oscar-winning Chris Terrio) and a wonderful cast. These key elements were assembled by the producers George

Clooney, Grant Heslov and, yes, Ben Affleck. So, surely, it should be the producers who get the glory in this instance (which they did). The directing itself was just a matter of tying the ends together, however proficiently.

Look at another film – say, *Life of Pi* – and the story is very different. Many people, *most* people, said that Yann Martel's 2001 novel was unfilmable. Yet Ang Lee not only took a difficult literary work and made it digestible, entertaining and inspiring; he also made it supremely cinematic. Now that takes some directorial sleight of hand.

Another American actor who has turned to directing recently is Dustin Hoffman. Thirty-five years Affleck's senior, Hoffman took on the British film *Quartet*, another ensemble piece but of a very different aspect. An adaptation of Ronald Harwood's play of the same name, the film is a funny, bittersweet thing set in a retirement home for opera singers and musicians. The accent is on the thespian and the comic, which happens to be a far cry from the flavour of most British films directed by actors.

Take Gary Oldman, Tim Roth, Peter Mullan and Paddy Considine. This quartet of British actors all unleashed their directorial skill on decidedly dark material. Oldman's *Nil by Mouth* (1997) was a harrowing, semi-autobiographical portrait of a London family crippled by crime and alcoholism. Roth's equally brilliant *The War Zone* (1999) was a stark, emotionally numbing look at incest. Peter Mullan's *The Magdalene Sisters* (2002) was a bleak, deeply disturbing examination of the sordid lives of young women detained in the so-called Magdalene Asylums of Ireland. And Paddy Considine's stunning *Tyrannosaur* (2011) – starring Peter Mullan – was a brutal depiction of alcoholism and domestic abuse. Completing the circle, Considine himself co-starred in *Submarine*

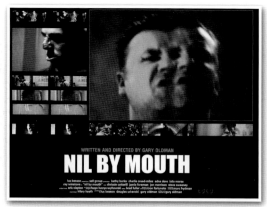

WRITTEN AND DIRECTED BY GARY OLDMAN

NIL BY MOUTH

FROM AWARD-WINNING DIRECTOR
PETER MULLAN

THE
Magdalene
SISTERS

IN A PLACE THAT DEFIED BELIEF
THEIR ONLY HOPE WAS EACH OTHER

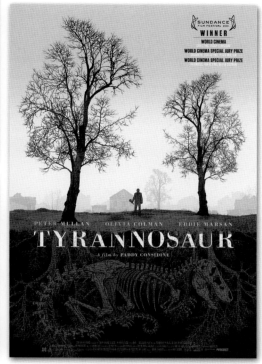

Hard-hitting
directing ventures
for (clockwise)
Gary Oldman,
Paddy Considine
and Peter Mullan.

(2010), directed by the actor Richard Ayoade, which set itself apart from the other films by being a smart, touching and very funny picture of first love (among other things).

Dexter Fletcher, a former child actor and co-star of *Lock, Stock and Two Smoking Barrels* (he played 'Soap'), is directing Peter Mullan in his upcoming musical *Sunshine on Leith*. Fletcher's first film as director, *Wild Bill* (2011), brought enormous charm and freshness to the crime-wracked streets of London's East End.

One may be forgiven for thinking that this world is an old boys' network – and one wouldn't be wrong. Hell, Ray Winstone starred in both *Nil by Mouth* and *The War Zone*, playing abusive fathers on each occasion. But why the doom and gloom? They say that, for an actor, laughter is harder to pull off than tears, so maybe tragedy is an easier career step for an aspiring filmmaker.

Thus, full marks must go to Alan Rickman, whose next film as a director (he previously made *The Winter Guest*, with Emma Thompson) has nothing to do with despair or even England. *A Little Chaos* is set in Versailles and concerns the

rivalry of two gardeners competing for the right to design a fountain for King Louis XIV. Rickman himself will play the monarch, with Kate Winslet as one of the designers.

Incidentally (or not), Winslet and Rickman previously appeared together in a film called *Sense and Sensibility*, which was directed by Ang Lee. So let's just hope that Rickman was paying attention when the great Taiwanese filmmaker was putting him through his paces.

Looks and smiles:
Richard Ayoade
gets the picture
for his *Submarine*.

Another Direction

Michael Darvell rounds up some of the other actors who've turned to directing.

Buster Keaton

Film actors have been doing it for years; turning to direction, that is.

Charles Chaplin and **Buster Keaton** began appearing in films in 1914 and 1917 respectively, both of them moving into writing and directing almost immediately. Since then it's been open house for actors to turn director. Here, then, are 101 of the best remembered – not including the examples cited on the preceding pages by James Cameron-Wilson.

Alan Alda has directed four features, all starring himself, among them *Sweet Liberty* and *Betsy's Wedding*.

Lloyd Bacon acted in silent movies prior to directing 130 films, including *42nd Street*. **Drew Barrymore**, acting in films from age three, has also directed *Whip It*. Her illustrious forebear **Lionel Barrymore** directed early talkies like *The Unholy Night* and *The Rogue Song*. Italian actor **Roberto Benigni** has nine directing credits to his name, including *Life is Beautiful*. **Peter Bogdanovich**, still acting, has directed 32 titles, including *The Last Picture Show* and *Paper Moon*. **Kenneth Branagh**'s 12 feature films as director include *Henry V* and *Hamlet*. **Marlon Brando** racked up just one directorial credit, *One Eyed Jacks*. **Matthew Broderick** has directed one film, *Infinity*, and **Albert Brooks** seven, including *Modern Romance* and *Lost in America*. **Mel Brooks**, a TV writer turned performer, has made 12 films, including *Blazing Saddles* and *Young Frankenstein*.

Kenneth Branagh

Dennis Hopper

Sofia Coppola

Steve Buscemi has directed such features as *Trees Lounge* and *Interview*.

James Cagney's only title as director was *Short Cut to Hell*. **John Cassavetes** directed a dozen features, among them the seminal *Shadows* and *A Woman Under the Influence*. **George Clooney** is the director of five films, including *Good Night, and Good Luck*. Occasional child actress **Sofia Coppola** has since directed four titles, including *Lost in Translation* and *The Bling Ring*. **Billy Crystal** has two features in his director's CV, namely *Mr Saturday Night* and *Forget Paris*.

Terence Davies, formerly a TV actor, is now Britain's most personal director, with 12 films including *The Long Day Closes* and *The Deep Blue Sea*. **Robert De Niro** has directed *A Bronx Tale* and *The Good Shepherd*. **Vittorio De Sica** had been acting for over 20 years before directing his first film in 1940. **Danny DeVito** has directed 18 films, including *The War of the Roses* and *Matilda*. **Johnny Depp** directed *The Brave* with Marlon Brando. **Kirk Douglas** directed *Posse* and *Scalawag*. **Robert Duvall**, veteran actor of nearly 150 films, has directed three features and a documentary.

Initially an actor, **Blake Edwards** subsequently turned out *Breakfast at Tiffany's*, *The Pink Panther* and many more. Horror star **Robert Englund** has directed, among others, *976-Evil*.

Jon Favreau, still an actor, is a director of 16 titles, his latest being *Cowboys and Aliens*. **José Ferrer** made seven films as director, the last being *State Fair*. **Mel Ferrer** (no relation) directed *Green Mansions*, among others. **Ralph Fiennes** has so far directed *Coriolanus* and *The Invisible Woman*. After acting assignments, **Bryan Forbes** directed such films as *Whistle Down the Wind* and *The Whisperers* and briefly took charge of Elstree Studios. **Walter Forde**, Britain's foremost silent comedian, became the distinguished director of such talkies as *Rome Express* and *Chu Chin Chow*. **Bob Fosse** appeared in a few 1950s musicals before crafting *Cabaret* etc. **Jodie Foster**

has directed three films, beginning with *Little Man Tate*.

Andy Garcia was writer-director-star of *The Lost City*. British actor-playwright **Peter Godfrey** directed such creepy Hollywood thrillers as *The Two Mrs Carrolls* and *Cry Wolf*. **David Greene** exchanged acting for directing films like *I Start Counting* and *Godspell*, plus a slew of TV movies.

Tom Hanks has headed up two films, *That Thing You Do!* and *Larry Crowne*. **Ed Harris** has *Pollock* and *Appaloosa* under his director's belt. **Charlton Heston** directed *Antony and Cleopatra* and *Mother Lode*, while **Dennis Hopper** directed seven features, starting with *Easy Rider* in 1969. British TV star **Peter Howitt**'s directorial career began with *Sliding Doors*. **Anjelica Huston** has directed a couple of features, unlike her father **John Huston**, who acted from 1929 onwards and also directed over 40 films, from *The Maltese Falcon* in 1941 to *The Dead* in 1987.

Silent pioneer **Ralph Ince** acted for 30 years (1907-37), also keeping up a phenomenal directorial career beginning in 1912.

Lionel Jeffries, stalwart British character actor, directed *The Railway Children* among others. In addition to TV films, **Tommy Lee Jones** has four feature credits, including *The Three Burials of Mesquiades Estrada*.

Diane Keaton has directed the theatrical features *Unstrung Heroes* and *Hanging Up*. **Gene Kelly** directed many films, including *Singin' in the Rain* and *Hello, Dolly!*

Burt Lancaster put his name to *The Kentuckian* and *The Midnight Man* and **Charles Laughton** to *The Night of the Hunter*. **Mélanie Laurent** has so far directed one feature, *The Adopted* (see Releases of the Year). **Jerry Lewis** directed 13 films from *The Bellboy* in 1960 to *Cracking Up* in 1983. **Ida Lupino** directed eight, including noir favourite *The Hitch-hiker*, plus multiple TV shows.

Madonna has directed *Filth and Wisdom* and *W.E.* **Penny Marshall** has seven features as director, from *Jumpin' Jack Flash* to *Riding in Cars with Boys*. **Elaine May**'s directing debut was the hilarious *A New Leaf*; her last (but don't mention it) was *Ishtar*. **Patrick McGoohan** directed *Catch My Soul* and **Eddie Murphy** *Harlem Nights*. **Bill Murray** was producer-director of *Quick Change*.

Paul Newman directed six films beginning with *Rachel, Rachel*. **Jack Nicholson**'s handful of directorial credits include *Drive He Said* and *Goin' South*. **Leonard Nimoy** has directed 12 films, including *Three Men and a Baby* and some of the *Star Trek* movies. **Edward Norton**'s one shot at directing, so far, was *Keeping the Faith*.

Laurence Olivier amassed nine films as producer, directing six, including *Hamlet* and *Richard III*.

Al Pacino has directed three films, including the documentary *Looking for Richard* (III). **Sean Penn** has made several films, starting with *The Indian Runner*. **Anthony Perkins** did *Psycho III* and *Lucky Stiff*. **Sydney Pollack** was an actor turned producer who also directed 36 films, among them *Tootsie* and *Out of Africa*. **Dick Powell** mostly acted from 1932-54, then directed, from 1953, a total of 58 films and TV shows. **Edmund Purdom** directed the infamous Santa slasher *Don't Open 'Til Christmas*.

Richard Quine swapped acting for directing such films as *The Solid Gold Cadillac* and *The World of Suzie Wong*.

Harold Ramis has directed ten movies, including *Analyze This* (and *That*). Father and son **Carl Reiner** and **Rob Reiner** were both actor-writers prior to moving into directing. **Jason Reitman** was a child actor before directing such blockbusters as *Juno* and *Young Adult*. **Mickey Rooney** directed a few films, starting with *My True Story*.

David Schwimmer has directed one film, *Run, Fatboy, Run*. Playwright **Sam Shepard**, with 60-odd acting credits, has directed just two films, *Far North* and *Silent Tongue*. **Charles Martin Smith**'s nine features began with *Trick or Treat* in 1986. **Kevin Spacey** has directed two films, *Albino Alligator* and *Beyond the Sea*. Apart from appearing in them,

Sylvester Stallone has directed some of the *Rocky* and *Rambo* films. Mr Comedy Central, **Ben Stiller**, is also a film and TV director (*Zoolander* etc). **Barbra Streisand** has directed films such as *Yentl* and her own TV documentaries.

At first acting for others, **Jacques Tati** was the inspired writer-director-star of *Jour de fête*, *Mon Oncle* etc. 1950s star **Don Taylor** subsequently directed *Escape from the Planet of the Apes* and others. **Stanley Tucci** has taken charge of five films from *Big Night* in 1996.

Liv Ullmann has directed *Sofie* and *Faithless*, among others. **Peter Ustinov** directed occasional films such as *Vice Versa* and *Billy Budd*.

Erich von Stroheim started as an actor (and is now best remembered for *Sunset Blvd*) but was also a titan of the silent era as writer-director of *Foolish Wives*, *Greed* and various others.

Tom Walls, star of the Aldwych farces in the 1920s and '30s, also directed some of the film versions. Comedian brothers **Damon Wayans** and **Keenen Ivory Wayans** both have several directorial credits on their CVs. **Cornel Wilde**'s occasional directorial assignments included *The Naked Prey* and *No Blade of Grass*.

Mai Zetterling was a stylish Swedish actress turned director, making, among others, *Doktor Glas* and *Scrubbers*.

Finally, for several more examples – **Leonardo Favio**, **Al Freeman Jr**, **Ben Gazzara**, **Erland Josephson**, **Zalman King** and **Eric Sykes** – turn to our In Memoriam section on page 188.

Jacques Tati

Erich von Stroheim

2012 (Subtitled)

Mansel Stimpson *reports on the year's most significant foreign language films.*

Michael Haneke directs Emmanuelle Riva and Jean-Louis Trintigant in *Amour*.

Not so long ago an article of this kind could spotlight, if not always at length, almost all of the foreign films distributed here over a period of 12 months. Things have changed. With the enormous increase in the number of weekly cinema releases in this country, the proportion of subtitled films hasn't dropped. Consequently we now have something like a hundred works of this kind per year, so it is simply not practical to reference all of them.

While I am naturally keen to include the films which were the best in my eyes (not least if they were somewhat overlooked in the flood of new work), I want also to remind readers of the titles that were most discussed, even if there wasn't always agreement among viewers as to whether or not they ranked with the year's best. Thus I make mention here of several titles which were greatly admired by others (but less so by me) because, whether I am right or wrong about them, they can justly be thought of as being among the year's key releases.

Despite the large number of foreign films seen in 2012, one stands out and that is Michael Haneke's *Amour*. As the latest work of a major auteur, it would have made a mark in any case, but two aspects meant that its impact was exceptional. One was the stunning quality of the performances: veterans Jean-Louis Trintignant

and Emmanuelle Riva were quite outstanding as an elderly couple faced with the tragedy of the wife's decline after a stroke. The other significant factor was that it broke through the barrier which usually keeps foreign films in their own ghetto. I refer to Riva being nominated at the Oscars for Best Actress; had she won it would have coincided with her 86th birthday and many were surprised that she lost out to Jennifer Lawrence. Further recognition included the London Critics' Circle selecting *Amour* as the best film of the year ahead of every English language contestant.

Haneke's previous films include several which, even when brilliant, might justify his work being thought of as the cinema of cruelty. With *Amour*, however, even the title suggests that he wanted to create a positive and moving portrayal of the couple's love, not least the husband's care for his wife when she is in extremis. For me, however, that aspect was overridden by the relentless worsening of the situation and, just because the film has been so highly praised, I have not held back from a review that takes account of the fact that *Amour* is the most depressing film I have ever seen (the runner-up being the 2005 Romanian film *The Death of Mr. Lazarescu*). That does not in any way detract from my admiration for the actors, but it's a reaction to the film worth stating since many older viewers may agree.

The poster for *Tabu* and Jafar Panahi in his highly personal *This is Not a Film*.

Two other films which found me more critical than many of my colleagues were amongst the most talked about of 2012. Denmark's Thomas Vinterberg returned with a drama about a man wrongly accused of paedophilia by a young school girl: *The Hunt* had powerful subject matter but grew increasingly unpersuasive in its detail. The other was Jacques Audiard's *Rust and Bone*. It was admirably acted by the ever splendid Marion Cotillard and newcomer Matthias Schoenaerts and was remarkable in portraying so graphically a legless woman overcoming the trauma of that loss. However, the second half of the film moves into much less telling territory and there is no excuse for the sentimentality and contrivance of the film's conclusion.

Elsewhere, however, I was at one with others in enthusing over films of very different kinds. The Iranian Asghar Farhadi made *About Elly* before his success with *A Separation*, but its belated release here was amply justified, while France's Robert Guédiguian was on good form with *The Snows of Kilimanjaro* (despite the title it's another drama set in Marseille, his home town). France also gave us a number of films in popular vein that worked well on their own terms. *Untouchable* was one such, with its wonderful star performance from César winner Omar Sy. In contrast, *Delicacy* was undervalued but provided an ideal vehicle for Audrey Tautou and the little-seen *The Women on the 6th Floor* was a pleasing divertissement. Turn to drama and *You Will Be My Son* boasted a novel setting among the French vineyards, while Alain Corneau bowed out with *Love Crime*, a neatly set-up piece reminiscent in tone of Fritz Lang's *Beyond a Reasonable Doubt*.

Given the success of *The Girl with the Dragon Tattoo* and its sequels, it wasn't surprising that distributors should buy into more Scandinavian works in similar vein. The best of these was *Headhunters*, but Noomi Rapace, the original Lisbeth Salander, did well in a contrasted role in *Babycall*, even if the film as a whole was less effective. A neater example of a thriller which went in for twists and surprises was *ID:A*, which used Copenhagen as its principal location.

Documentaries this year ranged from a moving view of families in Palestine caught up in the conflict with Israel (*5 Broken Cameras*) to the visually astounding Chilean work *Nostalgia for the Light*. As for films dealing with gay subject matter, we had the stunning South African work *Beauty* and the cynical Swedish drama *She Monkeys*, neither being shy of offering portrayals that many would find discomfiting. If some gay men could be disturbed by the former and some lesbians by the latter, they could find reassurance in such pieces as *Yossi* from Israel and *Circumstance* set in Iran.

Another area of filmmaking that flourished in 2012 was that of avant-garde cinema. All-out examples included Béla Tarr's self-declared last film *The Turin Horse* and Sokurov's *Faust*, while less familiar names such as Aleksei Fedorchenko (*Silent Souls*) and Yorgos Lanthimos (*Alps*) seemed to be following in this tradition. Not quite as demanding but not easy viewing either, Miguel Gomes' extraordinary and very impressive *Tabu* was a Portuguese film of total originality.

Three other films deserve mention here, even if only on the verge of being avant-garde. The long and slow, and therefore demanding, *Once Upon a Time in Anatolia* is the latest film by Nuri Bilge Ceylan and is one of the year's finest works. Those who find themselves on its wavelength will discover that by its close it has made many pertinent points about how people behave to others. Also from Turkey and very haunting is Reha Erdem's *Kosmos*: it's a truly artistic endeavour that encourages an audience to speculate on its meaning. Easier to grasp, but minimalist in style, is the Austrian film *Breathing* by Karl Markovics, a sensitive study of a young offender played to perfection by Thomas Schubert. Before moving on I add one more title, and it's a work that cannot be compared with any other: Jafar Panahi's *This is Not a Film* is the Iranian director's brave response to being denied by the authorities the right to make a movie. We simply see him at home, reading from a script he wasn't allowed to shoot; if not exactly a film as we know it, this work certainly deserves applause.

Foreign animation films also appeared during the year. The most original was *Tatsumi*, illustrating stories by the Japanese artist in a biographical context, but the one that delighted

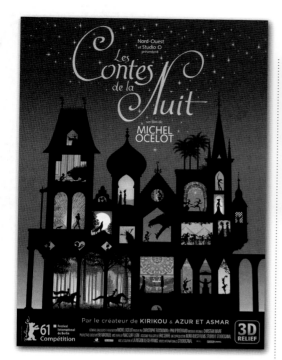

Far left: The French poster for *Tales of the Night*.

Left: Kylie Minogue in Leos Carax' extraordinary *Holy Motors*.

me was *Tales of the Night*, a collection of contrasted pieces by my favourite animator, Michel Ocelot. As for period films, we had work as contrasted as the Belgian 18th century drama *A Royal Affair* and Bertrand Bonello's portrayal of a Parisian brothel on the cusp of the 20th century in *House of Tolerance*. Another period tale, Dominik Moll's *The Monk* with Vincent Cassel, I regarded as underrated, but the potentially interesting *Mozart's Sister* from René Féret, although sincere, lacked dramatic life.

Before concluding with three more titles that are among my favourites of the year, I should mention in passing a number of new works from established directors. In this category we have *Le Havre* from Aki Kaurismäki, *The Kid with a Bike* from the Dardenne Brothers, the Polish wartime drama *In Darkness* from Agnieszka Holland and the return of Leos Carax with the extraordinary *Holy Motors*. Other names more recently to the fore include Ursula Meier (*Sister*), Pablo Trapero (*Carancho*), Christian Petzold (*Barbara*), Bruno Dumont (*Hadewijch*), Christophe Honoré (*Beloved*) and Eran Riklis (*Zaytoun*).

As for those three remaining achievements, they all deserve to be better known and each one gave me special pleasure. First there's the most memorable release to reach us this year from Japan: Miike Takashi's remake of Kobayashi's 1962 classic, *Hara-kiri: Death of a Samurai*. It makes adroit use of 3D but it's not just a film of action, being essentially a character-led period drama telling a powerful story involving both moral and social issues. It's one of the few remakes that measures up to the original and was well received.

In the case of Ismaël Ferroukhi's *Free Men*, however, critical responses here were unfairly lukewarm. I mentioned it in last year's annual in the Afterword section and have seen it again since then. It's a film centred on a Paris mosque during the Occupation (the year is 1942) and, in telling a story of collaboration against the Germans by Muslims and Christians, Ferroukhi's humane concerns, already apparent in his first feature *Le Grand Voyage*, surface once more. Michael Lonsdale is an outstanding presence here and, if anything, I admired the film even more on a second viewing.

Even less well known is Leonard Retel Helmrich's *Position Among the Stars*. For me this is the film of the year, as was confirmed when I went back to it for a second look. This portrait of an Indonesian family is the final part of a trilogy but stands on its own. It is directed with the freedom and imagination usually reserved for fictional works, and Helmrich, who photographed it himself, has a wonderful eye which results in scenes that are truly poetic. But there's no romanticising of the Sjamsuddin family's struggles in the harsh urban setting that is modern-day Jakarta. Because of that, the ever-hopeful grandmother, seen initially in the village home to which she returns at the end of the film, is a wonderful heart-warming presence. Indeed, the last few minutes of this film, reuniting her with a neighbour and allowing us to share the chance to savour the natural world absent in the city ("You can't see the stars in Jakarta"), come across as one of the greatest scenes in all cinema.

If you are in tune with *Position Among the Stars*, you will appreciate why the only word I can find to describe this final sequence is 'sublime'.

A scene from Leonard Retel Helmrich's *Position Among the Stars*.

Herbert Lom (see page 201)

In Memoriam
2012
by Jonathan Rigby

Given the hundreds of film personalities who died during 2012, the following selection of just 71 is, inevitably, a purely personal one. Pressure of space has excluded numerous important people, over 250 of whom are noted in supplements to the main entries.

CELSO AD CASTILLO

Born: *12 September 1943, Siniloan, Laguna, Philippines.*
Died: *26 November 2012, Siniloan, Laguna, Philippines.*
Variously hailed as the enfant terrible or even half-demented Messiah of Filipino cinema in its 1970s heyday, Celso Advento Castillo began by writing the mid-'60s 007 spoofs *James Ban-dong* and *Dr Yes*, then turned director for *Mission Dangerous* in 1965. The 1971 releases *Nympha* and *Asedillo* established him as a young maestro able to infuse lyricism into sex and action scenarios respectively, after which he mastered mid-1970s horror (*Let's Frighten Barbara to Death*, *Maligno*) and confirmed his provocateur status with his masterpiece, the multi-award-winning *Burlesk Queen* (1977). Later titles, interspersed with acting roles in other people's films, include *The Legend of Julian Makabayan* (1979), *Brown Emmanuelle* (1982), the extraordinary *Snake Sisters* (1984), *Isla*, *Paradise*

Celso Ad Castillo

Inn (both 1985), *Secrets of Madonna* (1997), a *Nympha* remake (2003) and, his last, *666* (2010).

❧ Other notable Filipino filmmakers who died in 2012 included award-winning writer-directors **Mario O'Hara** (in June, aged 66) and **Marilou Diaz-Abaya** (October, 57). **Linda Estrella**, a big star with Sampaguita Pictures in the 1940s and '50s, died in February, aged 89.

MAC AHLBERG

Born: *12 June 1931, Stockholm, Sweden.*
Died: *26 October 2012, Cupra Maritima, Italy.*
In 1965 Mac Ahlberg directed Essy Persson in *Jeg – en kvinde*, which as *I, A Woman* made a sensational impact worldwide. Ahlberg quickly turned out two sequels, together with a Swedish version of *Fanny Hill*, bringing to his erotic odysseys a visual sophistication that remained unimpaired even when the 1970s market demanded hardcore material. (For these latter duties he adopted the pseudonym Bert Torn.) In the late '70s he moved to Hollywood, working as a cinematographer on titles like *Hell Night* and *Chained Heat* in addition to shooting 29 films – among them, the horror classic *Re-Animator* – for producer Charles Band. He also photographed such 1990s mainstream titles as *Striking Distance*, *The Brady Bunch Movie* and, for John Landis, *Oscar*, *Innocent Blood* and *Beverly Hills Cop III*.

MERRY ANDERS

Born: *22 May 1934, Chicago, Illinois, USA.*
Died: *28 October 2012, Encino, California, USA.*
For former model Mary Helen Anderson, the early 1950s yielded only small parts in Hollywood films like *Les Misérables* and *Phffft*. But things looked up when she played Jayne Mansfield's role in the West Coast production of *Will Success Spoil Rock Hunter?* Next, she scored an eye-catching scene with Spencer Tracy in *Desk Set* and starred in the TV spin-off of *How to Marry a Millionaire*. (She'd had a bit in the original film.) Together with loads more television, she turned up thereafter in numerous low-end Westerns – *The Dalton Girls*, *Young Jesse James*, *The Gambler Wore a Gun* etc – and occasional horrors like *The Hypnotic Eye*, *House of the Damned* and (her last film, aged 36) *Blood Legacy*.

Aurora Bautista

THEODOROS ANGELOPOULOS

Born: *27 April 1935, Athens, Greece.*
Died: *24 January 2012, Piraeus, Greece.*
The allegorical style of Greece's most award-laden writer-director was characterised by mournfully atmospheric landscapes, virtuoso tracking shots, sustained (sometimes ten-minute) takes and yet more sustained (sometimes four-hour) running times – and the occasional use of international names like Marcello Mastroianni, Bruno Ganz and Harvey Keitel. Trained in Paris and initially a left-wing film critic, he made his first feature, *Reconstruction*, in 1970. Subsequently, *Days of '36*, *The Travelling Players* and *The Hunters* formed a 1970s trilogy succeeded, first, by a 1980s triptych – *Voyage to Cythera*, *The Beekeeper* and *Landscape in the Mist* – and then by two 1990s masterworks, *Ulysses' Gaze* and *Eternity and a Day*. A 21st century trilogy, beginning with *The Weeping Meadow* and *The Dust of Time*, remained unfinished; Angelopoulos died while shooting *The Other Sea*.

❧ Other directors of international repute who died in 2012 included Russia's **Eldor Urazbayev** (in February, aged 71), Bulgaria's **Hacho Boyadzhiev** (April, 80), Iran's **Iraj Ghaderi** (May, 77), Brazil's **Carlos Reichenbach** (June, 67), Holland's **Ruud van Hemert** (July, 73) and Turkey's **Yusuf Kurçenli** (February, 65) and **Metin Erksan** (August, 83). From Portugal, **Fernando Lopes** died at 76 in May and **Paulo Rocha** at 77 in December, while Spain lost **César Fernández Ardavín** (September, 89) and **José Luis Borau** (November, 83).

AURORA BAUTISTA

Born: *15 October 1925, Villanueva de los Infantes, Valladolid, Spain.*
Died: *27 August 2012, Madrid, Spain.*
This award-laden Spanish icon started out majestic and remained so. As Queen Juana la Loca in Juan de Orduña's *Locura de amor* (1948) she was the centrepiece of a Franco-sanctioned epic that sparked off several other florid vehicles, including Spain's first Scope film, *La Gata* (1956). As Spanish cinema loosened up, the asexual historical heroines she'd become famous for fed into her devastating portrait of a sexually repressed surrogate mother in Miguel Picazo's *El tía Tula* (1964), mutating later into her puritanical serial killer in Eugenio Martín's Gothic shocker *Una vela para el diablo* (1973). She was majestic, too, on stage, starring in plays by Arrabal, Lorca and Tennessee Williams; she made her last film, *Tiovivo c 1950*, in 2004. (NB: she shouldn't be confused with Spaghetti Western actress Aurora Battista.)

❧ Other Spanish performers who died in 2012 included actor-producer **Juan Luis Galiardo** (June, 72) and actors **Sancho Gracia** and **Carlos Larrañaga** (both 75, both in August). Spanish-born Mexican actress **Manola Saavedra**, best known for playing the title role opposite Cantinflas in the 1956 film *El bolero de Raquel*, died in August at 76. Argentine-born Mexican actress **Lucy Gallardo**, who appeared in Buñuel's *El ángel exterminador*, also died in August, aged 82. Also from Mexico: actors **Joaquín Martínez** (January, 81) and **Julio Alemán** (April, 78). And from Brazil: **Regina Dourado** (October, 59) and **Joel Barcellos** (December, 76).

JOSÉ BÉNAZÉRAF

Born: *8 January 1922, Casablanca, French Morocco.*
Died: *1 December 2012, Chiclana de la Frontera, Spain.*
This intellectual provocateur specified "taste, culture and perversion" as the essentials of a good sex film. Originally a producer, he moved into directing in 1960 with the groundbreaking *L'Éternité pour nous*, following it with titles like *Le Concerto de la peur*, *Cover Girls*, *Sexus* and *Joe Caligula* (which was banned the day before its release date). Disdaining scripts, he headed into the 1970s with oneiric, bourgeois-baiting fantasies like *Le Désirable et le sublime* and *Frustration*, then – cocking a snook at censors as comprehensively as he could – moved into hardcore with *Les deux gouines* (1975). Unfortunately, thanks to a changing market and what he called his "réputation diabolique," he found that he couldn't get out. A shame, as his early films had been striking enough to attract the attention of *Cahiers du cinéma*.

❧ Also mixing eroticism and political content was director **Kōji Wakamatsu**, known as the 'Pink Godfather' for his decisive role in the development of Japan's pinku eiga genre; he died in October, aged 76.

RICHARD RODNEY BENNETT

Born: *29 March 1936, Broadstairs, Kent, England.*
Died: *24 December 2012, New York City, New York, USA.*
The extraordinary breadth of composer Richard Rodney Bennett's work, embracing the atonal avant-

garde and a latterday career as jazz pianist and singer, is made all the more remarkable by his numerous elegant film scores, which started in 1957 with *Interpol*. As well as embracing British horror (*The Man Who Could Cheat Death*) and comedy (*Heavens Above!*), he was a favourite of directors John Schlesinger and Joseph Losey and was three times Oscar-nominated. Titles include *The Devil's Disciple, Blind Date, Only Two Can Play, Billy Liar, The Nanny, Far from the Madding Crowd, Billion Dollar Brain, Secret Ceremony, Figures in a Landscape, Nicholas and Alexandra, Lady Caroline Lamb, Murder on the Orient Express* (for which he won a BAFTA), *Equus, Yanks* and, in the 1990s, *Enchanted April* and *Four Weddings and a Funeral*. He was knighted in 1998.

❧ Other composers who died in 2012 include exploitation specialists **Joel Goldsmith** and **Robert O Ragland**, both in April, aged 54 and 80 respectively. Spanish composer **Bernardo Bonezzi**, who scored several of Almodóvar's early films, died at 48 in August. The legendary Indian musician **Ravi Shankar**, whose western film commissions ranged from *Charly* (1968) to *Gandhi* (1982), died in December, aged 92.

TURHAN BEY
Born: *30 March 1922, Vienna, Austria.*
Died: *30 September 2012, Vienna, Austria.*
Fleeing the Nazis in his late teens, Turhan Bey ended up in Los Angeles and studied acting at the Pasadena Playhouse. Launched on picturegoers as the so-called 'Turkish Delight', he joined Sabu and Maria Montez in Hollywood's select group of wartime exotics, with numerous torrid titles ranging from *Arabian Nights, The Mummy's Tomb* and *Ali Baba and the Forty Thieves* to *Dragon Seed, White Savage* and *Sudan*. His continental suavity was also showcased in more offbeat projects like *The Amazing Mr X* (1948), but by the mid '50s he'd returned to Europe to become a photographer. Forty years later, a brief return trip to Hollywood yielded a career revival in TV series like *Babylon 5* and *Murder, She Wrote*, plus the 1994 feature *Healer*.

ANITA BJÖRK
Born: *25 April 1923, Tällberg, Sweden.*
Died: *24 October 2012, Stockholm, Sweden.*
Anita Björk's intense performance in Alf Sjöberg's 1951 Strindberg adaptation, *Fröken Julie*, took her to Hollywood for Hitchcock's *I Confess*; when the Warner Bros brass realised she was an unmarried mother, she was sent back home and replaced by Anne Baxter. But a 'new Garbo' had been scented and a further attempt to launch her internationally followed in *Night People* (playing opposite Gregory Peck). She remained in Sweden, however, working regularly for Sjöberg, Gustaf Molander and Arne Mattsson, also enjoying an association with Ingmar Bergman stretching from *Kvinnors väntan* (Waiting Women, 1952) to the TV film *Bildmakarna* (The Image Makers, 2000), in which she starred as novelist Selma Lagerlöf. She also acted for Bo Widerberg (*Ådalen 31*, 1969) and Mai Zetterling (*Loving Couples*, 1964; *Amorosa*, 1985), as well as becoming a grande dame of Swedish theatre.

Ernest Borgnine

ERNEST BORGNINE
Born: *24 January 1917, Hamden, Connecticut, USA.*
Died: *8 July 2012, Los Angeles, California, USA.*
Though his natural niche – memorably showcased in early titles like *From Here to Eternity* and *Bad Day at Black Rock* – was that of the hard-faced villain, Ernest Borgnine won fame, and an Oscar, as the sensitive title character in *Marty* (1955). A varied roster of star roles – among them, *The Catered Affair, The Vikings* and *Summer of the Seventeenth Doll* – was followed by an early '60s stint in the TV sitcom *McHale's Navy*, after which he roared back in commercial heavyweights like *The Dirty Dozen, The Wild Bunch* and, in the 1970s, *The Poseidon Adventure*. Later roles were rather a mixed bag, distinguished by *Emperor of the North, Hustle, Convoy, Deadly Blessing, Spike of Bensonhurst, Gattaca* and Sean Penn's segment of the multi-director portmanteau *11'09"01*. Whatever the circumstances, Borgnine's burly, gap-toothed presence was never less than charismatic.

❧ Also dying in July (aged 86) was US TV star **Andy Griffith**, who was featured among the 'Rising Stars' in this annual's 1959 edition for his role in Elia Kazan's *A Face in the Crowd*. Other US actors who died in 2012 included **Jerome Courtland** (also a producer-director; in March, aged 85) and **Biff Elliot**, the original Mike Hammer in *I, the Jury* (1953), who died at 89 in August. Dying at 88 the day after Elliot was stage star **William Windom**, whose film career began with a showy role in *To Kill a Mockingbird* (1962).

RAY BRADBURY
Born: *22 August 1920, Waukegan, Illinois, USA.*
Died: *5 June 2012, Los Angeles, California, USA.*
America's pre-eminent 20th century master of lyric

fantasy published his first professional story in 1941 and 12 years later was introduced to filmgoers via two classics released just three weeks apart – *It Came from Outer Space* and *The Beast from 20,000 Fathoms*. His first screenplay, for John Huston's *Moby Dick* (1956), was followed by adaptations of his own work – *The Picasso Summer* (1969), *Something Wicked This Way Comes* (1982) and *The Wonderful Ice Cream Suit* (1998). Otherwise, his books were transferred to the screen by others, encompassing *Fahrenheit 451* (1966), *The Illustrated Man* (1969), the massive TV mini-series *The Martian Chronicles* (1980) and *A Sound of Thunder* (2005). He was also honoured with his very own 1980s TV anthology series, *The Ray Bradbury Theatre*.

❧ Actor-writer-director **Jean-Louis Richard** – who collaborated with François Truffaut on *Fahrenheit 451* and three other films, as well as writing *Emmanuelle* (starring Sylvia Kristel, qv) – also died in June, aged 85.

CHRISTOPHER CHALLIS

Born: *18 March 1919, London, England.*
Died: *31 May 2012, Bristol, England.*
Cinematographer Christopher Challis brought a vivid visual sense to titles as diverse as *Genevieve* (1953), *Windom's Way* (1957), *Never Let Go* (1960), *Chitty Chitty Bang Bang* (1967), *The Private Life of Sherlock Holmes* (1969), *Villain* (1971), *The Riddle of the Sands* (1978) and *Top Secret!* (1983). After early experience with Gaumont British News and the RAF Film Unit, he graduated to DP on *The End of the River* (1947), continuing with the Powell-Pressburger team on, among others, *The Small Back Room*, *The Tales of Hoffmann* and *Oh… Rosalinda!* His lushly inventive style was also popular with Stanley Donen, bringing Challis a BAFTA award for *Arabesque* in 1967. He was BAFTA-nominated, too, for *The Victors* (1963), *Those Magnificent Men in Their Flying Machines* (1965) and *The Deep* (1977). His 1995 autobiography was entitled *Are They Really So Awful?*

HAL E CHESTER

Born: *6 March 1921, New York City, New York, USA.*
Died: *25 March 2012, London, England.*
As a teen actor 'Hally' Chester made his debut opposite Humphrey Bogart in the 1938 film *Crime School*, thereby earning membership of the Dead End Kids which in turn led to a stint as one of Monogram's East Side Kids. Post-war he turned producer for a series of Monogram quickies based on the comic strip character Joe Palooka, later raising his game with titles like *The Underworld Story*, *Models Inc* and the imperishable *Beast from 20,000 Fathoms*. Having moved to London, he then made indelible contributions to the fields of British horror and comedy respectively with *Night of the Demon* (1956) and *School for Scoundrels* (1959). Later films included *His and Hers*, *The Double Man* and (his last, in 1970) *Take a Girl Like You*.

PHYLLIS DILLER

Born: *17 July 1917, Lima, Ohio, USA.*
Died: *20 August 2012, Los Angeles, California, USA.*
Presenting herself as a shock-haired grotesque, Phyllis Diller sprang to fame in the mid-1950s with her pricelessly acerbic stand-up routine. Her film debut in Elia Kazan's *Splendour in the Grass* followed in 1960, after which she co-starred with Bob Hope (whose deadpan style hers somewhat resembled) in *Boy Did I Get a Wrong Number!*, *Eight on the Lam* and *The Private Navy of Sgt O'Farrell*. She also top-lined *The Fat Spy* ("It's a Killer… a Diller… a Blast of Laffs!"), *Did You Hear the One About the Traveling Saleslady?* ("It's as Wild as Her Hair!") and in 1969 went to Britain for a rare dramatic role in *The Adding Machine*. Her voice performance in *Mad Monster Party?* (1966) presaged many more, notably *A Bug's Life* (1998) and, on TV, *Family Guy* (2006-07).

Ray Bradbury

Phyllis Diller

Michel Duchaussoy

Michael Clarke Duncan

MICHEL DUCHAUSSOY

Born: *29 November 1938, Valenciennes, Nord, France.*
Died: *13 March 2012, Paris, France.*
Though Michel Duchaussoy's reputation was founded
on his long association with the Comédie Française,
bringing him the Légion d'honneur in 2011, he also
appeared in well over 100 films, starting with Louis
Malle's *Vie privée* in 1961. That he was an unusually
compelling actor was made clear in Chabrol's *Que la
bête meure* (1969), as a man single-mindedly stalking
his son's murderer. He was also directed by Chabrol
in *La Femme infidèle, La Rupture, Nada* and (after 30
years apart) *La Demoiselle d'honneur*. There were fruitful
engagements, too, with Alain Jessua (*Jeu de massacre,
Traitement de choc, Armaguedon*), Malle again (*Milou
en mai*) and Patrice Leconte (*La Veuve de Saint-Pierre,
Confidences trop intimes*). Among his final films were
Le petit Nicolas, Sarah's Key and *L'Age de raison*.

❧ Other French performers who died in 2012 included
Rosy Varte (in January, aged 88), **Jacques Duby**
(February, 89), **Pierre Tornade** (March, 82), **Maurice
Chevit** (July, 88), **Christian Marin** (September, 83), and –
both in December – **Paul Crauchet** (92) and **Jean Topart**
(90). **Tsilla Chelton**, who gained fame in her seventies
in the title role of *Tatie Danielle*, died in July, aged 93.
And **Pierre Mondy**, who starred as Napoleon in Abel
Gance's 1960 film *Austerlitz* and in later years became
TV's Commissaire Cordier, died at 87 in September.

MICHAEL CLARKE DUNCAN

Born: *10 December 1957, Chicago, Illinois, USA.*
Died: *3 September 2012, Los Angeles, California, USA.*
This former bouncer and bodyguard (to such stars
as Will Smith and Jamie Foxx) got his acting break
opposite Bruce Willis in *Armageddon* (1998). As well as
appearing with Willis in three further films (*Breakfast of
Champions, The Whole Nine Yards* and *Sin City*), he was
indebted to Willis for recommending him to director
Frank Darabont for *The Green Mile*, in which Duncan's
touching 'gentle giant' characterisation earned him
a 1999 Oscar nomination as Best Supporting Actor.

His massive (6'5") frame and distinctive baritone
were also showcased in *Planet of the Apes, The Scorpion
King, Daredevil, Talladega Nights, School for Scoundrels,
Slipstream, The Slammin' Salmon* and *Redemption Road*,
while his numerous voice credits included *Cats and
Dogs, Dinotopia* and *Kung Fu Panda*.

❧ Other US character actors who died in 2012 included
Sam Coppola (79), **Peter Breck** (82), **Phil Bruns** (80),
Russell Arms (92) and **Dick Anthony Williams** (77), all
in February, plus in March **Leonardo Cimino** (94) and
Warren Stevens (92). **George Murdock** died in April
at 81, **Frank Cady** in June at 96, and, in July, **Morgan
Paull** (67), **Sherman Hemsley** (74), **Chad Everett** (75),
Norman Alden (87) and **RG Armstrong** (95). **Jeffrey
Stone** (85), **Steve Franken** (80) and **Joe Lewis** (68) all
died in August, followed by **Lance LeGault** (77) and
Johnny Lewis (28), both in September, **Gary Collins** (74)
and **Russell Means** (72), both in October, and **Larry
Hagman** (81) and **Pat Renella** (83), both in November.
Greg McClure, **Cliff Osmond** and **Harry Carey Jr** all
died in December, aged 97, 75 and 91 respectively.

CHARLES DURNING

Born: *28 February 1923, Highland Falls, New York, USA.*
Died: *24 December 2012, New York City, New York, USA.*
This brilliant Irish-American character star, having
come to filmgoers' attention in the 1973 hit *The Sting*,
was nominated for a Golden Globe two years later for
Dog Day Afternoon and in the early 1980s received two
Oscar nominations back to back – for *The Best Little
Whorehouse in Texas* and *To Be or Not to Be*. A D-Day
veteran, his other credits include *Breakheart Pass,
Starting Over, The Muppet Movie, True Confessions, Dick
Tracy* and *The Music of Chance*. He also worked with

Charles Durning

Brian De Palma (*Sisters*, *The Fury*), the Coen brothers (*The Hudsucker Proxy*, *O Brother Where Art Thou?*) and scored a comic-poignant bullseye as Dustin Hoffman's deluded suitor in *Tootsie*. Nine-times Emmy-nominated for his television work, his Big Daddy in a 1990 Broadway revival of *Cat on a Hot Tin Roof* brought him a Tony award.

❧ TV star and occasional film actor **Jack Klugman** died, aged 90, on the same day as Durning. **Garry Walberg** – Klugman's nemesis in the TV series *Quincy ME* and, like him, an occasional film actor – died at 90 in March.

JAKE EBERTS
Born: *10 July 1941, Montreal, Quebec, Canada.*
Died: *6 September 2012, Montreal, Quebec, Canada.*
Investment banker Jake Eberts became fascinated by the film business while setting up the animated film *Watership Down* in the mid-1970s. He then founded Goldcrest with David Puttnam and presided over the British film industry's brief 1980s revival. The Goldcrest zenith was reached when *Chariots of Fire* and *Gandhi* won Best Picture Oscars in consecutive years, though by 1990 Eberts was charting the company's (post-Eberts) collapse in his book *My Indecision is Final*. Other films with Eberts' name attached include *The Name of the Rose*, *Hope and Glory*, another pair of consecutive Best Pictures – *Driving Miss Daisy* and *Dances with Wolves*, *A River Runs Through It*, *City of Joy*, *Super Mario Bros*, *Grey Owl*, *Chicken Run* and *The Way Back*.

MARLA ENGLISH
Born: *4 January 1935, San Diego, California, USA.*
Died: *10 December 2012, Tucson, Arizona, USA.*
Signed to a Paramount contract in 1952, beauty queen Marla English was promoted on the strength of her resemblance to Elizabeth Taylor. Various bit roles (including one in Hitchcock's *Rear Window*)

were followed by loaned-out leads in such 'B' projects as *Shield for Murder*, *Desert Sands*, *Hell's Horizon* and as one of *Three Bad Sisters*. In 1955 she was offered the lead in *The Mountain* opposite Spencer Tracy, but turned it down. ("It's the dumbest thing I've ever done," she later admitted.) Paramount dropped her and she appeared instead in the cult AIP quickies *She Creature* and *Voodoo Woman*, both of which featured a slumming Tom Conway and an identical monster suit. She then retired at the tender age of 21.

NORA EPHRON
Born: *19 May 1941, New York City, New York, USA.*
Died: *26 June 2012, New York City, New York, USA.*
Nora Ephron was the daughter of screenwriters Henry and Phoebe Ephron, who based their 1961 Broadway comedy *Take Her, She's Mine* on Nora's rebellious youth. (She was played by Sandra Dee in the film version.) Destiny, perhaps, played a part in her 1980s transition from caustically witty columnist to successful screenwriter. After the Meryl Streep vehicles *Silkwood* and *Heartburn* (the latter autobiographical, with Streep playing Nora this time), Ephron had a huge hit in 1989 – and won a BAFTA – with *When Harry Met Sally*. Continuing to redefine romantic comedy for the 1990s, she then directed as well as wrote *Sleepless in Seattle* and *You've Got Mail*. A three-time Oscar nominee, her last film – in 2009, again with Streep – was *Julie and Julia*.

LEONARDO FAVIO
Born: *28 May 1938, Luján de Cuyo, Mendoza, Argentina.*
Died: *5 November 2012, Buenos Aires, Argentina.*
Leonardo Favio enjoyed an early reputation as Argentina's James Dean via Leopoldo Torre Nilsson films like *El secuestrador* (1958), and in the following decade became a popular balladeer, producing such

Marla English

hits as 'Fiuste mía un verano' and 'Ella ya me olvidó'. He also consolidated his reputation by turning writer-director on the highly regarded films *Crónica de un niño solo*, *El romance del Aniceto y la Francisca* and *El dependiente*. A member of Juan Perón's inner circle, he fled the country after the military coup of 1976; he'd recently made Argentina's most successful film, an intriguing lycanthropic allegory called *Nazareno Cruz y el lobo*. On his return he made films like *Gatica el mono* and *Aniceto* (a 2008 remake of his earlier work), and in 2010 was appointed Ambassador of Culture.

❖ **Lydia Lamaison**, whose 70-year career included Leopoldo Torre Nilsson's 1958 film *La caída*, died in February, aged 97. Another Argentine star – **Olga Zubarry**, who at 16 caused controversy by appearing partially nude in Carlos Hugo Christensen's *El ángel desnudo* – died in December at 83.

JON FINCH
Born: *2 March 1942, Caterham, Surrey, England.*
Death discovered: *28 December 2012, Hastings, Sussex, England.*
After *The Vampire Lovers* for Hammer in 1970, Jon Finch was a strikingly intense *Macbeth* for Roman Polanski and was rewarded with the 'wrong man' lead in Hitchcock's penultimate film, *Frenzy*. There were further showy roles in *Lady Caroline Lamb* and *The Final Programme* (for Robert Fuest, qv), but Finch passed on playing both James Bond in *Live and Let Die* and Aramis in *The Three Musketeers*. Later he was invalided out of Ridley Scott's *Alien* (John Hurt replaced him), rounding off the 1970s instead with *Death on the Nile* and *Breaking Glass*. Uninterested in stardom, he popped up in such disparate latterday titles as *Darklands*, *Anazapta* and (reunited with Scott in 2004) *Kingdom of Heaven*.

Nora Ephron

Jon Finch

WILLIAM FINLEY
Born: *20 September 1940, New York City, New York, USA.*
Died: *14 April 2012, New York City, New York, USA.*
William Finley earned cult immortality in the dual role of Winslow Leach, the guileless composer tragically transmogrified into *The Phantom of the Paradise* in Brian De Palma's 1974 rock opera. A classmate of De Palma's, he had appeared in several of the director's early experimental films before lending his uniquely disconcerting presence (slick-haired, pasty-faced) to De Palma's breakthrough picture, *Sisters* (1972), thereafter featuring in *The Fury* and as the killer's voice in *Dressed to Kill*. There were also three assignments for Tobe Hooper (*Death Trap*, *The Funhouse*, *Night Terrors*), a memorable mad scientist in the Chuck Norris vehicle *Silent Rage* and a 21st century swan song in De Palma's *The Black Dahlia*. But – wastefully – not a lot else.

HARRY FOWLER
Born: *10 December 1926, London, England.*
Died: *4 January 2012, London, England.*
British filmmakers looked upon Harry Fowler, he observed philosophically, "as the obligatory cockney, just as you had the obligatory 'negro' in American films." This native of Lambeth Walk was plucked from a Piccadilly news-stand in 1941 to appear in *Those Kids from Town*, turning up thereafter in Ealing classics like *Champagne Charlie*, *Hue and Cry* and *I Believe in You*. Scores of 'B' pictures and the occasional 'A' ensued, perhaps most notably *The Pickwick Papers* in 1952 (as Sam Weller). He also became a household name via the 1960s sitcoms *The Army Game* and *Our Man at St Mark's*. Typed or otherwise, Fowler became one of the quintessential faces of post-war British cinema, in recognition of which he was made an MBE in 1970.

❖ Other British character players who died in 2012 included **Frederick Treves** (January, 86), **John Fabian**

In Memoriam

Al Freeman Jr

(April, 84), **Anthony Bate**, **James Grout** (both June, both 84), **Geoffrey Hughes** (July, 68), **John Moffatt** (September, 89), **John Clive** (79) and **Joe Melia** (77), both in October, and, in November, **Clive Dunn** (92) and **Roger Hammond** (76).

AL FREEMAN JR
Born: *21 March 1934, San Antonio, Texas, USA.*
Died: *9 August 2012, Washington DC, USA.*
Al Freeman Jr's smouldering intensity on stage made him a significant figure in the burgeoning Civil Rights movement. One of the plays he starred in, Leroi Jones' *Dutchman*, became a 1967 film that memorably pitted Freeman against Shirley Knight. Other 1960s film appearances included *This Rebel Breed*, *Black Like Me*, *Ensign Pulver*, *The Detective*, *Finian's Rainbow* and *Castle Keep*, and in 1970 Freeman directed as well as starred in another Jones adaptation, *A Fable*. Preoccupied by the daytime soap *One Life to Live*, he nevertheless played Malcolm X in the 1979 mini-series *Roots: The Next Generations* and 13 years later gave an award-winning performance as Elijah Muhammad in Spike Lee's *Malcolm X*. Other 1990s credits included *Once Upon a Time … When We Were Colored* and Maya Angelou's *Down in the Delta*.

❧ Pre-dating Civil Rights, dancer **Jeni LeGon** found herself typed as maids in most of her Hollywood appearances; she died in December, aged 96. **Jamaa Fanaka**, director of the 1980 hit *Penitentiary* and a tireless critic of the limited opportunities available to African-American filmmakers, died in April at 69.

ROBERT FUEST
Born: *30 September 1927, Croydon, England.*
Died: *21 March 2012, London, England.*
The visual flair characteristic of Robert Fuest's films first

Robert Fuest

became apparent when he was production designer (and later director) on the classic ABC television series *The Avengers*. His first feature as director – *Just Like a Woman* in 1966, for producer Bob Kellett [qv] – was followed by the queasy thriller *And Soon the Darkness*, shot in France in 1969. He was then taken up by the British arm of American International, for whom he made *Wuthering Heights* and the studiedly camp Vincent Price vehicles *The Abominable Dr Phibes* and *Dr Phibes Rises Again*. Then, after the cult Michael Moorcock adaptation *The Final Programme* (starring Jon Finch, qv), he went to Mexico in 1975 for *The Devil's Rain* and thereafter returned largely to TV.

❧ Prolific TV directors **John Rich** and **Paul Bogart**, both of whom worked on the classic 1970s sitcom *All in the Family*, also had theatrical features to their name; Rich (*Wives and Lovers*, *Roustabout*) died in January at 86 and Bogart (*Marlowe*, *Torch Song Trilogy*) in April, aged 92. Another TV director, **William Asher** (*I Love Lucy*, *Bewitched*), ventured into cinema as a gangster (*Mobs Inc*) and beach party (*How to Stuff a Wild Bikini*) specialist; he died at 90 in July. Finnish-born **Vivi Friedman** died aged 44 in January, four months after the release of her single feature, *The Family Tree*. And **Danny Steinmann**, writer-director of cult 1980s exploiters like *Savage Streets* and *Friday the 13th: A New Beginning*, died at 70 in December.

BEN GAZZARA
Born: *28 August 1930, New York City, New York, USA.*
Died: *3 February 2012, New York City, New York, USA.*
The powerful presence of this Actors Studio graduate, already showcased on Broadway as the original Brick in *Cat on a Hot Tin Roof*, burst onto cinema screens in *The Strange One* (1957) and, two years later, *Anatomy of a Murder*. Subsequent films made less impact but, after a lengthy spell in TV, Gazzara joined up with actor-director John Cassavetes for the seminal, semi-improvised 1970s triptych *Husbands*, *The Killing of a Chinese Bookie* and

Ben Gazzara

Marvin Hamlisch

Opening Night. Prolific in later years, his appearances included *Saint Jack, Tales of Ordinary Madness, They All Laughed, Road House, The Big Lebowski, Buffalo 66, Summer of Sam, Dogville* and (reunited with his Cassavetes colleague Gena Rowlands) *Paris, je t'aime*. He also directed the barely seen Italian feature *Oltre l'oceano* (Beyond the Ocean, 1990).

❖ Like Gazzara, character actor **John P Finnegan** was a Cassavetes regular; he died in July, aged 85. **Mel Stuart**, director of *If It's Tuesday This Must Be Belgium* (in which both Gazzara and Cassavetes appeared) and *Willy Wonka and the Chocolate Factory*, died at 83 the following month.

ULU GROSBARD

Born: *9 January 1929, Antwerp, Belgium.*
Died: *19 March 2012, New York City, New York, USA.*
Having been assistant director on such films as *The Hustler* and *The Pawnbroker*, Ulu Grosbard was Tony-nominated for directing the Frank Gilroy play *The Subject Was Roses*, which ran on Broadway for two years (1964-66) and in 1968 led to a film version, also directed by Grosbard. In the 1970s he teamed up with his old off-Broadway stage manager, Dustin Hoffman, for the Hoffman vehicles *Who is Harry Kellerman and Why is He Saying Those Terrible Things About Me?* and *Straight Time*, in the 1980s with Robert De Niro for *True Confessions* and *Falling in Love*, and in the 1990s rounded out his brief but impressive filmography with *Georgia* and *The Deep End of the Ocean*. In the meantime, his ongoing Broadway career yielded premieres of plays by Arthur Miller and David Mamet.

TONINO GUERRA

Born: *16 March 1920, Santarcangelo di Romagna, Italy.*
Died: *21 March 2012, Santarcangelo di Romagna, Italy.*
Dialect poet Tonino Guerra established himself as Italy's master screenwriter through more than 100 films and a truly remarkable series of collaborations.

For Antonioni he wrote, among others, *L'avventura, La notte, L'eclisse, Il deserto rosso* and *Blow Up*, which brought him one of three Oscar nominations; the others were for Monicelli's *Casanova '70* and Fellini's *Amarcord*. He also worked with Fellini on *And the Ship Sailed On* and *Ginger e Fred*, with Francesco Rosi on *Il caso Mattei, Lucky Luciano, Cadaveri eccellenti* and *Cronaca di una morte annunciata*, with Vittorio de Sica on *Matrimonio all'italiana* and *I girasoli*, and with the Taviani Brothers on *La notte di San Lorenzo, Kaos* and *Good Morning Babylon*. Beyond Italy, he co-wrote *Nostalgia* for Tarkovsky and no fewer than eight films, culminating in *The Dust of Time*, for Theo Angelopoulos [qv].

❖ **Maria Pia Casilio**, star of de Sica's *Umberto D* in 1952, died in April, aged 76. **Olimpia Cavalli**, who acted for Visconti and Rossellini, died at 81 the previous month. Writer-director **Giuseppe Bertolucci** (Roberto's younger brother) died at 65 in June. **Luigi Bazzoni**, writer-director of giallo pictures and Euro Westerns, also died in March, aged 82. Other Italian names who died in 2012 include Slovene-born Spaghetti Western regular **Andrea Bosic** (in January, aged 92), actor **Mario Maranzana** (also January, at 81) and actress **Alida Chelli** (in December, aged 69). Italian poster artist **Arnaldo Putzu**, whose work in Britain ran the gamut from *Get Carter* to *Carry On Abroad* and innumerable *Look-in* covers, died in September, aged 85.

MARVIN HAMLISCH

Born: *2 June 1944, New York City, New York, USA.*
Died: *6 August 2012, Los Angeles, California, USA.*
En route to being positively festooned with Oscars, Emmys, Tonys, Grammys and even a Pulitzer, composer Marvin Hamlisch began his film career with *The*

Swimmer in 1968. There followed *Take the Money and Run*, *Bananas*, *Kotch* and then, in 1974, three Oscars in one night, for *The Sting* and *The Way We Were*. Heading towards and into the 1980s, the titles, and awards, proliferated – *The Spy Who Loved Me*, *Same Time Next Year*, *Ice Castles*, *Ordinary People*, *Sophie's Choice*, *A Chorus Line* (based on his Broadway original), *Romantic Comedy*, *Three Men and a Baby*, *Shirley Valentine* and, in 1991, *Frankie and Johnny*. After several years away from film, he returned with Steven Soderbergh's *The Informant!* in 2009; he was about to start work on Soderbergh's *Behind the Candelabra* when he died.

CELESTE HOLM

Born: *29 April 1917, New York City, New York, USA.*
Died: *15 July 2012, New York City, New York, USA.*
Though generally a second lead, the wryly humorous Celeste Holm was often more watchable than the firsts. Having made a huge impact in the original Broadway production of *Oklahoma!* in 1943, she was snapped up by Hollywood and won an Oscar for her third film, *Gentleman's Agreement* (1947). Two further nominations followed – for the forgotten *Come to the Stable* and immortal *All About Eve* – but she only returned to Hollywood at the behest of Frank Sinatra, with whom she co-starred in the mid-'50s duo *The Tender Trap*

and *High Society*. In later years she was Terry-Thomas' fiancée in *Bachelor Flat* (1961), the title character's aunt in *Tom Sawyer* (1972), Ted Danson's mother in *Three Men and a Baby* (1987) and Brendan Fraser's grandmother in *Still Breathing* (1996).

WHITNEY HOUSTON

Born: *9 August 1963, Newark, New Jersey, USA.*
Died: *11 February 2012, Beverly Hills, California, USA.*
With seven consecutive Number One singles to her name and all-round record sales topping the 200 million mark, Whitney Houston was a pop music phenomenon. She also made films, with chart-busting soundtrack albums affixed to each one. Having come to fame in 1985, her film debut was delayed until 1992, when she starred in *The Bodyguard* with Kevin Costner and acquired her signature tune, 'I Will Always Love You'. *Waiting to Exhale* and *The Preacher's Wife* followed a few years later, plus a TV movie version of Rodgers and Hammerstein's *Cinderella*. Having produced *The Princess Diaries* and its sequel in the interim, she returned to acting (and producing) in 2011 with *Sparkle*, which was released posthumously.

❧ **Davy Jones**, The Monkees' British member and co-star of Bob Rafelson's *Head* (1968), died at 66 in February. **Dick Clark**, the legendary television DJ whose film appearances ranged from *Disc Jockey Jamboree* to *Confessions of a Dangerous Mind* 45 years later, died at 82 in April. **Robin Gibb**, who as one third of The Bee Gees gave *Saturday Night Fever* its epoch-making soundtrack and then co-starred in the disastrous *Sgt Pepper's Lonely Hearts Club Band*, died in May, aged 62. **Tony Martin**, the hit-making crooner whose films included *Ziegfeld Girl* (1941) and *Till the Clouds Roll By* (1946), died at 98 in July. Another classic crooner, **Andy Williams** – who starred opposite Sandra Dee in *I'd Rather Be Rich* (1964) – died in September, aged 84.

POLA ILLÉRY

Born: *15 October 1908, Corabia, Romania.*
Died: *15 February 2012, Scranton, Pennsylvania, USA.*
In last year's *Film Review* we pronounced Barbara Kent "the last surviving person to have starred in silent films as an adult." We spoke too soon. Outliving Kent by four months was the diminutive Paula Iliescu, who chose her screen name in tribute to Pola Negri. Her debut, in the 1928 film *Le Désir*, was followed by Alberto Cavalcanti's *Le Capitaine Fracasse* the same year. In 1929 she made her last silent, *Illusions*, and played opposite the wolfish Jean Renoir in Cavalcanti's *Le petit chaperon rouge*. She then starred in René Clair's first sound film, *Sous les toits de Paris*, which was an international smash. She also appeared in Romania's first talkie, *Parada Paramount*. After several more films she emigrated to the USA to avoid Nazi persecution.

❧ **Vondell Darr**, child actress in US silents, died in September at 93. **Jack Hanlon** – 'Our Gang' member and last surviving actor from Buster Keaton's *The*

Celeste Holm

Pola Illéry

Erland Josephson

General – died at 96 in December. Another 'Our Gang' veteran, **Peggy Ahern**, died in October, aged 95. **Louise LaPlanche**, last survivor of the 1923 *Hunchback of Notre Dame* (she played the child Esmeralda), died the previous month, aged 93.

ERLAND JOSEPHSON

Born: *15 June 1923, Stockholm, Sweden.*
Died: *25 February 2012, Stockholm, Sweden.*
Erland Josephson was 16 when he first worked with Ingmar Bergman; by the turn of the century he was playing 'Bergman' in Liv Ullmann's Bergman-scripted *Faithless*. After trial runs in Bergman films like *So Close to Life* (1958), *A Passion* (1969) and *Cries and Whispers* (1971), Josephson's mournful, weatherbeaten visage became a Bergman signifier via his blistering performance in *Scenes from a Marriage* (1973), followed by *Face to Face*, *Autumn Sonata*, *Fanny and Alexander* and finally a 30-years-later follow-up to *Scenes* called *Saraband*. In the meantime he acted for Makavejev (*Montenegro*), Tarkovsky (*Nostalgia*, *The Sacrifice*), Kaufman (*The Unbearable Lightness of Being*), Szabó (*Hanussen*), Greenaway (*Prospero's Books*), Ullmann (*Sofie*) and Angelopoulos [qv] (*Ulysses' Gaze*). He was also director of Stockholm's Royal Dramatic Theatre (succeeding Bergman) and writer-director-star of *One on One* (1978) and *Marmalade Revolution* (1980).

❧ Swedish actor-writer-directors **Stig Ossian Ericson** and **Hans Lindgren** died in July and November, aged 88 and 80 respectively. Other Swedish actors who died in 2012 included **Bertil Norström** (September, 88) and **Göran Stangertz** (October, 68).

BOB KELLETT

Born: *25 December 1927, Lancaster, Lancashire, England.*
Died: *27 November 2012, West Sussex, England.*
In 1964, Bob Kellett was writer-producer of the 55-minute comedy *San Ferry Ann*. Pursuing this line,

he joined forces with Ronnie Barker for the wordless featurettes *A Home of Your Own* and *Futtock's End*, directing the latter. For producer Ned Sherrin he then directed the Frankie Howerd vehicles *Up Pompeii*, *Up the Chastity Belt* and *Up the Front*, as well as the more thoughtful comedy drama *Girl Stroke Boy*. As the '70s wore on, he also directed Danny La Rue in *Our Miss Fred*, Leslie Phillips and Terry-Thomas in *Spanish Fly*, and the TV spin-offs *The Alf Garnett Saga* and *Are You Being Served?* Latterly, he worked on the Lewis Gilbert films *Haunted* and *Before You Go* as co-writer and producer respectively.

❧ British producer **Frank Godwin**, whose films ranged from *Woman in a Dressing Gown* to *Sammy's Super T-Shirt*, died at 95 in September. British animation producer **John Coates** (*Yellow Submarine*, *When the Wind Blows*, *The Snowman*) died at 84 the same month. And TV director **Jim O'Brien** – whose one theatrical feature was *The Dressmaker* in 1988 – died in February, aged 64.

RAJESH KHANNA

Born: *29 December 1942, Amritsar, Punjab, British India.*
Died: *18 July 2012, Mumbai, Maharashtra, India.*
Rajesh Khanna's elevation to the position of Bollywood's first bona-fide superstar put him, according to 'Gadfly' of *India Herald*, "in an unreachable stratosphere but also uncharted territory." Struggling to come to terms with this, he was soon superseded by the more contemporary figure of Amitabh Bachchan; even so, his charismatic screen presence had created an unprecedented fan-worship phenomenon. Leading ladies like Mumtaz and Sharmila Tagore were envied throughout the subcontinent and, starting with *Aradhana* and *Do Raaste*, he racked up a still-unbroken record of 15 consecutive hits between 1969 and 1971 alone. Other titles from his massive filmography include *Safar*,

Rajesh Khanna

Anand, Kati Patang, Amar Prem and (from a 1980s second wind) *Souten, Bewafai* and *Swarg*. He received a Filmfare Lifetime Achievement award in 2005.

❧ Posthumous recipient of the same award, director-producer **Yash Chopra** directed Khanna in *Ittefaq* and *Daag* as well as making several vehicles for Amitabh Bachchan; he died in October, aged 80. Other Indian film personalities who died in 2012 included producer **KCN Gowda** (October, 84), director-producer **Navodaya Appachan** (April, 87) and actor-director **Joy Mukherjee** (March, 73). Among directors, **V Madhusudhan Rao** (89) died in January, followed by **Raj Kanwar** (50) and **OP Dutta** (90), both in February, **KSR Das** (June, 76), **BR Ishara** (July, 77) and **Subhash Dutta** (November, 82). Others included composer **Anthony Gonsalves** (January, 84), screenwriter **T Damodaran** (March, 77), cinematographer **Ashok Mehta** (August, 64), editor **MS Shinde** (September, 83), actor **Karibasavaiah** (February, 52) and actresses **Kalpana Mohan** (January, 65) and **Preeti Ganguly** (December, 59).

ZALMAN KING

Born: *23 May 1942, Trenton, New Jersey, USA.*
Died: *3 February 2012, Santa Monica, California, USA.*
As an actor, Zalman King had mid-1970s features like *The Passover Plot* (in which he played Jesus) and the horror classic *Blue Sunshine* on his résumé. In 1985 he produced (and with his wife, Patricia Knop, co-wrote) Adrian Lyne's *9½ Weeks*, which provided a blueprint for the high-toned erotica (with a pronounced female

focus) that would become his legacy as writer-director-producer. The theatrical releases *Two Moon Junction* and *Wild Orchid* were followed by a hugely profitable cable feature, *Red Shoe Diaries* (1992), that spun off into a series. In the same back-lit, music video-inflected vein, his later films included *Delta of Venus*, *Shame Shame Shame* and *Women of the Night*. Such was his softcore supremacy that he was consulted by Kubrick on the latter's final film, *Eyes Wide Shut*.

ELYSE KNOX

Born: *14 December 1917, Hartford, Connecticut, USA.*
Died: *15 February 2012, Los Angeles, California, USA.*
Having established herself as a *Vogue* cover girl Elyse Knox was snapped up by Twentieth Century-Fox but barely used by them. She had better luck at RKO and, particularly, Universal, starring opposite such wartime luminaries as Roy Rogers (*Sheriff of Tombstone*), the Dead End Kids (*Keep 'Em Slugging*), Lon Chaney Jr (*The Mummy's Tomb*), the Andrews Sisters (*Moonlight and Cactus*) and Abbott and Costello (*Hit the Ice*). Lou Costello, in particular, she credited as a major supporter, though it was under his patronage that she downgraded to Monogram, where she appeared in a clutch of Joe Palooka potboilers. Among her last films was the underrated 1948 noir *I Wouldn't Be in Your Shoes*. Her children – Kelly Harmon, Kristin Nelson and Mark Harmon – all became actors.

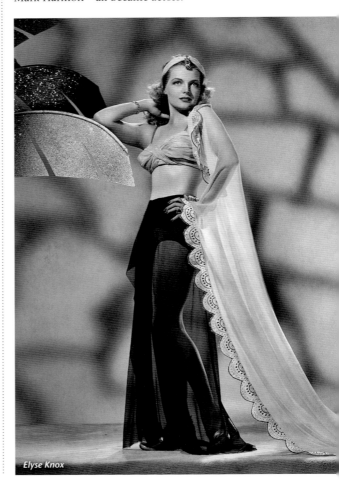

Elyse Knox

Sylvia Kristel

❖ Other US actresses of the 1940s and '50s who died in 2012 included **Martha Stewart** (in February, aged 89), **Carol Adams** (April, 94), **Margie Stewart** (also April, 92), **Kay Christopher** (June, 86), **Susan Luckey** (November, 74) and **Gloria Pall** (December, 85).

SYLVIA KRISTEL

Born: 28 September 1952, Utrecht, Netherlands.
Died: 18 October 2012, Utrecht, Netherlands.
Sitting semi-naked in a rattan armchair and holding a pearl necklace to her lips, Sylvia Kristel became the dominant erotic image of the 1970s in Just Jaeckin's *Emmanuelle*. From this Bangkok softcore classic she moved to Hong Kong for *Emmanuelle 2* and the Seychelles for *Goodbye Emmanuelle*, also appearing in Robbe-Grillet's *Le Jeu avec le feu*, Vadim's *Une Femme fidèle*, Borowcyzk's *La Marge* and Chabrol's *Alice ou la dernière fugue*. In the early 1980s she starred in Jaeckin's *Lady Chatterley's Lover* in Britain and the phenomenally successful *Private Lessons* in the US, later devolving into turkeys like *Mata Hari* and *Dracula's Widow*. In her 2006 memoir, *Undressing Emmanuelle*, she summed up her commodified career in the poignant phrase "I belonged to dreams."

HERBERT LOM

Born: 11 September 1917, Prague, Bohemia, Austria-Hungary.
Died: 27 September 2012, London, England.
Having fled the Nazis, this charismatic Czech-born actor became one of the classic faces of British cinema, first coming to prominence in the 1945 hit *The Seventh Veil*. Thereafter, his films included *Night and the City*, *Hell is Sold Out*, *The Ladykillers*, *Hell Drivers*, *No Trees in the Street*, *Spartacus*, *El Cid*, *Mysterious Island* and a haunting Phantom in Hammer's *The Phantom of the Opera*. He was a two-time Napoleon – in *The Young Mr Pitt* (1942) and *War and Peace* (1956) – and, starting with *A Shot in the Dark* in 1964, became indelibly associated with the twitchy Commissioner Dreyfus in a half-dozen Pink Panther films. There were also plenty of continental exploitation horrors, most notoriously *Hexen bis aufs Blut gequält* (Mark of the Devil, 1970). Latterday credits included *The Dead Zone*, *Whoops Apocalypse* and *The Pope Must Die*.

❖ Also born in Prague, **Zita Kabátová** was a pre-war star in her homeland and kept acting until 2009; she died in May, aged 99. Other Czech performers who died in 2012 included **Eva Klepácová** (79) and **Jaroslava Adamová** (87), both in June, **Radoslav Brzobohaty** (79) in September, and **Antonie Hegerliková** (89) in December.

STANLEY LONG

Born: 26 November 1933, London, England.
Died: 10 September 2012, Denham, Buckinghamshire, England.
An undisputed master of British sexploitation, Stanley Long started as cinematographer on the cheeky 1959 featurette *Nudist Memories*. Through the 1960s he variously photographed and/or produced *Nudes of the World*, *Take Off Your Clothes and Live*, *Secrets of a Windmill Girl* and *This, That and the Other!* Via Tony Tenser, he also served as cinematographer on *Repulsion* (uncredited), *The Sorcerers* and *The Blood Beast Terror*. After the staggering success of *The Wife Swappers* in 1970, he added directing to his armoury with titles

Susanne Lothar

Richard Lynch

> German actors **Peter Carsten** and **Rainer Penkert** both died in April, aged 83 and 90 respectively. **Günther Kaufmann**, a regular in Fassbinder's films, died at 64 in May. Also from Germany, actor-director **Vadim Glowna** died in January, aged 70.

RICHARD LYNCH
Born: *12 February 1940, New York City, New York, USA.*
Died: *19 June 2012, Yucca Valley, California, USA.*
In a long list of strange roles, perhaps Richard Lynch's strangest was the hermaphrodite Messiah in Larry Cohen's bizarre 1975 film *God Told Me To*. Eight years earlier, this striking Irish-American actor had set himself on fire in Central Park under the influence of LSD. As a result, his ravaged features dictated a film career devoted almost exclusively to eye-catching exploitation villains; this despite Broadway appearances opposite Anne Bancroft, Jason Robards and Vanessa Redgrave. Starting in 1973, films included *Scarecrow*, *The Seven-Ups*, *Open Season*, *Deathsport*, *Steel*, the TV movie *Vampire*, *The Ninth Configuration*, *The Formula*, *The Sword and the Sorcerer*, *Invasion USA*, *Little Nikita*, *Bad Dreams*, *Necronomicon*, *Crime and Punishment* and the 2007 *Halloween*.

> Two other cult actors, **James Farentino** and **Luke Askew**, died in January and March respectively. Amid much TV, Farentino's films included *The Pad and How to Use It* (for which he won a Golden Globe) and *Dead & Buried*; he was 73. Best known for *Easy Rider*, Askew was also a memorably mean antagonist in films like *Cool Hand Luke* and *Rolling Thunder*; he was 80.

CHRIS MARKER
Born: *29 July 1921, Neuilly-sur-Seine, France (?).*
Died: *29 July 2012, Paris, France.*
As well as transposing documentary into poetry, Christian François Bouche-Villeneuve cultivated so dense a cloud of personal mystery that even his birth

like *Naughty!*, *Sex and the Other Woman* and the 'Jack the Lad' sauciness of the *Adventures* films (… *of a Taxi Driver*, *Private Eye*, *Plumber's Mate*: 1975-77). His company, Alpha Film Distribution, also gave exposure to films by, among others, Cronenberg, Fassbinder and Altman.

> Beastie Boy **Adam Yauch**, who died at 47 in May, founded the distribution company Oscilloscope Laboratories, ensuring release for indies like *The Messenger* and *We Need to Talk About Kevin*. Another distributor who died young was **Sage Stallone**, actor son of Sylvester Stallone and co-founder of Grindhouse Releasing; he died at 36 in July.

SUSANNE LOTHAR
Born: *15 November 1960, Hamburg, Germany.*
Died: *21 July 2012, Berlin, Germany.*
A regular at the Deutsches Schauspielhaus in her native Hamburg, elfin character star Susanne Lothar won a German Film Award for her screen debut, *Eisenhans* (Strange Fruits, 1982). She was nominated for another for her second film, *Winckelmanns Reisen* (1990), and thereafter gained three further nominations, winding up with Michael Haneke's *Das weisse Band* (The White Ribbon) in 2009. Latterly, she appeared in such international projects as *The Reader* and *Anna Karenina*, but it is for her four Haneke collaborations that she will remain best remembered. The others were *Das Schloß*, *Funny Games* and *La Pianiste*; in the first two of these she co-starred with her husband Ulrich Mühe, who predeceased her in 2007.

place is a question mark; he claimed Mongolia, others demurred. His post-apocalyptic half-hour photo-montage *La Jetée* (1962) contained only one 'motion' shot and has proved profoundly influential. Emerging from the same Left Bank coterie as Agnès Varda and Alain Resnais, he had been a pioneer of the 'film essay' in the 1950s, directing *Olympia 52*, *Les Statues meurent aussi* (with Resnais), *Dimanche à Pekin* and *Lettre de Siberie*. Developing his unique style, he later created such striking works as *¡Cuba sí!* (1961), *Le joli mai* (1962), *Le Fond de l'air est rouge* (1977), *Sans soleil* (1982), *A.K.* (a portrait of Akira Kurosawa, 1985) and *One Day in the Life of Andrei Arsenevich* (about Tarkovsky, 2000).

❧ American avant-garde filmmakers **Robert Nelson** (*Oh Dem Watermelons*, 1965) and **Stephen Dwoskin** (*Central Bazaar*, 1976) died in January and June, aged 81 and 73 respectively.

RALPH McQUARRIE

Born: *13 June 1929, Gary, Indiana, USA.*
Died: *3 March 2012, Berkeley, California, USA.*
This Korean War veteran and Boeing technical artist little knew what awaited him when asked by George Lucas in 1974 to prepare conceptual art for an upcoming space fantasy. The result, released three years later, was *Star Wars*, its characters, settings and even locations meticulously mapped out in advance by McQuarrie – and further developed by him in the follow-ups *The Empire Strikes Back* and *Return of the Jedi*. His intensely visual imagination was also called upon by Steven Spielberg (*Close Encounters of the Third Kind*, *Raiders of the Lost Ark*, *E.T.*, **batteries not included*), as well as in *Star Trek IV: The Voyage Home* and the TV series *Battlestar Galactica*. In 1985 he won a Best Visual Effects Oscar for *Cocoon*.

Patricia Medina

❧ **Matthew Yuricich**, who was Oscar-nominated for *Close Encounters* the year after winning a Special Achievement Oscar for the visual effects in *Logan's Run*, died at 89 in May. Conceptual artist **Jean Giraud** (*Alien*, *The Abyss*) died at 73 in March, and award-winning visual effects producer **Eileen Moran** (*The Lord of the Rings*, *Avatar*) died in December, aged 60.

PATRICIA MEDINA

Born: *19 July 1919, Liverpool, England.*
Died: *28 April 2012, Los Angeles, California, USA.*
A dash of exoticism in Patricia Medina's otherwise porcelain good looks (she was half-Spanish) saw her adding smoulder to numerous Hollywood swashbucklers, but she started out in British productions like *Simply Terrific* (1938), *The Day Will Dawn* (1942), *Don't Take It to Heart* and *Hotel Reserve* (both 1944). Transplanted to the US, she appeared in comedy (*Francis*, 1950) and 3D Gothic (*Phantom of the Rue Morgue*, 1954) but mainly in titles like *The Fighting O'Flynn*, *Aladdin and His Lamp*, *Lady in the Iron Mask*, *Siren of Bagdad* and *Pirates of Tripoli*. Other credits included *Botany Bay* (1953), Orson Welles' *Mr Arkadin* (1955) and, her last notable film, *The Killing of Sister George* (1968). Married latterly to Joseph Cotten, she embarked with him on several US stage tours.

CLAUDE MILLER

Born: *20 February 1942, Paris, France.*
Died: *4 April 2012, Paris, France.*
Though he was assistant director to Bresson, Demy and Godard, it was Claude Miller's numerous production manager duties for François Truffaut that most influenced him. He made his first feature as writer-director, *La meilleure façon de marcher*, in 1975, following it six years later with the highly successful policier *Garde à vue*. As well as winning four Césars, this film gave notice of the grim world view that would permeate Miller's later work, much of which focused on the injustices suffered by children. In the process he boosted Charlotte Gainsbourg (in *L'Effrontée* and *La petite voleuse*, the latter an unrealised Truffaut project)

Claude Miller

Mila Parély

and, later, Ludivine Sagnier (*La petite Lili*). Other titles included *Mortelle randonée*, *L'Accompagnatrice* and the Cannes prize-winner *La Classe de neige*. His last film, *Thérèse Desqueyroux*, was released posthumously.

MILA PARÉLY

Born: *7 October 1917, Paris, France.*
Died: *14 January 2012, Desertines, Auvergne, France.*
Memorable for her aristocratically fine-boned features, the one-time Olga Colette Peszynski numbered Fritz Lang's *Liliom* among the films she made as a teenager, subsequently appearing in such classics as Renoir's *La Règle du jeu* (1938), Bresson's *Les Anges du péché* (1943), Cocteau's *La Belle et la bête* (1946) and Ophüls' *Le Plaisir* (1952). She also replaced Arletty in Sacha Guitry's *Remontons les Champs-Élysées* (1938) and played George Sand in the Liszt biopic *Rêves d'amour* (1946). Later she went to England for the Gainsborough thriller *Snowbound* (1948) and the fledgling Hammer 'B' *Blood Orange* (1953), retiring soon afterwards to look after her injured husband, Scots racing driver 'Taso' Mathieson. She returned only twice; for *Comédie d'été* (1989) and the 1991 TV movie *La grande dune*.

❧ Also born in Paris, Folies Bergère dancer **Olympe Bradna** went, not to England, but Hollywood, making several exotic Paramount appearances between 1936 and 1941; she died in November, aged 92.

FRANK PIERSON

Born: *12 May 1925, Chappaqua, New York, USA.*
Died: *22 July 2012, Los Angeles, California, USA.*
Having gained writer-producer-director experience via the CBS television series *Have Gun – Will Travel*, Frank Pierson followed up in 1965 with a Best Screenplay Oscar nomination for the droll Western *Cat Ballou*. Two years later he received another for Stuart Rosenberg's classic *Cool Hand Luke* (which contained the immortal line "What we've got here is a failure to communicate"), then in 1975 he finally won – for Sidney Lumet's *Dog Day Afternoon*. An earlier Lumet

heist picture, *The Anderson Tapes*, was also written by Pierson, who in the meantime had moved into direction himself with *The Looking Glass War* (1969), *A Star is Born* (1976) and *King of the Gypsies* (1978). Latterly he wrote *Presumed Innocent* (1989) and was a producer on the hit TV series *Mad Men*.

❧ Playwright **William Hanley**, writer of numerous TV movies and the 1969 feature *The Gypsy Moths*, died in May, aged 80. Also in May, novelist **Frederick E Smith** (whose work inspired two very different British films, both made in 1963 – *Devil Doll* and *633 Squadron*) died at the age of 93. And Australian actor **Jonathan Hardy**, who was Oscar-nominated in 1980 for co-writing *Breaker Morant*, died at 71 in July.

CLAUDE PINOTEAU

Born: *25 May 1925, Boulogne-Billancourt, France.*
Died: *5 October 2012, Neuilly-sur-Seine, France.*
In the film industry from 14, Claude Pinoteau became assistant director to, among others, Jean Cocteau (*Orphée*) and Max Ophüls (*Lola Montès*). In 1972 he graduated to writer-director in his own right with *Le Silencieux*, the first of four collaborations with craggy character star Lino Ventura. The second, *La Gifle*, won the Prix Louis-Delluc and launched 18-year-old Isabelle Adjani. Confirming his popular touch, Pinoteau then scored a massive hit in 1980 with *La Boum*, which in turn launched 13-year-old Sophie Marceau. It also became a cult film to an entire generation and was followed by two further Marceau vehicles, *La Boum 2* and *L'Étudiante*. For his final film, Pinoteau starred Isabelle Huppert and Philippe Noiret in *Les Palmes de M Schutz* (1996).

Claude Pinoteau

French writer-director **Pierre Schoendoerffer** (who won an Oscar for the 1967 Vietnam documentary *The Anderson Platoon*) died at 83 in March, while writer-actor-director **Jean Henri-Roger** died in December, aged 63.

MARTIN POLL

Born: *24 November 1922, New York City, New York, USA.*
Died: *14 April 2012, New York City, New York, USA.*
In reviving New York's old Biograph facility as Gold Medal Studios, Martin Poll put the city back on the filmmakers' map and in 1959 became 'Borough Commissioner of Motion Picture Arts'. Three years later he turned producer in his own right with the Glenn Ford vehicle *Love is a Ball*. There followed the multi-Oscar-winning 1968 hit *The Lion in Winter*, after which he put his name to *The Possession of Joel Delaney*, *Night Watch*, *The Man who Loved Cat Dancing*, *Love and Death* and *The Sailor who Fell from Grace with the Sea* – offbeat 1970s showcases for Shirley MacLaine, Elizabeth Taylor, Burt Reynolds, Woody Allen and Kris Kristofferson respectively. Later titles included *Nighthawks*, *Haunted Summer* and a 2003 TV remake of *The Lion in Winter*.

Lee Rich, whose producer credits ranged from *Helter Skelter* and *The Choirboys* to *Just Cause* and *The Score*, died at 93 in May. **Hank Moonjean** – producer of *The Great Gatsby*, *Dangerous Liaisons* and half-a-dozen Burt Reynolds vehicles – died in October, aged 82. Broadway producer **Martin Richards**, whose screen ventures ranged from *The Boys from Brazil* (1978) to *Chicago* (2002), died at 80 in November. Canadian producer **John Kemeny** (*Atlantic City*, *Quest for Fire*, *The Gate*) died the same month, aged 87. Also from Canada, director-writer-producer **Roman Kroitor** – the documentarist who co-invented the IMAX process – died at 85 in September.

DEBORAH RAFFIN

Born: *13 March 1953, Los Angeles, California, USA.*
Died: *21 November 2012, Los Angeles, California, USA.*
Though an iconic face of the 1970s, Deborah Raffin's cinema career never quite took off. Starting as Liv Ullmann's daughter in *40 Carats* (1973), she received a big publicity push the following year in *The Dove*, leading directly to the torrid potboiler *Once is Not Enough* (in which her mother Trudy Marshall also appeared). After a mid-'70s detour into horror (*God Told Me To*, *The Sentinel*), she missed out on the lead in *Grease*; then, after *Touched by Love* in 1980, she retreated in the main to TV. By the time she starred in the 1993 film *Morning Glory* (which she co-wrote with *Dove* director Charles Jarrott), she had co-founded a highly successful 'talking books' business, named (in honour of her breakthrough film) Dove Books on Tape.

Other US actresses who died in 2012 included **Dimitra Arliss**, who died at 79 in January, **Janet Carroll** (May, 71), **Lupe Ontiveros** (July, 69), **Leigh Hamilton** (September, 62) and actress-dancer **Zina Bethune** (February, 66). **Sammi Kane Kraft**, who played the Tatum O'Neal role in the 2005 remake of *The Bad News Bears*, died in October, aged 20.

CARLO RAMBALDI

Born: *15 September 1925, Vigarano Mainarda, Italy.*
Died: *10 August 2012, Lamezia Terme, Calabria, Italy.*
Long before the advent of the CGI effects he so eloquently loathed, this animatronics pioneer began as he meant to go on – with a fire-belching dragon in the 1957 Siegfried retread *Sigfrido*. As special effects guru for horror masters Mario Bava, Lucio Fulci and Dario Argento, he added such shockers as *Terrore nello spazio* (1965), *Una lucertola con la pelle di donna* (1971) and *Profondo Rosso* (1974) to his resumé, then got his Hollywood break via Dino De Laurentiis' *King Kong* remake. Having won his first of three Oscars, he staked his claim to immortality with *Alien* (realising HR Giger's creature designs) and, for Steven Spielberg, *Close Encounters of the Third Kind* and *E.T.* (realising his own). Later titles included *The Hand*, the tentacled sex monster in Zulawski's *Possession*, *Cat's Eye*, *Dune* and *Silver Bullet*.

Gerry Anderson, Britain's inspired creator of 'Supermarionation' via classic TV series like *Fireball XL5* and *Stingray*, was also writer-producer of such 1960s feature films as *Thunderbirds Are GO* and *Doppelgänger*; he died in December, aged 83.

Deborah Raffin

TRACY REED

Born: *21 September 1942, London, England.*
Died: *2 May 2012, West Cork, Ireland.*

Daughter of one film director (Anthony Pelissier), step-daughter of another (Carol Reed), grand-daughter of Fay Compton… It was perhaps inevitable that Tracy Reed became an actress. After plenty of TV work as a teen, she had the distinction of being the only woman in the 1963 Kubrick classic *Dr Strangelove*. Her Titian-haired beauty was then featured in the Clouseau sequel *A Shot in the Dark*, the quaint vampire opus *Devils of Darkness*, the Michael Winner comedy *You Must Be Joking!* and such modish titles of the day as *Casino Royale*, *Maroc 7* and *Hammerhead*. A few sex comedies (*Percy*, *Fun and Games*) were followed by *The* (rock-bottom) *Deadly Females* in 1976, upon which she retired.

LINA ROMAY

Born: *25 June 1954, Barcelona, Cataluña, Spain.*
Died: *15 February 2012, Málaga, Andalucía, Spain.*

Rosa María Almirall Martínez first encountered the maverick Spanish director Jesús Franco in 1971. Their first film together was *La maldición de Frankenstein* and Franco immediately saw in her an uncanny echo of his recently deceased muse Soledad Miranda. Taking the name of the Mexican-American singer Lina Romay, she then made a major impact on Euro-cult fans with her uninhibited performance in Franco's *Les Avaleuses*, playing Irina Karlstein – 'The Bare-Breasted Countess' of one of the film's numerous alternative titles. Over 30 years later she was Dr Van Helsing in Franco's impoverished *Snakewoman*, having long since become not only his partner but also a fetishist icon in his wildly unpredictable films. They eventually married in 2008.

❖ **Nathalie Perrey**, longtime associate (both before and behind the camera) of France's fetish-fantastique director

Jean Rollin, died in March, aged 83. **Frank Braña**, veteran of numerous Spaghetti Westerns and Spanish horrors, died the previous month at 77. **Bill Hinzman**, the celebrated 'cemetery ghoul' of George Romero's *Night of the Living Dead*, also died in February, aged 75.

ANN RUTHERFORD

Born: *2 November 1917, Vancouver, British Columbia, Canada.*
Died: *11 June 2012, Beverly Hills, California, USA.*

As a teenager, Ann Rutherford starred in 'B' Westerns opposite John Wayne and Gene Autry prior to being signed by MGM. In addition to titles like *Of Human Hearts* and *Pride and Prejudice*, she played Mickey Rooney's feisty but faithful girlfriend in the studio's long-lived Andy Hardy pictures, plus Red Skelton's wife in *Whistling in the Dark* and two sequels. She was also loaned out to play Vivien Leigh's younger sister in *Gone with the Wind*, later leaving Metro and appearing opposite Danny Kaye in *The Secret Life of Walter Mitty* and Errol Flynn in *The Adventures of Don Juan*. After 1950 she confined herself to TV, reappearing in a couple of 1970s features but declining the role of Kate Winslet's older self in the 1997 blockbuster *Titanic*.

FREDERICA SAGOR

Born: *6 July 1900, New York City, New York, USA.*
Died: *5 January 2012, La Mesa, California, USA.*

Frederica Sagor was one of the last survivors of the silent era. As a screenwriter, she tangled with such moguls of the day as BP Schulberg, Carl Laemmle and Harry Rapf while crafting Jazz Age 'youth appeal' hits like *The Plastic Age*, *Silk Legs*, *The Waning Sex*, *Rolled Stockings* and *Red Hair* – in the process helping to promote such stars as Clara Bow, Madge Bellamy, Louise Brooks and Norma Shearer. She married Ernest Maas in 1927 but they had no luck in touting themselves as a screenwriting team until

Tracy Reed

Ann Rutherford

Frederica Sagor

Dinah Sheridan

Darryl F Zanuck bought their story for *The Shocking Miss Pilgrim* in 1945. Sagor's 1999 memoir bore the same title and – given her conviction that the "SOBs are all below" – was an unsparing exposé of early Hollywood.

❧ In addition to 111-year-old Sagor and 103-year-old Pola Illéry [qv], other centenarians who died in 2012 included Chinese director **Tang Xiaodan** (January), US actress **Fern Persons** (July) and German director **Kurt Maetzig** (August), all at 101. **Alma Bella**, sexy siren of early Filipino cinema, died in March, aged 102, and Spanish actress **Carmen Martínez Sierra** in November, at 108.

HARRIS SAVIDES
Born: *28 September 1957, New York City, New York, USA.*
Died: *9 October 2012, New York City, New York, USA.*
Having lit music videos for Madonna, Nine Inch Nails and REM, Harris Savides shot the title sequence of David Fincher's *Se7en* in 1995 and thereafter was DP on Fincher's *The Game*. Via a fruitful collaboration with Gus Van Sant (*Finding Forrester*, *Gerry*, *Elephant*, *Last Days*, *Milk*, *Restless*), Savides perfected a boldly minimalist style governed by his method of lighting spaces rather than faces. Much in demand, he also worked with Noah Baumbach (*Margot at the Wedding*, *Greenberg*), James Gray (*The Yards*), Ridley Scott (*American Gangster*), Woody Allen (*Whatever Works*) and with Jonathan Glazer on perhaps Savides' most texturally striking work, *Birth*. In 2005 he rejoined Fincher for the innovative digital filming of *Zodiac*, later working with Sofia Coppola on *Somewhere* and (his last film, released posthumously) *The Bling Ring*.

TONY SCOTT
Born: *21 June 1944, North Shields, Northumberland, England.*
Died: *19 August 2012, San Pedro, California, USA.*
Like his elder brother Ridley, Tony Scott came up via art school and eye-catching commercials to direct

a clutch of box-office heavy-hitters with a generous helping of visual flash. After the sombrely untypical *Loving Memory* (1970), his first Hollywood feature, the Sapphic vampire saga *The Hunger*, appeared in 1983, whereupon Scott put his boldly kinetic stamp on the Tom Cruise vehicles *Top Gun* (1986) and *Days of Thunder* (1990), interleaving these with *Beverly Hills Cop II* (1987). After the dazzling, Tarantino-scripted ensemble piece *True Romance* (1993), Scott's style sobered somewhat for *Crimson Tide* (1995), the first of numerous collaborations with Denzel Washington; the last of these was also Scott's last film of all, *Unstoppable* (2010). Other titles include *Revenge*, *Enemy of the State* and *Domino*. His suicide, jumping from an LA bridge, shocked the film community.

❧ **Bob Brooks**, American guru of British advertising and director of the 1981 feature *Tattoo*, died in September, aged 84.

DINAH SHERIDAN
Born: *17 September 1920, Hampstead Garden Suburb, England.*
Died: *25 November 2012, Northwood, Middlesex, England.*
Of German-Russian extraction, Dinah Sheridan met Jimmy Hanley on the 1936 film *Landslide* and married him six years later. As well as being cast opposite Hanley in several further projects, she also appeared

in, among others, *Get Cracking* (with George Formby), *Calling Paul Temple*, *The Story of Shirley Yorke* and *The Huggetts Abroad*. Then a clutch of early 1950s titles – *Where No Vultures Fly*, *The Sound Barrier*, *Appointment in London* and particularly the evergreen comedy *Genevieve* – promised major stardom. But at this point she married the tyrannical Rank chief John Davis, who terminated her career. Her dryly humorous charm was only seen again as the Edwardian mother in *The Railway Children* (1970), though plenty of latterday TV yielded the 1980s sitcom *Don't Wait Up*.

❧ Other English actresses who died during the period under review included **Lila Kaye** (in January, aged 82), **Faith Brook** (March, 90), **Stella Tanner** (also March, 87), **Charlotte Mitchell** (May, 85), **Dorinda Stevens** (October, 80), **Dolores Mantez** (November, 76) and **Daphne Oxenford** (December, 93). Irish-born stage star **Joyce Redman** (who died in May, also aged 93) made only five films but was Oscar-nominated for two of them (*Tom Jones* and *Othello*). Another Irish actress, **Maureen Toal**, died at 81 in August. And French ballerina **Katherine Kath**, whose British screen career yielded the role of La Goulue in John Huston's *Moulin Rouge*, died in November at 92.

KANETÔ SHINDÔ

Born: *22 April 1912, Hiroshima, Japan.*
Died: *29 May 2012, Hiroshima, Japan.*
The fact that writer-director Kanetô Shindô was born in Hiroshima and served in World War II resonated throughout much of his work. Man's inhumanity to man, rendered in limpidly atmospheric monochrome, was the keynote of his international breakthrough films, *The Island* (1960) and *Onibaba* (1964); the latter was sufficiently grim (intensely so) to be lionised by horror aficionados, leading to Shindô's more straightforwardly supernatural *Kuroneko* (1968). Having begun in the industry in 1934 and trained under Kenzo Mizoguchi, he directed his first films – *Story of a Beloved Wife* and *Children of Hiroshima* – in the early 1950s; starring in these, and almost all his work until her death in 1994, was his lover (and eventual third wife) Nobuko Otowa. His last film, *Postcard*, was released in 2011 and set in the aftermath of World War II.

Kanetô Shindô

❧ Actor-producer **Taketoshi Naitô**, who appeared in Shindô's *An Actress* and *Lucky Dragon No 5* and in Kon Ichikawa's *The Burmese Harp*, died in August, aged 86.

VICTOR SPINETTI

Born: *2 September 1929, Cwm, Ebbw Vale, Wales.*
Died: *18 June 2012, Monmouth, Monmouthshire, Wales.*
Of Italian extraction, the brilliant comic actor Victor Spinetti came to prominence as a member of Joan Littlewood's Theatre Workshop, winning a Tony Award when her production of *Oh! What a Lovely War* reached Broadway. He also starred opposite Jack Klugman in the West End première of *The Odd Couple*. In the interim he had been lionised by The Beatles, who insisted on him being cast in their films *A Hard Day's Night*, *Help!* and (on TV) *Magical Mystery Tour*. His other films included *Sparrows Can't Sing*, *The Taming of the Shrew*, *Start the Revolution Without Me*, *Under Milk Wood* (for which he was a natural), *The Return of the Pink Panther*, *Voyage of the Damned*, *Emily*, *Under the Cherry Moon* and *The Krays*.

❧ Two other Welsh character players, **Peter Halliday** and **Philip Madoc**, died in February and March, aged 87 and 77 respectively. Ireland's **David Kelly** died in February at 82, while Canadian **Ronan O'Casey** (89) and Greek-Cypriot **Paul Stassino** (82) – both much employed in post-war British films and TV – died in April and June respectively. And **John Forrest**, the American-born but very British teen actor who played Flashman in the 1951 version of *Tom Brown's Schooldays*, died in May, aged 80.

BRUCE SURTEES

Born: *3 August 1937, Los Angeles, California, USA.*
Died: *23 February 2012, Carmel, California, USA.*
Son of the Oscar-winning cinematographer Robert Surtees, Bruce Surtees was himself Oscar-nominated for the smoke-wreathed chiaroscuro of *Lenny* (1974). His first film as full-fledged DP – lighting the creepy Southern Gothic of *The Beguiled* (1970) – marked the beginning of long associations with director Don Siegel and actor-director Clint Eastwood, throwing up an impressive list of titles that included *Play Misty for Me*, *Dirty Harry*, *High Plains Drifter*, *The Outlaw Josey Wales*, *Escape from Alcatraz*, *Honkytonk Man* and *Pale Rider*. As one of the quintessential 1970s cinematographers, he also shot *Blume in Love*, *Night Moves*, *The Shootist* and *Big Wednesday*. The last of these, along with '80s credits like *Risky Business* and *Beverly Hills Cop*, proved that he was just as capable of glitz as gloom. His last film, in 2001, was *Joshua*.

❧ Surtees' contemporary **Ric Waite** – whose credits as cinematographer included *The Long Riders*, *Footloose* and *Red Dawn* – died in February at 78. Other US filmmakers who died in 2012 included costume designer **Richard Bruno** (January, 87), production designer **J Michael Riva** (June, 63), documentarist **George C Stoney** (July, 96), editors **Neil Travis** (March, 75) and **Dann Cahn** (November, 89), and Polish-born documentarist **Irving Saraf** (December, 80).

Eric Sykes

Joan Taylor

ERIC SYKES

Born: *4 May 1923, Oldham, Lancashire, England.*
Died: *4 July 2012, Esher, Surrey, England.*
One of the greatest names in post-war British comedy, Eric Sykes got his start writing scripts for Frankie Howerd, then in the 1960s became a TV star in his own right via the BBC's *Sykes and a...* series, in which he formed a winning partnership with Hattie Jacques. Feature films inevitably followed, among them *Kill or Cure*, *Heavens Above!*, *One Way Pendulum*, *Rotten to the Core*, the big-budget marathons *Those Magnificent Men in Their Flying Machines* and *Monte Carlo or Bust!*, his own 'silent' featurette *The Plank*, *Shalako* and *Theatre of Blood*. Despite having been deaf for decades and latterly blind, he continued to appear in complicated stage farces together with such 21st century films as *The Others* and *Harry Potter and the Goblet of Fire*.

◆ Sykes' comic contemporary **Max Bygraves**, who died at 89 in August, starred in four films, among them *Charley Moon* and *Spare the Rod*.

JOAN TAYLOR

Born: *18 August 1929, Geneva, Illinois, USA.*
Died: *4 March 2012, Santa Monica, California, USA.*
Trained at the Pasadena Playhouse, Joan Taylor was plucked from there, aged 19, to star alongside Randolph Scott in *Fighting Man of the Plains*. More Westerns followed, playing opposite Charlton Heston (*The Savage*), Robert Stack (*War Paint*), Lloyd Bridges (*Apache Woman*) and Lex Barker (*War Drums*). She also appeared in the Bob Hope comedy *Off Limits*, the MGM musical *Rose Marie* and two SF classics, *Earth vs the Flying Saucers* and *20 Million Miles to Earth*, released in 1956 and 1957 respectively. After much television, she retired in 1962 but, on the death of her husband Leonard Freeman, assumed control of the TV show he'd created, *Hawaii Five-O*. Latterly, she had writing credits on a few TV movies plus the 1997 feature *Fools Rush In*.

PHYLLIS THAXTER

Born: *20 November 1919, Portland, Maine, USA.*
Died: *14 August 2012, Orlando, Florida, USA.*
After Broadway experience (during which she was romantically involved with Montgomery Clift),

Phyllis Thaxter made a big impact in her first film – as the wife of war hero Van Johnson in *Thirty Seconds Over Tokyo* (1944). Thereafter, however, she was cast rather interchangeably as sympathetic helpmeets to, among others, Robert Ryan, Burt Lancaster, Randolph Scott, Gary Cooper, Gig Young and Ronald Reagan. More interesting roles surfaced in *Bewitched* (as a split personality) and especially the Ernest Hemingway adaptation *The Breaking Point* (as John Garfield's level-headed wife). Previously signed to Metro, her Warners contract was terminated in 1952 when she contracted polio. After lots of television, she returned in 1978 (courtesy of her son-in-law, producer Ilya Salkind) as the title character's adoptive mother in *Superman*.

SUSAN TYRRELL

Born: *18 March 1945, San Francisco, California, USA.*
Died: *16 June 2012, Austin, Texas, USA.*
Smoky-voiced queen of midnight movies, Susan Tyrrell was a member of the Warhol set prior to gaining an Oscar nomination as alcoholic Oma in John Huston's 1972 release *Fat City*. Thereafter she became typed in offbeat roles in equally offbeat films, among them *Bad* (for Warhol), *Forbidden Zone*, *Tales of Ordinary Madness* (opposite Ben Gazzara, qv), *Angel*, *Big Top Pee-Wee* (as a

Gore Vidal

The American film critic **Andrew Sarris** (who in 1962 propagated the auteur theory) died in October, aged 83. The anti-auteurist critic **Judith Crist**, famous for her appearances on NBC's *Today* show, died in August at 90. Another influential American critic, **Elliott Stein** – who acted in such films as *Secrets of Sex* (in Britain) and *Les Apprentis sorciers* (in France) – died at 83 in November. And England's own **Philip Jenkinson** – presenter of the BBC's *Film Night* and latterly an archivist – died in March, aged 76.

SIMON WARD

Born: *19 October 1941, Beckenham, Kent, England.*
Died: *20 July 2012, Taunton, Somerset, England.*
Like his contemporary Jon Finch [qv], Simon Ward started his film career with Hammer (*Frankenstein Must Be Destroyed*, 1969) and then was given a major push in 1972; in Ward's case it was the heroic lead in Richard Attenborough's epic *Young Winston*. Also like Finch, he followed up with prestige projects (*The Three Musketeers*, *All Creatures Great and Small*, *Aces High*) before devolving into continental obscurities like *Die Standarte* (in which they both appeared). Later titles included *Zulu Dawn*, *The Monster Club* and *Supergirl*, while in his last film, *Wuthering Heights* (1992), he was aptly cast as his daughter Sophie's father. He also reprised his Winston Churchill in the massive Turkish mini-series *Kurtulus* (1994).

British actress **Angharad Rees** (*Under Milk Wood*, *Hands of the Ripper*) died the day after Ward, aged 68. Five days later, **Mary Tamm** (*The Odessa File*, *The Likely Lads*) died at 62.

ISUZU YAMADA

Born: *5 February 1917, Osaka, Japan.*
Died: *9 July 2012, Inagi, Tokyo, Japan.*
Perhaps best remembered in the West for her accusatory to-camera stare at the end of Mizoguchi's *Osaka Elegy* (1936) and her hair-raisingly atavistic consort to Toshiro Mifune in Kurosawa's *Throne of Blood* (1956), Isuzu Yamada signed up with the Nikkatsu company aged just 13. After making a few late silents, she became an iconic figure early on thanks to the transgressive young women she played for Mizoguchi in *The Downfall*, *Sisters of the Gion* and *Osaka Elegy*. She also made several films for Mikio Naruse and Teinosuke Kinugasa, plus one film – *Tokyo Twilight* – with Ozu. But it was the Noh-trained physical precision she brought to her Kurosawa films – including also *The Lower Depths* and *Yojimbo* – that brought her international attention. In 2000 she became the first actress to receive Japan's Imperial Order of Culture.

Keiko Tsushima (86) and **Noriko Sengoku** (90), both of whom appeared in Kurosawa's *Seven Samurai*, died in August and December respectively. **Hideji Ōtaki**, whose film appearances ranged from Kurosawa's *Kagemusha* to Itami's *Tampopo*, died at 87 in October, and action star **Hideaki Nitani** (best known for the 1966 yakuza film *Tokyo Drifter*) died in January, aged 81.

midget) and *Cry-Baby* (as Johnny Depp's grandmother). In 2000, shortly after playing a one-legged drunk in *Buddy Boy*, she lost both her legs to a rare blood disease. According to Stacy Keach (her co-star in *Fat City* and, four years later, *The Killer Inside Me*), "She was like the Billie Holliday of the dispossessed. She sang the blues with every word she spoke."

GORE VIDAL

Born: *3 October 1925, West Point, New York, USA.*
Died: *31 July 2012, Los Angeles, California, USA.*
This lordly mandarin of US letters published his first novel, *Williwaw*, aged 20. He was also a screenwriter, winning an Emmy for his TV work and then writing José Ferrer's 1957 film *I Accuse!* Later he had an uncredited hand in *Ben-Hur*, co-wrote René Clément's *Is Paris Burning?* and adapted his friend Tennessee Williams' *Suddenly, Last Summer*. His own plays, meanwhile, gave rise to the films *The Left Handed Gun*, *Visit to a Small Planet* and *The Best Man*. Then, at either end of the 1970s, his name became indelibly associated with the cinematic scandals *Myra Breckinridge* (sex-change extravaganza) and *Caligula* (*Penthouse*-sponsored porn fest). Latterly, he also acted from time to time, as in *Bob Roberts* and *Gattaca*, and in 1992 he published the moviegoing memoir *Screening History*.

Richard D Zanuck

RICHARD D ZANUCK

Born: *13 December 1934, Los Angeles, California, USA.*
Died: *13 July 2012, Beverly Hills, California, USA.*
Dying at the same age (77) as his father – Fox mogul Darryl F Zanuck – Richard D Zanuck had long since emerged from his intimidating shadow. After producing the Leopold and Loeb drama *Compulsion* in 1959, he took charge of Fox aged 27 and helped turn around the *Cleopatra* fiasco with *The Sound of Music*. In 1970, however, he was fired by Zanuck Sr and struck out on his own with production partner David Brown. They soon racked up a smash hit with *The Sting* and a bona-fide phenomenon with *Jaws*. Later titles included *The Eiger Sanction*, *MacArthur* and, in the 1980s, *The Verdict*, *Cocoon* and *Target*. Having picked up the 1989 Best Picture Oscar for *Driving Miss Daisy*, Zanuck's subsequent films included *Mulholland Falls*, *Road to Perdition* and a half-dozen Tim Burton pictures, culminating with the 2012 release *Dark Shadows*.

Other film personalities who died during the period under review included:

From Australia: performers **Grant Tilly** (April, 74), **Jon Finlayson** (September, 74) and **Patricia Kennedy** (December, 96), plus writer-director **Albie Thoms** (November, 71). In February, Australian deep-sea documentarist **Andrew Wight** (52) and his US counterpart **Mike deGruy** (60) died in the same helicopter crash. And New Zealand sound editor **Mike Hopkins** died in December, aged 53.

From mainland Europe: Danish actresses **Hanne Borchsenius** (76) and **Ulla Lock** (78) died in March and September respectively, and Dutch actress **Will van Kralingen** (61) in November. Czech animators **Břetislav Pojar** (89) and **Vladimir Jiranek** (74) died in October and November. Also: Belgian documentarist **Luc de Heusch** (May, 86) and Oscar-nominated Dutch production designer **Ben Van Os** (July, 67), together with Dutch actor **Piet Römer** (January, 83), Hungarian actor **Hugó Gruber** (July, 74), Danish actor **Henning Moritzen** (August, 84) and Romanian actor **Iurie Darie** (October, 83). Norwegian actors **Tom Tellefsen** (80) and **Per Sunderland** (87) died in January and June, and Norwegian producer **Tomas Evjen** (39) in September.

Turkish-born Greek actor **Athinodoros Prousalis** died at 85 in June, Turkish actor **Ekrem Bora** (78) in April and Egyptian actor **Ahmed**

Ramzy (82) in August. From Russia: actors **Anatoly Ravikovich** (April, 75), **Igor Kvasha** (August, 79) and **Alexander Belyavsky** (September, 80), actresses **Lyudmila Kasatkina** (February, 86), **Lyudmila Shagalova** (March, 88), **Marina Golub** (October, 54) and **Natalya Kustinskaya** (December, 74), and screenwriter **Eduard Volodarsky** (October, 71).

Chinese actresses **Zhang Ruifang** (94) and **Jacqueline Law** (45) both died in June, Chinese screenwriter **Szeto Kam-Yuen** (48) in October, and Taiwanese mogul **Yang Teng-Kuei** (74) in December. Finally, from Japan: Oscar-winning designer **Eiko Ishioka** died at 73 in January and 'pink' star **Nao Saejima** in September, aged 44.

Hanne Borchsenius

Afterword

by **Mansel Stimpson**

So, how is 2013 working out cinematically speaking? As I write this I have probably seen about half of the year's releases that will come my way, but most of the summer's big movies have yet to appear. The latest screen version of F Scott Fitzgerald's *The Great Gatsby* is one such, but, as now seems to have become inevitable, many of the films in this category are the latest instalments of established franchises. Regardless of what the weather was doing, summer came a little early this year with Tom Cruise in *Oblivion*, followed by *Olympus Has Fallen* in which the White House was threatened. But these were soon overshadowed by the first franchise addition in the shape of *Iron Man 3*, which, with the bonus of an unexpected stand-out performance from Sir Ben Kingsley, looked set to be a hit.

As for those currently on the horizon, it's anybody's guess which will be the winners and which the losers. There must be some people out there who can't wait to see *Fast and Furious 6*, but surely there are rather more who are eager to assess Henry Cavill's turn as Superman in *Man of Steel*. By the end of the summer the White House will be in danger yet again, this time in Roland Emmerich's *White House Down*, but in the meantime there's the little matter of saving the planet. Given its delayed appearance, *World War Z* with Brad Pitt is less obviously inviting than *Pacific Rim*, which has the cachet of being directed by Guillermo del Toro. Also due is *300: Rise of an Empire*, and for fans of *X-Men* there's *The Wolverine*. But for a fresh chapter in a well-established franchise *Star Trek Into Darkness* has led the way with aplomb.

Nevertheless, connoisseurs of futuristic tales might put their money on *Elysium* since it was directed by Neill Blomkamp, who made that cult hit *District 9*. The recent form shown by

Leonardo DiCaprio and Carey Mulligan in *The Great Gatsby*.

M Night Shyamalan holds out less promise for *After Earth*, but this science fiction piece does reunite on screen Will Smith and his son Jaden. The odd one out here features a figure from the remote past, but he's not to be ignored for *The Lone Ranger* reappears in the form of Johnny Depp.

Although fantasy action movies dominate in the summer months, 2013 does see entrants in other popular fields to rival them. Comedies lined up include *The Hangover Part III*, *The Big Wedding*, *Stand Up Guys* and *The Internship*, while we're back to the end of the world, viewed in rather different terms, in both *This is the End* starring Seth Rogen and *The World's End* featuring Simon Pegg (here reunited with director Edgar Wright). For some a high spot will undoubtedly be the arrival on the big screen of Steve Coogan's Alan Partridge character in *Alan Partridge: Alpha Papa*; also eagerly awaited is *Kick-Ass 2*. Meanwhile animation weighs in with such titles as *Epic*, *Despicable Me 2* and Pixar's *Monsters University*.

As ever, at the beginning of the year our cinemas were filled with the movies that would fight it out at the Oscars, and some of those contending were distinctly better than others. I would cite Tom Hooper's *Les Misérables* as a splendid example of how to give a stage musical real cinematic power. In contrasted mode, *The Sessions*, with its adult and sensitive handling of a polio victim's engagement with sex, deserved far more recognition than it got. As for *Django Unchained*, for better and for

worse it told you everything you need to know about Quentin Tarantino.

It would certainly have been a sin had *Lincoln* not carried off the Best Actor Oscar for Daniel Day-Lewis, but otherwise I found Spielberg's film dry. Similarly it was the acting more than the film that I admired in the case of *Zero Dark Thirty* – and in saying that I think of Jennifer Ehle no less than Jessica Chastain. Ditto when it came to Denzel Washington in *Flight* which, following its spectacular crash landing in the opening reel, turned into a saga about an alcoholic's reformation but failed to take off.

Indeed, it could be said that in 2013 many actors were seen doing great work in films that were interesting without being wholly successful. I think of Ryan Gosling acting Bradley Cooper off the screen in the three-part drama *The Place Beyond the Pines*, Jack Black in Richard Linklater's oddity *Bernie*, Frank Langella in the comic yet touching *Robot & Frank*, Jude Law in Soderbergh's *Side Effects*, Matthias Schoenaerts in the Belgian drama *Bullhead*, the Chinese actress Zhao Tao in the Italian movie *Sun Li and the Poet* and Ann Dowd stepping into a leading role with absolute assurance in *Compliance*.

Turning to films which consistently achieved more on their own terms, four other performances demand to be noticed. Richard Gere gave a career-best turn in the drama *Arbitrage*, while Matthew Goode displayed more star quality than ever before in *Stoker*, that eccentric but undervalued film from Chan-wook

Nick Frost, Eddie Marsan, Simon Pegg, Paddy Considine and Martin Freeman in *World's End*.

Helen Mirren and Anthony Hopkins in *Hitchcock*.

Ken Loach returned to documentary for *The Spirit of '45*.

Park. In *Before Sunrise* (1993) and its sequel *Before Sunset* (2004) Ethan Hawke and Julie Delpy proved a perfect team; in reuniting with their roles once more in *Before Midnight* they have now completed a trilogy that does them and their director Richard Linklater proud.

The early months of 2013 brought several films which, following in the wake of such hits as *The Best Exotic Marigold Hotel*, seem primarily aimed at older cinemagoers. Tom Courtenay brought distinction to *Quartet*, Vanessa Redgrave's sincerity did much for *Song for Marion* and Christopher Walken stole *A Late Quartet* from Philip Seymour Hoffman and Catherine Keener. British distributors also took up works from abroad that might appeal to just this audience.

One example was *Love Is All You Need* from Denmark's Suzanne Bier (set mainly in Italy and largely subtitled despite the presence of Pierce Brosnan), while *Populaire* was a French comedy set in the 1950s.

Also from France we had *Renoir*, a picturesque look at the tensions between the painter Auguste Renoir and his filmmaker son Jean. Hollywood put another director screen centre in the flawed yet immensely enjoyable *Hitchcock*, starring Anthony Hopkins and Helen Mirren.

Documentaries continue to flourish and in the 2013 crop we had another work about a notable filmmaker – that was *Michael H. Profession: Director*, in which Michael Haneke was a central if sometimes enigmatic figure. Equally concerned with cinema was *Side by Side*, a companion piece to 2012's *The Last Projectionist* in that it saw Keanu Reeves investigating the decline of film stock as digital takes over. Elsewhere, the subject matter on view could hardly have been wider. It included a remarkably revealing film about Israel's security service (*The Gatekeepers*), a chance for elderly gay men to talk about their lives (*The Invisibles*), a study of young ballet dancers (*First Position*), a devastating critique of the Catholic Church's response to paedophilia among the clergy (*Mea Maxima Culpa: Silence in the House of God*), a detailed look at a Tokyo restaurant owner (*Jiro Dreams of Sushi*) and a self-analytical portrait of a notable war photographer in *McCullin*.

Of special interest, however, was the film that marked Ken Loach's return to documentary: *The Spirit of '45*. This piece celebrating the Britain of the post-war period may have been too personal to

dogwoof presents

THE SPIRIT OF '45

A film directed by KEN LOACH

'A stirring film, it puts an eloquent and elegant case for a more humane society'
Stephen Schofield, The Observer

'Powerful, rousing and saddening'
Dave Calhoun, Time Out

SIXTEEN FILMS · FLY FILM · BFI · FILM4 · CHANNEL 4
producers STEPHEN STANDEN producer GEORGE FENTON film produced by JIM ANDERSON
associate IZZY CHAPMAN editor JONATHAN MORRIS sound EAMONN McMAHON
production REBECCA O'BRIEN · KATE OGBORN · LISA MARIE RUSSO director KEN LOACH

f /TheSpiritof45   @TheSpiritof45
www.TheSpiritof45.com

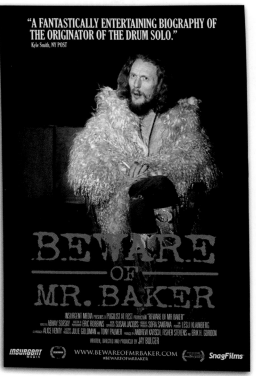

Posters for Pedro Almodóvar's *I'm So Excited!* and Jay Bulger's absorbing music documentary *Beware of Mr. Baker.*

be objective but it was a brilliant work technically and a clear labour of love from a born socialist.

One other feature that has stood out in 2013 is the large number of new works from well-established directors. Leaving aside those mentioned elsewhere, the list includes Almodóvar (*I'm So Excited!*), Assayas (*Something in the Air*), Bertolucci (*Me and You*), Boyle (*Trance*), Dumont (*Hors Satan*), Kassowitz (*Rebellion*), Kiarostami (*Like Someone in Love*), Kore-Eda (*I Wish*), Larrain (*No*), Mallick (*To the Wonder*), Mungiu (*Beyond the Hills*), Nair (*The Reluctant Fundamentalist*), Jeff Nichols (*Mud*), Ozon (*In the House*), Redford (*The Company You Keep*), Reygadas (*Post Tenebras Lux*), Soderbergh (*Behind the Candelabra*), Trapero (*White Elephant*), Van Sant (*Promised Land*) and Winterbottom (*The Look of Love*). By no means all of these directors were on their best form but it's quite a list nevertheless.

The films that impressed me most were often those that took me by surprise. Having no great interest in pop music, I did not expect to be bowled over by Jay Bulger's film about the drummer Ginger Baker. But, in confronting so well a man whose behaviour can seem deeply repellent yet who is remarkably engaging, *Beware of Mr Baker* was one of the best documentaries of the year thus far. It's a work so imaginatively assembled that an unusually prominent credit for its editor, Abhay Sofsky, is richly deserved. If it has a rival for best documentary that would be Andy Heathcote's *The Moo Man*, a feature made with all the quality previously suggested in Heathcote's short films. A deeply sensitive study

of a dairy farmer in Sussex, it is wholly successful in capturing the bond between the farmer and his animals. Heathcote's own photography is superb and Stephen Daltry contributes a splendid music score.

When it comes to dramas, the impact of Tobias Lindholm's *A Hijacking* was again something I had not anticipated. It deals insightfully with the problem that arises when negotiators have to cope with terrorists who are holding hostages, in this case the crew of a Danish vessel hijacked in the Indian Ocean. Instead of opting for melodrama, the film gives us a telling depiction of a situation in which whatever you do invites criticism. It's apt that a real-life negotiator takes on the role of his fictional equivalent here.

Several British films stood out too. Although I was disappointed by Michael Winterbottom's *The Look of Love* I greatly admired his quiet, intimate piece *Everyday*, about a family's situation when the man of the house is in prison. *Broken*, a remarkable film debut for theatre director Rufus Norris, was for much of its length a compellingly realised view of some of the worst aspects of life today in this country. Ironically we had to go to 1970s Belfast for uplift: that was in *Good Vibrations*, a portrait of Terri Hooley whose promotion of punk music was a counter to the violence in the streets. This was an encouraging second feature from Lisa D'Sa and Glenn Leyburn, whose *Cherrybomb* (2008) was sadly undervalued. Ireland was also the setting for a more troubling view of adolescence in Lenny Abrahamson's involving *What Richard Did*.

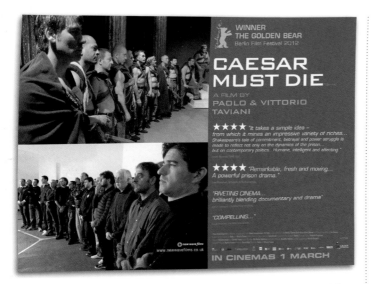

The poster for the Taviani Brothers' *Caesar Must Die*.

...ammed ...rkable ...djda.

Three films that I admired got less recognition than was their due. The Turkish film *Home*, otherwise known as *Yurt*, marked the directorial debut of the actor Muzaffer Ozdemir. Strictly for those who respond to minimalist cinema, it is a superbly composed and subtly balanced requiem for a lost Eden. Somewhat in the same mould was *Shell*, a haunting film about a father and daughter set in Scotland; touching on incest, it encourages us to note the names of its lead actress Chloe Pirrie and writer-director Scott Graham. Not quite so minimalist but initially slow-moving is So Yong Kim's American film *For Ellen*. It's a study of how an impending divorce affects the young child of a failed marriage, and the scenes between Paul Dano and Shaylena Lynn Mandigo as father and daughter are as true and touching as anything seen in cinema in recent times.

I liked, too, Baltasar Kormákur's Icelandic drama *The Deep* and could see why *Frances Ha*, a perfect vehicle for its star Greta Gerwig and a New York movie to rival those by Woody Allen, would appeal to young audiences sophisticated enough to appreciate a movie in black and white. But I want to end with two remarkable works by filmmakers who could not be more contrasted.

Caesar Must Die from Italy is the latest feature by the Taviani Brothers, now in their eighties. They have created a unique film. In so far as it shows prisoners in a high-security jail outside Rome acting in Shakespeare it is a documentary. But it is also a powerful abridged presentation of *Julius Caesar*, akin in its impact to what was achieved by Carlos Saura with his triumphant presentation of a Flamenco ballet in a rehearsal room in *Blood Wedding* (1981).

If this film confirms that the Tavianis are wise in their old age, the fact that wisdom can come earlier in life is evidenced by *Wadjda*, a first feature by Haifa Al-Mansour. Filmed on location in Riyadh, this is a film which shows us life in Saudi Arabia through female eyes. That's the case twice over since, in addition to the writer-director being a woman, she invites us to view events through the eyes of a young girl, quite magnificently played by Waad Mohammed. In post-war Italy Vittorio De Sica made a great film about a bicycle being stolen; now we have an equally involving tale of a girl of spirit trying to save enough money to buy a bike in a country where such a dream is an affront to tradition.

Wadjda is all the more shattering because it's so quiet and unpretentious. It's one of the film highlights of 2013.